THRIVING
ON AN
AGING WORKFORCE

Strategies for Organizational
and Systemic Change

THRIVING ON AN AGING WORKFORCE

Strategies for Organizational and Systemic Change

Edited
by
Paulette T. Beatty
and
Roemer M. S. Visser

KRIEGER PUBLISHING COMPANY
Malabar, Florida
2005

Original Edition 2005

"Building an Age-Friendly Workplace." Copyright Laura Markos.
"How to Become Employer of Choice for the Working Retired." Copyright Beverly Goldberg.

Printed and Published by
KRIEGER PUBLISHING COMPANY
KRIEGER DRIVE
MALABAR, FLORIDA 32950

Library of Congress Cataloging-In-Publication Data

Thriving on an aging workforce : strategies for organizational and systemic change / edited by
    Paulette T. Beatty and Roemer M.S. Visser.
        p. cm.
    Includes bibliographical references and index.
    ISBN 1-57524-200-1 (alk. paper)
        1. Older people—Employment—United States. 2. Age and employment—United States.
    3. Personnel management—United States. 4. Employees—Recruiting—United States.
    5. Employees—Training of—United States. I. Beatty, Paulette T. II. Visser, Roemer M. S.

    HF5549.5.O44T47 2004
    658.3'0084'6—dc22

                                                                        2004049018

    10 9 8 7 6 5 4 3 2

Contents

Acknowledgments

This book would not have been possible without the crucial support we received from others. First, we wish to gratefully acknowledge Texas A&M University's Department of Educational Administration and Human Resource Development for its unwavering encouragement and support from the start.

Secondly, we wish to thank all of the contributors to the book. We hope they will agree that their hard work and patience have paid off.

Last, but not least, we wish to thank all members of our expert panel (described in more detail in Chapter 1), the results of which form the very backbone of this book. The value of the panelists' insights, experiences, and knowledge cannot be understated, and without their willingness to participate, this project would have been very short-lived.

We are indebted to the following people.

W. Andrew Achenbaum, Dean of the College of Liberal Arts and Sciences at the University of Houston, and past president of the National Council on the Aging

James A. Auerbach, Senior Vice President, National Policy Association

Scott A. Bass, Distinguished Professor of Sociology and Policy Sciences, Dean of the Graduate School, and Vice President for Research at the University of Maryland, Baltimore County

Judith Brown, Director of Research with the International Public Management Association for Human Resources

Francis G. Caro, Professor of Gerontology and Director of the Gerontology Institute at the University of Massachusetts, Boston

Lawrence A. Crecy, Executive Vice President of the National Caucus and Center on the Black Aged, Inc.

Stanley P. DeViney, Department of Social Sciences at the University of Maryland, Eastern Shore

Rocki-Lee DeWitt, Dean of the School of Business Administration at the University of Vermont

Lisa M. Finkelstein, Associate Professor of Social-Industrial/Organizational Psychology at Northern Illinois University

Catherine D. Fyock, employment strategist and author of *America's Work Force Is Coming of Age* and *UnRetirement*

Beverly Goldberg, Vice President, The Century Foundation, a New York-based research institution, and author of *Age Works: What Corporate America Must Do to Survive the Graying of the Workforce*

Martin M. Greller, Professor of Management, University of Wyoming

Melissa A. Hardy, Bellamy Distinguished Professor of Sociology and Director of the Pepper Institute on Aging and Public Policy at Florida State University

Richard Knowdell, Executive Director, Career Planning & Adult Development Network (www.careernetwork.org)

Karl D. Kosloski, Professor of Gerontology and Reynolds Professor of Public Affairs and Community Service at the University of Nebraska at Omaha

Barbara S. Lawrence, Associate Professor at the Anderson Graduate School of Management, University of California at Los Angeles

Victor W. Marshall, Director of the University of North Carolina Institute on Aging, and Professor of Sociology at the University of North Carolina at Chapel Hill

Barbara R. McIntosh, Associate Professor, The School of Business Administration, University of Vermont

Philip H. Mirvis, independent consultant, and editor of *Building the Competitive Workforce*

Kelly Mollica, former Assistant Professor of Management at the Babcock School of Management at Wake Forest University, and currently president of Star Performance Consulting & Training

Emory W. Mulling, President of the Association of Career Transition Firms International, North America, and Chairman of the Mulling Companies/Lincolnshire International, an Atlanta-based family of firms handling outplacement, leadership development, and retained search with worldwide capabilities

Jan Mutchler, Professor of Gerontology and Senior Fellow with the Gerontology Institute at the University of Massachusetts, Boston

Van Doorn Ooms, Senior Fellow at the Committee for Economic Development, a research and policy organization of some 250 business leaders and educators

Angela M. O'Rand, Professor of Sociology at Duke University

Dave Patel, former Manager, Trends and Forecasting, with the Society for Human Resource Management

Amy Pienta, Assistant Professor at the Institute on Aging and the Department of Health Policy & Epidemiology at the University of Florida

Jill Quadagno, Professor of Sociology at Florida State University where she holds the Mildred and Claude Pepper Eminent Scholar Chair in Social Gerontology

Sara E. Rix, Senior Policy Advisor with the Economics Team of the Public Policy Institute of AARP

Christopher J. Ruhm, Jefferson-Pilot Excellence Professor of Economics at the University of North Carolina at Greensboro, and Research Associate with the National Bureau of Economic Research

Martha M. Russell, Secretary of the National Career Development Association, and independent career consultant since 1984

Patricia A. Simpson, Assistant Professor of Industrial Relations at the Institute of Human Resources and Industrial Relations, Loyola University Chicago

Harvey L. Sterns, Professor of Psychology and Director of the Institute for Life-Span Development & Gerontology at the University of Akron, and Research Professor of Gerontology at Northeastern Ohio Universities

William K. Wasch, Chair of the National Council On the Aging's Workforce Development Committee, and author of *Home Planning for Your Later Years*

Moreover, we would like to thank anonymous representatives of the following organizations for their participation.

The **Alliance for Retired Americans,** a nationwide organization of three million retirees and other older Americans working together to make their voices heard in the laws, policies, politics, andinstitutions that shape our lives (www.retired americans.org)

Business and Professional Women/USA, promoting equity for all women in the workplace through advocacy, education, and information (www.bpwusa.org)

The San Antonio District Office of the **Equal Employment Opportunity Commission.**

The Editors

Paulette T. Beatty, Ph.D., Emeritus Professor at Texas A&M University, retired recently after 25 years of service at the institution. She continues to teach in the Educational Human Resource Development graduate program and is developing a program to assist elders in writing and telling their life stories replete with life lessons learned. During her tenure, she chaired over 20 Masters and 50 Doctoral students through their graduate programs, served as Interim Head of the Educational Human Resource Development Department, and as Program Coordinator of the Adult and Extension Education Program. In addition to her other teaching responsibilities, she also developed a specialty in gerontology within the program and designed and taught its courses: Education and the Older Adult, Retirement Planning, and Managing the Aging Workforce. She has served as a member of the faculty for the Training and Development Certification Program. She has served on the Board of the American Association for Adult and Continuing Education, served as program chair for one of its International Conferences, and served as editor of its research-to-practice journal, *Adult Learning, An Omnibus of Research and Practice*. She also served several terms as Executive Board Member of the Commission of Professors of Adult Education. Her publications include *Connecting with Older Adults* (with Mary Alice Wolf) and numerous journal articles.

Roemer M. S. Visser holds a Master's Degree in Industrial/Organizational Psychology from the Vrije Universiteit in Amsterdam, the Netherlands. Upon graduation, he worked in corporate Human Resources departments in the Netherlands and subsequently in the United States. He holds the Society for Human Resource Management's PHR certification. Currently, he is finishing his Doctorate in Human Resource Development at Texas A&M University. He has presented at various conferences on the topics of qualitative research methodologies, aging workforce issues, and storytelling. For his dissertation, he has collected life stories from aging Dutch citizens who were college students during World War II. He has used narrative inquiry methods to explore the extent to which these life stories reveal repercussions that the wartime experiences have had for their subsequent lives. In the future, he hopes to use these methods to investigate the role of storytelling in organizational processes such as career development, employee socialization, training and mentoring, interview and selection processes, performance appraisals, and/or organizational development activities.

The Contributors

Scott A. Bass, Ph.D., is Dean of the Graduate School and Vice Provost for Research and Planning at the University of Maryland, Baltimore County (UMBC), where he also holds academic appointments of Distinguished Professor of Sociology and Policy Sciences. He is an expert in the field of gerontology and has published over 50 book chapters and 30 monographs or research reports on aging and aging policy.

Dennis Doverspike, Ph.D., ABPP, is Professor of Psychology at the University of Akron. He is the author or coauthor of two books and over 100 professional publications. He also has over 20 years of consulting experience and serves as Director of the Center for Organizational Research at the University of Akron. His research and teaching interests include personnel selection, testing, and the psychology of online behavior.

Suzanne Dunn, Ph.D., supervises instructional design efforts in the development of video- and computer-based courseware for use by traditional and nontraditional students nationally and internationally. She is the Director of Product Design for the LeCroy Center for Educational Telecommunications in the Dallas County Community College District. Prior to her current position, she spent 20 years in instructional design and multimedia production, plus researching and teaching at the university level.

Lisa M. Finkelstein is an Associate Professor in the Social-Industrial/Organizational Psychology program at Northern Illinois University in DeKalb. She earned her Ph.D. in Industrial/Organizational Psychology from Tulane University in New Orleans, Louisiana, in 1996. Her research interests include age identity, age stereotyping, age discrimination, and intergenerational issues, particularly focusing on socialization and mentoring contexts. She has been appointed Program Chair of the 2005 Society for Industrial and Organizational Psychology annual conference.

Paul Fronstin is a Senior Research Associate with the Employee Benefit Research Institute (EBRI). He is also Director of the Institute's Health Security and Quality Research Program. He has been with EBRI since 1993. Dr. Fronstin's research interests include trends in employment-based health benefits, consumer-driven health benefits, the uninsured, retiree health benefits, employee benefits and taxation, and public opinion about health care. He earned his Bachelor of Science degree in economics from SUNY Binghamton and his Ph.D. in economics from the University of Miami.

Howard N Fullerton, Jr., was at the Bureau of Labor Statistics from 1960 to 2003. As Senior Demographer Statistician, he has regularly prepared demographic projections of the U.S. labor force and research concentrated on the demography of an aging and more diverse workforce. He has contributed chapters for several books and has delivered scholarly papers in both demographic and economic forecasting forums as well as serving on several interagency committees.

Catherine D. Fyock, CSP, SPHR, is an employment strategist—a leader in providing insights and solutions for an aging and changing work force. For over 15 years she has combined her knowledge of workforce issues and her talents as speaker to help organizations attract top talent, reduce turnover, and improve productivity in a volatile labor market. She is the author of *America's Work Force Is Coming of Age* and *UnRetirement*. Contact her at: http://www.cathyfyock.com.

Beverly Goldberg is the author of *Age Works: What Corporate America Must Do to Survive the Graying of the Workforce* (The Free Press, 2000) and *Overcoming High-Tech Anxiety: Thriving in a Wired World* (Jossey Bass, 1999), as well as numerous articles on the subject of older workers and retirement. She is Vice President of The Century Foundation, a not-for-profit, New York-based research institution that examines economic, financial, and social issues.

Jennifer Reid Keene is an Assistant Professor of Sociology at the University of Nevada—Las Vegas. Her research interests include the work and family implications of the Sandwiched Generation, gender and the work-family nexus, the impact of informal spousal caregiving on well-being in widowhood, and gender differences in access to employer-provided health insurance. At UNLV, she teaches classes in the Sociology of Aging, Quantitative Research Methods, and Introductory Sociology.

Laura Markos, Ph.D., consults with organizations on systemic and cultural change. A former *Fortune* 500 executive, she is also an active professional and community volunteer, and founding coeditor of the *Journal of Transformative Education*, focusing on adult transformative learning environments and experience. She holds a doctorate in human and organizational systems from Fielding Graduate Institute, an M.A. in organizational development, and an M.B.A. in marketing. She lives in Santa Fe and online at LauraMarkosPhD@cs.com.

Dave Patel was Manager of Workplace Trends and Forecasting for the Society for Human Resource Management (SHRM). In this capacity, he was responsible for identifying and tracking major economic, social, political, legal, and demographic trends, as well as writing and speaking about how those trends affect the workplace. Prior to his work at SHRM, he worked as a legislative aide to U.S. Senator Orrin Hatch. He studied International Finance at Georgetown University and Political Economy at Utah State University.

Rudolph G. Penner is a Senior Fellow at the Urban Institute and holds the Arjay and Frances Miller chair in public policy. Previously, he was a Managing Director of the Barents Group, a KPMG Company. He was Director of the Congressional Budget Office from 1983 to 1987. From 1977 to 1983, he was a Resident Scholar at the American Enterprise Institute. Previous posts in government include Assistant Director for Economic Policy at the Office of Management and Budget and Deputy Assistant Secretary for Economic Affairs at the Department of Housing and Urban Development. Before 1975, he was a professor of economics at the University of Rochester.

Martha M. Russell, M.S., NCC, is a Career Consultant and since 1987, owner of Russell Career Services in Washington State. She is a frequent speaker nationally and internationally on topics of career managment, workplace issues, and retirement concerns. She is currently on the Board of Directors of the National Career Development Association. Published works include numerous journal articles, book chapters and Career Management Handbooks. She holds a Master's degree in Career Counseling from California State University, Sacramento.

Dallas L. Salisbury is President and CEO of the Employee Benefit Research Institute (EBRI). EBRI was founded in 1978 to provide objective, unbiased information regarding the employee benefit system and related economic security issues. He joined EBRI at its founding in 1978. He is also chairman and CEO of the American Savings Education Council (ASEC), a partnership of public- and private-sector institutions that undertake initiatives to raise public awareness regarding what is needed to ensure long-term economic and health security. ASEC is part of the EBRI Education and Research Fund.

Kenneth S. Shultz, Ph.D., Wayne State University, is Professor of Industrial and Organizational (I/O) Psychology and Director of the Master of Science Program in I/O Psychology in the Department of Psychology at California State University, San Bernardino. He also completed a one-year National Institute on Aging post-doctoral fellowship at the Andrus Gerontology Center at the University of Southern California in 1998/99. His current work focuses primarily on aging workforce and retirement issues.

Patricia A. Simpson is an Assistant Professor in Industrial Relations at the Institute of Human Resources and Industrial Relations, Loyola University Chicago. She received her Ph.D. from the Institute of Labor and Industrial Relations, University of Illinois. She has published scholarly articles in *Social Science Research, Industrial Relations Research Review, Feminist Economics*, the *Journal of Labor Research*, and the *Journal of Vocational Behavior*.

Susan J. Stabile, J.D., joined St. John's University as Professor of Law in 1993. Previously, she had been associated in New York and Hong Kong with the international law firm of Cleary, Gottlieb, Steen and Hamilton, first in the corporate and securities area and later specializing in employee benefits and executive compensation matters. She is a past Chair of the Association of American Law Schools Section on Employee Benefits and of the Labor and Employment Law Section of the Industrial Relations Research Association. She has written numerous articles on pensions and employee benefits and is coauthor of a Bureau of National Affairs book *ERISA Litigation*.

Anthony A. Sterns, Ph.D., is the Director of Research of Creative Action, Inc., in Akron, Ohio. He received his doctorate in the field of Industrial/Organizational Psychology with a graduate certificate in Gerontology from The University of Akron. His undergraduate degree was from the University of Michigan College of Engineering's Department of Naval Architecture and Marine Engineering. His research interests include a focus on older worker issues including training, career development, and human factors.

Harvey L. Sterns, Ph.D., is Professor of Psychology and Director of the Institute for Life-Span Development and Gerontology at The University of Akron. He is also a Research Professor of Gerontology at the Northeastern Ohio Universities College of Medicine. He is a faculty member in both the Applied Cognitive Aging and Industrial/Organizational Psychology graduate programs and chairs the specialization in Industrial Gerontological Psychology. He has published extensively on work and retirement, career development, training and retraining, and maintaining professional competence. He was President of Division 20, Adult Development and Aging of the American Psychological Association for 2002-2003.

Mary Anne Taylor is a Professor of Industrial/Organizational Psychology in the Psychology Department at Clemson University in Clemson, South Carolina. She has published empirical and theoretical work on the factors that impact postretirement adjustment, emphasizing the importance of retirement planning in this process. Her most recent work focuses on tailoring retirement planning programs to the needs of different demographic groups, incorporating traditional variables of health and finances along with nontraditional considerations such as social support.

PART ONE
PROLOGUE

Chapter 1

Introduction

Roemer M. S. Visser
Paulette T. Beatty

The American workforce is aging. By 2020, more than half of the workforce will be age 40 or older. Thus, the majority of the workforce will be protected by the Age Discrimination in Employment Act. The workforce is also not growing as fast as it used to – as a matter of fact, it is projected to slow to its lowest rate in history. Organizations are therefore likely to become increasingly dependent on older workers to meet their staffing and performance needs. The purpose of this book is to help organizations in the private and public sectors prepare for the consequences of this graying of the workforce. Some excellent resources are available on this topic, but by far most of them provide a limited – though valid – perspective. For example, some focus only on human resource (HR) strategies and processes, leaving the wider social and political contexts out of the picture. Others focus only on public policy issues such as health care or social security reform. Yet others reflect a specific academic discipline, such as psychology, economics, or gerontology. No publication is available that directly identifies and addresses the critical issues that our society will face with the aging of the workforce and the changing nature of the workplace.

In this book, we have tried to be comprehensive. We have done this in several ways. First, there is the way in which the issues were identified. Second, for each of the identified issues, we have asked two authors to contribute a chapter. In most cases, we have paired an academic author with a practitioner. Third, we have secured a wide variety of author affiliations: Some of the academic disciplines represented include industrial/organizational psychology, industrial gerontology, sociology, industrial and labor relations, and law, while other authors hail from government, professional associations, and think tanks. Several independent consultants have contributed as well.

The result of this approach is a mosaic which, when seen as a whole, provides a surprisingly coherent picture of the issues that U.S. organizations will have to confront when the baby boomers, those born between 1946 and 1964, reach retirement age. The road map, or agenda for practice, policy, and research, is equally clear.

Clear is, of course, not the same as simple. None of the issues identified stands alone; all are somehow interrelated. Our aim has been to reveal the complexity and interrelatedness of these issues rather than to present "Ten Steps to Success." If one thing has become clear to us as editors, it is that all relevant stakeholders, including employers, policy makers, researchers, professional associations, consultants, and special interest groups, must take a collaborative approach to tackling these issues. It is our sincere hope that this book will be useful to anyone with a vested interest in preparing for an aging workforce.

However, we realize that no resource is equally relevant to everyone. The primary target audience for this book consists of human resource management and human resource development professionals as well as line managers in organizations – those who have the authority and the responsibility to adapt their organizations to the changing workforce demographics. We have attempted to meet their needs by asking all of the authors, regardless of their backgrounds or orientations, to close their chapters with specific recommendations for practice, research, and/or public policy. The secondary target audience for this book consists of academicians, including graduate students, and those who are in a position to influence public policy.

Method

So how did we identify the issues that form the structure of this book? We could have listed some ourselves, but our personal backgrounds and affiliations with adult education would have limited the scope of the book. Instead, we decided to let "the field" tell us what the issues are.

For our purposes, "the field" consisted of those individuals and organizations that have made the aging workforce key to their careers or strategies and have significant relevant expertise and credibility. We divided the field into six major stakeholder groups: special interest groups, think tanks, professional associations, government, academicians, and consultants. To identify the relevant professional associations, special interest groups, and think tanks, the Encyclopedia of Associations (2001) was used. This reference book lists all recognized associations and includes a short description of them. If the description mentioned anything related to older workers, that organization was included in the list of experts.

For identifying academicians and consultants, a more elaborate strategy was used. First, those books on the market, relevant to aging workforce issues and copyrighted in 1990 or later, were reviewed (Auerbach & Welsh, 1994; Bass, 1995b; Bass, Caro, & Chen, 1993; Crown, 1996; Fyock, 1990; Goldberg, 2000; Hale, 1990; Judy & D'Amico, 1997; Mitchell, 1993; Schaie & Schooler, 1998; Shea, 1991). All authors of these books and of particular chapters were entered in a spreadsheet.

Next, the most recent book with an elaborate reference list, the Crown (1996) publication, was reviewed. From its reference list, all of the books and articles published between 1990 and 1995 were entered into the same spreadsheet. The purpose was to find the mainstream academic journals where these experts publish their research. Relevance of a particular article was determined based on its title.

The result was a list of articles published up to 1995. To include more recent articles, all the journals cited at least twice were reviewed from 1994 through 2001. Each relevant article subsequently found was also entered into the spreadsheet.

This resulted in a list of 368 articles, books, and book chapters, published between 1990 and 2001 and somehow related to the aging work-

force. Since the purpose was to identify the experts, those who had published only one article or book were taken off the list. The assumption was that those who had authored multiple articles were more likely to be considered experts than those who had only authored one. For the remaining names, their classifications, academician or non-academician, were checked and they were separated accordingly.

In the academic group, 123 publications remained. Selecting academicians for our panel based on the number of publications in the spreadsheet seemed inappropriate: it was, after all, very possible that certain publications had been overlooked. In order to ensure the most systematic and defensible approach, information was sought for each of the 39 academicians remaining on the list: curricula vitae, lists of publications, and research interests were gathered where possible, to confirm that they indeed had expertise and credibility related to the aging workforce. Moreover, they were categorized according to the academic discipline they represented.

Interestingly, there was not a single professor of management in the entire group. To make sure this discipline had not inadvertently been overlooked, all issues of the following journals published between 1994 and 2001 were reviewed: *Human Resource Development Quarterly, Training and Development Journal, Human Resource Management, Human Resource Management Review*, and the *Academy of Management Journal*. In these journals, seven more authors were identified who had relevant expertise. Interestingly, none of them had been referenced by the previous group of 39 academicians and vice-versa, indicating a schism within the academic community when it comes to the aging workforce.

To identify the consultants for our panel, the non-academicians taken from the list of authors were reviewed. For each author, information was sought on the Internet. The assumption was that independent consultants with credibility and expertise have a web site. When information was available that identified them as a consultant, they were included in the list of experts. All in all, the list of experts consisted of 60 academicians, consultants, and organizations. Of the 60 on the list, 36 participated (see the Acknowledgements section for a listing).

The method selected for mining their expertise was an on-line Delphi. In a Delphi, panel members participate by answering questions confidentially, after which each of the members is presented with all of the other members' answers. They are then asked to consider adjusting their original answers in the face of their peers' answers. Within three such rounds of feedback, this procedure tends to yield a reliable consensus among experts.

The Delphi opened with the following two questions: "In your opinion, what are the five most critical issues that organizations will confront through the year 2020, given the aging of the U.S. workforce?" and "Why?" To limit ambiguity, the following definitions and guidelines were used to guide the question:

1. The aging workforce consists of those age 40 and older, who are protected by the Age Discrimination in Employment Act
2. The scope of the problem is limited to the United States; international developments were not included unless they had specific relevance to U.S. conditions
3. Organizations specifically include not for-profit, for-profit, and government organizations
4. Critical issue: a major challenge that needs to be addressed by one or more stakeholder groups in order to most effectively realize the full potential of the aging workforce

Findings

This first round resulted in 171 answers with rationales, since not every panelist had actually listed five issues. Our initial intent had been to use the Delphi to isolate the five most important issues identified by the panel. However, when we examined the answers more closely, it became clear that they reflected a high degree of agreement and coherence. On the one hand, virtually all of the answers were corroborated by others. In other words, there were no stand-alone answers. Simultaneously, none of the answers was contradicted by any of the others. The answers collectively reflected a mosaic of challenges and we realized that their strength lay in their comprehensiveness. Asking panelists to rank them so that we could

focus only on the top five would have taken away from this quality. Therefore, we decided not to proceed with the second round of the Delphi as planned.

Instead, we analyzed the answers for content and categorized them. After repeated analyses, nine major categories of responses emerged. They are briefly introduced below, each with two examples for the purpose of illustration.

1. The Workforce of Tomorrow

All of the answers referring to demographic trends on a nationwide scale were placed in this category. Examples are:

- Address labor shortage. As the baby boom cohort exits the workforce, continuing low fertility rates will mean a shortage of workers.
- The demographic diversity of the workforce. The nation must pay greater attention to the growing significance of the Spanish-speaking population and other "new" immigrants. Variations in disability with advancing age affect the workforce population structure.

2. The Workplace of Tomorrow

The workplace of tomorrow category includes the responses pertaining to larger-scale national and international developments which impact organizations in the United States. Examples are:

- Keeping abreast of, and responding appropriately to, the myriad changes that will affect competitiveness – or, for the nonprofit sector, success. Organizations will have to run faster and faster just to keep in place. Having the resources to know what is going on and where – technological development, emerging markets, continuous development of skilled workforces abroad, etc. – and what to do about it will become increasingly difficult. The aging dimension of this relates, of course, to availability of skilled labor.
- New and rapid technological changes. Training programs and classes should be offered to ensure that there is a technological playing field for all workers.

Please note that for the purpose of this book, we use the term *workplace* in a broad sense. While to some, this may refer to desks, lighting, and workplace safety, we use it to refer to the workplace in the broadest sense. This includes organizational structures, policies and procedures, and culture. In other words, it is the general environment within which work duties are performed.

3. Recruiting and Retaining Older Workers

The generic references to the need to recruit and retain older workers (without specific mention of, for example, health care as a recruitment or retention tool) were included here. Answers related to benefits in general, to compensation and to performance evaluation policies were also included, as becomes clear from these examples:

- Restructuring the reward system associated with work to make it less dependent on seniority. Much of the contemporary reward system is based on time-in-grade considerations (e.g., seniority). The reality of the future, however, is that workers will likely change employers, if not careers, numerous times. There is a great disincentive in this system for older workers who essentially must start over when displaced.
- Retaining employees and offering incentives to stay on the job. Recruitment and retention are likely to be the two biggest workforce issues through at least 2006 and beyond, and organizations are going to need to redesign their approach to employment if they are going to attract and keep workers in this aging and changing environment.

4. Training Older Workers

All the answers pertaining to training were placed under this heading. This includes issues of access as well as issues of appropriateness of training methods. See the following examples:

- How do we create information technology literacy in an older workforce? Work content has increasingly become digitized, and the aging workforce has yet to be introduced to the technology in a systematic fashion.

- Will employer inservice training investments become age neutral? Experience has shown that many employers engage in skill disinvestment as workers age. The rationale given is that it is wasteful to invest in persons who will soon be leaving the workplace. As the overall workforce ages, it should be seen that potential longevity will no longer be a quality of younger workers.

5. Career Development for Older Workers

Several respondents referred to the need for a new conceptualization of the term *career*. This became the basis for this grouping and is illustrated by the following examples:

- Career self-management must be carried out by middle-aged and older workers. Identifying factors that predict success in maximizing employment opportunities and finding new employment when desired or necessary is critical. There is no formal research that really focuses on how successful people are with such self--management.
- The changing nature of a job and/or career. In the past, you could go to work for IBM right after college and be assured that you would be there until retirement.

6. Enhancing Intergenerational Relations

This group encompasses the widest variety of answers, all of which somehow relate to diversity issues, particularly ageism in the workplace. Also included are references to ergonomics (physical characteristics of a welcoming workplace), gender equity, and intergenerational relations in the workplace. All of these refer to an organizational culture that welcomes and embraces both young and old. The following examples illustrate this:

- Intergenerational relations in the workplace. It is often the case that people befriend others like themselves, which means that older workers befriend older workers and younger workers befriend younger workers. While in some circumstances that is unavoidable since interests will drive friendships, effort must be put into improving relations across the age groups, to ensure that age heterogeneity works well in task groups and that people of different ages continue to treat each other with respect.

- Age stereotyping. Inaccurate stereotypes about older workers may prevent them from getting jobs, or may contribute to them being a target of job reductions.

7. Health and Older Workers

This category includes all answers pertaining to health care for older workers, including home health care, as the following examples show:

- What kinds of workplace benefits best meet the needs of an older workforce? The cohort has a need for health care access for themselves, may need access to family care for both their children and parents, and may need work hours flexibility to directly participate in caregiving.
- Health costs. Rapid cost escalation is problematic and an aging workforce will exacerbate this problem.

8. Pensions and Older Workers

This group is relatively self-explanatory:

- The retirement of workers before age 70. The decline of defined benefit pensions and their replacement by defined contribution pensions are individualizing the retirement decision. Some economists are projecting that some baby boom cohort members will delay retirement because of concerns over their defined contribution retirement accounts and this may present difficulties for employers who cannot discriminate against workers on the basis of age. In some sectors the aging of the workforce may affect organizational flexibility and responsiveness to changing environmental factors, such as the markets.
- Providing private pension and related retirement benefits at minimal risk to employees. Look at what happened at Enron Corporation (the energy company whose bankruptcy decimated the retirement savings of many of its employees).

9. Redefining Retirement

All of the entries suggesting the need to reconceptualize current, mainstream definitions and models of retirement were included in this group:

- Retirement flexibility. In most instances, retirement is an all-or-none proposition. Many older workers would be willing to continue working if there was sufficient flexibility in the workplace to enable them to enjoy the benefits of retirement and still participate in the labor force.
- Enhance work flexibility. In order to meet workforce demands, there is a need to make it more possible to pursue phased retirement and similar flexible routes to remaining in the labor force at least part-time.

Interpreting the Findings

The total score for the nine categories of responses is found in Table 1.1. A quick glance reveals that enhancing intergenerational relations, recruiting and retaining older workers, training older workers, and health care for older workers are the four largest categories in terms of the amount of responses they encompass. The relative size of these categories

Table 1.1
Categories Derived from the Delphi Panelists' Responses

Category	Frequency (Total: 171)
The Workforce of Tomorrow	14
The Workplace of Tomorrow	6
Recruiting and Retaining Older Workers	30
Training Older Workers	24
Career Development for Older Workers	9
Enhancing Intergenerational Relations	40
Health and Older Workers	24
Pensions and Older Workers	9
Redefining Retirement	15

should not be taken too literally, for two reasons. First, the size of the categories depends in part on our interpretation of particular answers. Our way of organizing the responses is one among many possible and legitimate ways of doing so. One should therefore be careful to conclude that recruitment and retention of older workers is more important than training older workers because it encompasses six more responses. Second, the particular make-up of the expert panel also influences the distribution of answers; for example, having several panelists more concerned with health care than with pensions clearly would impact the relative sizes of these categories as well.

In spite of this ambiguity, the answers do warrant a conclusion that becomes obvious when the categories themselves are grouped. The first two, the workforce of tomorrow and the workplace of tomorrow, can be placed together into a larger group referring to societal trends. These trends play out at nationwide and global levels and cannot be directly influenced by individual organizations. Thus, these two trends provide the broader contexts within which aging workforce issues are embedded. The other seven categories of responses reflect crtical issues that can and must be addressed. Moreover, these seven issues cover responsibilities that specifically fall under the purview of human resource management (HRM) and human resource development (HRD). Thus, it is safe to say that HRM and HRD will be the most important agents of change for organizations who wish to attract, retain, and develop an aging workforce. For sure, the degrees of freedom they have may at times depend on legislation (for example, in the case of Social Security reform), but as Part Three of this book shows, it certainly does not preclude them from initiating change within their organizations.

Nominating Authors

The nine groups of responses were presented to the panelists. Each of the panelists was asked to recommend an author with expertise on that particular group. Of the sixteen chapters covering these issues, seven were written by members of the expert panel. The other nine are written by authors who were recommended by panel members.

How to Read This Book

The responses from the panel revealed a web of interrelated issues. In order to preserve the wholeness and complexity of these findings, we decided to dedicate two chapters to each of the seven HR-related issues. The assumption was that illuminating each of these from two distinct perspectives would add to our understanding of the issues and would prevent any oversimplification. This has resulted in the current book structure.

The remainder of this book is divided into three parts. Part Two, consisting of Chapters 2 and 3, sets the stage. These two chapters reflect the first two categories of responses that were found: the workforce of tomorrow and the workplace of tomorrow. Taken together, they paint a coherent picture of societal changes that will continue to have a significant impact on organizations. They substantiate the basic premise of this book: with the workforce aging and its growth slowing, the next economic upturn may very well increase organizations' dependence on older workers for their continued success. Combined with a shift to an information/service economy, continued influx of technology, and continuing globalization, this places a variety of demands on organizational policies and strategies when it comes to recruiting, retaining, and developing older workers. After Chapter 3, we provide a synthesis of the two preceding chapters by superimposing the various trends identified in those chapters on each other and explore some of their consequences for the workforce and the workplace.

Part Three forms the core of the book as it deals with the seven HR-related categories – the critical issues – that emerged from the panel responses. Each of these issues is covered by two chapters. While in most cases an academically oriented (research-based) chapter is paired up with a practitioner-oriented one, the issues relating to intergenerational relations and health are exceptions to this. The reason is that within both of these groups of responses, two distinct substrands were visible. In the case of intergenerational relations, there was one clear emphasis on intergenerational relations as an inter-individual phenomenon. For example, what is it like for a younger worker to mentor an older one? The other emphasis was on ageism as a manifestation of organizational culture. We decided to retain these different emphases rather than merging them into one. The same is true for the health issue. While many of the responses referred to the increasing cost of health care, particularly for older workers, others brought attention to the phenomenon of the sandwich generation: those baby boomers who have dependent children in the home and have eldercare obligations for their aging parents. Since this reflects more of a work-life balance issue than one of strictly cost and access, again we decided to maintain this distinction in the two chapters on health and older workers.

Much like the synthesis at the end of Part Two, we provide a brief synthesis at the end of each pair of chapters in Part Three. These syntheses, in turn, help set the stage for the final chapter in this book (Part Four).

The observant reader will notice occasional font changes. At times, our authors are asking you to project yourself into the future. Whenever a hypothetical future scenario is described, we have chosen to switch to italics. Moreover, there are multiple practical, real-world examples and case studies in this book. To distinguish them from the rest of the text, they are printed in a sans serif font.

One final note: Our operational definition of the aging workforce consists of those aged 40 and up. Currently, they make up a substantial part of the workforce already. However, imagine the year 2020: Those who turn 40 that year are those born in 1980. They are now in the early stages of their careers. The point is that the scope of this book is not limited to those who are currently retired or to any other section of the workforce; it is about *everyone* currently in the workforce. We hope you will find that this book contributes to an increased understanding of the issues to be tackled and possible ways to tackle them.

PART TWO

SETTING THE STAGE

Introduction

Setting the Stage

Part Two, Setting the Stage, provides the backdrop for a review of seven issues that have been identified as critical nationally in accommodating a progressively aging workforce.

In Part One, the introductory chapter, the editors highlight the focus of this publication: the exposition of those issues critical in maximizing the potential of an increasingly aging workforce. It should be noted that a research-based approach undergirds this publication and buttresses our efforts in providing a comprehensive perspective of the issues and challenges that organizations and their human resource professionals will be addressing in the future.

In Chapters 2 and 3 our authors present the contexts within which these issues increasingly will be embedded. Chapter 2, The Workforce of Tomorrow, elaborates upon three trends in the demography of the workforce that will be playing out during the first two decades of this century; namely, the slowdown in the growth of the labor force, the aging of the workforce, and the increasing diversity in the profile of the workforce. Chapter 3, The Workplace of Tomorrow, details three major developments shaping the workplace of today and tomorrow; namely, the move from a production to an information and service-driven economy, the increasing pervasiveness of technology in the society at large and in the world of work, and the globalization of all sectors of society, especially critical in the world of work. The changing realities of both the workforce and the workplace have significant implications for organizations and their human resource professionals.

Chapter 2

The Workforce of Tomorrow

Howard N Fullerton, Jr.

The oldest baby boomer will turn 62 in 2008; the youngest member of the baby boom cohort will be 67 in 2031. Over the 23-year period between 2008 and 2031 baby boomers should witness as dramatic a change in the labor force as the period over which they entered the labor force, which extended from the late 1950s to the late 1980s. This demonstrates the scale of time over which demographic phenomena take place. A 1980-2020 time frame thus encompasses a period in which the baby boomers finished entering the labor force and a period in which it will begin leaving the labor force. What can be expected in the second half of such a dynamic period? The workforce should grow more slowly. The labor force should age. The labor force should also be more diverse.

Please note that the labor force projections in this chapter are not based on the recently completed 2000 census. This is because the Current Population Survey (CPS) – source of the historical data on the labor force for these articles and the basis of the Bureau of Labor Statistics (BLS) labor force projections – does not reflect the 2000 census. A population projection based on the 2000 census was not available at the time this chapter was written. These projections also do not reflect the new race categories promulgated by the Office of Management and Budget in "Revisions to the Standards for the Classification of Federal Data on Race and Ethnicity," Directive 15, October 30, 1997.

Overview

Over the 2000-2020 time period, the workforce is projected to increase by 17 percent or 24 million. This increase is only half the 32-percent increase over the previous 20-year period, 1980–2000, when the labor force grew by 34 million. (See Table 2.1.) These labor force projections were first presented in Fullerton and Toossi (2001) and in Toossi (2002).

In 2001, half the labor force was aged 40 or older; this characteristic should continue through 2020 (see Table 2.2). Labor force change is affected by the aging of the baby boom generation, persons born between 1946 and 1964. In 2020, the baby boom cohort will be ages 56 to 74; this age group will show significant growth over the 2000–2020 period.

Race or Hispanic origin groups have shown – and are projected to continue to show – widely varied growth rates because of divergent rates of population growth in the past. The Asian and other labor force is projected to increase most rapidly. The Hispanic labor force, which is larger than the black labor force, is projected to increase almost as quickly. Despite slower than average growth, white non-Hispanics will continue to comprise almost two-thirds of the workforce.

Slower Labor Force Growth

Labor force change is generally analyzed by considering separately the effects of population change and of change in the labor force participation rate – the proportion of a population in the labor force. In practice, population growth accounts for most labor force growth.

Slower Population Growth

Populations grow when births exceed deaths (natural increase) or when in migration exceeds out migration (net immigration is positive). The three population pyramids in Figures 2.1 through 2.3 illustrate the changing composition of the population.

When fertility drops, the population grows more slowly unless there is a large increase in immigration. For example, in the United States, there were 4 million births and 1.2 million immigrants in 1999.

Table 2.1

Civilian Labor Force by Sex, Age, Race, and Hispanic Origin, 1980 to 2000 and Projected, 2020

Group	Level (in thousands)			Share (in percent)			Change (in thousands)		Annual growth rate (in percent)	
	1980	2000	2020	1980	2000	2020	1980-2000	2000-20	1980-2000	2000-20
Total, 16 years and older	106,940	140,863	164,681	100.0	100.0	100.0	33,923	23,817	1.4	0.8
Men	61,453	74,247	85,430	57.5	53.4	51.9	13,794	10,183	1.0	0.6
Women	45,487	65,616	79,250	42.5	46.6	48.1	20,129	13,634	1.8	0.9
16 to 24	25,300	22,715	25,653	23.7	16.1	15.6	-2,585	2,938	-0.5	0.6
25 to 34	29,227	31,669	37,905	27.3	22.5	23.0	2,442	6,236	0.4	0.9
35 to 44	20,463	37,838	35,277	19.1	26.9	21.4	17,375	-2,561	3.1	-0.3
45 to 54	16,910	30,467	32,406	15.8	21.6	19.7	13,557	1,940	3.0	0.3
55 to 64	11,985	13,974	25,195	11.2	9.9	15.3	1,989	11,221	0.8	3.0
65 and older	3,054	4,200	8,243	2.9	3.0	5.0	1,146	4,043	1.6	3.4
65 to 75	2,619	3,410	7,045	2.4	2.4	4.3	791	3,635	1.3	3.7
75 and older	435	790	1,198	0.4	0.6	0.7	355	408	3.0	2.1
White	93,600	117,574	130,881	87.5	83.5	79.5	23,974	13,307	1.1	0.5
Black	10,865	16,603	21,856	10.2	11.8	13.3	5,738	5,254	2.1	1.4
Asian and other[1]	2,476	6,687	11,944	2.3	4.7	7.3	4,211	5,257	5.1	2.9
Hispanic origin	6,146	15,368	26,321	5.7	10.9	16.0	9,222	10,953	4.7	2.7
Other than Hispanic origin	100,794	125,495	138,359	94.3	89.1	84.0	24,701	12,864	1.1	0.5
White non-Hispanic	87,633	102,963	107,043	81.9	73.1	65.0	15,329	4,080	0.8	0.2

[1] The "Asian and other" group includes (1) Asians and Pacific Islanders and (2) American Indians and Alaska Natives. The historical data are derived by subtracting "Black" and "White" from the "Total, 16 years and older" group; projections are made directly, not by subtraction.
NOTE: Detail may not equal total or 100 percent due to rounding.
Source: Fullerton & Toossi (2001) and Toossi (2002).

Table 2.2

Distribution of the Population and Labor Force by Age, 1980 to 2000 and Projected, 2010-2020

Group	Population (in percent)						Labor force (in percent)					
	1980	1990	2000	2010	2015	2020	1980	1990	2000	2010	2015	2020
Total, 16 years and older	100.0	100.0	100.0	100.0	100.0	100.0	100.0	100.0	100.0	100.0	100.0	100.0
16 to 24	22.2	17.7	16.4	16.8	16.0	15.2	23.7	17.9	16.1	16.1	15.6	15.6
25 to 39	30.1	33.3	28.4	25.0	25.1	25.3	37.8	42.0	35.7	31.1	32.5	34.0
40 and older	47.7	49.1	55.2	58.2	58.9	59.4	38.6	40.1	48.2	49.8	50.5	50.4
65 and older	14.5	15.5	15.6	15.8	17.7	20.0	2.9	2.7	3.0	4.3	5.0	5.0
75 and older	5.4	6.1	7.1	7.0	7.1	7.8	0.4	0.4	0.6	0.6	0.7	0.7

NOTE: Detail may not equal total or 100 percent due to rounding.
Source: Fullerton & Toossi (2001) and Toossi (2002). More detail is available at http://www.bls.gov/emp/emplab1.htm .

Λ 5 percent drop in births (200 thousand) would require a 16 percent increase in immigration to offset it. Generally, immigration does not offset the drop in births and the population ages.

In 1980, population groups aged birth to 14 were smaller than the age groups 15 to 34, reflecting the drop in fertility following the end of the baby boom (Figure 2.1). Ages 45 to 49 reflected the birth dearth which occurred around 1930. More generally, the shape shows the effect of mortality on the population. When populations change from a high-fertility, high-mortality regime to a low-fertility, low-mortality one, the shape changes from a pyramid to a skyscraper with a pyramid on top. The pyramid shape of the 1980 population shows the beginning of this process. By 2000, the population is approaching the vertical, skyscraper shape for ages below 50, with notches reflecting the post-baby boom birth cohorts (Figure 2.2). By 2020, the vertical part is approaching age 70 (Figure 2.3).

It is possible to follow the baby boom genera-

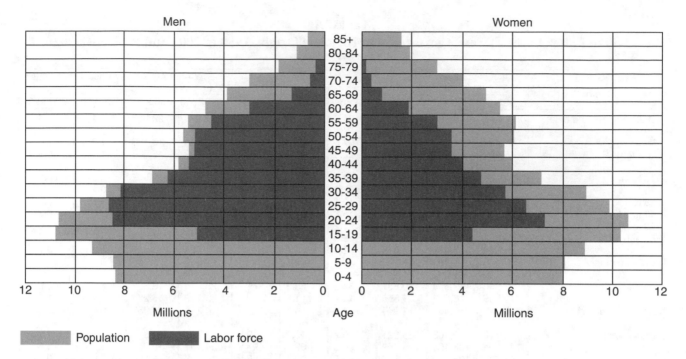

Figure 2.1 Population and labor force, 1980.

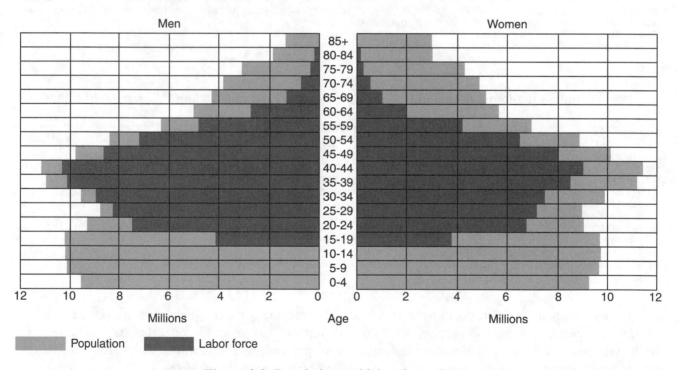

Figure 2.2 Population and labor force, 2000.

tion through the period by following the upward movement of the bulge from 1980 to 2000. Mortality will begin to affect the size of the baby boom cohort by 2020. These projections do not show the baby boom generation remaining in the labor force to a much greater extent than earlier groups, though labor force participation rates of all older age groups are projected to increase.

The civilian noninstitutional population will continue to increase over the 2000–2020 period, at

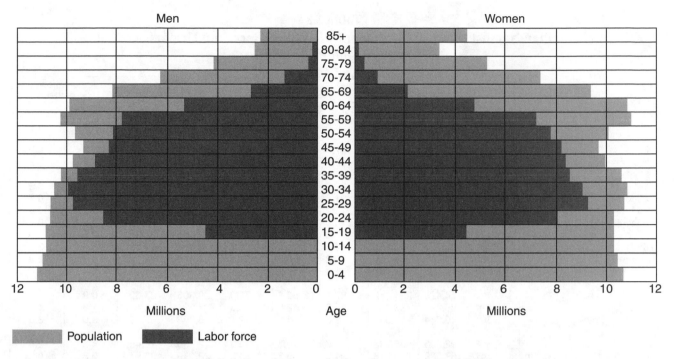

Figure 2.3 Population and labor force, projected 2020.

a slightly lower rate of growth than the previous 20 years. Table 2.3 provides three snapshots of the population at 20-year intervals over the 1980–2020 period. This analysis of changes in the civilian noninstitutional population is based on the Census Bureau's middle population projection scenario of the resident population (United States Bureau of the Census [USBC], 2000c). The civilian noninstitutional population includes civilian residents of the 50 states and the District of Columbia not in institutions (such as prisons and nursing homes). Thus, the analysis does not cover some members of the older population. The civilian noninstitutional population includes those people likely to work or seek work in the market economy. (Prison workers and draftees are not in the market economy.)

The various race and ethnic groups also exhibit differential rates of population growth. Either natural increase or net immigration—or both—can be a factor in the different growth rates. The effects of migration on the demographic composition of the population can be seen in two ways in Table 2.3. The first is reflected in the very rapid growth rate of the Asian and other and Hispanic populations. The projected growth rates of these groups are expected to be greater than those of the other race

groups over the 2000-2020 period. The second way migration affects the composition of the population is by age distribution. For example, persons aged 25 to 34 numbered 36.6 million in 1980. Twenty years later, this same cohort was larger, 36.9 million. The only way these cohorts could increase is through net migration. Because the overwhelming reason for migration is the opportunity to work, the population at these ages is affected significantly by migration (Massey et al., 1993).

The Hispanic and black populations are also growing faster than the overall population because of higher fertility. This is projected to continue during the 2000-2020 period. Because of this, Hispanics, which were 6 percent of the 16 and older population in 1980, are expected to be 15 percent in 2020. The Asian and other share of the population is projected to increase from 2 percent to 7 percent over the same period. Blacks, whose population share has been increasing a percentage point a decade since 1950, are expected to have their share grow by only 2 percentage points over the 2000-2020 period. White non-Hispanics, who were more than 80 percent of the 1980 population, will see their share drop to 66 percent by 2020 (see Table 2.3). These differential rates of population growth lead to differential rates of labor force growth.

Table 2.3
Civilian Noninstitutional Population by Sex, Age, Race, and Hispanic Origin,
1980 to 2000 and Projected, 2020

Group	Numbers (in thousands)			Share (in percent)			Change (in thousands)		Annual growth (in percent)	
	1980	2000	2020	1980	2000	2020	1980-2000	2000-20	1980-2000	2000-20
Total, 16 years and older	167,745	209,699	253,069	100.0	100.0	100.0	41,954	43,370	1.1	0.9
Men	79,398	100,731	121,569	47.3	48.0	48.0	21,333	20,838	1.2	0.9
Women	88,348	108,968	131,500	52.7	52.0	52.0	20,620	22,532	1.1	0.9
16 to 24	37,178	34,453	38,550	22.2	16.4	15.2	-2,725	4,098	-0.4	0.6
25 to 34	36,558	37,417	43,120	21.8	17.8	17.0	859	5,712	0.1	0.7
35 to 44	25,578	44,605	40,767	15.2	21.3	16.1	19,027	-3,838	2.8	-0.4
45 to 54	22,563	36,905	38,594	13.5	17.6	15.3	14,342	1,689	2.5	0.2
55 to 64	21,520	23,615	41,472	12.8	11.3	16.4	2,095	17,857	0.5	2.9
65 and older	24,350	32,705	50,557	14.5	15.6	20.0	8,355	17,852	1.5	2.2
65 to 75	15,365	17,809	30,764	9.2	8.5	12.2	2,444	12,954	0.7	2.8
75 and older	8,988	14,896	19,793	5.4	7.1	7.8	5,908	4,897	2.6	1.4
White	146,122	174,428	201,452	87.1	83.2	79.6	28,306	27,024	0.9	0.7
Black	17,824	25,218	33,625	10.6	12.0	13.3	7,394	8,407	1.8	1.4
Asian and other[1]	3,801	10,054	17,992	2.3	4.8	7.1	6,253	7,938	5.0	3.0
Hispanic origin	9,598	22,393	38,793	5.7	10.7	15.3	12,795	16,400	4.3	2.8
Other than Hispanic origin	158,147	187,306	214,276	94.3	89.3	84.7	29,159	26,970	0.8	0.7
White non-Hispanic	136,847	153,111	166,313	81.6	73.0	65.7	16,264	13,202	0.6	0.4
Age of baby boom:	16 to 34	36 to 54	56 to 74							

[1] The "Asian and other" group includes (1) Asians and Pacific Islanders and (2) American Indians and Alaska Natives. The historical data are derived by subtracting "Black" and "White" from the "Total, 16 years and older" group; projections are made directly, not by subtraction.
NOTE: Detail may not equal total or 100 percent due to rounding.
Source: Fullerton & Toossi (2001) and Toossi (2002).

Slower Labor Force Growth

Clearly, there were more men in the labor force than women in 1980. By 2000, the age distributions of men and women were more similar. By 2020, their distributions will exhibit similar shapes—thus nearly equal labor force numbers, until the older ages. Older women in 2020 are projected to be less likely than men to be in the labor force. However, it is at the older ages when the number of women in the population exceeds the number of men. This is seen in Figures 2.1 through 2.3, which display the labor force with the population.

Since the labor force, as measured in the Current Population Survey, concerns only those ages 16 and older, a change in births operates with a long lag on the labor force. For example, the baby boom started in 1946, but effects were not really noticed in the labor force until the late 1960s. Similarly, births dropped over the late 1960s and early 1970s while the labor force was growing at an increasing rate.

The period over which the baby boomers entered the labor force was one characterized by increasing labor force growth. This reflects both that the later years of the baby boom saw more births than the earlier years and the rise in labor force participation of women. The departure of the baby boomers will result in successively lower rates of growth in the labor force according to Bureau of Labor Statistice (BLS) projections (see Table 2.1). The labor force growth, which had averaged 2.6 percent annually over the 1970s, decreased to a rate of 1.6 percent a year over the 1980s. The growth rate of the 1990s, 1.1 percent annually, is also the projected rate for the first decade of this century. After that, the rate is projected to drop to below a percentage point a year in the 2010-15 period and to just above zero for the next five years.

Typically, the growth rate for the labor force of men has been lower than for their population; this is expected to continue during the 2000-2020 period. This implies decreasing labor force participation. Women, whose labor force participation rates have been increasing, have labor force growth rates higher than their population; this is not expected to continue after 2010. The female labor force has typically grown faster than that of men; this should continue until 2015, when the older age structure of the female population affects the growth of their labor force. Older women have lower labor force participation rates than younger women.

White non-Hispanics were the largest group in the labor force in 1980, accounting for 82 percent of the total. However, over the 1980-90 and 1990–2000 periods, this group had the lowest growth rates—1.1 and 0.5 percent a year—among the groups analyzed. The smallest group, Asians and others, had the highest growth rate. Indeed, growth rates were inversely related to ranking by size, and the rankings were the same for men and women. Asian and other women and men each were the fast-est growing labor force group over the 1980–2000 period. Moreover, all minority groups increased their share of the labor force. Hispanics increased their share from 5.7 percent to 10.9 percent, Asians and others increased their share from 2.3 percent to 4.7 percent and blacks increased their share from 10.2 percent to 11.8 percent. By contrast, white non-Hispanics decreased their share of the labor force from 82 percent to 73 percent (See Table 2.1). The pattern of labor force growth rates is more reflective of changes in the population than the changes in labor force participation rates.

The Hispanic population has been growing and is expected to continue to grow faster than the black population; as a result, the Hispanic labor force will be larger than the black labor force by 2010. Given that projections have errors and the possibility that the method for enumerating race and Hispanic origin could change, the specificity of the year should be viewed with caution. The male Hispanic labor force exceeded that of black men in 2000; the female black labor force greatly exceeded that of Hispanic women.

The Asian and other group's population is also growing rapidly. However, it is expected to remain the smallest of the four labor force groups well beyond 2020. Similarly, the white non-Hispanic group, which is growing slowly, will remain the largest group. Its share of the 2020 labor force is

expected to be 66 percent and would be 4.1 million larger than that in 2000, despite dropping by 2 million between 2015 and 2020. The remaining three groups are expected to add 19.7 million persons to the labor force over the same period. White non-Hispanics will remain by far the largest group of the labor force for years after 2020 (Table 2.1).

Immigration, although not offsetting the drop in fertility, has changed the race and ethnic composition of the population and labor force.

Consequences of Slower Labor Force Growth

Slower population growth leads to slower labor force growth; the slower population growth is due to lower fertility. It is unlikely that net immigration will offset the drop in fertility rates. Will slow labor force growth lead to worker shortages? BLS has illuminated the problems of identifying shortages (Veneri, 1999). The United States has experienced two decades with labor force growth rates of 1.1 percent annually. The 1950s ended with a recession and there was no perception of supply shortages. The end of the 1990s concluded the longest peacetime economic growth the United States has ever experienced and there was a perception of supply shortages, even with substantial immigration. It is reasonable to conclude that if the first decade of the current century does experience growth of 1.1 percent yearly, the perception of supply problems will depend on the rate of economic growth.

For the period after 2010, there is no analogy. The labor force will grow slowly because a large segment of the population, the baby boom cohort, will be at the ages at which retirement is expected. There have not been sufficient births in the United States to replace these workers. Since people in their 60s and 70s are now healthier than in the past, and since the physical aspect of much work is less challenging, it is tempting to think that the BLS projection of labor force participation rates for older workers will prove to be too low. Given the low rates of savings of the U.S. population, many workers may not be able to retire. Other workers, with defined contribution pension plans, are at the mercy of the stock and bond market. A prolonged upswing in the market would induce retirement; a stock market that does not change will defer retirement. However, a prolonged stock market boom would probably accompany an economic boom and attract workers. A period of slow economic growth would likely accompany a sluggish stock market, so there might not be high demand for workers.

Alternatively, the almost unprecedented growth in labor productivity since 1995, virtually unaffected by the 2001 recession and by the events of September 11, 2001, may mean that strong economic growth is possible even with a slowing growth in labor supply. Obviously many factors, some with high degrees of uncertainty, will be important in determining whether or not worker shortages develop between now and 2020.

Aging of the Workforce

A population generally ages because fertility drops; when mortality at older ages also improves, the effect is reinforced. In the United States, such a decrease in fertility was experienced at the end of the baby boom. Although fertility has increased since the mid 1970s, rates have never been above replacement for an extended period of time. Fertility for whites—the major population group—has not been above replacement since the late 1970s. The current population projection does not have white non-Hispanic fertility at replacement levels in the 2000-20 period.

As the baby boomers age, the labor force will also grow older. When the baby boomers entered the labor force, the median age dropped; thereafter, it rose as the baby boom cohort itself aged. The workforce is expected to continue aging: whether this is expressed in terms of median age or the proportion of the labor force that is over some threshold age, such as 40 and older, or 65 and older (Table 2.2). If aging is defined as an increase in the proportion of the population (or labor force) 40 and older, then aging will peak in 2010 at 50.4 percent and then drop modestly. At the same time, the population will continue to age.

The departure of the baby boomers from the labor force will lessen the aging of the workforce. This is because the older population is less likely to be in the labor force. Table 2.4 shows the labor force career of the baby boom cohort over the 1980-2020 period.

It is easy to see that the share of the labor force is related to the pattern of labor force participation by age. Right now, the baby boom cohort is as great a share of the labor force as it will ever be. By 2020, it will not have that much impact on the labor force. However, the baby boomers will still be around, generating demand and the population will continue to age.

Another way to indicate that the labor force is aging is to study trends in the median age of the labor force. The median age is that age at which half the labor force is younger and half older—the middle. It may seem odd to look at the middle, but if the median age of the labor force is at or above what is considered "old," then the labor force must have aged. The median age of the labor force, at 40.5 years in 1962 (the highest level attained before the baby boomers entered the labor force), dropped steadily until 1980, and since then, it has been rising. With the population projected to continue aging as rapidly as in the past, the median age of the labor force in 2010 is projected to just exceed the level reached in 1962, then decrease. Table 2.5 provides median ages for the labor force aged 16 and older.

The median age of both the population and the labor force is increasing, but the median age of the former is increasing more than that of the latter. The median age of the labor force is less than the population's because the labor force participation rates of older persons are much lower than the rates of young workers. The growth of the older population combined with the increase in their participation rates results in the median age of the 2010 projected labor force being significantly lower than the median age of the 16 and older population.

Historically, white participants in the labor force have been older than the rest of the labor force. This is projected to continue, with the difference reaching 0.5 year in 2020. Compared with whites, the black and Hispanic groups are younger, reflecting their higher birth rates. As a result, their youth are projected to claim a somewhat larger share of their respective populations. Black participants in the labor force have been about 1.5 years to 3.1 years younger than the overall labor force; this age gap is projected to continue through 2020. In 2000, the median age of Asian and other participants in

Table 2.4
Labor Force Status of the Baby Boomers

Group	1980	1990	2000	2010	2020
Civilian labor force (in thousands)					
16 to 24	25,300				
25 to 34	29,227	35,929			
35 to 44		32,145	37,838		
45 to 54			30,467	36,783	
55 to 64				21,204	24,200
65 to 74					7,045
Baby boomers	54,527	68,074	68,305	57,986	31,245
As a share of the labor force (in percent)	51.0	54.1	48.5	36.8	19.0
Civilian noninstitutional population (in thousands)					
16 to 24	37,178				
25 to 34	38,558	42,976			
35 to 44		37,719	44,605		
45 to 54			36,905	43,894	
55 to 64				34,846	39,303
65 to 74					30,764
Baby boomers	73,736	80,695	81,510	78,740	70,066
As a share of the population (in percent)	44.0	44.8	38.9	33.7	27.7
Labor force participation rate (in percent)					
16 to 24	68.1				
25 to 34	79.9	83.6			
35 to 44		85.2	84.8		
45 to 54			82.6	83.8	
55 to 64				60.9	61.6
65 to 74					22.9
Baby boomers	73.9	84.4	83.8	73.6	44.6

NOTE: Detail may not equal total or 100 percent due to rounding.
Source: Fullerton & Toossi (2001) and Toossi (2002).

Table 2.5
Median Age of the Labor Force Actual 1980-2000, and Projected, 2010-2020

Group	1980	1990	2000	2010	2015	2020
Total	34.6	36.6	39.3	40.6	40.5	40.2
Men	35.1	36.7	39.3	40.6	40.5	40.2
Women	33.9	36.8	39.3	40.6	40.7	40.7
White	34.8	36.8	39.7	41.3	41.1	40.7
Black	33.3	34.9	37.3	37.7	38.0	38.2
Asian and other	34.1	36.5	37.8	38.7	38.8	38.8
Hispanic origin[1]	32.0	33.2	34.9	36.4	36.6	36.7

[1] Persons of Hispanic origin may be of any race.
Source: Fullerton & Toossi (2001) and Toossi (2002).

the labor force was 1.5 years less than the median age of the overall labor force. This difference is expected to continue through 2020. Hispanic participants generally have been younger, due to their higher fertility rate. This group is projected to continue having a lower median age than the overall labor force, but it is projected to age from a median of 34.9 years in 2000 to 36.7 years in 2020, reflecting the aging of earlier immigrants. The median age of all race and Hispanic groups is expected to increase during the 2000–2010 period.

Characteristics of Older Workers

What are the current characteristics of the older labor force? To some extent that has been addressed. From Figures 2.1 to 2.3 (the population and labor force pyramids) it is clear that older men are more likely to be in the labor force than older women. For every 100 women in the labor force in 2000 aged 40 and older, there were 114 men; for every 100 women in the labor force aged 75 and older, there were 146 men. Given that the older population has more women than men, the labor force participation rates of older women are lower than those of men. In 2000, the labor force participation rates of men 45 to 54 were 12 percentage points higher; those of men 65 and older were 8 percentage points higher. The differences for ages 45 to 54 and 55 to 64 are projected to decrease, but the difference for ages 65 and older is expected to persist. The labor force participation rates for both groups are projected to increase by about the same amount.

Older workers are less likely to be unemployed. This reflects their seniority; in mass layoffs, older workers take more time to find a new job and it is likely to have significantly lower pay than the earlier job. In 2000, workers 65 and older had an unemployment rate of 3.1 percent; the overall rate was 4.0 percent. Younger "old" workers had even lower unemployment rates, those 45 to 54 and 55 to 64 both had a rate of 2.5 percent. For workers over the age of 61, there is an alternative to unemployment: retirement. For a few workers under the age of 62, retirement is also an alternative, although it is clear that most pensions for persons that age are quite low.

Older workers are also more likely to be self-employed. Workers 45 and older represented 45 percent of employment in 2000, but 52 percent of the self-employed.

Given that workers 40 and older represent almost half the labor force and will soon be more than half, they are likely to be comparable to the overall labor force in many ways. As workers age, their share of part-time employment increases: a quarter of those 55 and older were employed part-time; for those aged 65 and older, more than half were part-time. For workers 75 and older, 60 percent were employed part-time, or more interestingly, 40 percent were employed full-time. Workers aged 65 and older were about 10 percent of the part-time labor force.

Educational Attainment of Older Workers

If there will be a need for workers in the future and if there will be older people available to work, will there be a match between those workers and the jobs? Or to put it another way, what will the education levels be of the older labor force in 2020?

One way to consider the level of education of the older labor force in 2020 is consider the date of birth of some groups. Those who will be 40 in 2020 would have been born in 1980; those who will be age 55 would have been born in 1965; and those who will be 65 were born in 1955. So, 40-year-olds in 2020 would have graduated from high school around 1998; 55 year-olds would have graduated in 1983; and those who would be 65 would have graduated in 1973. Many of the 40-year-olds in 2020 are still in the process of completing their college work; few have completed graduate school. This suggests that most older workers will have educational levels comparable to today's workforce.

Educational attainment is typically measured for the 25 and older population; for those who will be 40 in 2020, the first measurement will be in 2005. For the other two groups, it is possible to give some indication of their education. To quote the U.S. Bureau of the Census (1984):

> In March 1981, about 70 percent of all adults 25 years old and over were high school graduates. Ten years earlier, the figure was 58 percent, and 1950, only 34 percent were high school graduates. The change reflected the rapidly increasing high school graduation rate

of young people, mortality among the older, less well-educated population and the larger relative size of the younger cohorts. Of young adults 25 to 29 years old, 86 percent were high school graduates in 1981, and only 53 percent were high school graduates in 1950 (p. 1).

Almost 90 percent of the population has completed high school and the number of people completing college has been increasing. The number of jobs that typically require a college degree has been increasing and is expected to increase. This suggests that the supply and demand for educated workers may be in rough balance in the 2000-2020 period. Since BLS does not project the educational attainment of the labor force, it is not possible to be more specific. However, if the techniques that have been used to project the educational attainment of the population were employed for the labor force, the conclusions reached about the population in 2020 would be reached for the 2020 labor force.

Consider that more educated people have higher labor force participation rates than less educated people; further, consider that younger cohorts in the labor force are more highly educated than older cohorts (in 1990, 55 percent of the 65 and older population had completed high school). Finally, given that the older cohorts are less likely to be in the labor force, the labor force should have at least the same education level as the population. Of course, since different race, Hispanic origin groups have varying levels of educational attainment, differential growth rates of the various groups could affect the educational attainment of the population. The population is projected to have a gradually increasing level of educational attainment.

There are two conclusions about the increasing age of the population. First, the labor force will age through 2010; then measures of aging will decrease slightly. Second, the older labor force in 2020 will be more educated than the older labor force of 2000.

Increasing Diversity of the Workforce

The workforce of the future not only will grow more slowly and become older, it will become more diverse. In 1980, white non-Hispanics accounted for 82 percent of the labor force; by 2020 they will be only 65 percent (Table 2.1). Their labor force is projected to drop in size after 2015. In other words, the minority share will increase from 18 percent to 35 percent, almost a doubling in share. The relative rankings will also change, with those of Hispanic origin being the largest minority. The older labor force will be more diverse in the future than now; all race, Hispanic-origin groups will age.

Taking "older" to be those aged 40 and older, in 1980, white non-Hispanics accounted for 84 percent of older workers; by 2000, this share had dropped to 77 percent and in 2020, they are expected to account for 69 percent. White non-Hispanics, of all ages, are expected to account for 66 percent of the 2020 labor force.

Blacks, the second largest group in the 2000 labor force, made up 11.5 percent of the labor force or a total of 16.6 million. With a net change of 5.7 million, the group will increase in number, and by 2020, their share of the labor force is expected to be 13.3 percent, up 1.5 percentage points from 2000. In 1980, blacks comprised 9 percent of the 40 and older population; by 2020, this should increase to 12 percent.

In 2000, Hispanics (of all races) were the third largest labor force group, with 15.4 million workers representing 10.9 percent of the labor force. Because of their higher levels of migration, the Hispanic labor force is projected to increase by 9 million over the 2000–2020 period. By 2010, the Hispanic labor force is projected to be greater than the black labor force. The Hispanic labor force is projected to increase to 26 million persons in 2020. Hispanics were 5 percent of the older labor force in 1980; by 2020, they should account for 13 percent.

In 2000, the smallest racial group in the labor force was Asian and other. This group's labor force is projected to increase by 5.3 million over the 2000-2020 period, almost doubling in size (79 percent). This group was only 2 percent of the older population in 1980; in 2020, their share should have increased to 7 percent.

To demonstrate that each race or Hispanic origin group is aging, we can look at the share those 40 and older have of their labor force in 1980 or 2020. In 1980, older white non-Hispanics were 40 percent of their labor force; by 2020, 53 percent of the white non-Hispanic labor force should be older. Older persons were 35 percent of the black labor force in 1980; this is expected to increase to 46 percent by 2020. Older Asians had about the same proportions of their labor force in 1980 and the share of older Asians in their labor force is expected to increase by 13 percentage points by 2020. Hispanics had the youngest labor force in 1980, with only 30 percent aged forty and older; in 2020, older Hispanics are projected to account for 42 percent of the labor force. Thus, each of the race, Hispanic-origin groups is aging.

Education and Skills

Discussions of labor force shortages often turn to skill shortages; discussions of immigration, the source of much of the increase in diversity, turn to the "quality" of immigrants. "Quality" is measured by the level of education the immigrant has. Often, it seems that skill is also measured by years of formal schooling. It is well known that immigrants have bi-modal levels of education: a higher proportion than native-borns have a bachelors degree or higher and a greater proportion than native-borns have not completed high school.

Returning to supply issues, the changing racial and ethnic composition of the labor force has raised questions about education levels in the future. BLS has not prepared a projection of the labor force by educational attainment, but the Census Bureau has prepared one for the population (USBC, 2000b). The results of this projection, which is consistent with the labor force projection, indicate that the massive immigration we have sustained and are expected to experience will not have an adverse effect on education levels. The authors list four concerns about the future level of education and training, including ethnic shifts in the composition of the U.S. population and the high levels of immigration. Depending on their "high" or "low" projection, high school completion would increase by 4 to 7 percentage points and college graduation by 4 to 5 percentage points. Also, a higher proportion of the population would have some college education (USBC, 2000b, p. 9). Each of the various groups—

native born or foreign born—will exhibit an increase in educational attainment.

Just as earlier it was important to consider demand as well as supply in looking at worker shortages, so in considering skill shortages it is important to consider demand. BLS has not made any projections of the number of jobs demanded for the year 2020, but has for 2010 (Hecker, 2001). For each of the 700 occupations for which BLS made a projection, one of 11 typical levels of education or training was assigned. The results are aggregated by the levels (Table 2.6). Approximately 21 percent of jobs in 2000 typically had a bachelor's or higher degree. This share is expected to increase by a percentage point by 2010. Those occupations that typically have on-the-job training accounted for more than 70 percent in 2000; they are expected to account for just under 70 percent in 2010. If the rates of growth from 2000 to 2010 are applied to each of the 11 categories, the distribution does not change much; for example, the jobs with work-related training would drop to 68 percent. Jobs requiring a bachelor's degree or higher would increase to 23 percent. This raises the question: in the face of slow labor force growth, will such modest change in demand as reflected in the shares have a detrimental effect on economic growth?

Summary

The 2000-2020 period should experience labor force growth significantly lower than experienced in U.S. history; the labor force will age. Indeed, a majority of the labor force will be over the age of 40. The workforce will be more diverse; but, white non-Hispanics will continue to be a majority of the labor force.

Reviewing the skills issue: first, aside from years of formal schooling, there are no current data on the skills level of jobs; second, what murky information that is available on the demand side indicates that the proportions of jobs requiring an education will not change dramatically; third, the educational attainment of the population should increase. This is not to say that there is no reason to be concerned, but rather that the challenges appear to be manageable.

Table 2.6
Employment and Total Job Openings, 2000-2010, by Education and Training Category

Education and training category	Employment		Change	
	Number (in thousands)		Number (in thousands)	Percent
	2000	2010		
Total, all occupations	145,594	167,754	22,160	15.2
Bachelor's or higher degree	30,072	36,556	6,484	21.6
First professional degree	2,034	2,404	370	18.2
Doctoral degree	1,492	1,845	353	23.7
Master's degree	1,426	1,759	333	23.4
Bachelor's or higher degree, plus work experience	7,319	8,741	1,422	19.4
Bachelor's degree	17,801	21,807	4,006	22.5
Associate degree or postsecondary vocational award	11,761	14,600	2,839	24.1
Associate degree	5,083	6,710	1,626	32.0
Postsecondary vocational award	6,678	7,891	1,213	18.2
Work-related training	103,760	116,597	12,837	12.4
Work experience in a related occupation	10,456	11,559	1,102	10.5
Long-term on-the-job training	12,435	13,373	938	7.5
Moderate-term on-the-job training	27,671	30,794	3,123	11.3
Short-term on-the-job training	53,198	60,871	7,673	14.4

NOTE: Detail may not equal total or 100 percent due to rounding.
Source: Hecker (2001).

Chapter 3

The Workplace of Tomorrow

Dave Patel

The aging of the workforce, as discussed in the previous chapter, is only one of many changes that organizations will face in the next 20 years. Although these changes cannot be predicted with certainty, general trends can be extrapolated into the future. The purpose of this chapter is to examine possible future implications of the following trends: the shift to an information/service economy; the increased pervasiveness of technology; and continued globalization. After introducing these three trends in more detail, possible implications are discussed.

The Information/Services Economy

There is no better signal of the shift to a service economy than the growth of Wal-Mart Stores into the largest corporation in America, as rated by the *Fortune 500*. Wal-Mart became the first service company to rise to No. 1 in the history of the *Fortune 500* in 2002, and unseated perennial kings GM and Exxon (Murphy, 2002). One of those two industrial giants had held the top position every year since the list was established in 1955.

The U.S. economy will continue the long-term shift from a largely goods-producing economy to an information/services-producing economy. Industries such as finance, insurance, real estate, transportation, communications, and wholesale and retail trade are expected to account for approximately 20 million of the 22 million new wage and salary jobs generated over the 2000-2010 period, according to the Bureau of Labor Statistics (BLS). The services and retail trade industry divisions will account for nearly three-fourths of total wage and salary job growth. The BLS reports that professional occupations will grow the fastest, adding more new jobs than any other major occupational group. Technology, health care, and education and training will contribute the most

growth within the professional occupations (Hecker, 2001).

Technology

Communications Technology

At the dawn of the 21st century, it is difficult to fathom that such ordinary workplace tools as laptops and cell phones were exotic luxury items just 10 years before, and e-mail and the Internet were not yet commercially available. By 2010, universal Internet access, at least in the United States, may be taken for granted, and wireless broadband may be available to a large majority of the business community. Telecommunications technology such as GPS tracking devices and miniature computing and communications devices may be universally available, and required for many workers.

Within the next 5 to 10 years, voice-activated computers with wireless, broadband access to the Internet could connect the user to a vast database of information. Ray Kurzweil (1992), author of *The Age of Intelligent Machines*, predicts that within the next 10 years, computer screens will be placed directly on the retina, on eyeglasses, or on clothing. Web sites and chat rooms could become three-dimensional meeting places. Kurzweil also predicts that telephones that can simultaneously translate languages will be perfected, allowing two different language-speakers to communicate instantly, greatly enhancing global communications.

Certain professions will lead the way in the uses of these new technologies. For example, physicians and aerospace technicians could be the first to embrace virtual reality technology, discarding the thick manuals they have used for decades. Virtual reality will allow them to see three-dimensional blueprints of the human body or an airplane literally before their eyes.

Robots and Artificial Intelligence

Imagine a future where everyone will have a robot house-helper that will take care of the mundane household chores that take so much of our time, like cleaning the house or washing clothes or even cooking meals. And imagine working side by side with robots that perform repetitive or dangerous jobs, such as building skyscrapers.

If you think this is just a Hollywood fantasy, think again. Robots already perform many tasks that used to be performed by humans, and in our lifetime will take over many more duties.

Robots that look very much like the characters from movies are already being used by hospitals to deliver drugs, food trays, and laboratory specimens. Hospitals operate around the clock and face severe labor shortages, so robots that can perform some of the more routine tasks 24 hours a day, 7 days a week are a tremendous boon. More advanced robots are being used to do some kinds of surgery. As artificial intelligence technology improves the capabilities of machines to perform more complicated tasks, it is not difficult to imagine robots entirely taking over either the less skilled tasks, like delivering mail or cleaning windows, but also physically dangerous tasks such as fighting fires, drilling for oil, or working in mines.

Further out in the future, there may be an interesting melding between machines and humans. Today, people already use machines such as cochlear implants for better hearing. Retinal implants are not far behind. Nano-technology and robotics will one day provide amazing prosthetics that can essentially replicate the functions of human limbs.

People may one day walk around with computer microchips that allow them to see in the dark, or perform repetitive motions without tiring. Although some of these ideas sound far away, their importance for the workplace cannot be underestimated: In a 2002 survey, the Society for Human Resource Management (SHRM) found that "the impact of technology is foremost on the minds of human resource professionals" (p. 31).

Globalization

Despite the ebb and flow of political and cultural tensions, global economic interdependence will continue. A global economy, aided by a revolution in telecommunications technology, the spread of English as a *lingua franca*, the presence of large regional free-trade zones, increasing labor mobility, and unprecedented cross-border merger and acquisition activity, will create a truly global marketplace of goods, capital, and labor.

Global corporations will continue to be created through mergers and acquisitions of unparalleled scope. These megacorporations will achieve immense economies of scale and compete for goods, capital, and labor on a global basis, driving down prices and presenting a plethora of options for consumers and for workers. Large corporations will assert more power on the global stage. As of 2000, 51 corporations were among the 100 largest economies in the world. Only 22 countries had gross domestic products (GDPs) larger than the 2000 sales of each of the top five corporations: General Motors, Wal-Mart, Exxon Mobil, Ford Motor, and Daimler Chrysler (Institute for Policy Studies, 2000).

In this global marketplace, English will become the second language of the world. In 2000, English was spoken by an estimated 1.5 billion people—a quarter of the world's population. *Time* estimates that during 2000, three-quarters of the world's mail was written in English, and more than a billion people were learning English. More than 60 countries counted English as their official or dominant language, and at least 80 percent of Internet sites were in English (Geary, 1997). The dominance of English as the language of the global economy will continue to rise in a self-fulfilling cycle as more people see the necessity of being conversant in English. Already, countries such as India have built a considerable economy based on the knowledge of English. India's huge talent pool of English-speaking software engineers has led many technology companies, including Microsoft and Oracle, to create development centers in India.

As English becomes the universal business language around the world, Spanish will become the second language of the United States. The Hispanic population in the United States grew by more than 60 percent during the 1990s, becoming the largest ethnic minority in the country (United States Bureau of the Census [USBC], 2001). The Census Bureau predicts that Hispanics will account for a quarter of the total U.S. population by 2030, and this increase will be reflected across age groups, gender, and socioeconomic strata. This suburbanization of diversity will lead to a necessity to learn Spanish, which will be critical for certain groups such as health care workers and public safety officials. Knowledge of Spanish will also prove to be a competitive advantage for employers, businesses, and politicians.

Implications

These three trends, by themselves and in combination, are likely to continue to radically transform the workplace as we move deeper into the 21st century. There are eight implications for the workplace that emerge from extrapolating these trends further into the future. Arguably, the first of these is the most far-reaching.

1. From Bureaucracy to the "New Organization"

With marketplaces going increasingly global and competitive, with technological advances speeding up over time, and with increased workforce mobility, the one thing that becomes clear is that the pace of change will continue to increase. Surviving, let alone thriving, in such an environment will place a heavy premium on flexible, nimble organizations that have a sound capacity for learning and adaptation (Senge, 1990).

Kanter (1989) predicts that winning organizations are those that emphasize "four F's: being Focused, Fast, Friendly, and Flexible" (p. 344). They can do so by becoming flatter, stressing responsiveness, and striving for synergies and teamwork. This involves a smaller, fixed core, which is consistent with the projected growth of the contingent labor force; it involves being embedded in a network of reliable business partners that can share resources or complement skill sets; and it suggests the demise of bureaucracy and hierarchy as we have known them in the past. Whereas the old corporate strategy was to get as big as possible to attain economies of scale, "increasingly today the corporate ideal lies in how *small* an organization can be and still get the job done" (p. 352). The strategic challenge is to do more with less. Two major tensions need to be addressed, however. One is between organiza-

tional flexibility and individual job security, while the second is between workplace overload and family commitments. Kanter makes 10 recommendations for national policy that can address these tensions and facilitate the transition to the new economy. They are:

> [A] human resource development tax credit; industry-level training partnerships; accelerated technology and language education; union management partnerships to plan workplace changes; incentives for profit-sharing and performance bonuses; stronger safety nets for displaced employees; day care; flex-year opportunities; flexible use of severance and unemployment benefits; and portable pensions (p. 370).

Ancona, Kochan, Scully, Van Maanen, and Westney (1999) reason along a similar vein when they argue that the "traditional bureaucratic form stresses distance and buffering from the external environment while the new form is constantly and tightly linked to other firms, both competitors and allies" (p. 6, Introduction). They propose that the shape of the "new" organizational form is becoming visible over time and can be described in terms of five features. Each is described briefly below.

Networked. Within the organization, there is a strong emphasis on cross-functional teams as the core unit of activity. There are systems that allow the free exchange of information along horizontal and vertical lines.

With respect to the environment, close and direct relationships with customers, suppliers, and other partners are important. This can be evident in an integration of business processes for increased efficiency and flexibility at reduced cost.

Flat. The new organization does more than just cut out layers of management structure. It also seeks "empowerment" of the operating levels of the organization, pushing decision-making down to the "front line" of the company" (p. 9, M-1). This has been facilitated by improved information technology, a need for a more rapid response, and pressures to cut cost.

Flexible. To some extent, flexibility is achieved with increased dependence on temporary structures such as projects and task forces, and on an increasingly contingent workforce. Flexibility also involves a shift away from standard approaches toward custom-made solutions, tailored to the unique needs of each customer.

Diverse. This characteristic flows from the previous three and addresses "the need for the new organization to accommodate a diversity of perspectives and approaches, career paths and incentive systems, people and policies within its boundaries" (p. 10, M-1). Moreover, the organization must be able to work with an increasingly diverse group of stakeholders.

Global. This feature of the new organization flows directly from the previously identified trend of increased globalization and economic interdependence. The networks mentioned above stretch across international borders and time zones. Factories are built outside of the home country, while marketing strategies are increasingly tailored to specific local customs and preferences.

Certainly, transitioning from the old, bureaucratic model to the new organization with these five features is a perilous path fraught with ambiguity and paradox. Ancona and associates point out these four contradictory consequences:

1. Flattening or downsizing the organization requires increased commitment and effort from employees, while reducing their job security.
2. Power is shifted "downwards" to teams on the front line, while at the same time a strong leader takes control and makes executive decisions.
3. The needs of the organization (in terms of staffing, for example) may be in conflict with those of the social environment in which it functions.
4. While shifting to the new organization model requires an emphasis on long-term results, pressures for improved performance continue to play out in the short term.

Nevertheless, the authors suggest that in spite of these problems inherent in transitioning from the old to the new organization form, this model is increasingly becoming accepted as the ideal form for the new economy and workplace realities.

Besides this "new organization," there are seven other implications of the three major trends for the workplace. They are introduced next.

2. Growing Skills Gap

The shift in the economy means that there will be more demand for high-skilled jobs than for low-skilled jobs. According to the BLS, employment in occupations requiring at least a bachelor's degree is expected to grow 21.6 percent; jobs requiring an associate's degree are projected to increase by 32 percent; and those requiring a postsecondary vocational award will grow 24.1 percent (see Figure 3.1). All but 2 of the 50 highest paying occupations will require a college degree (Hecker, 2001). New jobs will increasingly require both general and occupation-specific skills, will be more demanding, will involve more teamwork and worker participation, and will be in occupations that allow people to think and be creative on the job.

The fastest employment growth will occur in highly paid professional occupations. Growth in

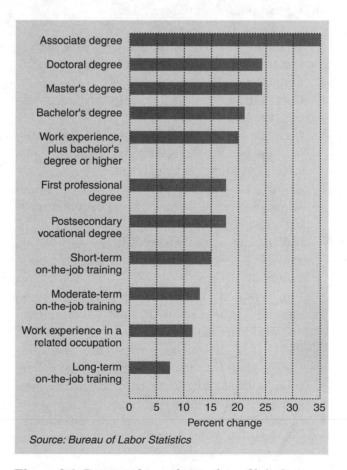

Source: Bureau of Labor Statistics

Figure 3.1 Percent change in number of jobs by most significant source of education or training, projected 2000-2010.

professional services jobs covers knowledge worker categories such as information technology (IT), business consulting, some health care services, and financial services. Because most of these occupations require more skills, faster relative growth in these occupations will drive a need for better workplace training.

The shift in the American and global economy means that those who lack education beyond high school or do not possess specific technology skills will find their opportunities and economic mobility severely restricted. The knowledge and service-based economy will require a level of knowledge and skill that, for the most part, can be gained only through programs offered beyond high schools. This is corroborated by a study conducted by the League for Innovation in the Community College (2000), in cooperation with the Pew Charitable Trusts. Their project identified the following eight clusters of critical life skills needed for students to survice and flourish in the digital age:

1. Technology skills – acquiring computer literacy and Internet skills, retrieving and managing information via technology
2. Communication skills – reading, writing, speaking, listening
3. Computation skills – understanding and applying mathematical concepts and reasoning, analyzing and using numerical data
4. Critical thinking and problem solving – evaluating, analyzing, synthesizing, decision making, creative thinking
5. Information management skills – collecting, analyzing, and organizing information from a variety of sources
6. Interpersonal skills – developing teamwork, relationship management, conflict resolution, and workplace skills
7. Personal skills – understanding self, managing change, learning to learn, taking personal responsibility, understanding, aesthetic responsiveness, and wellness
8. Community skills – building ethical, citizenship, diversity/pluralism, and local, community, global, and environmental awareness

The growing skills gap is perhaps best summed up by a Hudson Institute finding that 60 percent of jobs in 2020 will require skills that only 20 percent of the workforce currently possesses (Judy & D'Amico, 1997). Education reform in the nation's primary, secondary, and higher education systems is one way to tackle this problem. But rapid changes in a technology-reliant economy and the increasing transitory nature of the workplace mean that corporate training and development programs will also play a big role in skills development.

Enrollments in higher education institutions are expected to continue to increase by 15 percent to 17.7 million by 2012, up from 15.3 million in 2000 (National Center for Education Statistics, 2002). Continuing education does not necessarily mean just the pursuit of more formal degrees. Individual courses, certificates, and professional certification programs lasting anywhere from a few days to a few months are available through a myriad of public and private institutions, and increasingly available on the Internet.

Corporate training and development programs may also increase partnerships with nonprofit or for-profit educational institutions to tailor courses or entire programs for specific skills or proprietary knowledge. Many large companies already provide an institutionalized framework of study for their employees. These corporate universities include everything from highly technical courses to courses representing a broad overview of general business skills, and have gained a significant amount of attention in the past 10 years.

Training for subgroups such as the elderly or those with disabilities will also need to be tailored to their specific needs. Numerous studies cite the challenges the elderly face in dealing with technology, and as this group continues working well past traditional retirement age, their comfort with technology will need to be addressed. Additionally, only one-quarter of persons with disabilities who work have a computer at home. Since the information economy creates new work opportunities for those with disabilities, their training in working with emerging technology will also need to be tackled.

In sum, in a world where machines perform work previously done by humans, it will become imperative for workers (the human kind) to develop skills and for employers to provide training so that people can perform the jobs that require abstract thinking, reasoning, and problem solving.

3. Growing Contingent Workforce

The move to an information and services economy, together with technology advances and changes in generational attitudes regarding work, will continue to increase the numbers of non-full-time workers, and may change the very nature of the relationship between employer and employee.

Definitions of and estimates for alternative staffing arrangements, including part-time workers, temporary workers, project workers, and independent workers, vary greatly. The GAO (General Accounting Office, 2000) estimates that up to 30 percent of the U.S. workforce could be considered contingent workers. The GAO figure includes part-time workers as contingent. The BLS estimates that there are 12.2 million "nontraditional workers" as of 2000, including 8.2 million independent contractors; 2 million on-call workers; and 1.2 million temporary workers. An additional 769,000 were considered "workers provided through contract firms" (Hipple, 1998).

Meanwhile, Daniel Pink (2002), author of *Free Agent Nation*, says that 10 to 16 percent of the American workforce should be considered contingent workers. But while differing definitions abound as to what constitutes a non-full-time employee and how many workers should be included in what categories, the reasons for workers and employers opting for non-traditional methods of work seem to be crystallizing.

The Employment Policy Foundation (2000) reports that only 15 percent of the 5.6 million contingent workers in 1999 felt they had no other choice; the others chose contingent work for a variety of reasons, including flexibility in work schedule, family obligations, opportunities to get training and experience, and the possibility that the temporary assignment becomes permanent. As for the employers using contingent wokers, 81 percent of them indicated that they did so "to provide labor flexibility to meet demand fluctuations." Fort-eight percent used contingent workers "to aquire specific skills" lacking in their permanent workforce.

Amidst this menagerie of employment conditions, the nature of full-time work may also undergo significant changes, as flexible schedules and global teams create workplaces where few workers are full-time employees. Technology, globalization, and labor mobility are already creating virtual workforces spread in different locations, further throwing the concept of unified and singular workplaces into chaos. With vast amounts of workers becoming independent contractors or free agents, the traditional workplace that grew out of the Industrial Revolution will become obsolete, replaced by a marketplace where skills are sold as commodities.

4. Increased International Labor Mobility

The creation of political and economic zones of cooperation, such as the North American Free Trade Agreement, the European Union, and the pending Free Trade Area of the Americas (FTAA), is a manifestation of continued globalization and will significantly affect international labor mobility.

Large corporations such as Ford, GM, and Nestlé already employ more people outside of their headquarter countries than within those countries. Smaller companies will join the movement toward employing workers in multiple countries to take advantage of labor availability, cost savings, and market penetration. Advances in telecommunications technology will promote the practice of global teams that can work on projects around the clock.

Labor mobility will also not just be a one way "brain drain" of highly skilled professionals from developing countries to developed countries. According to a study by the Public Policy Institute of California (PPIC), the brain drain may be evolving into a "brain circulation" linking people, countries, and capital (2002). The PPIC study found that highly skilled, foreign-born IT professionals working in the United States maintain extensive ties to their native countries, advise companies and arrange business contracts there, meet with their home countries' government officials, and invest their own money in business ventures in their countries of origin. While the increasing occurrence of immigrants establishing business networks in their countries of origin offers solid evidence of the impact of global economic trends on the American workplace, it also will have profound consequences for economic development in developing countries. It could also present immigration policy challenges for employers and the government in the United States.

5. Increased Ethnic Diversity

A report from the United States Bureau of the Census (2001) reveals that the nation's foreign-born population in 2000 was 28.4 million, about 1 in 10 U.S. residents, and the BLS (Toossi, 2002) forecasts that by the year 2050, the U.S. labor force will be 23 percent Hispanic and 11 percent Asian. Census Bureau figures reveal that over 75 percent of immigrants coming into the United States come from Latin America and Asia.

For example, recent data indicate that Indian software engineers account for up to 30 percent of the U.S. information technology workforce, with Chinese software engineers not far behind. U.S. companies have heretofore relied on importing these skilled professionals to meet demand. As companies base operations abroad, and as foreign-born professionals become more involved with their native countries, labor shortages in the technology industry could increase.

Far from being a monolith, immigrant populations are as varied as the countries they come from. Educational attainment by immigrants is dependent on region, with 84 percent of Asians graduating from high school, as opposed to 37 percent for those from Central America. And even within the Latino population, wide disparities exist depending on country of origin and time spent in the United States.

Globalization will also have a considerable impact within the United States due to increasing ownership by non-U.S. based companies. A good example of this phenomenon is in the South, where the once ubiquitous textile mills are increasingly being replaced by automobile manufacturing plants, including those of BMW, Honda, Mercedes-Benz, Nissan, and Toyota. Small towns in Tennessee, Alabama, and Mississippi are experiencing new life as these automakers bring in thousands of jobs with above-average wages, attracting hundreds of related businesses.

An article in the *Washington Post* (Pressley, 2001) detailing the economic transformation of the South noted that the arrival of foreigners, or even their anticipated arrival changed the local culture. Seminars offered by local colleges and universities, advised, among other things, toning down "touchy-feely" southern effusiveness out of respect for the more formal Asian and German cultures.

All of these changes, from immigrants coming to the United States to foreign companies opening plants in small towns, will increase exposure to a wide variety of cultural practices.

6. Increased Bifurcation in Immigrant Workforce

While forecasts from the BLS predict a tremendous need for technology workers over the next decade, any lessening in the availability of educated, immigrant workers could present great challenges for employers and for human resource professionals. At the same time, the need for low-skilled workers, mainly in the farming and construction industries, will remain, and most likely will continue to be filled by immigrants. Many of these immigrants come into the United States illegally, and work illegally, often under deplorable conditions. This trend is likely to continue, absent any serious initiatives by the federal government.

7. Increased Bifurcation in Domestic Workforce

As technology continues to change the way we work, we will also have to remain cognizant of workers and workplaces that are not defined by cutting-edge technology. Labor forces may increasingly include low- and semi-skilled workers who are uncomfortable with technology and knowledge workers providing professional services who are entirely reliant upon and comfortable with technology. Clearly, as more people use technology to conduct day-to-day activities, being digitally connected will become ever more critical to economic, educational, and social advancement. At the same time, people who lack access to those tools will be at a growing disadvantage. This bifurcation may present new challenges for employers in creating unified and productive workforces.

8. Anytime, Anywhere Work

As the information and service industry becomes an ever-larger part of the U.S. economy, and as more work is done with the assistance of portable technologies, workers could be freed from going to a specific location for work, and from traditional work schedules. But these same technologies may also promote 24/7 work cultures.

Aggregate studies of the entire U.S. workforce point to slowly rising work hours over the 1990s, and surveys of U.S. workers reveal that workers themselves feel they are working much more than in the past. At the same time, family and personal needs and longer commutes create increasing stress on workers to balance work demands with family or personal needs. Work/life policies such as flextime and distance work, including telecommuting, have become a staple of the workplace in recent years, giving great flexibility to workers trying to juggle demands of work and home. But the very technologies—e-mail, home Internet access, mobile phones—that make possible flexible work time also enable employers to reach workers regardless of time and location. The use of "electronic leashes" seems to be increasing, extending even to employee vacations. The issue is also a concern for employees who have difficulty turning off or shutting out work.

As the economy becomes increasingly based on information and service industries, more dependent on wide access to technology as well as a get-it-done-yesterday culture that continues to blur the lines between work and non-work, work/life opportunities and constraints presented by the use of technology will continue to vex employers and workers. This push and pull between work and non-work will lead to customized employment contracts, where employees designate specific times and days for work; to project-based work, where employees work based on project deadlines; or even to contingent work.

The availability and use of technology in the workplace may also greatly decrease the importance of a specific physical location of work. Distance work, whether done in company-leased business centers or done at home through telecommuting, will increase due to the availability of technology and the acceptance of the practice by management. Safety and security concerns as well as the stress of commuting will also play a big role in the rising popularity of distance work. An estimated 25 million Americans regularly or occasionally telecommuted during 2000, according to the International Telework Association and Council (2001), and these numbers are likely to only continue increasing in the future with better and cheaper technology.

Although no one can accurately predict the future of the American economy or the shape of the ideal organization, the signs all point in the direction of the following changes in the workplace:

- Pervasive, personal technology will be available for all workers.
- Use of telecommuting and occurrence of distance work will increase.
- The existing bifurcation between skilled and unskilled work and workers will intensify.
- International labor mobility and ethnic diversity will increase.
- The use of contingent workers will increase.
- A growing skills gap could create the need for learning organizations.
- The line between work and non-work will continue to blur.
- Global competition will reward networked, flat, flexible, diverse, and global organizations.
- The pace of change will continue to increase.

Summary

The workplace of the future will be greatly changed by the demographics of the workforce, the information/services economy, the pervasiveness of technology, and continuing globalization.

Forecasts from the U.S. Bureau of Labor Statistics predict that the overwhelming job growth from 2000-2010 will be in the information and services sectors. As brain power replaces muscle power, workplaces too will change from factory floors to cubicle farms.

The workplace of tomorrow will also be replete with technology uses, from cutting-edge use of robotics and artificial intelligence machinery to perform many routine or hazardous tasks to the use of telecommunications equipment such as portable and powerful personal communications and computing equipment.

In turn, the revolution in technology, especially in telecommunications technology, will lead to a globalization of labor. The global economy of goods and capital will become the global economy of goods, capital, and labor, as corporations not only compete for customers in the global marketplace, but also compete for employees.

But this new global marketplace will also mean

that workers will need to keep up with the necessary skills to succeed in a changing environment. The pace of change could also produce tension within the workforce, as older workers not comfortable with the pervasiveness of technology work alongside younger workers who have always used the Internet and mobile phones.

These developments will also have far-reaching implications for the way corporations are organized. The first signs of the "new organization" appear to be emerging: key features are the extent to which the organization is networked, flat, flexible, diverse, and global.

Synthesis

Setting the Stage

Part Two sets the stage for the remainder of this book by asserting its central premise: U.S. organizations (for-profit and not-for-profit alike) will increasingly depend on older workers to meet their staffing and performance needs while facing continued pressure to adjust to global economic trends, continued technological innovation, and increased globalization.

Chapter 2 shows that the workforce is aging and diversifying and that its growth will slow to its lowest rate in history between 2010 and 2020. Chapter 3 sheds light on three global trends that are affecting the American workplace as well: the shift to an information/services economy, continued globalization, and continued technological innovation. These trends make for a tremendously challenging environment within which organizations will need to thrive.

The increased role of services in the economy will lead to increased bifurcation within the workforce, in terms of the "haves" and the "have-nots," the digitally connected and the digitally deprived, and between the higher and lower educated workers. Moreover, it will lead to an increased bifurcation in the job market. The gap between the low-end service jobs that require little formal education and the professional jobs occupied by the knowledge workers will continue to grow.

Communications technology is rapidly making the notion of geographic location irrelevant, because of the increased use of global, virtual project teams. In turn, this will help increase the cultural and ethnic diversity of the workforce and it will stimulate continued globalization. With time zones being crossed real-time at light speed, the 24-hour economy will continue to evolve and work-life boundaries will continue to blur. One implication is that organizations will have to be responsive and adaptable, in turn leading to lower hierarchy and increased flexibility. In turn, this is projected to lead

to increased growth of the contingent workforce.

If we superimpose all these trends on each other, we find that both aging workers (those age 40 and older, protected by the Age Discrimination in Employment Act) and organizations in the United States are likely to face major challenges in the upcoming decades.

Older workers are at risk of being relegated primarily to the lower end of the employment spectrum. Consider the following: Older workers are at higher risk of suffering from skills obsolescence than younger workers are. They are also less likely to have the computer skills so vital for success in any professional job. Many of them have not saved sufficiently for their retirement and will be faced with an economic necessity to remain in the workforce. Moreover, there are persistent stereotypes regarding the capability of older workers to perform and to learn. Therefore, older workers are the most likely candidates for the growing contingent workforce, covering the graveyard shift at a low-end service job with little or no prospect for training, job security, fringe benefits, work/life balance, job challenge, or any other aspect of the regular full-time job that the younger manager occupies. Clearly, this means that aging workers will have to be proactive about their own continued professional development. Advocacy groups such as AARP and the Alliance for Retired Americans will likely play an important role in how this plays out in the future. And of course, the challenge will at least in part be met at the voting booth.

The focus of this book, however, is less on the consequences for the aging workers themselves than it is on the consequences for employing organizations. With unemployment levels currently lower than in other recessions, one can only wonder what will happen during the next economic upturn. What will organizations do when the job growth outpaces the workforce growth? With increased labor force participation from women and ethnic and racial minorities, the only labor pool largely left untapped consists of the older workers. Enticing them not to take retirement when they become eligible will be a formidable challenge, let alone enticing the retired to come out of retirement and rejoin the workforce.

Fast forward to the year 2020. It might look like this:

The American workforce includes proportionately more women and racial and ethnic minorities than it did in 2000. The States of Florida, Texas, and California now require proficiency in Spanish for more than half of their government jobs. The proportion of officially bilingual companies in the United States is on the rise and is estimated at 10 percent. In 2012, the median age of the workforce exceeded the previous record (held at 40.5 years), reached in 1962. And for the last 10 years, the workforce has been growing by a paltry 0.4 percent per year. While innovations in technology have helped to increase productivity and facilitated economic growth, job growth has been outpacing workforce growth for the last six years, putting serious pressure on staffing departments to fill their positions. The reforms in Social Security, Medicare, and Medicaid, enacted at the end of the first decade of the century, removed disincentives for people to remain employed past the age of 65. The shifts in pension and health care plans that were identified 20 years ago have continued, resulting in Americans carrying increased responsibility for their retirement income and benefits. These reforms and trends have led to the current average retirement age of 72, in part because workers cannot afford to retire, and in part because they are still healthy and energetic, and they enjoy contributing

meaningfully. With increased flexibility in employment contracts, and people working anywhere from 10 to 60 hours per week, the Bureau of Labor Statistics has had to redefine retirement and now considers workers retired if they collect Social Security benefits and their workload drops below 20 hours per week. A by-product of this adjustment has been that the projections of the workforce's age composition released in 2000 seriously underestimated the true increase in median age. After all, they were based on the assumption that at age 65, workers would retire and leave the workforce. With the current average retirement age at 72, and the whole idea of retirement essentially outdated, the median age of the workforce is currently projected to rise to around 50 by 2040.

Considering this hypothetical context in 2020, what will your organization look like at that time? Or rather, what *should* it look like? Will it be an employer of choice for the older worker? Is there a good level of synergy between older, experienced workers and younger, eager ones? Are turnover rates for older workers similar to those of younger ones? Do older workers participate in and benefit from training as much as any others? Are your older employees referring others to your company? Do they have as much flexibility to care for their aging parents as younger ones have to take care of their young children?

Unless your organization is one of the few that has already made this vision a reality, you may wonder how to get there. This is what Part Three is all about. It addresses the issues identified by the expert panel described in Chapter 1 and each chapter offers specific steps for making progress toward achieving success in transitioning to an age-friendly workplace.

PART THREE
CRITICAL ISSUES

Introduction

Critical Issues

Part Three, Critical Issues, presents the seven issues that were identified by our Delphi panel of experts as described in Chapter 1. Two chapters are devoted to each issue and the authors have provided uniquely differing perspectives for the issue under consideration.

The issue of recruiting and retaining older workers is the focus of Chapters 4 and 5. In Chapter 4, the primary charge to the authors was to present the academic backdrop against which guidelines for practice, discussed in Chapter 5, could be superimposed. Chapter 4, Academic Perspectives on Recruiting and Retaining Older Workers, provides a comprehensive overview of the knowledge base and the state of the art in recruiting and retaining older workers. Three specific recruiting strategies are highlighted as are three specific retention strategies in working with older adults. The chapter concludes with recommendations covering the spectrum from research to practice. Chapter 5, Effective Strategies for Recruiting and Retaining Older Workers, closely parallels Chapter 4 and is replete with practical strategies for recruiting, selecting and interviewing, and retaining older adults. It also offers a special caution of the importance of reviewing personally held assumptions about older adults and their desire to continue in the workforce. The author closes by providing a roadmap that will facilitate human resource personnel in the effective recruitment and retention of older workers. Chapter 5 contains an instructive case example of this in practice.

The issue of training older workers is the focus of Chapters 6 and 7. The same charge was provided the authors of this issue as was provided to the authors of the previous issue. Consequently, in the paired chapters, Chapter 6 and 7, we have a presentation of the research base followed by a compendium of practical strategies for human resource professionals. Chapter 6, Academic Perspectives on Training Older Workers, provides a concise recapitulation of the research relating to three critical questions; namely, is it feasible to train older workers, are older workers being trained, and are older workers and their firms benefiting from the training that is provided? Chapter 7, Effective Strategies for Training Older Workers, follows up with a series of effective strategies for developing age-friendly training infrastructures and learning climates and tailoring training programs to the older age cohort. This chapter too provides the human resource professional with a case illustrating effective approaches to training.

The issue of career development for Older Workers is the focus of Chapters 8 and 9. Again, the charge to the authors of these paired chapters was in the first instance to set the stage and pose the challenge for career development undertakings in the coming years, and in the second instance to provide a road map for the future for maximizing the career potential of older adults during the times of great transition in the society and in the workplace. The challenge for the field of career development is to research and develop models that are congruent with current and emerging developments in the world of work and to consistently foster career self-management. Chapter 8, Past and Future Directions for Career Development Theory, presents a succinct distillation of career development theory and practice over a historic window beginning in the 1940s. It elaborates upon the factors, both internal and external, that serve to explain career development behavior in practice. Then, recommendations for both research and practice are offered the reader. Chapter 9, Partnering Career Development and Human Resources, reviews the complex issues that must be articulated as human resource professionals engage in career development initiatives within their organizations. It introduces and refutes five major barriers to the successful implementation of career development programs frequently encountered in the workplace: the presence of stereotyping and ageism, the lack of executive support and commitment, the utilization of outdated career development theories, the lack of knowledge within the human resource profession regarding organizational career development, and the lack of integration between human resource and career development processes within the organization.

The issue of enhancing intergenerational relations was framed in a somewhat different perspective in Chapters 10 and 11. While the first of the two chapters still has more of a research emphasis, both reflect different ways of looking at intergenerational relations. Chapter 10, Intergenerational Issues Inside the Organization, takes a social-psychological perspective on the issue and primarily examines intergenerational behavior between individuals belonging to different generational groups. It focuses upon three work contexts where the mix of generations typically occurs and may matter; namely, newcomer socialization, mentoring relationships, and work teams. The chapter concludes by presenting three approaches for more effectively understanding and facilitating these intergenerational groups: generational identity, manipulation of contexts, and multiple sources of diversity. Chapter 11, Building an Age-Friendly Workplace, takes a more systemic, holistic approach and views ageism as a manifestation of an organizational culture that transcends interactions between individuals. This chapter calls attention to the dangers of treating older workers as members of homogeneous groups and the concern that such an effort would simply add to diversity training woes. Arguments are put forward to convince the skeptical. We are then presented with three approaches for developing an organizational culture that is age-friendly; namely strategies for identifying organizational and individual assumptions, assessing attitudes and values both espoused and in practice, and reviewing organizational structures and processes.

Like the issue of enhancing intergenerational relations, the issue of health and older workers was framed in a somewhat different perspective. Rather than address the research and then the practice arena, we took two different dimensions to the challenge of fostering employee health and well-being

and charged authors for each of the paired chapters to set the stage and provide recommendations for practice. The first chapter takes the primary perspective of the employee while the second chapter takes the primary perspective of the employer. Chapter 12, Balancing Work and Caregiving, identifies the trends that well could result in a crisis of care if the family-friendly organization does not emerge to attend to the demands that its employees have for family caregiving, especially given the aging workforce. Specifically highlighted is the disproportional burden placed upon women to meet the caregiving needs of the family and the challenges faced in meeting both work and family demands. An array of recommendations is provided ranging from research to practice. Chapter 13, Rising Health Care Costs and the Aging Workforce, takes the perspective of the demand upon the organization in providing health care benefits to its employees and retirees. These costs are driven in part by the aging of the workforce and in part by the increased technology available in meeting the health care needs of the population. Insurance options and cost considerations are reviewed. Also reviewed are six trends in retiree health benefits and the outlook for future benefits for both active and retired workers. Recommendations are provided for consideration.

The issue of pensions and older workers is addressed in Chapters 14 and 15. Chapter 14, Adapting Pensions to Demographic Change, addresses the barriers or limitations within the law as well as within organizations that mitigate against making adaptations to pension programs. The role played by Social Security entitlements also contributes to the mix helping to dictate decisions regarding if and when to retire. Recommendations are provided to assist stakeholders in making the necessary adaptations to the pension systems in operation. Chapter 15, Retirement Security in a Post-Enron Environment, addresses the shift from defined benefit to defined contribution plans and the attendant shift in risk not only for the individual retiree but ultimately the public at large when employer securities are overinvested and when market downturns occur. Recommendations are provided.

Finally, the issue of redefining retirement is addressed in Chapters 16 and 17. Chapter 16, New Models for Post-Retirement Employment, discusses the shift in our societal understanding of retirement and the structural lag that exists between contemporary expectations about retirement and the social structures and models that could support such expectations. Models are provided to accommodate these new expectations and recommendations that span the public, private, and philanthropic sectors. Chapter 17, How to Become Employer of Choice for the Working Retired, again highlights the realities of the third age population and couples those realities with those models of working already in existence in many workplaces that could be adapted to retirees. The author further offers an array of options to the traditional pattern of retirement. Lastly, a series of action items is provided to position an employer to become an employer of choice for the working retired.

ISSUE 1

RECRUITING AND RETAINING
OLDER WORKERS

Chapter 4

Academic Perspectives on Recruiting and Retaining Older Workers

Mary Anne Taylor
Kenneth S. Shultz
Dennis Doverspike

As documented in detail elsewhere in this book, compelling demographic data clearly point to the need for companies to recruit and retain older employees. In 2010, baby boomers (i.e., individuals born between 1946 and 1964) will begin to retire in large numbers (Judy & D'Amico, 1997). This change in cohorts among those of retirement age will have significant, wide-ranging effects. Given the aging of the population, it is estimated that labor force participation by those over 55 would have to increase by 25 percent to maintain a constant ratio of employees to the population from 2005 onward (Penner, 1998; Wellner, 2002). The need to replace retiring employees is even greater in the public sector, and particularly severe for the federal government (Doverspike, Taylor, Shultz, & McKay, 2000). As a result, both private-sector and public-sector employers will have to develop proactive strategies for recruiting new employees from the older adult population, both those currently working and those already retired, and also for retaining their experienced workforce (Doverspike & Tuel, 2000; Taylor & Doverspike, 2002).

Unfortunately, traditional recruiting and retention strategies are often targeted at younger workers and are inappropriate for an older population (Arthur, 1998; Barber, 1998; Doverspike & Tuel, 2000; Loi & Shultz, 2002). The older segment of the population has unique needs, preferences, and concerns that are not addressed by traditional human resource development methods. The purpose of the present chapter is to review the findings of applied and academically oriented research in order to develop suggestions for effective recruiting and retention strategies with regard to our aging workforce.

Recruiting Strategies

In order to develop an effective recruiting strategy for use with older adults, employers need to evaluate and modify their entire recruitment system. However, in this chapter we will concentrate on a few, selected key areas:

- Identifying and meeting needs
- Engaging interest and attracting applicants
- Building and maintaining a relationship during the application process (Cober, Brown, Blumental, Doverspike, & Levy, 2000)

Identifying and Meeting Needs

In order to effectively manage recruitment, employers must identify and understand both the organization's needs and the needs of older adults. As with most organizational interventions, a redesign of the recruitment system should begin with a job and organizational analysis. An analysis of the personnel needs of the firm can assist the human resource professional in identifying which occupations may be understaffed in the future and, therefore, what areas should be targeted for enhanced recruitment efforts. In addition to identifying potential areas of need, the organizational analysis should identify what resources the organization has available that may prove attractive to the older employee.

Once an organization understands its own strengths and needs, it must develop an understanding of the needs of the older worker. This analysis should go beyond simple number crunching and should include an attempt to understand the work-related aspirations and desires of the diverse older worker population. As a group, boomers are more educated than previous cohorts, have accumulated a great deal of wealth, and are healthier than previous generations of older workers (Blumental, Cober, & Doverspike, 2000; Kausler & Kausler, 1996; Zemke, Raines, & Filipczak, 2000).

Although baby boomers have some characteristics in common, they constitute a diverse group, and an analysis of the baby boomer population reveals wide diversity in terms of background and needs (AARP, 2000a; Loi & Shultz, 2002; Zemke et al., 2000). Significant variability in a number of factors exists within and between age cohorts (National Academy on an Aging Society, 2000b). For example, the older cohort of baby boomers, born between 1946 and 1954, differs in many ways from the younger cohort, born between 1955 and 1964. Boomers in the older cohort were not influenced by the wage stagnation of the 1970s, and they accumulated more wealth than younger boomers during their careers. Women and African-Americans are much more likely to be financially disadvantaged than Caucasians across baby boomer groups (Dailey, 1998; National Academy on an Aging Society, 2000b). As might be expected, education is correlated with salary. African-American and female retirees tend to have lower levels of education than their white male counterparts.

For upper-income groups, financial considerations are less of a concern. As a result, organizations need to emphasize other characteristics of work including the social climate, the challenge of the job, and the opportunity to contribute to the community (Adams & Beehr, 1998; Pogson, Cober, Doverspike, & Rogers, 2003; Taylor & Shore, 1995). Feeling bored, feeling not useful, and missing co-workers are listed as some of the chief concerns in the 51-59 year old group of retirees (National Academy on an Aging Society, 2000b), and baby boomers expressing an interest in part-time or bridge employment indicate that they will work mainly for the social aspects and pure pleasure of working, rather than financial reasons (AARP, 1999). This suggests that recruiters who assume that wealthier older workers would not be interested in employment may be in error.

For those companies who wish to target recruiting efforts toward disadvantaged groups, careful consideration of financial incentives is a must, and health insurance along with other benefits, including retirement benefits for those who are not yet retired or lack sufficient coverage, may drive the decisions of those retirees who are interested and able to return to work. However, emphasizing solely money as a way of attracting older employees has two major drawbacks. First, while health care provisions and salary are important considerations in attracting an older worker into a position, the employer may have less flexibility and control in the area of financial incentives. Second, for a significant percentage of the older worker population, social and job-related factors may be more important than money in determining attraction to a company (AARP, 1999; Herz, 1995; Weckerle & Shultz, 1999).

Alternative work options may also appeal to older workers (Rosen & Jerdee, 1985, 1988). This is especially true for those who have already retired; of those retirees who wish to return to work, 71 percent want part-time employment. The options open to employers encompass part-time work or partial retirement and cover a range of functions from mentoring younger workers to performing entry-level jobs (Wellner, 2002). One of the most popular options among older workers is a phased work schedule that entails cutting the 40-hour work-week back to 20 or fewer hours. A closely related work option is flextime, where employees have control over the time and number of hours worked. Other options include job sharing and employing older workers as consultants. Maintaining flexibility in the number of hours worked seems to be a critical component in the success of most recruitment programs aimed at older adults, regardless of the type of work involved or whether the company is pursuing workers internally or in the outside labor market (Sterns & Miklos, 1995).

Prospective older workers are a diverse, heterogeneous group (AARP, 2000b; Luttropp, 1993). Organizations must understand the needs of the older workers they are trying to recruit, and target their efforts toward these individuals. Of course, another effective strategy is to recruit older workers from within the organization. This topic will be discussed in the retention section of this chapter.

Engaging Interest and Attracting Applicants

In order to recruit employees, it is necessary to first attract them, a process which often involves advertising. Of course, the type of advertising which appeals to new entrants into the workforce may not work with older workers. Thus, it is critical that the organization analyze and evaluate its advertising materials and its methods for finding applicants. Relevant aspects of advertising include the photographs used, the actual content of the advertisement, and the placement and type of recruiting advertisement (AARP, 1993a; Doverspike et al., 2000).

It is critical that organizations create a positive first impression with the older worker (Doverspike & Tuel, 2000). Thus, the message of the advertisement should send a positive signal to older employees. This message can be conveyed through a number of modalities including television, radio, newspapers, and face-to-face appeals.

Regardless of the medium, the content of advertisements and other recruiting appeals should be monitored to ensure their appropriateness for an older audience. Portraying older employees as vibrant and strong is important in marketing appeals (AARP, 2000b; Luttropp, 1993). The photographs or videos used in recruiting materials should incorporate older employees and create the impression that older people are valued employees. Advertisement copy can be worded so as to convey the impression that past work experience is valued through the use of terms such as *experienced* and *mature* (Fyock, 1990; Lefkovich, 1992). Job descriptions and posting notices should be written so as to make clear to older individuals that the job would be suitable for them.

Thus, the medium and the message should be one that will prove attractive to the older worker. It should respond to the older worker's needs and create a positive first impression. Of course, to be effective, the message must be delivered in a fashion such that it reaches the eyes and ears of the older worker.

Older workers and retired individuals may be more difficult to reach than the younger, entry-level worker. However, many options are available to the inventive employer. Groups such as AARP and the National Council on the Aging offer job posting and related services. Locations that can be targeted include adult education centers, temporary agencies, company retiree fairs, senior centers, civic groups, neighborhoods with a large percentage of older people, malls and libraries, and government employment centers (AARP, 1993a; Fyock, 1990; Lefkovich, 1992). In addition, companies can sponsor job fairs for older workers. Effective use of the Internet is just as important with older workers as it is with younger workers. However, again its use

should be tailored to the older worker, for example, by using large text and fewer detailed graphics (Cober et al., 2000).

Building and Maintaining a Relationship

Once applicants are attracted, the organization must then build a relationship with the job candidate until the point is reached where a job offer is extended (Cober et al., 2000; Doverspike & Tuel, 2000). Within a limited window of time, the organizations must screen the candidate for an appropriate job-person fit, while also creating a positive image of the company and job. As part of creating a more attractive environment for older employees, human resource managers should address the issue of the company's attitude toward older employees, reviewing relevant personnel policies and practices, and illustrate how the company can meet the job candidate's needs.

A major concern of older adults is potential age discrimination. Unfortunately, this fear may be well founded, since researchers often find that employers are ambivalent about hiring older employees and may have negative attitudes toward older workers (AARP, 2000a). For example, stereotypes of older workers indicate that they are often viewed as inflexible, averse to change, and resistant to learning and understanding new technology. Thus, recruiters need to address and quell such fears as soon as possible in the recruitment process.

Personnel policies should be reviewed to ensure that they are not discriminatory. Rather, they should encourage older applicants to consider employment with the company. When possible, older employees within the company should be consulted and integrated into the staffing, advertising, and recruiting processes (AARP, 2000b; Luttropp, 1993). Organizations should engage in training and development efforts with recruitment personnel to address any possible negative beliefs about the capabilities of older workers and to encourage positive attitudes toward older adults. Such proactive interventions can ensure that a supportive environment is provided for older employees, and that a positive impression of the company is conveyed beginning with the initial interview process. A review of employment policies can ensure that they are age-neutral (AARP, 2000a).

In designing an interview to attract older adults, companies can benefit by reviewing and revising the content of interviews including the types of questions, the choice of interviewers, and the description of the company and the job provided during the interview. When describing the company and the job to the older applicant during the initial interview, personnel should emphasize the aspects of work that are likely to be most appealing to older workers including the flexibility of scheduling, social aspects, and money and health benefits (AARP, 1999; Herz, 1995; Weckerle & Shultz, 1999). An appropriately designed interview is a critical step in maintaining and managing the relationship between the older applicant and the organization.

Overall, the success of the organization's recruiting efforts will depend heavily on its ability to create a culture where the older applicant feels valued and respected. This same climate will also be a major asset in the retention of current older employees.

Retention Strategies

In the 2000s, organizations appear to have returned to an emphasis on employee commitment and retention. In part, this is a response to the virtual organization trend of the 1990s, where employees were viewed as independent contractors and employee mobility and limited job security were accepted as part of the cost of reshaping the employment contract. Of course, as detailed in our introduction, it is also partially a response to a realization that the retention of talent, both young and old, is a necessity for organizations wishing to remain competitive in the face of a decline in the supply of potential employees.

In a wildly impractical sense, retention is easy; simply ask employees what they want and then give it to them. However, in the real world, the ability to simply give employees what they want is limited by budgetary factors and the diversity of individual needs and desires. As with recruitment, in order to develop an effective retention strategy for use with older adults, employers need to evaluate and modify many elements of their human resource systems. In addition, the issues involved in retaining that segment of the older population considering retirement are quite different than the issues involved in

retaining those who have not yet reached retirement age. Nevertheless, we believe that we can start our analysis by concentrating on several key issues:

- Identifying and meeting needs
- Increasing commitment to the organization
- Recruiting from within

Identifying and Meeting Needs

As we discussed in the section on recruitment, in order to develop effective strategies for retaining older employees, organizations must begin with a thorough analysis of their own strengths and needs and also the needs of the older employees. A simple employee attitude survey will provide a wealth of data on why employees are satisfied or dissatisfied with their jobs and the organization. Analyses of career ladders and training programs should provide information on fighting obsolescence and skill decay. Job analyses can lead to the redesign of jobs so as to make work more enriching and also suggest ergonomic alternatives so as to make work less physically taxing for the older employee.

An adequate analysis of workforce data can also lead to the identification of areas where specific retention strategies can be directed. In particular, higher wages and greater satisfaction with pay are often associated with more positive attitudes toward retirement and earlier anticipated retirement dates (Feldman, 1994; Weckerle & Shultz, 1999). Thus, it may well be that those employees an organization most needs to keep in the workforce are also the most likely to terminate employment at an early date.

Given that pay rate is associated with more skilled employment and higher education level, the workforce shortage is likely to be felt earliest in the most skilled occupations. Profiles of anticipated retirement rates by year and by occupation can focus organizational efforts on those older employees with the highest likelihood of early exit from the organization. As with recruitment, retention strategies should also be tailored to different occupational levels, different types of workers, and different demographic groups (Loi & Shultz, 2002).

Increasing Commitment to the Organization

Employees who are committed to the organization and enjoy their jobs are less likely to terminate their employment. One sure way to decrease commitment among older employees is for the organization to send the message to older employees that they are not valued. This message is often communicated to older employees through unbalanced pay polices or through the perception that the organization is ambivalent to, or even worse, encourages perceived age discrimination. Although many factors have an impact on commitment, we believe that total compensation and the organization's attitude toward older employees are two critical variables that influence retention rates among older employees.

Total compensation includes base pay, variable pay, benefits, and the psychological aspects of the job. If employees see their total compensation as high, then they are likely to:

- Feel more committed to their job and the organization
- Experience greater levels of job satisfaction
- Be less likely to seek out other employment
- Be more likely to delay retirement

If employees see their total compensation as lower than equitable or than desired, then they are likely to:

- Feel less committed to their job and the organization
- Experience lower levels of job satisfaction
- Be more likely to seek out other employment
- Be more likely to consider early retirement
- Be more likely to see a violation of the psychological contract between employer and employee

As mentioned above, total compensation has many components. An obvious one is the level of pay as compared to the market. Organizations should ensure that their pay policies either match or lead the market. Of course, this attention to market should be applied evenly across employee demographic groups. Organizations often pay too much attention to market in their entry-level pay decisions, while at the same time allowing their merit pay to lag behind the market. As a result, older employees experience pay inequity, as the entry-

level pay of younger employees increases at a higher rate than does the merit-based pay of current employees (Griffeth & Hom, 2001). This problem is best exemplified in the extreme levels of salary compression often found in faculty jobs, although this phenomenon also affects a range of industries from information technology to nursing.

Benefits and pensions are an important part of any total compensation package. As employees become older, the benefits of greatest interest and importance tend to shift. Benefits that are likely to be attractive to older employees include seniority pay; paid sick days; eldercare; work-life benefits; health, wellness, and prevention programs; and pensions and retirement programs (Taylor & Doverspike, 2003).

Nontraditional benefits also can serve as an attractive option in a total compensation package. Older employees often experience a variety of work-home conflict, especially if they have to care for older parents or a disabled spouse. In response, organizations can offer family and medical leave and a variety of eldercare programs, including resource and referral services and long-term care insurance.

As a direct means of retaining employees, organizations are offering a variety of retention bonuses or golden handcuffs (Griffeth & Hom, 2001), including profit sharing and stock options. Retention bonuses are contingent upon the employee remaining with the organization for some specified time period. However, a problem with attempting to induce people to stay through retention bonuses is that it may be viewed as a bribe, or in the terminology of social psychology, as a problem of overdependence on continuance commitment.

Whether based in reality or not, older employees often perceive themselves to be the victims of age discrimination (Committee for Economic Development [CED], 1999; Forteza & Prieto, 1994; Mor-Barak, 1995; Reio & Sanders 1999; Shultz, Sirotnik & Bockman, 2000; Sterns & Gray, 1999). The available research suggests that this perception may have a basis in reality as older workers, as compared to younger workers, are often perceived as harder to train, less motivated, less creative, less productive, less physically able, less able to change or learn new tasks, more likely to be sick or absent from work, more expensive, and technically outdated (Bennett-Alexander & Pincus, 1998; Haefner, 1977; Hansson, DeKoekkoek, Neece, & Patterson, 1997; Reio & Sanders, 1999; Rosen & Jerdee, 1976a; Sheblak, 1969; Waldman & Avolio, 1993).

This is not to suggest that all individuals hold negative stereotypes nor that positive stereotypes associated with older employees are completely lacking. However, given the findings of laboratory and field research, organizations need to be aware of the possibility that older employees may perceive themselves as being victims of negative attitudes and age discrimination.

Recruiting from Within

Recruiting from within is an option that should be considered by all organizations. By recruiting from within, we are referring to a variety of strategies for encouraging older employees considering retirement to remain with the company. Older employees considering retirement can be recruited from within through either the option of reduced or flexible work hours, or through bridge employment.

One of the most popular ways to retain older employees is through flexible work arrangements. Although flexible work arrangements can be used with all types of workers, there is a special benefit to considering tapping retired employees of the organization to fill the organization's work needs (Lindbo & Shultz, 1998; Shultz, 2001). Some examples of types of flexible work arrangements include the following (Rosen & Jerdee, 1985, 1988).

Permanent part-time jobs. Refers to jobs that have permanent individuals who work less hours than traditional full-time workers. These types of jobs can be quite beneficial to individuals with work-life conflicts, including older workers.

Phased retirement. Refers to the gradual reduction of work hours, and responsibilities, until the point of full retirement. This method allows for a gradual exit from full participation in the workforce.

Consulting. Refers to an employment arrangement where the older employee serves as a consultant either to the former employer or to new clients. An advantage is that younger employees are less likely to see the older consultant as a competitor for their jobs, and older managers will be receptive to the peer value of such a relationship. For the older employee, this type of arrangement allows for

a great deal of flexibility (Levinson & Wofford, 2000). Companies should also consider offering entrepreneurial training in order to help older employees build and broaden their consulting practices.

Job-sharing. Refers to an arrangement whereby two employees share one job. In theory, the two individuals split the hours, responsibilities, and benefits of a full-time position.

Job redesign. Refers to a scientific or technological process for studying and systematically changing the tasks, duties, or characteristics of a job. In the case of older workers, this redesign would often be for the purpose of creating a greater fit between the job demands and the current level of knowledge, skills, abilities, or physical abilities, possessed by the employee. Individuals whose jobs are redesigned may require retraining.

Retraining. Refers to a variety of training programs aimed at fighting obsolescence and encouraging new skill development. Training should be offered to employees regardless of age. Programs should be tailored to the learning strategies of the older worker. Cross-generational training allows all workers to benefit from the different experiences of workers of various ages.

Sabbaticals. Refers to a situation where an older employee is granted a leave of absence from the company in order to renew, refresh, and revitalize skills and competencies. This type of work arrangement may be especially appropriate for mid-career employees, individuals suffering from burnout or fatigue, and for employees approaching retirement who wish to enter consultant roles.

It should be noted that although these strategies are discussed here in the context of retention, flexible work arrangements are also a valuable recruiting tool (Doverspike et al., 2000). Flexible work arrangements are also an effective recruiting and retention tool when used in combination with bridge employment.

Bridge employment refers to employment that occurs between one's career job and permanent workforce withdrawal or retirement. This employment is often in a new career area and may involve a variety of flexible work arrangements (Doeringer, 1990; Employee Benefit Research Institute [EBRI], 1999; Quinn, 2000).

Research by Adams and Lax (2002) suggests that demographic variables and self-evaluation factors are important in understanding job seeking during bridge employment. In addition, organizational variables, including the degree of emotional and instrumental social support, are hypothesized to influence bridge employment decisions.

Feldman (1994) developed a decision tree framework for understanding bridge employment in terms of individual difference variables (e.g., work history, marital status, health status, and attitudes), opportunity structures (e.g., type of industry, primary or secondary labor market, and experience with age-related discrimination), organizational factors (e.g., financial rewards, early retirement counseling programs, and organizational flexibility), and the external environment (e.g., uncertainty regarding the economic environment, social security, and pension regulations). Feldman's theories have received at least partial support in a number of research studies (Feldman & Kim, 2000; Heindel, Adams, & Lepisto, 1999; Kim & Feldman, 1998, 2000; Weckerle & Shultz, 1999). However, it should be noted that minority and other disadvantaged groups are less likely to have access to bridge employment opportunities (Feldman & Kim, 2000; O'Rand & Henretta, 1999; Quinn & Kozy, 1996; Ruhm, 1989).

Thus, organizations need to find ways to encourage bridge employment as a method of both retaining current older employees and recruiting older adults from the general working population. Bridge retirement and flexible work options can be presented to older employees during unretirement fairs. Unretirement fairs are very similar to college recruitment fairs, except that the target audience consists of older employees considering retirement. During the unretirement fair, older employees are presented with information on bridge employment and flexible work arrangements available within the firm. Another option is the use of retiree job banks. With the retiree job banks, older and retired employees can review bridge employment opportunities and also make themselves available for part-time and bridge employment (Lindbo & Shultz, 1998; Shultz, 2001).

Recommendations

In this section, we present some basic research, policy, and practical recommendations. Given the academic orientation of this chapter, we first suggest some ideas for future studies, along with related statements concerning limitations in the current literature. We then discuss the likely impact of anticipated policy changes at the national level. Finally, we outline some recommendations for applying the findings from this chapter to practical, human resource problems.

Recommendations for Research

What little research has been done on recruiting and retaining older workers has been cross-sectional (one-time) in nature. As a result, we end up with a snapshot (or still) picture instead of the complete movie of how best to recruit and retain older workers. To the extent recruiting and retention represent the ends of a very long continuous process, we know very little about what happens between these two points on the continuum when cross-sectional research designs are used. The ability to obtain and analyze longitudinal data would greatly enhance our ability to look at recruitment and retention of older workers as a process, rather than as individual and independent events, as typically occurs.

As noted above, there are multiple influences on the recruitment and retention process. However, most research has focused on either the individual being recruited or the organization doing the recruiting. Future research needs to be able to look across multiple levels of analysis (e.g., individuals, departments, organizations, industries) to examine how these different factors interact to create the context for effective recruitment and retention. Somewhat related, as more and more organizations take on an international scope, cross-cultural issues need to be addressed. That is, the recruitment and retention strategies used in the United States (an individualist culture) may not work in a country such as Japan, where a collectivist culture dominates (Usui, 1998). Therefore, we have to determine which strategies are going to be most effective in which cultures if we hope to make broader policy recommendations.

Recommendations for Policy

Broad policy recommendations such as changing pension and social security eligibility criteria may help or hinder us with regard to both recruitment and retention of older workers. For example, the recent removal of the earnings limit on social security for those between ages 65 and 69 should help in efforts to recruit older workers. On the other hand, the progression from defined benefit to defined contribution pension systems is more likely to foster earlier exits from the labor force, thus harming retention efforts, in that defined contribution pension plans do not require a combination of years of service and/or age to obtain a sufficient pension income. As a result, decisions regarding retirement are less tied to age in these increasingly prominent pension plans.

In addition, policy changes to encourage work (thus retention) at older ages might include tax credits to employers for hiring older workers. Tax credits or tuition subsidies to both employers and individuals for engaging in job skills updating and retraining (Shultz et al., 2000) would encourage work at older ages. Such subsidies would encourage employers to target recruitment strategies to older workers. To the extent that employers are "rewarded," via policy changes for offering many of the alternative work arrangements noted above, there should then be a corresponding change in the willingness of organizations to engage in recruitment and retention efforts aimed at older workers.

Recommendations for Practice

Public and private sector organizations will soon be faced with the problem of how to best recruit older adults. A comprehensive campaign for the recruitment of older workers should incorporate:

- Methods for identifying the needs of both older workers and the organization and corresponding means of meeting these needs
- The appropriate design of recruiting efforts aimed at older employees so as to engage interest and attract applicants
- The appropriate design of the selection process so as to build and maintain relationships during the application process

Similarly, in order to maximize their retention efforts, organization should utilize:

- Methods for identifying the needs of both older employees and the organization, and corresponding means of meeting these needs
- Interventions that increase the commitment of older employees to the organization
- Recruitment from within

Summary

In the case of older workers, the numbers speak for themselves; competition for the competencies and expertise possessed by older workers will increase in the coming years. Unfortunately, traditional recruiting and retention strategies may not be appropriate for the older adult. In response, in this chapter we have reviewed the applied and academic research related to the recruitment and retention of older workers.

In our review of the research on recruitment, we found that older workers have unique needs and that organizations must first identify and then strive to meet these needs. Recruiting materials and campaigns should be designed so as to interest and attract older applicants. Finally, the selection process should be designed so as to build and maintain relationships.

In our review of the literature on retention, we found that again organizations need to identify and respond to the unique needs of older employees. In addition, employers should develop programs so as to increase the commitment of older employees to the organization. Finally, employers need to recruit from within and develop a range of alternative work arrangements for older workers.

It is always difficult to predict the supply and demand for labor. As soon as companies begin to worry about recruiting, it seems like the economy weakens, the demand for labor decreases, and organizations shift their interest back to retention. Fads are also common in the world of human resources, and some of those fads stick around. Nevertheless, the forward-thinking organization will make appropriate investments in its intellectual and human capital, and will emphasize both the recruitment of talent and the retention of valued employees. Organizations that begin now to invest time and effort in the development of recruiting and retention plans targeted for this segment of the population will have a clear competitive advantage.

Chapter 5

Effective Strategies for Recruiting and Retaining Older Workers

Catherine D. Fyock

Two key forces are converging to make the recruitment and retention of older workers a necessity today. On the one hand, employers are still finding that recruiting and retaining top talent are major priorities. They are realizing that recruitment and retention are two of their greatest issues, with such remarks as:

- I can't find the qualified people I need, and I don't want to lower my hiring standards.
- I can't fill open positions.
- It's taking me twice as long to fill vacancies.
- I have high turnover, adding to my labor costs, and lowering productivity.
- I can't open my business without qualified workers.

According to a survey conducted by the Society for Human Resource Management (SHRM) and Commerce Clearing House (CCH)(1999), today's candidates are often insufficiently qualified; they also tend to negotiate for higher beginning salaries and for benefits. Furthermore, the growth of the workforce will slow to its lowest rate in U.S. history. As a recent survey conducted jointly by the SHRM and AARP (1998) shows, human resource professionals are aware of this situation, as they acknowledge that by the year 2010, we may experience a greater shortfall of workers.

On the other hand, baby boomers who are now reaching their 50s are considering retirement, but are finding that they may be unable to retire because of lack of savings. As Pollan and Levine (1995) report, boomers are saving less than their parents did and are ill-prepared for the financial burdens of retirement. They conclude that for most, retirement at the traditional retirement age is neither financially feasible nor responsible.

As for the boomers who have properly prepared for retirement, it is also believed that many of them would prefer to continue working. According to a 2002 Harris Interactive Poll, 95 percent of workers aged 55 to 64 said that they planned to work in some capacity after age 65 (Taylor, 2002).

Given these two converging issues – a future need for more qualified workers and the availability of older workers who wish to remain employed past the normal retirement age – employers will come to recognize the potential value of aging employees for their business goals. However, many employers currently are unaware of this. Unprepared for this shift in thinking, many organizations still boast early-out programs and foster cultures that promote youth.

According to the SHRM and AARP survey (1998), employers already recognize the benefits of employing older adults – "golden agers" – yet they do little to encourage their return to the workplace or to actively retain them. More than 1000 human resource managers responded to the survey, and commented on the positive features of employing older adults. Among the benefits: less absenteeism (65 percent), greater motivation (62 percent), and excellent mentoring abilities for younger workers (60 percent). HR managers also commented on the flexibility of older adults, and their willingness to work part-time and temporary assignments.

The survey also demonstrated that in spite of this favorable attitude toward employment qualities of older adults, few organizations are developing initiatives to actively support the continued employment of older individuals. Fewer than 3 out of 10 employers maintain specific programs to encourage older workers to stay on the job.

Recruiting Older Adults

What can employers do to encourage these "golden" employees to consider new job opportunities within the organization? How can employers entice older adults to remain an active part of the workforce? Consider these strategies for discovering the gold in the graying of America.

Develop Targeted Messages to Attract Mature Workers

Older adults tend to respond to messages that appeal directly to them, and that let them know they are specifically wanted for employment opportunities. Recruitment messages that specify *mature*, *experienced*, and *reliable* all let the older readers know that they are being sought after for employment opportunities. This is especially important since many older adults have faced age discrimination or ageism, and are reluctant to actively seek new employment opportunities unless the employer has clearly indicated that their experience and maturity are valued. Employers such as Kelly Services, Days Inn, and Wal-Mart, who have developed targeted recruitment strategies and publicized their efforts in this arena, are also the companies with the greatest success stories in the employment of older adults.

Recruitment success hinges in part on the choice of words in advertising efforts. The terms used to refer to people 40 and over must be appropriate. For example, the term *senior* or *senior citizen* is inappropriate, as it generally refers to those people who are 65 years of age or older. The term *elderly* further segments those people 70 years of age and older. Be aware that the terms used in recruitment advertising will be interpreted in different ways by people of different ages. For example, one employer used the term *senior citizens* in targeted recruitment advertisements, but failed to attract older adults until it switched to a campaign that simply used the term *mature* (Fyock, 1990, p. 31). A testimonial approach may also be a good way to show older adults you want them for employment. Feature an older employee in the advertisement who talks about positive experiences in working with your organization.

Besides the language used in advertising, visual elements are perhaps equally crucial. One employer recently examined the company's recruitment literature only to discover that not one photograph featured an older adult. Organizations interested in targeting older adults will need to include pictures of older adults at work in annual reports, recruitment brochures, and advertising campaigns to successfully attract this labor market segment.

Companies such as Hardee's Food Systems based in Rocky Mount, North Carolina, have been successful in developing a series of targeted messages, including "Tired of being retired?" (depicting a bored older man holding his golf bag), and "How to ease back into the labor pool" (showing a middle-aged woman posing at the end of a diving board). Hardee's found that by using targeted messages, it was not only able to attract an older employee group, but also to reduce turnover and improve restaurant performance in those restaurants hiring older workers (Fyock, 1990).

As older adults most often respond to recruitment messages that meet their needs, consider using the following:

- Your skill, experience and maturity are valued.
- Join other mature individuals—just like you.
- Flexible hours—the hours you want to work.
- Job accommodation to meet your special needs.
- You can work—and still keep your Social Security.
- Stay active—and keep young.
- An opportunity to make new friends . . . in a friendly place.
- A growth opportunity—for your second or third career.
- Fringe benefits—especially health and life insurance.
- You already have the skills and experience to do the job.
- No training required.
- On-the-job training provided.
- Keep on giving, and help others.
- Now that you have raised your family . . . raise some cash!
- Did you retire too soon?

Use Appropriate Recruitment Activities and Resources

Besides developing targeted recruiting messages, it is also important to rethink traditional recruitment activities and venues when targeting older adults. Since older adults may be reluctant job seekers, more active or intrusive forms of recruitment may be more effective, such as telemarketing, direct mail, and other activities directed at older adults. Here are some other cost-effective ideas for recruiting older adults.

Offer "unretirement parties." The Travelers, based in Hartford, Connecticut, has done this to entice their own retirees as well as other older adults to join the pool of part-time and temporary workers to meet the organization's temporary staffing needs (Fyock & Dorton, 1994).

Participate in open houses and (second) career fairs. Specifically for older adults, these activities can be quite successful. They are often sponsored by organizations such as AARP and other organizations sponsoring the employment of older adults.

Make presentations to senior centers. Target those senior centers that include active older adults as members. Talk about your benefits and flexible work options when addressing these groups.

Advertise in uncommon newspaper sections. Since many older adults are not actively seeking employment, consider advertising in sections other than the help-wanted section. Alternate sections, including the sections on lifestyle, television, food, sports, or even the obituaries! Also, consider different newspapers, including local and community papers, church bulletins, club publications, and convenience store bargain shoppers such as the *Thrifty Nickel* or the *Penny Pincher*.

Appeal to coffee klatches. Coffee klatches (or "clutches") often gather in local eateries and fast-food restaurants. Often these are sociable and active older adults who may be open to your employment opportunity.

Approach "mall walkers." These are groups of active, healthy older adults—especially those who walk near your place of business.

Host open houses. An open house is an event sponsored by the employer, either at the business location, at a community center, or at a hotel. Open houses are particularly effective in attracting older workers who may be considering reentering the work force, or entering the job market for the first time. An open house environment gives these people the opportunity to check out what you have to offer without committing to the formal job interview.

Hold information seminars. Older individuals often want and need information on health concerns, financial issues, and other matters. Conduct such an event, perhaps in conjunction with an older worker organization (such as AARP, the National Council on the Aging, or a local organization that supports the employment of older workers), and include second career and job information.

If you are already employing older workers, ensure that these individuals are a part of the program. Older candidates can then see that you are not just providing lip service to this issue, but have a commitment to providing opportunities for older employees.

Television. Television can be affordable when you tap into dollars available through Public Service Announcements (PSAs). Check with your local station to see if such announcements may be available at no cost. Another option is to investigate the use of cable television bulletin boards for low-cost recruitment advertising.

Radio. Radio is an excellent medium to attract older adults. Check listener demographics for the station with the right potential candidate "mix" to meet your recruitment needs. Public Service Announcements may also be available.

Radio messages should appeal to the concerns of older adults, and should demonstrate how work will help meet their needs—through competitive pay and benefits, in a friendly and supportive work environment, and with an opportunity to use life experiences in a positive and productive way.

Direct mail. Mailing lists can be purchased that permit you to target older adults within certain zip code locations, with specific technical or professional experience, or with industry-specific certifications or licenses. To identify mailing list vendors, look in your yellow pages phone book under "Mailing Lists," call professional organizations, or contact your recruitment advertising agency.

Appeal to older readers by showing you understand their needs. The caption, "Have you retired too soon?" may capture the interest of many older individuals. Also, talk about flexible hours and the ability to manage work hours so that Social Security benefits are not impacted if you can offer this benefit.

Posters. Posters can reach a large number of older adults in places they visit every day. Consider the post office, grocery stores, banks, laundromats, churches, pharmacies, senior centers, and community centers. Include a mini-application blank that includes contact information.

Be sure to use pictures of older individuals in the poster. In this way, the older adult identifies with the advertisement, and will be more likely to respond.

Referral program/task force. Talk with your current employees to see if they might refer some good workers, or have some suggestions on how to recruit other older adults. Offer incentives for referrals that result in a hire.

Rehire retirees. Consider this option, particularly if they possess industry-specific experience. Work with an employee leasing company if your pension program does not encourage post-retirement reemployment.

Career fairs. Join forces with other employers and host a career fair. Be competitive with an upscale booth. Offer a "freebie" to attract candidates to your booth, or better yet, have candidates register for a prize drawing, and collect name, address, and phone number to follow up at a later time. Often job fairs are sponsored by older worker organizations, so develop contacts with these organizations to be included in these events.

Networking. Let churches, community groups, senior centers, your own retirees, and others in your community know of your staffing needs and your interest in qualified older workers.

Door hangers. Using recruiting messages on door hangers can be a method to attract older individuals within a specific geographic area. Select communities with high concentrations of older adults for the best results. If your company has a consumer product or service, combine recruitment messages with product and service messages to enhance response rates. Offer a coupon for your product or service, and entice the older adult to become a customer and an employee!

Partners. There are many potential partners that can assist in attracting older workers, including ten national sponsors of the Seniors in Community Service Employment Project (SCSEP). These ten national sponsors, that may have local programs in your community, include:

1. AARP
2. National Urban League
3. National Council on the Aging
4. National Indian Council on Aging
5. National Pacific/Asian Resource Center on Aging
6. National Association for Hispanic Elderly
7. Green Thumb
8. National Council of Senior Citizens
9. National Caucus and Center on the Black Aged
10. National Association of State Units on Aging (Fyock & Dorton, 1994)

Contact your state employment office or One Stop Center for guidance on additional local programs that support the employment of older workers within the community. There are state funds that are allocated for the employment of older adults; contact your state agency or bureau on aging for information on programs in your area.

Interviewing Older Adults

Recruiting and attracting older workers only gets them in the door for the interviewing and selection process. The messages sent (intentionally or not) to the older applicant during the interviewing process must be consistent with those sent in the advertising campaign, especially given many older applicants' previous exposure to various forms of ageism.

Unfortunately, the reality is that many managers are so used to interviewing young workers that they ask inappropriate and sometimes discriminatory questions during the selection process. This can easily undo all the work that went into piquing applicants' interest in that employer in the first place!

Job applicants over the age of 40 are protected by the Age Discrimination in Employment Act (ADEA). It prohibits the use of age as a determination of terms or conditions of employment. Since many claims of age discrimination against applicants are based upon the employer making age-related inquiries, most employers have had to revamp their employment applications and pre-employment interviews to eliminate age-related questions that may be illegal. In addition to removal of date of birth and high school graduation dates, employers have also had to train their hiring managers and supervisors to avoid the following potentially illegal questions:

- How old are you?
- What is your birthdate?
- When did you graduate from high school? (or any other questions that tend to identify the age of the candidate)
- Do you receive Social Security?
- What do you think about working for a younger boss?
- Can you physically handle the job? (This is not permissible if it is asked only of older adults.) Instead, it is better to ask all candidates, "Can you perform the essential functions of this job, with or without accommodation?"

Rather than concentrating on avoiding illegal questions, a better approach may be to focus on questions that demonstrate respect for the older adults' wealth of knowledge and years of experience. Examples are:

- How has your experience in this industry prepared you for a role in this organization?
- What is the greatest lesson you've learned at work?
- What have you discovered to be the most important element in teamwork?
- Tell me about a time when you had to share your knowledge about a process or task with your supervisor in order to move the project ahead?
- Describe for me a time when you had to deal with difficult customers or coworkers? What did you do?
- What has been the most important ingredient for your success?
- What is most important for you right now in terms of your career search?

There is an analogy between recruiting and interviewing that should also be pointed out. In designing the recruitment message, it is important to consider both the content (language) and the package (picture, medium) of the message. The same holds true for the interviewing process. On top of showing respect for older adults' age and experience by asking questions such as those listed above, consider introducing the applicants to older workers currently employed. This may help future socialization and it will also allow the applicants to

see for themselves that older workers are indeed valued. In other words, you could implement an effective recruiting campaign and ask the right kinds of questions in an interview, but if the older applicants are interviewed only by younger workers, all may be for naught.

Retaining Older Workers

Great! So you've passed all these hurdles and successfully recruited and hired promising older workers. Retaining them is where the real work begins. Remember, many of them work only because they want to, not because they have to. A good-faith effort to accommodate their needs in the workplace is a necessity for successfully retaining older workers. The following activities and strategies can prove valuable.

Provide Sensitivity Training on the Aging Dimension of Diversity

While many organizations have developed training initiatives for a culturally diverse workforce, few have considered aging as a diversity dimension. Yet many managers lack the skills and abilities to supervise the diversity of values, work ethics, and work styles demonstrated in the workplace today. Further, many managers may have negative perceptions about the abilities of older adults, and may be threatened by and show resistance to directing the work activities of individuals who are old enough to be their parents or grandparents.

Just as organizations have developed education programming and sensitivity training for the increased employment of individuals representing differing cultural and racial backgrounds, employers must seek the same kinds of programming to ensure the effective employment of workers of all ages (Brotherton, 2000).

Develop Task Forces and Focus Groups

Many organizations, such as Honeywell, have developed internal task forces to listen to employee groups to determine their specific needs and concerns. Honeywell's older worker task force, called the Older Worker League (OWL), provides information to management that is instructive in redesigning benefits, policies, and procedures with all employee groups in mind.

Examine Retirement Policies

Some older individuals find that they cannot continue working for their employer of many years because of the design of pension benefits. For example, older adults who wish to work reduced work schedules, or to work in lesser positions, may find their pension benefits jeopardized. Many organizations encourage their experienced workers to take early retirement, only to discover that the talents that left the organization are not readily replaced in the job market.

Adapt Training Programs to Older Adults

There are several strategies that businesses can adopt in order to facilitate the training process for older adults. Of course, employers are learning that the similarities between older workers and younger workers in terms of how they learn are far more numerous than the differences. Therefore, many of these strategies make it easier for all employees, regardless of age, to learn more quickly and effectively.

Allow self-paced learning. Since all adults tend to learn at varying rates of speed, and because some older adults in particular may have a slightly slower rate of processing new information, a learning process that permits the learners to proceed at their own pace is preferable. This will permit the learner to gain confidence, and overcome fears about the learning process.

Use training materials with bold typeface and high contrast colors. By using a typeface that is at least 12 points in size, all readers will be able to view the information more effectively.

Avoid posting notices and training materials above eye level. Since many older adults wear bifocals, posting posters and other materials at eye-level will facilitate reading.

Speak clearly and distinctly during training sessions. Trainers should ask hearing-impaired people to sit at the front of the room so that the speaker's face can be clearly seen. Remove distracting sounds that may interfere with listening.

Use adult learning principles to train older adults on new skills. A building-block approach to learning is preferred by older learners, since it permits them to build self-confidence while building upon past learning. A modular approach is excellent, in that it permits this building-block approach to learning, while it also facilitates many older workers' desires for part-time work. Shorter training segments enable workers to exercise a more flexible schedule.

Implement Flexible Work Arrangements

The SHRM/AARP survey indicated that 20 percent of the employers who did not have programs designed to retain older adults said that their older workers had no interest in remaining on the job. While it is true that many older adults seek retirement options, there are still many individuals who want and need to work. Other older individuals desire continued employment when it meets their needs, through scheduling options and other conditions of employment that meet their motivations and lifestyles (SHRM & AARP, 1998).

Organizations that have offered scheduling options, including job-sharing, phased retirement, flex-scheduling, telecommuting, and other alternative staffing programs have found these options of high interest not just to older adults, but to many employees seeking greater flexibility in the need to balance home and work responsibilities. Consider these options.

Flex scheduling. Flex week, flex month, and even flex year are options being offered by employers. With flex scheduling, employees opt to work a certain set of hours or days within the week, month, or year. By allowing employees to set their own schedules, employees are more productive as they now have time to balance hobbies, leisure activities, care-giving responsibilities, and other personal issues.

Job-sharing. This happens when two (part-time) employees "share" one (full-time) job. While job-sharing is most common in professional and technical positions, new industries and occupations are offering this option. Older adults enjoy this job option when paired with a younger coworker in a mentoring relationship, and are able to pass on knowledge and skills.

Part-time work. Employers are now offering less-than-40-hour schedules for a large number of employee roles, including entry-level and professional and managerial positions.

Temporary workers. For projects and short-term assignments, employers are turning to temporary employees to fill these needs. While temporary placement agencies are being used for many temporary needs, many employers are exploring the use of contractual workers.

Telecommuting. Work-at-home arrangements, when the worker does not have to be at the job site the entire work period, are gaining in popularity. Some workers are working one day a week at home; others are working almost entirely out of their homes. With the advent of low-cost office equipment (copiers, fax, computers, modems) telecommuting is gaining in popularity among employers and employees. Telecommuting is a favorable option when mobility and transportation issues make it more difficult for the older adult to travel to the physical work location.

Job shops. Job shops are temporary employment agencies for professional and technical occupations. Job shops permit the retired worker to put professional skills and abilities to work without the hassle of independently marketing and bidding each new assignment.

Leasing. Employee "leasing" companies are becoming popular as employers seek to employ their retirees, but find that pensions are barriers to continued employment. These leasing companies hire the employer's workers, and "rent" them to the employer for a fee.

Case Study:

Gray-Haired Whiz Kids Demonstrate Success Throughout Their "UnRetirement"

Organizations typically struggle long and hard in finding high-tech employees who are knowledgeable regarding state-of-the-art technology. Yet, few organizations work as hard to keep talent that is now adept at internal systems, the culture, and applications. The case that follows is unusual in that this organization has developed unique scheduling options to help keep valued high-tech, mature employees.

Dot heads to work on Monday to her job as a computer operator for St. Joseph Hospital in Lexington, Kentucky. On Tuesday she gets in 18 holes of golf. Wednesday she'll spend some time with her family after work. And over the weekend she'll play duplicate bridge with her club.

Thanh flies in to town from 900 miles away and stays with his son. He'll return to work the next day in his job as a computer programmer/analyst. Just before coming to town, Thanh was in Dallas, where he was spending a month with his family.

What's so unusual about Dot and Thanh, and what do they have in common? Dot and Thanh are both older adults who have gone back to school during their 50s to learn their high-tech craft, and have continued to work into their 70s within this dynamic field. They have overcome skepticism from friends, colleagues, and employers about their abilities to learn and stay current in the ever-changing field of mainframe computers. Both have negotiated unusual work schedules with their employer, providing each with the opportunity to "unretire"—to re-define work in a way that meets their needs, motivations, and lifestyle issues beyond "normal" retirement age.

Dot's Story

Before becoming a computer operator, Dot Hellard was a librarian in Mason County, Kentucky. Upon leaving her library job after years in the field, she decided to embark upon a new career direction, and attended Lexington Community College in Lexington, Kentucky, studying computer science. After graduation, Dot mailed out 70 resumes, and was told by one agency that her age was holding her back.

She eventually took the only computer operator job offered to her—on the night shift. While it was difficult for her (she confesses that she's not a "night person"), "There wasn't a moment when I was going to quit," she proudly states. After four successful years on third shift, she transferred to day work, and has been in this position ever since.

Because of Janie Fergus, Dot's department director, who had gone to bat for her, Dot was able to work a reduced work schedule of 20 hours per week at a point in time when Dot wanted to balance her work life with some of her life's passions—golf and bridge. This past summer she managed to participate in 20 golf tournaments, maintaining her handicap of 10 to 12.

Working a 20-hour week also permits Dot the opportunity to spend more time with her grandson, James. "Sometimes I just need a 'James-fix'," she explains. "My work schedule gives me the opportunity to fit all the things I love into my life."

Thanh's Story

Thanh Son Le fled to the United States in April 1975, just one day before the collapse of the Vietnamese government. After spending seven months in a refugee camp, he researched a variety of career fields before deciding upon computers. In Vietnam Thanh had a law degree and taught law at the police academy where he was a police colonel for 30 years.

Thanh attended Lexington Technical Institute and the University of Kentucky, and then went to work for his current employer. After 16 years of service, Thanh works a nontraditional schedule of one month on, and one month off.

This schedule was necessitated by a family decision to move to Dallas in order to provide medical services for Thanh's wife. Thanh wanted to retain his job, and, after talking with his supervisor he was able to reach a decision that permitted each to meet their mutual needs.

Why does Thanh continue to work? "I like my job, and I like to work," Thanh replies. "After relaxing for a month with my family, I return feeling fresh. I deal with complicated problems, and it keeps my mind active."

The Business Issue

"We have always tried to do whatever it takes to keep our excellent employees, but in these situations we had to think out of the box," states Janie Fergus, who is Dot and Thanh's department manager. "Both employees had unique needs and concerns, and we had to be creative in developing schedules that would allow us to keep two highly qualified and productive employees. This schedule was, and still is, very innovative. It helps the organization keep valued employees, while helping the

employees meet their personal needs. We couldn't be happier with the arrangement, although it took some time to sell top management on the concept."

Recommendations

Today's workforce is indeed coming of age. In order to successfully create and implement a plan to employ and manage an aging workforce effectively, businesses need to begin making strategy plans now to address these issues. Today's businesses must seek methods to make the continued employment of its aging workforce a meaningful, productive, and positive experience for everyone involved. This is not only because it is the proper thing to do, but also because there is much riding on its success. Effectively recruiting and retaining older workers may very well be a crucial competitive edge in an increasingly competitive labor market. Smart business leaders will begin to initiate strategies to make the effective employment of older workers a solution to many of the changes taking place in the workforce today. The action steps that companies should undertake to recruit and retain older workers include the following.

1. Get educated! The needs and concerns of the aging workforce are different from the needs and concerns of yesterday's workforce. Strategies to recruit and select, train, manage, and retire older workers are different for this new labor market segment. Companies need to look for ways to stay updated on aging issues that will affect the management of these workers.

2. Use local, regional, and national resources. Many employers do not realize that there are myriad outside resources to provide information, guidance, and counseling on older worker issues.

3. Gain total management support. The effectiveness of many corporate programs can be measured immediately by the degree of involvement, commitment, and support by top management. The initiative to respond to the needs of an aging workforce demands high-level involvement.

4. Eliminate barriers to the employment of older workers. There are a great many barriers, internal and external, that prohibit employment of older workers within the corporate environment. Internal barriers include age discrimination or the more subtle ageism, inflexible work options, and outdated job designs, personnel policies, and procedures. Examples of external barriers are perceptions that the organization does not want to employ older workers and recruitment messages that do not reach the older adult.

5. Implement methods to attract and retain older workers. The increased and effective employment of an aging workforce does not just happen. It comes about from careful planning that incorporates an understanding of the desires of older adults.

6. Train supervisors for managing a changing and aging workforce. Managers today are largely unprepared for the challenges of supervising a diverse older workforce. They need additional training.

7. Keep communication lines open. Listening and responding to employee issues remains one of the most important steps a company can take in increasing productivity and morale.

Summary

An increasingly important issue facing organizations today is how to find and keep qualified, motivated employees. Most human resource professionals note recruitment and retention as top priorities, yet few are tapping into their own growing resource—older workers. This chapter has outlined key ideas for recruiting and retaining one of America's most undervalued and underutilized resources—older adults. It has provided specific suggestions for redesigning messages and improving activities for attracting older adults, as well as strategies for keeping this valuable resource. Smart business leaders will begin now to develop steps to ensure that older adults are not only recruited but also properly managed and motivated. In turn, this will lead to increased retention and productivity from an increasingly aging workforce.

Synthesis

Recruiting and Retaining Older Workers

The preceding chapters on recruiting and retaining older workers show remarkable agreement in spite of the differences in the authors' affiliations. It seems that they can be captured in the following five observations.

1. When it comes to tapping into nontraditional labor pools for recruitment purposes, it is necessary to use nontraditional media as well as nontraditional messages.
2. When it comes to retaining older workers, flexibility is essential. While the scope of this book is the aging workforce as a whole, we must remain aware that older workers do not form a homogeneous group. Each subgroup, and ultimately, each individual, has unique needs that must be met. The stories of Dot and Thanh in Chapter 5 are powerful illustrations of such tailoring to individual needs.
3. Ageist assumptions and attitudes that may pervade the organization must be identified and adequately addressed. This leads to the next observation.

4. There is a training imperative. Older workers may need to be (re)trained in order to improve productivity and morale. Design and delivery of such training interventions need to be age-neutral, a formidable challenge in itself. Moreover, human resource practitioners, managers, and supervisors may need training on ways in which ageism manifests itself within the workplace.
5. Finally, it is clear that recruitment and retention are not only intertwined with each other, but also with the other critical issues discussed later in this book. The authors document the importance of pension and health care plans for retirement decisions. Moreover, without addressing ageism, recruitment efforts may be a waste of time and money. Lastly, the different forms of employment suggested by the authors, clearly positioned as retention tools, form the basis of the redefining retirement issue discussed later in this book.

ISSUE 2
TRAINING OLDER WORKERS

Chapter 6

Academic Perspectives on Training Older Workers

Patricia A. Simpson

Perhaps one of the most important labor supply trends of the 21st century in the United States will be the aging of its workforce. In a recent study predicting labor force characteristics into the new millennium, the U.S. Bureau of Labor Statistics (BLS) estimated that an additional 7.5 million labor force participants will be 55 and older in 2008. Further, older workers will comprise 16 percent of the workforce in 2008, a considerable increase from a representation figure of 12.7 percent in 1999. The BLS also predicted that the median age of the workforce will increase to a historically unprecedented level of 40.7 years (Fullerton, 1999a, b). Other studies have also pointed out that the age group experiencing the greatest growth between 2000 and 2010 will be those aged 55-64 (Barber, Crouch, & Merker, 1992; Barth, McNaught, & Rizzi, 1993).

Multiple factors appear to be behind these trends. Perhaps most influential is the aging of the United States population in general, particularly of the large baby boom cohort. Additionally, new exigencies are compelling the current cohort of older workers to remain in the workforce longer than the cohorts that immediately preceded them. As life expectancy has risen, there is an increased probability that pension systems, even those supplementing Social Security income, cannot provide a sufficient long-term income to retirees (Hall & Mirvis, 1994). Relatedly, because the aging of the population could eventually lead to a situation where too few current workers must support too many publicly supported pensioners, reformers have argued for pushing back the normal and early retirement eligibility ages for Social Security benefits (Committee for Economic Development, 1999). New attitudes on labor force participation have certainly been documented among workers over 50 years of age. A recent study conducted by the AARP indicated that 80 percent of baby boomers expect to continue to work after a first retirement (AARP,

1998). Other surveys have garnered similar results (National Institute on Aging, 1993; Employee Benefit Research Institute [EBRI], 1997). Indeed, AARP's Public Policy Institute (2002) has charted an increasing labor force participation rate for workers 55 and older since 1985. The trend has been especially strong for women, but even the steady decline in men's retirement ages since 1950 leveled off after approximately 1985 (EBRI, 1999). Herz (1995) and Ruhm (1990) have demonstrated that the incidence of full- and part-time work among "retired" men younger than 65 has increased significantly since 1984.

These demographic and participation trends have been gathering momentum in a period of dramatic change within the American business community. Movement toward flatter, less hierarchical, and team-based work structures emphasizing job rotation and pay for skills acquisition have increased the need to retain employees who are suitable for retraining, demonstrate flexibility, and can adapt to fast-paced work environments (Mirvis & Hall, 1996). Skills obsolescence has also become an increasing concern in the face of the ongoing technological revolution (Bartel & Sicherman, 1993). Computerization has necessitated that employees acquire new technical and intellectual competencies in order to avoid redundancy (Jones & Bayen, 1998). In short, continual skills upgrading is absolutely imperative to remain employable in the new economy. This imperative should hold special meaning for current and future generations of older workers, especially given the factors motivating them to extend their work lives. Yet, common stereotypes about older workers often lead to misperceptions concerning the feasibility, incidence, and value of older worker training.

The purpose of this chapter is to review the existing academic literature on the topic of training older workers. I will address three major questions in discussing this topic as follows:

1. Is it feasible to train older workers?
2. Are older workers training?
3. Do older workers and their firms benefit from training?

Is It Feasible to Train Older Workers?

One of the most common stereotypes regarding older workers is the belief that they are have a reduced capacity for acquiring new skills and competencies, indeed, for learning in general in comparison to younger workers (Rosen & Jerdee, 1976a, b). Studies have shown that managers identify older workers as being "inflexible and difficult to train" (AARP, 2000a; Barth et al., 1993; Hall & Mirvis, 1994). Older employees have themselves expressed anxiety about their retraining capabilities, especially in comparison to younger workers and when the focus of skills acquisition is the newer technologies (Costello, 1997).

Admittedly, psychologists and gerontologists examining this issue have uncovered some evidence to support the view that cognitive functioning does vary by age (for a review, see Jones and Bayen, 1998). One stream of research has indicated that there is a general slowing of cognitive processes over the life course (Ponds, Jolles, & van Boxtel, 2000; Salthouse, 1996; Spirduso & MacRae, 1990). For example, older adults perform at a slower pace than younger adults on the Wechsler Adult Intelligence Scale-Revised (WAIS-R) Digit-Symbol Substitution Test (Wechsler, 1981). This slowing of cognitive processing arguably explains a substantial portion of measured age differences in cognitive functions such as long-term memory, analytical reasoning, and spatial abilities.

Another line of research posits that cognitive aging results from problems associated with attentional capacity and working memory. Working memory has been defined as a "system for the short-term storage and simultaneous processing of information" that is drawn upon when learning and reasoning (Jones & Bayen, 1998). Evidence confirms that older adults do less well at working-memory tasks (Dobbs & Rule, 1989; Salthouse & Babcock, 1991) and at tasks that draw heavily upon attentional capacity (for a review, see Hartley, 1992).

These dimensions of cognitive aging become even more pronounced when the complexity of the assigned tasks increases (Cerella, Poon, & Williams, 1980).

Older adults also appear to have greater difficulty filtering out irrelevant information. Some have argued that the problem corresponds with a decline in the efficiency of what has been identified as "inhibitory attention mechanisms" (Hasher & Zacks, 1988; Zacks & Hasher, 1994), but others have offered a more positive view. Older adults may have more difficulty ignoring extraneous thoughts simply because their comparatively greater breadth and scope of experience leads to a broader activation of stored material when presented with a stimulus (Jones & Bayen, 1998).

Finally, certain visual impairments become more pronounced over the life course. These can include difficulty focusing on short distances, a limited range of color vision, increased sensitive to glare, and, of course, greater susceptibility to disorders such as glaucoma and cataracts (Baltes & Lindenberger, 1997; Corso, 1987; Fozard, 1990; Whitbourne, 1985).

The implications of the cognitive aging literature for older workers are limited due to a number of factors. First, much of the research has been conducted in laboratory, rather than field settings. Indeed, empirical field studies on the relationship between age and job performance have never been able to uncover substantial variation in job performance by age (McEvoy & Cascio, 1989; Sterns & McDaniel, 1994). Presumably if age-related declines in cognitive functioning mattered in the workplace, then worker productivity and performance should correspondingly decline with age. This seeming contradiction may be resolvable, however. Based on results from two earlier empirical studies (Schaie, 1990; Sullivan & Duplaga, 1997), Greller and Simpson (1999) have also suggested that the effects of cognitive aging really only become pronounced at a point where most individuals have exited the work force. This means that the effects of cognitive aging are largely irrelevant to job performance. Certainly it is common in the cognitive aging literature to see research samples that include individuals 17 to over 90 years of age and that uncover significant cognitive functioning differences between the youngest age group (20-25 years) and the oldest age groups (over 65 years). Most recently Schaie (1990) and Sullivan and Duplaga (1997) have confirmed that significant declines in most mental processes only manifest themselves well into the 70s. There is also evidence that life experience can moderate the relationship between cognitive functioning and age. For example, Shimamura, Berry, Mangels, Rasting, and Jurica (1995) found that college professors were less likely to suffer working memory losses than people in other occupations. Finally, it is possible that in real-world settings where performance on actual work tasks is being measured, the tendency of older workers to entertain extraneous thoughts in experimental settings may actually be a bonus, allowing them to quickly access and evaluate multiple problem-solving strategies (Czaja & Sharit, 1998).

Ultimately, however, the most relevant literature is that which has looked directly at the relationship between age and job-related training performance. In a recent meta-analytic review of over 32 studies covering the period between the late 1950s and the mid-1990s, Kubeck, Delp, Haslett, and McDaniel (1996) concluded that important age differences in training performance did exist. Older individuals demonstrated less mastery of training material in post-test evaluation and required more time to complete training programs than younger adults. Further, the results suggested that there was a progressive linear deterioration in training performance. The overall distribution of the sample suggested that 30, 40, 50, 60, and 70 year olds fell into the 57th, 47th, 37th, 28th, and 20th percentiles, respectively. However, as Sterns and Gray (1999) have observed, at least one empirical study tested the assumption that one of the problems for older employees was less pre-test mastery of training material, thus putting them at a disadvantage compared to younger employees at the beginning of training (Gray, Boyce, Hall, & McDaniel, 1996). The study also more precisely examined how the effects of age might change in the presence of essential controls. Results confirmed that age differences in post-training knowledge were, at least in part, a function of parallel differences in pre-training knowledge. Further, the portion of age differences that could not be explained by pre-training knowledge differences was significantly decreased once education was included as a control. Factors

relating to the unique life experiences of individuals from different generational cohorts appear to also play a role in the age differences.

Because age differences do not disappear completely in the face of controls, the effects of cognitive aging cannot be discounted entirely, however. Consequently, gerontologists have undertaken to outline targeted training strategies and approaches that can easily and cost-efficiently accommodate the realities of cognitive aging. Strategies that address the reality that older adults take longer to complete training have been particularly popular and include:

1. Providing a slower pace of instruction with frequent pauses and ample time for discussion
2. Breaking up the verbal presentation of material with hands-on exercises
3. Minimizing the amount of required reading
4. Reducing the amount of material covered over the course of the training
5. Letting students learn at their own pace, something that has become relatively easier to achieve in an era of computerized instruction (Dennis, 1988; Gist, Rosen, & Schwoerer, 1988; Hogarth & Barth, 1991; Jones & Bayen, 1998; Knowles, 1987; Shea, 1991)

Another line of research also indicates that older employees do better when they are trained separately from younger workers (Knowles, 1987; Mullan & Gorman, 1972). This approach is not always economically feasible, but there is some evidence that it overcomes the frustrations and distractions that older employees feel when they realize that younger students master tasks and material at a faster pace (Charness, Schumann, & Boritz, 1992).

In summary, the answer to our original question: "Is it feasible to train older workers?" is a resounding "Yes." With only minor adjustments to training design, older workers learn just as well as younger workers. The stereotypes find absolutely no support in the research literature.

Are Older Workers Training?

Until recently the conventional wisdom both among academics and practitioners fed expectations of low rates of training among older workers. Developed by economists operating within the neoclassical tradition, early applications of human capital theory offered a particularly gloomy assessment of employers' willingness to offer training to older workers and of older workers' willingness to seek training opportunities. Economists rely heavily on a present value cost-benefit framework in understanding how both employers and employees make decisions regarding human capital investment. The core present value formula is based on the discounted net returns from training over the employee's remaining years of labor market participation.

Applying a present-value framework, neoclassical economists argue that prohibitively high indirect opportunity costs explain employer reluctance to train older employees. They reason that all else being equal, older workers are often too valuable in their current jobs to warrant further training or development. Given that older workers are often comparatively more productive because of their accumulated experience, pulling them from their duties for training incurs a higher opportunity cost in lost productivity than it does for younger persons (Andrisani & Daymont, 1987; Straka, 1992). A present-value framework also leads to assumptions regarding the effects of a limited payback period. Older employees have fewer years left of possible continued employment with the firm compared to younger employees. For this reason, employers prefer to make training investments in younger workers because they can expect that returns on their investment will be spread out over a longer period of time when younger workers are targeted for training (Becker, 1964; Polachek, 1981).

This understanding of employer decision making leads to another question. While it might not be in the employer's interest to train older workers, why would older workers not seek training on their own? The traditional human capital view was that workers apply the same logic as their employers. Older employees are equally concerned that both the direct costs of tuition and the indirect opportunity costs of foregone wages (presuming they take time off from work to retrain) will not be offset when the payback period on training investments is limited. In addition, they recognize that ageism in the external market may further reduce the potential returns from new skills acquisition.

At least for on-the-job training, most previous empirical research conducted in the United States confirmed that older workers did indeed train comparatively less (Booth, 1993; Duncan & Hoffman, 1979; Frazis, Gittleman, & Joyce, 1998; Lillard & Tan, 1986; Lynch, 1992; Royalty, 1996). Similarly, surveys repeatedly confirmed that employers were reluctant to provide training opportunities to older workers (Barth et al., 1993).

However, new data are emerging that challenge the expectations of traditional human capital theory. Rates of training participation among older workers have been rising dramatically in recent years. The increase is particularly apparent when off-the-job training formats are analyzed along with on-the-job training formats, something that was too often overlooked in previous analyses. For example, the enrollment of individuals aged 40 years and above in higher education grew by 235 percent between 1970 and 1993 (Elman, 1998). Elman (1998) notes that the rate of increase was even higher for older adults participating in vocational training and other work-related education formats of typically shorter duration. Government data suggest that the majority of courses older adults take across all possible educational or training settings are job-related in some fashion (Office of Technology Assessment, 1986). While little direct evidence currently exists to suggest that older workers are training more than younger workers, Simpson, Greller, and Stroh's (2002) analysis of a national sample confirmed that individuals 40 and older were more likely than younger individuals to participate in specific types of work-related education like on-the-job computer training. They were even more likely to enroll in formal credentialing programs for purposes of job or career advancement than those younger than 40. In contrast, younger workers were more likely to enroll in core courses like ESL, basic skills, and GED to improve their employability. Further, when only labor force participants are included in the sample, the overall incidence of training is higher for older workers than for younger workers (Simpson & Stroh, 2001). Finally, a recent survey found that a surprisingly high number of employers are providing training to older workers. Over 44 percent of 405 employers contacted by the AARP indicated that they offered training to older workers (AARP, 2000a).

Sociologists and gerontologists offer possible explanations for these changing training patterns. Models and frameworks that emphasize structural sources of change hold the greatest promise in this regard. Specifically, technological and related production process transformations occurring in modern industrial economies are thought to be at the heart of the altered training environment.

For example, Elman (1998) argues that within the United States, production process transformations and the introduction of new technologies have repeatedly elicited widespread changes in the makeup of student populations, educational delivery systems, and curriculum content within the United States. Most recently, the technological revolution has coincided with the rapid expansion of new educational delivery systems that have probably contributed to reducing the opportunity costs older workers face when retooling. Often incorporating nontraditional scheduling approaches, an expansive adult education system allows growing numbers of adults to enroll in classes and courses in their nonwork hours. Further, adult education providers often incorporate nontraditional pedagogical approaches that tend to appeal to older learners (Sterns, 1986; Sterns & Doverspike, 1988).

Elman and O'Rand (1998) have also linked increasing training participation among older adults to an effort to maintain labor market status and advantage in the face of structural sources of job insecurity. Similarly, in his life-span career development model, Sterns (1986) discusses how profound economic or technological change can generate new attitudes and behaviors among cohorts of workers toward training. In his view, because older workers tend to be the most vulnerable to obsolescence when new technologies are being rapidly introduced, the number of them seeking retraining rises commensurately. Certainly substantial evidence now exists to suggest that older workers have been facing intense labor market pressures since the 1980s. Older workers were targeted during the downsizing and restructuring efforts that typically preceded organizational restructuring and retooling during this period (Farr, Tesluk, & Klein, 1998; Sterns & Miklos, 1995). Proportionately more older workers than younger workers were laid off during the major downsizing phase that took place between 1986 through 1991 (Hall & Mirvis, 1994). Moreover,

when reemployed, the older workers experience considerable declines in compensation and status (Doeringer & Terkla, 1990; Gustman & Steinmeier, 1985).

Also with the structural sources of change perspective, Simpson and Stroh (2002) have demonstrated that a high comparative rate of training among older women workers in the 1990s is correlated with occupational segregation by gender. They conjecture that this correlation is a function of employers' need to offer training in the new computer technologies to women in administrative support positions.

While the prima facie evidence is supportive, few studies have directly analyzed the proposition that intensified training activity among older workers is a function of an altered workplace environment. One possible pathway to confirming this proposition requires further clarification of precisely which groups of older workers are training. For example, what evidence exists of a comparatively greater likelihood to train among older workers in industries, firms, and occupations that have been particularly impacted by production process and technological changes? Also, when does training take place? Is it prior to, but in anticipation of job loss, or following voluntary or involuntary job loss and in preparation for bridge jobs? Further, even within rapidly changing sectors of the economy, are certain types of workers more likely to train than others? Elman and O'Rand's (1998) status maintenance model suggests that professional and technical workers might be more prone to retrain as a means to preserve access to high-paying jobs with favorable working conditions. Psychologists remind us that individual attributes and dispositions impact the decision to retrain and retool. Shearer and Steger (1975) found that lower levels of career expectations and need for achievement were correlated with greater redundancy among older workers. Older workers were also more likely to be obsolete if they evidenced a stronger external locus of control. Other researchers have emphasized the importance of being interested in one's work (Richardson & Kilty, 1992) and openness to change (Mullan & Gorman, 1972; Thomas & Thomas, 1990). For review of the individual factors that might influence older workers' willingness to seek retraining, see Sterns and Gray (1999) and Yeatts, Folts, and Knapp (2000).

In short, unraveling the causal dynamics underlying intensified training activity among older workers should clearly be a top priority in future research agendas on older workers. An important first step in reaching this goal is a more precise delineation of the demographic and psychological characteristics of those older individuals who choose to train and of their location within the labor market.

"Are older workers training?" The answer to our second question seems to be not only that they are training, but that they are training in surprisingly, seemingly unprecedented numbers. Now the task before the research community is to clarify how and why this trend developed in recent years.

Do Older Workers and Their Firms Benefit from Training?

What labor market rewards, if any, do older workers gain through participation in training? Regrettably, systematic analysis of this question is unknown in the academic literature. The same can be said with regard to the firms that employ retrained older workers. To my knowledge, no rigorous empirical study has yet tackled the critical issue of whether training older workers enhances their productive value and adds to business revenues and profits.

Alternatively, there is a growing body of largely anecdotal case studies that shed some light, however indirectly, on these issues. As far back as 1977, the Aerospace Electronics Systems Department at General Electric (GE) set up a special training program for its older engineers. This effort was designed to introduce the older engineers, originally schooled in the world of analog technology, to the world of digital technology. The program was evaluated to be quite successful by GE management (Jacobsen, 1980). Another firm with a strong history of providing employee training demonstrated the value of targeted training techniques for older workers. The Russell Corporation adapted computer-based learning to its production of clothing and apparel and brought in certified adult education specialists to offer on-site classroom instruction with a strong hands-on component to the training (Jacobsen, 1980). Because of the success of this program, the company expanded its training efforts to include computer-based self-paced instruction for all its workers. This approach was deemed even more successful by management.

Perhaps the program that has garnered the most coverage in academic and popular texts is that provided by the Days Inn hotel chain. Rapid expansion of the chain in the 1980s created serious problems in staffing its sophisticated, computer-based national reservation system. Given their labor supply problems, the hotel chain launched a training program designed to teach computer illiterate individuals how to use the system. At first they found that older trainees took considerably longer to complete the training. Eventually, company trainers made adjustments to the program to accommodate the special needs of older adults. They included a brief orientation to the basics of computer technology for the older adults that had, in most cases, never seen a computer before the training. After this adjustment, older employees learned just as quickly as younger employees. More importantly, the costs of training the older adults were actually lower, because in this firm the turnover rate for older workers was lower. Thus, in contrast to the conventional human capital view, the payback period for employers to cover the costs of training was actually longer for the older workers than for the younger workers. Older workers were also more likely to have made a successful reservation upon completion of a phone call (McNaught & Barth, 1992).

The identified case studies suggest that older workers reap labor market rewards from training, at least in the sense that select firms have been more likely to retain them post-training. A recent empirical study also provides indirect evidence on this point. Utilizing government databases that provide cross-sectional samples for the entire U.S. population, Friedberg (2001) explored the relationship between computer usage among older workers and retirement. She found clear evidence to suggest that computer users retire later than those who do not use computers. As the author observes, if there is a causal relationship between retirement age and computer use, its directionality is unclear. On the one hand, those who have acquired computer skills may choose to retire later. Computer users probably have relatively greater access to jobs with higher levels of extrinsic and intrinsic rewards. Because computer users minimize the risk of being labeled obsolete by their employers and coworkers, they are also less likely to experience overt and subtle pressures from their employers and their coworkers to retire.

On the other hand, the correlation between computer use and retirement age may arise because individuals who plan to retire later choose to acquire computer skills. This kind of trajectory conforms rather well to the evidence regarding new economic pressures compelling older workers to remain in the workforce longer and new expectations among baby boomers that they will retire later than the generation that immediately preceded them. These realities motivate select older workers to seek to retrain as a means to maximize the probability that they will stay employable for a longer period of time in a rapidly changing economy. Of course, undertaking retraining does not guarantee that one's work life will be extended. This is why, however inconclusive, the documented link between computer skills acquisition and longer working lives for older workers is heartening.

As this overview clarifies, the answer to our third question, "Do older workers and their firms benefit from training?" is uncertain. Indeed, researchers have a wide-open field in regard to this topic. Evaluative field studies that examine older worker productivity levels pre- and post-training are clearly in order. Macro-researchers can look at longitudinal data bases that include questions on training participation to look more directly at the relationship between participation by older workers and post-training improvements in their wages, benefits, working conditions, and labor force participation, perhaps at 5-to-10-year intervals. Doctoral students and young scholars interested in industrial gerontology should take note; virtually uncharted territory is open to exploration.

Recommendations

Several major recommendations emerge from this overview of the literature on older workers and training. First, researchers exploring the topic of training older workers are well-advised to adopt a more comprehensive definition of training that incorporates both on-the-job and off-the-job training activities, including nontraditional adult education options with a vocational emphasis. Second, a larger number of empirical studies should be devoted to systematic analysis of the individual and environmental determinants of training participation and nonparticipation among older workers. In the context of projected future labor shortages and individual and societal interest in prolonging productive work lives, a clearer understanding of these determinants is especially important. Such knowledge might shed light on public policy alternatives that sustain optimal levels of older worker training participation. Third, as affirmed earlier in this chapter, the accumulated wisdom on the benefits that accrue to older workers and their firms when they retrain is woefully inadequate at this juncture. This oversight needs to be redressed as quickly as possible.

Perhaps research branches of entities like the National Institute on Aging and AARP can devote in-house and grant resources to the identified topics in the near future. Advocacy organizations also need to continue to educate the general public about both the feasibility of training older workers and the pedagogical strategies and techniques that work best with this population. The business community is especially deserving of targeted attention in this regard. Finally, business leaders must assess the hidden costs to their firms of failing to update older employee skills and aptitudes and the existing organizational barriers, formal or informal, which inhibit older worker access to training.

Summary

Prolonging worklife productivity has become a critical labor market imperative as the workforce ages, the potential for skilled labor shortages increases, attitudes and behavior regarding the "normal" age of retirement change, and the pace of technological innovation accelerates in the U.S. economy.

Little solid empirical evidence exists to suggest that older workers under 70 suffer from deficits in cognitive functioning that seriously inhibit their capacity for retraining. Further, the empirical studies are almost exclusively experimental in nature and fail to examine how factors like occupation can moderate the relationship between aging and cognitive functioning. Declines in cognitive functioning, for example, are less likely to occur among college professors.

Perhaps the most credible finding in the literature linking aging to cognitive functioning indicates that aging results in modest declines in working memory and information-processing speed. However, additional studies confirm that at little or no additional cost, training programs can be redesigned to address the special learning needs of older workers. Favored training strategies include (1) a slower pace of instruction with ample discussion time; (2) the incorporation of hands-on exercises and experiential techniques; (3) less required reading material; (4) self-paced instruction, including the innovative use of computers.

Contrary to what researchers previously expected and typically found based on studies of on-the-job training, recent research suggests an unexpectedly high level of training among older workers in major industrialized nations during the 1990s. In one study of U.S. trends, older workers trained more than younger workers in both on-the-job and off-the-job training categories. However, there is evidence to suggest that nontraditional adult education options are particularly attractive to older workers who seek further vocational training. Future research must therefore embrace a comprehensive definition of retraining that accommodates these options.

Although this line of research is largely preliminary, older workers appear to be motivated to retrain when they have a high need for achievement, possess a strong internal locus of control, and report that they are interested in their work. Older workers in professional and technical categories also retrain more, as do workers in industries associated with high growth rates and the rapid infusion of new technologies in recent years.

Case study evidence offers repeated examples of firms that have successfully retrained older workers, generally in an attempt to overcome labor shortages. They suggest that older workers may be higher-quality, more productive employees than younger workers after retraining. At least one study indicates that older workers who acquire computer skills retire at a later age than those who do not. Further research is clearly needed, however, to determine the value of training for both older workers and their employers.

Chapter 7

Effective Strategies for Training Older Workers

Suzanne Dunn

Sharon is a 35-year-old training manager for a quick-printing franchise company. In an effort to improve their franchisee support services, her employer has decided to start a 24/7 call center. The center is to be staffed by 27 employees (operating in three teams of eight covering three shifts with one team leader per shift). Sharon has been charged with training the call center employees for full deployment in eight weeks. She has determined through a job task analysis that the call center employees will require knowledge and skills in four areas: telephone customer service, team communication and problem solving, franchise products and services, and general computer operation. The HR department has informed Sharon that it will be actively recruiting older adults for the daytime shifts due to the demographics of the available applicant pool. Sharon has heard that older adults are typically not computer literate and are not really motivated to learn technical skills. Sharon has also heard that it is almost impossible to teach older adults something new in a short amount of time. She has some real concerns about how to train these older adults for the call center positions in just two months. How would you advise her?

Sharon's situation illustrates the types of challenges that training practitioners will face with increasing frequency as demographic change shapes human resource needs in 21st century organizations. According to Wallace (1999), "Nowhere will the age quake strike harder than in the workplace. Yet nowhere seems less prepared for the challenge" (p. 129). During the last decade of the 20th century, workers over 50 comprised the fastest growing segment of the American workforce (Walsh, 1995). Of the current working-age population, 52 percent is made up of baby boomers, 23 percent of which are between the ages of 47 and 51 (Caudron, 1997).

Current projections for the year 2005 indicate that Americans 55 or older will represent 30 percent of the working-age population. This proportion will increase to 40 percent by the year 2020 (Hall & Mirvis, 1994). In a recent poll, AARP and the National Council on the Aging found that "the closer [today's] workers get to retirement age, the more they want to keep working, and that 40 percent of [currently] retired people would rather be working" (Dychtwald, 1990, p. 175).

How can HRD practitioners like Sharon help their employers proactively anticipate and effectively embrace the inevitable changes that will result from this shift in workforce demographics? Sharon wants to start by reexamining the current training methods used and the learning environments that exist at her company. Her subsequent considerations should include plans for (1) establishing an age-friendly training infrastructure and learning climate in her workplace environment, and (2) accommodating the effects of age in training program design and delivery to keep up with the pace of changing technology and economic environments.

Age-Friendly Training Infrastructures and Learning Climates

In thinking about the task with which she is charged, Sharon considers a number of questions. How can she create an age-friendly learning climate so that trainees will be motivated to learn in just eight weeks what they will need to know and be able to do on the job? Are there older workers currently employed in other areas of the company that might want to transfer to the call center positions and require retraining or skill upgrading? How will she justify the return on investment (ROI) for training and/or retraining the older workers who get the call center positions? Sharon decides her first step is to acquire more information about age-friendly training infrastructures and learning climates and formulate a plan.

As is the custom of many training practitioners tasked with developing new training programs, Sharon first looks for a model of best practices. She searches for information about companies that successfully recruit and hire older workers. Her search produces a list of studies like the Louis Harris & Associates Laborforce 2000 Survey. Unfortunately, these studies are mostly about companies that avoid hiring or training older workers altogether despite the fact that relatively few jobs today require the ability to perform hard physical labor (Carnevale & Stone, 1994; Hale, 1990; O'Brien, Robinson, & Taylor, 1986; Useem, 1997). This finding prompts Sharon to wonder why companies are so reluctant to recruit and hire older workers especially given that, like the call center positions, most jobs require cognition, experience, and wisdom. Research indicates that these are qualities that can be presumed to increase with age and are considered important competencies for many managerial and decision-making roles (Sterns & Sterns, 1995a). Much of the underutilization of older Americans as workers – both those currently working and those wanting to work – is the result of "rigid corporate and government policies and practices" (Barth, McNaught & Rizzi, 1995, p. 61). Workers in their 50s and early 60s are perceived by others in a manner consistent with what people falsely assume about very old age. For example, others often incorrectly assume a greater decline in their abilities and productivity than reality would indicate, and tend to expect increased illnesses and absenteeism, or a rise in accident rates and diminished levels of productivity (Peterson & Wendt, 1995). The result of this transference of negative stereotypes is that retirement age is typically viewed as a cutoff point for one's working capabilities, and some baby boomers admit to grappling with prejudices about older workers when making hiring and personnel decisions (Carnevale & Stone, 1994; Steinhauser, 1998). Consequently, many companies will not assign older workers to retraining because of these existing stereotypes, which assume that the older worker is less capable, less efficient, less productive, more irritable, and poorer in health. These unjustified assumptions affect older workers in a particularly negative way when it comes to competing with younger people for training (Carnevale & Stone, 1994). For example, older employees are often refused training opportunities, despite working in organizational cultures that value those who maintain and improve their skills. Some human resource managers believe that older workers are less flexible, are unwilling to learn or change their ways, and have work styles that conflict with the work styles of younger workers (Sterns & Sterns, 1995a). These unjustified assumptions often lead to rationalizations based entirely on "the bottom-line":

> Investing in older workers – whether by hiring them, training them, broadening their skills by varying work assignments, or retaining them – yields a poor return for the company resources expended. Ironically, when any of this holds true, it is largely because management or company policy has created a self-fulfilling prophecy. By devaluing its older workers, especially by denying them training, management creates a depressing work environment that encourages neither high quality nor productivity. (Carnevale & Stone, 1994, p. 105)

Other effects of workplace ageism include the potential for lower employee morale and productivity as well as a rising number of costly lawsuits. Sharon is concerned for several reasons that these ageism-produced effects will render a negative long-term impact on her efforts to train and maintain productive call center teams comprising an intergenerational mix of employees.

Employee Morale and Productivity

Workplace ageism promotes feelings of inadequacy among older workers (Carnevale & Stone, 1994). Employees who work in an environment influenced by ageist suppositions tend to believe that at a certain age they will, or have suddenly become, useless. In many cases, these feelings of inadequacy and loss of purpose conflict with an aging worker's growing need for the intrinsic rewards of work (e.g., job satisfaction, congenial coworker relationships, or participation in meaningful activity) (Sterns & Sterns, 1995a). Cleveland, Shore, and Murphy

(1997) write that "Many of the problems and challenges faced by older workers are likely to be the result of others' reactions to and beliefs regarding the individual's age rather than a result of age per se" (p. 240).

Companies and managers who accommodate ageist myths about older workers often discourage them from participating in training opportunities that would keep their skills up-to-date. In such environments, it is often the case that older workers also believe the myths, and self-select themselves out of training. "It's a self-image problem; they feel they can't learn" (Kaeter, 1995, p. 64). The probability that older workers who lack access to training opportunities will find themselves obsolete and, eventually, out of a job is greater than for their peers who are able to keep their skills and knowledge current. According to one estimate, more than 50 million workers will need to upgrade their skills to perform tomorrow's jobs (Carnevale & Stone, 1994). Between 30 and 40 percent of workers currently over 40 years of age feel they need training to update their skills (Kaeter, 1995). One study revealed that workers in the year 2020 will need to be retrained "up to 13 times to keep pace with technological changes in the work environment" (Fyock, 1991, p. 22).

Sharon knows that the computer operation component of her call center training curriculum will need to be updated as the technology and supporting software changes. This also means that call center employees will need a training update every time new hardware or software is installed. This anticipated ongoing investment required to maintain the call center teams' technology-related proficiencies could be directly affected by workplace ageism. It has been Sharon's experience that employees with low levels of morale and productivity – regardless of age – are more costly to train and maintain.

Costly Litigation

Despite the Age Discrimination in Employment Act, enacted in 1967, many older workers continue to be denied opportunities for training, development, and promotion in both private and public employment. This situation has developed because of age prejudice and because employers have assumed that most workers would retire before age 65 (National Committee on Careers for Older Americans, 1979, p. 24).

> Much ado has been made recently about early baby boomers turning 50. For employers, the number to watch is 40 – when employees become eligible for protection under the Age Discrimination in Employment Act (ADEA). Now that nearly a quarter of [43 million] boomers has reached that magic number, [human resource practitioners] must be even more vigilant about avoiding age-discrimination lawsuits. (Flynn, 1997, p. 105)

The numbers of individual and class-action law suits alleging age discrimination filed by older workers in the United States reached a high of 22,800 in the first half of 1992 alone (Hassell & Perrewe, 1995). "If businesses are going to avoid costly litigation, they should recognize age bias and discrimination as a pervasive, escalating issue and immediately expand preventative training on age bias" (ThirdAge, 1998).

Sharon realizes that in order to keep her call center teams productive post-training, the workplace environment is a critical component in the total mix. Like other HRD practitioners, Sharon must confront age-related stereotypes that have germinated in the workplace over the past several decades (AARP, 1993b). One such common stereotype of older workers is that "they are slow and are progressively less able to handle intellectual tasks" (Driver, 1994, p. 196). As training manager for her company, Sharon realizes that one way to get senior management's attention about the value of an age-friendly workplace environment is to help them understand the potential costs of workplace ageism beyond the direct impact on training investment return. She decides to plan for development of a training program to counter age bias. Increasing awareness is the first step she can take to help her company avoid costly litigation related to age discrimination. She finds ample research to support her plan.

Diversity Training Programs

The 1987 Hudson Institute report, *Workforce 2000*, made "diversity" a household word (Karp &

Sutton, 1993). While that report focused on racial and ethnic diversity, some experts suggest that age diversity has now become a more pressing issue:

> Workplace 2000 is here. A bigger issue has superceded the concerns of racial, gender, and ethnic diversity: age diversity. There are four age cohorts in the workplace now and a fifth coming on by the year 2005. These five groups share some traditional work values but differ on such important ones as the role of managers, employer/employee loyalty, telecommuting, technical competence, and what constitutes a good day's work. (M. M. Kennedy, personal communication, 1999)

In organizations that value diversity and treat ageism as a diversity issue, younger employees are sensitized via diversity training to interact effectively with older workers. According to Kaeter (1995), the "attitude of the company is critical" (p. 65). As a result of their work, Zemke, Raines, and Filipczak (2000) suggest that "there are two keys to creating a successful intergenerational workforce: aggressive communication and difference deployment." The latter refers to "the tactical use of employees with different backgrounds, experiences, skills and viewpoints to strengthen project teams, customer contact functions, and, at times, whole departments and units" (p. 153). In other words, rather than viewing (generational) difference as a liability, it is considered a strength, and project teams are managed accordingly. In aggressive communication, "generational conflicts and potential conflicts are anticipated and surfaced," assuming that surfacing them "takes a giant step toward resolving them" (p. 153). Monsanto Chemical is an example of a company with a successful intergenerational workforce. It has a *Process for Diversity Management* program "aimed at making people more efficient and effective in their interpersonal relationships on the job" (Galagan & Cummins, 1993, p. 45).

In her search for successful age diversity programs, Sharon succeeds in locating some studies about employers who don't share ageist beliefs about older workers (Barkin, 1970; Bové, 1987; Brubaker & Powers, 1976; Carnevale & Stone, 1994; Clark, 1994; Czaja, 1995; Driver, 1994; Galagan

& Cummins, 1993). In fact, she finds a number of contemporary companies like the Oracle Corporation, Chevys Fresh Max, TGI Friday's, Ben & Jerry's Homemade, Inc., West Group, and Lucent Technologies that have successfully developed age-friendly workplaces (Goldberg, 2000; Zemke ct al., 2000).

Sharon also learns that, among employers who do offer training, there is evidence that older workers want to learn. This finding leads Sharon to conclude that stereotypical thinking about older workers' suitability for training is more of a statement about managers' calculations of immediate return on investment than about the workers themselves (Dixon, 1990; Phillips, 1996, 1991). Another one of the costs that such companies typically overlook in their training investment calculations is the cost of replacing workers versus retraining them. The Corning Glass Company reports a replacement cost of $40,000 per worker, and Merck and Company estimates that training a replacement for a lost worker can cost as much as one-and-one-half times that person's average salary (Goldberg, 2000).

Sharon now realizes that the difference between organizations that value older workers and those that don't seems clearly to be a function of the degree to which ageism in the workplace is present. Sharon's investigation convinces her that she and her fellow human resource practitioners should be concerned with the effects of workplace ageism for several reasons. Not only are age and ageism frequently central variables in hiring decisions, but ageism can strongly influence the morale and productivity of older workers and their younger counterparts. Ageism can be costly to employers in terms of age discrimination litigation. Furthermore, the changing nature of the workforce age composition may force employers to increase their training investments at the expense of other strategically planned expenditures.

In order to maximize her return on investment associated with training the call center employees, Sharon's strategy must include the post-training workplace environment because that's where the transfer of knowledge and skills to the job occurs. Sharon realizes that without an understanding of the effects of workplace ageism, she, like many other human resource practitioners, is ill-prepared for effectively troubleshooting the negative outcomes as they occur. The environment must be age-friendly in order to encourage high employee morale and productivity on the job. For future success in ongoing technology retraining and upgrading, the workplace environment must be free of age bias that would limit or discourage older employees from accessing and participating in additional training opportunities.

Sharon includes the following components in her plan for establishing an age-friendly training infrastructure and learning climate. First she reports her findings to senior management to make them aware of the potential negative effects of workplace ageism on the bottom line, and to ensure their ongoing support of training and retraining older workers. She also proposes a company-wide age diversity program to redress the negative stereotypes associated with the value of older workers. This will help foster an age-friendly workplace environment to keep the older workers' levels of productivity and morale high following training and job deployment.

Age-Tailored Training Programs

In order to accommodate the needs of her older trainees, Sharon turns her attention to gathering more information about designing and delivering age-tailored training curriculum. She wants to be sure that she doesn't discriminate against younger workers who will also need to be trained since there will be an intergenerational mix of workers filling the call center positions.

Based on what Sharon found out about the pervasive effects of workplace ageism, she begins her search for answers to a number of questions. How should programs be designed to accommodate the needs of older workers without discriminating against younger workers? What is important for training practitioners to understand about the effects of aging on cognitive processing? How do negative stereotypes about older workers influence training program design? Does research support what Sharon has heard about older workers being neither computer literate nor motivated to learn technical skills?

Sharon's questions lead her to discover a variety of well-entrenched myths about what older workers can and cannot do. Three common myths identified by the Department of Health and Human Services, as cited in Rolander (1988) include:

> Myth 1. Older workers are less productive than the average worker.
> Myth 2. It costs more to prepare older workers for a job than it does for younger workers.
> Myth 3. Older workers are unwilling to learn new jobs and are inflexible about the hours they will work. (p. 19)

Many training practitioners, like Sharon, do not believe that younger and older trainees differ in psychological needs, physical limitations, and learning styles. They maintain that a good instructor can train anyone using the same methodology, presentation styles, and instructional tools. Occasionally, when such practitioners are misinformed about studies of age differences in performance, the physical limitations of an older trainee, coupled with the time constraints of the program, become an irritant for everyone involved (Mintz, 1986). For example, using timed tests and not using real-world tasks are examples of "age-bias" factors resulting from studies of age differences in performance that are often misinterpreted by those who are less knowledgeable (Johnson, 1994). In other situations, older employees' needs are acknowledged in broad, philosophical goal statements, but they are handled poorly at the point of contact. Many human resource practitioners sometimes view age or prior experience as a hindrance, and devalue the experience-referenced contributions of their older trainees.

Through her research, Sharon realizes that many of the age-related stereotypes that have germinated in the workplace over the past several decades are a result of myths fostered by misinformation and failed experiments (Elliot, 1995). An example of a failed experiment is the 1973-1978 government project to retrain 2,500 air traffic controllers, whose average age was 45. The program cost over $100 million, and yielded a success rate of only 7 percent, based on the number of controllers who found second careers. The air traffic controllers responded poorly not because they were too old to learn, but rather because the classes were designed for participants in their 20s, not experienced 40-year old males (Carnevale & Stone, 1994). Misconceptions about training older workers that are based on past failures add to this problem that concerns everyone (i.e., trainers, supervisors, and workers who are, or someday will be, older members of the workforce) (Gilsdorf, 1992, p. 77). Sharon directs her search away from the myth-laden literature and toward empirically based research concerning training older workers.

Training Older Workers: Research Versus Myth

Sharon finds a growing body of evidence that clearly disproves many of the myths and stereotypes that she has heard and read about training older workers. For example, there is a pervasive myth that older workers are afraid of technology and do not want to learn new skills (Harkness, 1999). But many companies that have invested in computer training for their older workers have been pleasantly surprised by the results (Shields, Hentges, & Yaney, 1990; Thornburg, 1995). The research (Arthur, Fuentes, & Doverspike, 1990; Baldi, 1997; Barth et al., 1995; Caffarella & Barnett, 1994; Goddard, 1987; Mintz, 1986; Rolander, 1988) also indicates that older and younger workers generally show equal levels of productivity, and older workers do meet the productivity goals of their companies. Creative and intellectual achievements tend not to decline with age. Older people can be trained or retrained as effectively as anyone if programs are appropriately age-tailored. Vocabulary, general information, and judgment either rise or do not fall before age 60, and even then continue to develop in the majority of people. Senior workers, if treated with respect, show greater critical judgment, insight, and patience, and in general, are actually better able to transfer their knowledge and skills to their jobs. Older workers are eager to learn and are no more or less inflexible than the rest of the organization.

Sharon's review of other studies comparing performances between younger and older adults in the work setting (Barkin, 1970; Mintz, 1986) reveals that older adults typically perform better than 30 percent of the young adults. Older trainees differ from younger ones in terms of their psychological needs, physical limitations, and learning styles. Older adults experience problems processing information when it is presented at a fast pace, when contextual cues are not provided, and when the individual cannot consider competing information

provided simultaneously (Mintz, 1986). Although many age-related deficits have been identified (visual and auditory functions decrease on average with age), close to 90 percent of perceptual functioning remains intact (Mintz, 1986). A significant body of research has indicated a substantial learning ability for healthy persons at any age (Peterson & Wendt, 1995).

For many work-related cognitive abilities, such as working memory, there are no age variations across the years. Research over the past 40 years on the physiological and mental capabilities of older adults (Bass, 1995a; Driver, 1994; Howard, 1994; Shields et al., 1990; Sterns & Sterns, 1995a) indicates that:

1. Older adults learn as well as younger adults; where deficiencies occur with age is in speed of information processing.
2. As workers grow older, their learning styles and modalities change to accommodate the effects of age.
3. Intellectual capacity is sustained as we age.
4. If people are healthy and motivated, then age-related memory and learning problems are nonexistent or mild. Mental disorder, or dementia, does not become frequent until past age 75 (20% incidence), and the disorder does not become a real problem until past 85 (50% incidence).

Through her research, Sharon begins to realize that she and other training practitioners should accommodate the physiological effects of aging, particularly diminished vision and hearing capability. A training environment with "reasonable lighting and sound systems, comfortable temperature and seating, and clear and safe walking surface would compensate for most of the physical problems" (Shields et al., 1990, p. 3).

She also discovers the limits of the self-fulfilling prophecy (Rosenthal & Jacobson, 1968). Current thinking is that one can influence one's performance level and that of others by one's level of expectation (Howard, 1994). For example, negative stereotypes of the computer-illiterate older adult have not been supported by the research. Older adults' attitudes toward the computer do improve with positive experiences with the computer. Also, training studies show that older adults can learn how to use the computer, but need approximately twice as long to complete training as young adults (Baldi, 1997; Garfein, Schaie, & Willis, 1988; Kaeter, 1995). Another study (Hayslip et al., 1996) refutes the stereotype that older workers cannot adjust to a work team environment (i.e., team training involving older workers).

Accommodating Older Learners

Sharon decides to assemble a list of best practices from companies that have developed successful age-tailored programs. Sharon generates a list of companies that include the following: Triton International Management Consulting; General Electric Aerospace Electronics Systems Department in Utica, New York; Days Inn; Travelers Companies in Hartford, Connecticut; Russell Corporation; and Motorola Corporation (Carnevale & Stone, 1994; Fyock, 1991; Kaeter, 1995; Shaver, 1977).

Sharon finds other companies that have taken steps through age-tailored training programs to ensure that older workers do not fall behind rapidly changing technology. These companies include Crouse-Hinds, a New York manufacturer of electrical products; AT&T; Control Data Corporation, a Minneapolis-based computer manufacturer; and Kelly Services, Inc., a large temporary services firm (Bové, 1987).

From further investigation of the list of companies she generates, Sharon learns that when training programs are tailored to the age, knowledge, and experience of older workers, training proves just as effective as and no more expensive than it does for younger workers. The successful training programs always considered cost-effectiveness, practicality, and relevance regardless of the trainee's age. In fact, Sharon realizes that, based on her research so far, all of the accommodations that would be appropriate for "age-tailoring" a training program would enhance the overall quality of the training experience for all of her trainees, regardless of age.

Realizing that if ageist attitudes and behaviors can be put aside, Sharon concludes that the question is not, Can older adults learn? but rather, What is the best way to teach them? Peterson and Wendt (1995) suggest that "motivated older individuals can acquire new facts, skills, behaviors, and attitudes, but specific adjustments in the instruction given to them must be made for learning to be most effective" (p. 233). Based on what Sharon has learned about the negative effects of workplace ageism, the pervasive myths about how well older workers can learn something new and how misinformed most training practitioners are when it comes to designing age-tailored training programs, she is ready to generate a plan for developing her call center training curriculum.

Sharon's Plan

Sharon's plan includes a list of 12 specific research-based prescriptions that will improve the probability of producing the measurable learning outcomes she needs to maximize the return on investment of her call center training curriculum (Carnevale & Stone, 1994; Fyock, 1991; Johnson, 1994; Jones, 1984; Litwin, 1970; Peterson & Wendt, 1995).

She knows that her training curriculum needs to address competencies in four areas: 1) telephone customer service; 2) team communication and problem solving; 3) franchise products and services; and 4) general computer operation. She wants to incorporate all that she has learned about training older workers, and "age-tailor" her call center training curriculum. By doing so, Sharon will improve the probability of successful transfer of knowledge and skills to the job. Her return on investment will also improve, especially if she can effectively deploy an age diversity program throughout her company to foster an age-friendly workplace environment. Sharon plans to incorporate the following prescriptions in her call center training curriculum:

1. Create a learning environment that encourages self-confidence. If her older trainees have bought into the myths about their ability to learn, helping them gain self-confidence will mitigate the negative effects of the self-fulfilling prophecy.
2. Use modular training programs, especially with the computer operation training component. Break skills into small tasks and then build upon that knowledge; a building block approach to facilitate learning. Present one idea at a time. Summarize frequently.

3. Use easy-to-read printed training materials (high-contrast colors and large, bold typefaces). The older trainees will tend to place credibility on the printed word and will want to take work home to study and review.

4. Before using video-based training materials (e.g., for the team communication and problem-solving components), first make sure that the older trainees are comfortable with operating the video equipment.

5. For the computer-based training materials, provide tutorials to make sure older trainees are comfortable with operating the computer and navigating the training program interface design.

6. Design activities for the training curriculum that acknowledge and draw upon the older trainees' life experiences and build on that expertise. If there are incumbent employees who are transferring to the call center positions from other jobs in the company, utilize their years of experience with the company in the component on franchise products and services.

7. Be sure that the learning activities are purposeful, mindful, and relevant because all of the trainees, regardless of age, need to see the relevance of the training experience to their jobs and understand specific ways of applying it to their work situations. Eliminate any company jargon, especially for any trainees new to the company, because jargon creates barriers and perpetuates a we/they mentality.

8. For the telephone customer service skills component, use age peer instruction and coaching, small group work, and provide opportunities for lots of discussion and Q&A. Older trainees will respond more positively to an instructor who is sensitive to their needs for clarification, repetition, and application. To reinforce team communication and problem-solving skills, have the trainees work in teams when possible to solve problems.

9. Effective instruction accommodates a variety of learning style preferences so use a variety of delivery methods: verbal instruction, role modeling, self-directed or self-paced learning, and more time for practice and skill acquisition. Age-related physiological changes in the older trainees will cause them to prefer training that is self-paced or modified to accommodate their needs. Some of the older trainees with less than a high school education will be motivated to learn by concrete, real-life examples. Include activities that stimulate and motivate through involvement, such as case studies and problem analysis. In recognition that cognitive processing tends to slow with age, avoid using timed tests or exercises with the older trainees as these create unnecessary stress that interferes with learning efficiency.

10. Some of the older trainees may need help with study skills like reading, note-taking, reviewing, and organizing study materials because they have not been involved in learning situations in a number of years and have forgotten how to learn effectively. Build into the curriculum design the use of mnemonics, memory aids and any other tools to help the trainees organize information.

11. Create a supportive learning atmosphere for all of the trainees that (1) allows them to succeed, (2) provides positive and immediate feedback, and (3) encourages personal goal-setting and planning. Help the older trainees set specific measurable and realistic personal goals and formulate realistic plans for achieving those goals.

12. Finally, be sure that the training environment is free of distractions and provides opportunities for frequent breaks and social interaction. Select classrooms and seating arrangements that facilitate the older trainees' ability to hear the speaker and see the speaker's face. Advise the instructors to speak clearly and distinctly. Remove distracting sounds. Avoid posting training materials above eye level so that trainees with bifocals won't have difficulty seeing what is posted.

Summary

As shifting workforce demographics shape the training efforts of 21st century HRD practitioners, more and more situations will be created wherein younger instructors will be charged with training graying adults. The training infrastructure and learning climate are important factors for practitioners and their employers to consider to ensure the post-training morale and productivity of older workers. Human resource practitioners who understand the potential costs to the organization of decisions based on unbridled ageist stereotypes are better positioned for addressing the effects of ageism in the workplace.

It is important that HRD practitioners of all ages be better educated about research regarding learning abilities and work performance levels of older workers, rather than basing training decisions on myths propagated through the informal grapevine, or filtered through perceptions skewed by personal bias. Understanding how to age-tailor training programs will help employers proactively anticipate and effectively embrace the inevitable changes that will result from this shift in workforce demographics. Ultimately, knowledge about training older workers will enable 21st century HRD practitioners to maximize their employers' return on training investments, and help an aging workforce keep pace with rapidly changing technologies and economic environments.

Synthesis

Training Older Workers

The picture that emerges when Chapters 6 and 7 are analyzed and then synthesized is essentially the following:

1. There are persistent myths about older workers and their ability and willingness to learn. These myths may in part be fed by research that documents declines in cognitive functioning with age in a laboratory context.

2. However, the fact that research has not documented meaningful differences in work performance between older workers and younger workers certainly challenges the myth regarding older workers' ability to learn.

3. Those differences in learning that remain after other variables are accounted for are easily accommodated for by improving training design and delivery. It needs to be reiterated that such improvements are appropriate for *all* age groups. Therefore, making training age-friendly does not mean making it youth-unfriendly. This certainly applies to all the other action items that are called for elsewhere in this book.

4. The fact that many more older workers are training than is generally suspected certainly debunks the myth about their willingness to learn.

5. Those older workers who are indeed less willing to learn new skills may have internalized the stereotype themselves. Paradoxically, it may take training (specifically, a positive learning experience in the context of a training intervention) to rebuild self-confidence.

6. The extent to which older workers and their employers benefit from training interventions is unclear. However, Chapter 6 points out that many more older workers are engaged in training than suspected. It is highly unlikely that this trend would have developed if there were no benefit to either learner or employer. Additionally, Chapter 7 addresses the characteristics of the workplace within which new skills and knowledge are to be transferred. If the conditions are unfavorable, the benefit may be small or negligible. This suggests that the benefit enjoyed by both learner and employer may be driven more by organizational and context variables than by the age and expected tenure of the learner.

7. Finally, the issue of training older workers is interrelated with many of the other issues discussed in this book, in particular those of career development and intergenerational relations.

ISSUE 3

CAREER DEVELOPMENT
FOR OLDER WORKERS

Chapter 8

Past and Future Directions for Career Development Theory

Harvey L. Sterns
Anthony A. Sterns

For many decades we have been aware of the increasing numbers of older individuals in the United States. Increasing budgetary demands have put pressure on social policy planners to define the protections, entitlements, services, and benefits which this large and growing group will receive. Related to these issues is how these older Americans will participate in our economy and in our society, in particular in the context of employment.

Feldman (1988) documents a continuum of late career issues in his discussion of managing careers in organizations. He argues that more attention to the late career is important for three reasons. First, it represents a significant portion of one's career, potentially 15 to 20 years of an individual's working life. Second, it is likely that as older adults become a larger segment of the workforce, a larger percentage of the workforce will be in the later stages of their work life. Third, changes to the Age Discrimination in Employment Act ended mandatory retirement for many individuals and solidified protections that would allow individuals to work beyond the then standard retirement age of 65 years. Feldman also raises several issues with regard to career planning, including careful planning to ensure that one's late career provides for professional satisfaction, activity, and financial security.

Chapter 3 shows that besides the aging of the workforce, other trends are occurring as well. The shift to an information/services economy, the influx of communications technology, and increased globalization all will continue to impact the workplace. With lifetime employment no longer valued by employers or pursued by workers, and the pace of change only increasing, organizations have not remained static either and their processes for developing staff to be managers and managers to be executives have continued to advance. To remain on the cusp of market changes, organizations have instituted new structures and personnel development programs that facilitate remarkable adaptability to changes in the external environment. These learning organizations practice continuous renewal of their structures and processes (Lei, Slocum, & Pitts, 1999; Lord & Maher, 1993). Larger organizations are also seeking to identify areas for improvement at the personnel and organizational levels through feedback systems. These organizations have formal processes for getting feedback from subordinates, peers, supervisors, and customers. This information can drive the agenda for the types of training and career development processes embraced by an organization (London, 2002).

Clearly, there is a need for current and flexible models of career development that reflect this new reality. A life span developmental perspective on career development holds a promising future as it places a changing individual in a changing environment. This perspective has proven very robust in the work environment. The decision to pursue promotions, change jobs or careers, find new employment, or engage in career development activities may come about as a result of changes within the individual, the environment, or both in combination. The professional role of the older worker is being redefined in the rapidly changing environment of work in the 21st century. Industrial gerontologists have also redefined how they model career development from its beginnings in the 1940s to the present (Sterns & Huyck, 2001; Sterns & Sterns, 1995b). This chapter will review the major influences on career development theory of the past 50 years and propose some considerations and challenges for career development models as we move deeper into the century.

Models of Career Development

Feldman (2002) defines *career* as the progression of events of a person's work experience from the formation of career interests through retirement. *Career development* refers to those activities that pertain to managing the progression of a career. These activities may be initiated by employers (e.g., hiring and promotion policies), professional organizations (e.g., certifications), supervisors (e.g., performance appraisals), or the individual involved (e.g., self-directed study). Career development models attempt to summarize the progression of career events and decisions to two ends. First, these models are useful to predict the behavior of individuals. Second, and of more personal interest to each of us, these models can be used to better understand our own career behavior and provide recommendations that can aid each of us to maximize our personal growth and development during our working lives. The ultimate goal of a career development model should be to contribute to maximizing the potential of all individuals as they navigate their careers. How models have tried to achieve this has changed dramatically over the past half century.

1940s

The 1940s were dominated by what is often called the measurement revolution (Zunker, 1998). During World War II, the need for classifying large numbers of armed services recruits led to the development of large-scale tests. Upon return from the war, veterans were eligible for counseling to assist them in transitioning back to civilian life. These interventions, however, were based on the match between a particular vocation and the individual's (general) abilities. With abilities assumed to remain constant across the lifespan, this approach could not be considered developmental. In fact, the term *career development* did not appear until the next decade.

1950s

In 1957, Super proposed a theory that is still very influential today and is arguably one of the first developmental approaches to career. Recognizing that careers develop, he proposed a fixed sequence of career stages. Children from birth to age 14 develop certain interests and abilities by role-playing activities. This he termed the growth stage. Between ages 15 and 24, people are in a stage of

exploration, making tentative career choices and entering the labor market. From ages 25 to 44 comes the establishment stage in which occupational changes sometimes occur and an effort is made to stabilize the career. By ages 45 to 65 people are expected to hold on to what they have in the so-called maintenance stage. Finally, from age 65 on, the person enters into a stage of decline, where the pace is slowed and retirement occurs.

Super's theory stressed the interaction of personal and environmental variables. It included issues addressed in previous career development theories including individual differences, a person's potential for numerous occupations, ability patterns, and the influence of role models on career decisions. He also contributed several life span developmental considerations. Aspects such as the continuous adjustment to the environment, the dynamic influences of events common to different life stages, and the impact of job satisfaction on one's role in life were for the first time considered as elements in career development. As a result, however, the outlook for older workers in terms of access to training or other career development activities was bleak.

1960s

The early 60s continued to focus on a linear career path. Wilensky (1961) defined an orderly career as an endeavor in which a person can grow in responsibility and competence as well as income, can plan for the future, and can invest time and energy with the certainty of future gain (Havighurst, 1982).

The 1960s also led to the development of the person-environment fit model. Holland (1959, 1962) defined work using four characteristics: change, simplicity, instrumentation, and data. Holland proposed that a finite number of work environments exist within the American society. These environments are defined as realistic, investigative, social, conventional, enterprising, or artistic. This model focused on matching the individual with the work environment in terms of these characteristics.

1970s

The 1970s saw age and life stage as an important determinant of behavior and these elements were incorporated into career development theories. Numerous models suggested that the mobility rates of younger persons (up to around age 30) are much higher than those of older persons (Hall & Nougiam, 1968; Super, 1957; Veiga, 1973) as the younger generations move about seeking their niches in life and the older ones maintain theirs as they plan for retirement.

Schein (1971) describes three stages in a career: socialization, performance, and obsolescence versus the development of new skills. In the third stage, the obsolete person may be retained as "deadwood," with no options for mobility, or may be retrained, transferred into a lateral position, or forced into early retirement. Although career development could be helpful to the employee in all three stages, it seems likely that the person who would most strongly desire such help would be in a third stage of Schein's model. In terms of actual research, "mobility in the earliest stage of one's career bears an unequivocal relationship with one's later career" (Rosenbaum, 1979, p. 220). Thus, the person who is mobile early on most likely will be mobile in the latter career stages (Veiga, 1981, 1983).

Hall's model of career growth (1971) conceptualizes career planning from a goal-setting perspective. Once a career-goal decision – such as the decision to engage in training or retraining – is made, then goal attainment should lead to identity growth and enhanced self-esteem. Such enhanced self-esteem may then lead to greater commitment to future career-developmental goals. Goal attainment enhances self-esteem, which may increase perceptions of self-efficacy and future commitment to career-development activities.

Research on actual mobility rates seems to bear out these hypotheses (Bureau of Labor Statistics [BLS], 1967, 1975; Sommers & Eck, 1977; Veiga, 1983). Veiga (1983) also found that age correlated significantly and negatively with propensity to move. With regard to career development, Gould (1979) predicted that career planning would be highest during Super's stabilization period (age 31 to 44), when there is stable growth as the person attempts to secure his or her place within the occupation. Research support has not been found for this hypothesis.

In the late 70s, theories of career progression began to be criticized for following a "linear life plan," the pattern in which education is a task for the young, work is for the middle-aged, and leisure is for the elderly. The criticism of using the linear life plan as a basis for theory is that it perpetuates the notion that these are the appropriate tasks for each life stage, discouraging intermixing all three tasks across the life span.

The work of Levinson, Darrow, Klein, Levinson, and McKee (1978) added new dimensions to stage theories by incorporating biological, psychological, and social development constructs. Levinson et al. (1978) and Sheehy (1976) have contributed by popularizing the idea of midlife transition issues and raising the possibility of different career development patterns for males and females.

1980s

The life span orientation combines the above approaches with a recognition that behavioral change can occur over the entire life cycle. This approach emphasizes substantial individual differences in aging (Baltes, Reese, & Lipsitt, 1980). Individuals are influenced by normative, age-graded biological and environmental influences (physical and cognitive changes as one ages), normative, history-graded factors (generational events), and non-normative influences unique to every individual. The influences interact to determine an individual's career path. Over the course of a career, a person will be presented with increasingly complex work roles, which play a crucial role in stimulating the development of mental models of how people interact, how projects are successfully completed, and how to gain recognition from the organizations. Individuals begin with different potentials and will improve at differing rates.

Katz (1978) moved the focus of career development into the organizational setting. In a model of job longevity, Katz describes three successive stages: socialization, innovation, and adaptation. Stage I, socialization, occurs during the first few months on the job. During this stage, one tries to establish a situational identity, decipher situational norms, learn role expectations, build social relationships, and prove oneself as an important contributing member of the organization. Stage II, innovation, is characterized by a transition in employee job concerns. Occurring approximately between the sixth month and the third year of job longevity, the major concern is on achievement and accomplishment. Attempts are made to improve special skills, enlarge the scope of one's contributions, enhance visibility and promotional potential, and influence the organizational surroundings. Gradually, however, if promotion or movement does not occur, tasks become less challenging and more routine, and the person enters into Stage III, adaptation. In this stage the individual either adapts to remaining in that job or leaves the organization. If the organization is left, then the socialization phase (Stage I) is reentered in the new job. Thus, the socialization stage can occur throughout the span of the career.

Similarly, in 1984, Super updated his theory to include "mini-cycles" that revisit the career stages across the life span. Career growth, exploration, maintenance, and decline may occur at any or at many points in the life span. An individual can continue to grow, explore new interests and career directions, establish new competencies, maintain those new skills, and then disengage and take on a further set of new interests. The continued relevance of Super's theory hinges upon the notion of career adaptability—a construct that encompasses a willingness to plan a career, participate in ongoing exploration, and develop adaptive decisional skills (Savickas, 1997). Although research validating Super's theory has been sparse, numerous studies support its utility (Sterns & Subich, 2002).

The early 80s also brought research attention to personality variables. Need for achievement and locus of control were variables hypothesized to affect mobility and career development attitudes. Neapolitan (1980) investigated occupational changes in mid-career and found that people who made changes regardless of great obstacles tended to reflect an internal locus of control. A comparison group of people dissatisfied with their careers who did not make changes tended to perceive great risk beyond their control, which would doom any such efforts. According to Greenhaus and Sklarew (1981), exploration "is a proactive attempt to understand and influence one's life" (p. 2). Thus, we might expect internals to engage in greater career-planning activity than externals. Research by Beehr, Taber, and Walsh (1980) and by Gould (1979) tends

to support this hypothesis. We may conclude that persons with an external locus of control are less likely to view a career development program as beneficial to them and, hence, less likely to participate in one.

In the early 80s Veiga (1983) discussed individual barriers to moving in the context of seniority and age. Veiga suggested that perceptions of one's own marketability might strongly influence one's efforts to explore alternative career opportunities, both within one's own organization and in an outside firm. Since holding a particular position within the same organization for an extended period of time may only reinforce feelings of specialization and/or obsolescence, older workers are at higher risk of perceiving low marketability. Moreover, the longer people remain with a company and the older they get, the more likely they will be to think twice about risking any benefits accrued through the years in order to move to a new organization. The same may be true for the person who strongly values job security, regardless of age. In sum, if the perceived risks associated with career moves are too high, people are unlikely to participate in career development programs.

Veiga also identified five motives that significantly influenced propensity to leave: fear of stagnation; career impatience; and dissatisfactions with salary, recognition, and advancement. Again we assume that people with a desire to move will react positively to the initiation of a career development program that could conceivably help them on their way.

In the 80s life-cycle and stage theories were criticized for using male workers as the basis for the development. It is becoming increasingly evident that career progressions of women may be quite different from those of men, as the former juggle the roles of student, housewife, paid worker, mother, and so on. Life-cycle and stage approaches have also been criticized for failing to test propositions adequately. Particularly lacking is longitudinal research using subjects over age 50. A criticism of stage and with-job theories is that they tend to ignore the interaction of work and nonwork aspects of life (Sonnenfeld and Kotter, 1982).

Patchett and Sterns (1984) and Sterns and Patchett (1984) have attempted to develop and refine (Sterns, 1986) a model of adult and older adult

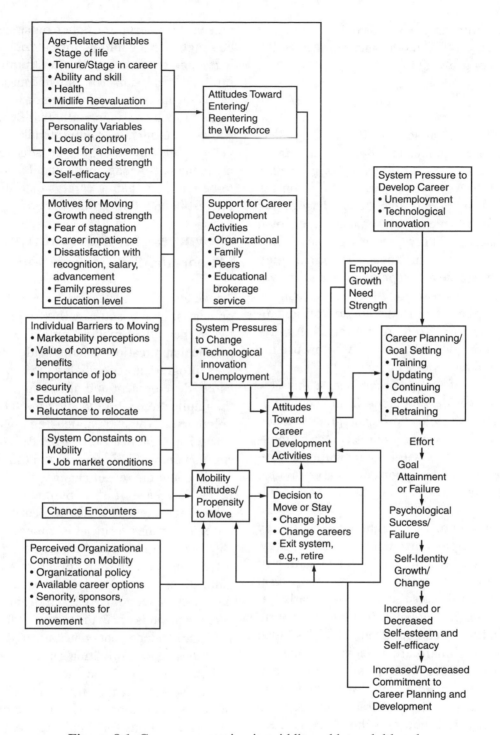

Figure 8.1 Career progression in middle and late adulthood.

career development that is not age-specific. The model assumes that transition in work life may occur many times throughout a career (See Figure 8.1).

The model shows that the decision to change jobs or careers or to exit the system is directly influenced by attitudes toward mobility and success or failure in previous career development activit-

ies. Numerous factors are hypothesized to affect mobility attitudes, such as employment, career stage or tenure, growth need, fear of stagnation, marketability perceptions, job market conditions, and chance encounters. The decision to change jobs or careers also may affect one's attitudes toward entering or reentering the workforce. The effects of various personality variables also could mediate any of these variables. The model incorporates Hall's model of career growth (1971).

1990s

Hall and his colleagues revisited Hall's (1971) goal-setting career model in 1996 with a popular book entitled *The Career is Dead – Long Live the Career* (Hall & Associates, 1996). Based on his 1970s goal-setting perspective, he emphasized the importance for people to now manage their own careers themselves. This represents a clear turning point, as previously it had been the organization that directed increases in responsibility and growth through training. Career growth and development were no longer confined to the context of the employing organization. To represent this shift in responsibility to individual workers, we now use the term *self-management* of careers.

Two schools of thought characterize this new approach to career development. In the context of Mirvis and Hall's (1996) "protean career" model, Hall now looks at advancing one's career by moving between as well as within organizations. Loyalty is to oneself and the opportunities are provided by the industry as a whole, not just by a single employer.

The other school of thought, represented by Sterns' self-management model (Sterns & Gray, 1999), emphasizes training and the acquisition of new skills through formal education, short-term training, and self-directed study. While early career theory assumed that key career decisions were made early in life, and models from the 1970s called attention to additional career decisions taken in midlife, Sterns' model recognizes that these decisions are taken throughout the lifespan. People are not bound to any particular track, as they can change employers, reenter school, learn new skills, or change careers at any point in their working lives. These decisions are influenced by a variety of factors, including technological change, evolving interests, or unexpected opportunities.

In the self-management model people engage in career planning and goal setting, leading to the necessary training and updating not only to maintain currency but also to set the stage for new employment opportunities. If employers do not provide those opportunities, then outside training must be sought. This could be formal (e.g., through colleges, universities, or computer training centers) or informal (e.g., subscriptions to journals or technical publications). Training offered by organizations tends to focus only on skills that benefit the company, while outside training tends to focus on developing the individual in a broader sense. According to the self-management model, people are likely to be ready to change careers or retire when their interest in updating skills declines.

Synthesizing Current Applied and Theoretical Issues into Future Models

As we enter the 21st century we find career development still in a state of flux, while the gap between theoretical models, empirical research, and practical application remains wide. We have made great progress in recognizing the cyclical nature of career development and have begun to understand the implications of a dynamic model of career development. However, much remains to be done. There is a great need for career development theories that are valid, have utility in practice, and take into account the recent changes that have occurred in the workplace. It is our belief that the concept of self-management has great potential for this purpose. To further refine this concept, the relationship between individual career decisions and their effects on the individual, on groups within the organization, and on organizations as a whole must be better understood. The environment in which career decisions are made (external factors) and the intrinsic elements that contribute to the individual's awareness and motivation (internal factors) must be better conceptualized, measured empirically, and tested to determine the utility and validity of emerging career development theory. Before presenting recommendations for future research and practice, we present a synthesis of career development research: What have we learned?

External Factors Which Contribute to Career Development Behavior

The organization that employs the older adult contributes in important ways to the desire of that worker to engage in career development activities such as training (Farr & Middlebrooks, 1990; Farr, Tesluk, & Klein, 1998). Because organizational factors are outside the individual, they are referred to as external factors.

Opportunities for training. Training opportunities are very different in the 21st century, with many new training modalities available through dramatic advances in networking and multimedia technologies. However, at least in the near term, older workers may be given fewer opportunities to train as they are likely to have greater responsibilities than younger workers and may not be given time or encouragement to continue to update skills. Often this decreased access is also rooted in a widely held assumption that older workers do not learn as fast as younger ones do. However, Czaja and Drury (1981) and Elias, Elias, Robbins, and Gage (1987) have demonstrated that both young and older adults benefit equally from training on real job tasks (word-processing and inspection).

Flexibility. Employees must feel free to approach their manager with new ideas and be encouraged to discuss, pursue, and apply them. This does not suggest a radical and global change every time an employee has an idea, but creating an environment that is flexible enough to discuss new ideas and to invest resources in learning about and trying new ideas. A flexible managerial style will encourage older and younger workers alike to learn about, develop, and implement conceptual and mechanical tools to improve performance, productivity, and profitability (Fossum & Arvey, 1990).

Reward systems. A reward system is necessary to encourage training behavior (Kaufman, 1990; Votruba, 1990). An organization must provide release time for updating skills (Votruba, 1990). This is especially important for middle and higher-level managers, as their large staffs and time-consuming responsibilities often leave them little time to train and update skills. Training periods often allow additional benefits by giving managers time to associate with peers and to exchange ideas and get expert feedback without the impression management often required in a formal office setting.

Challenging work. This is another key external factor (Willis & Dubin, 1990). A work situation of this nature provides intrinsic motivation for employees to seek out new strategies and tools to ac-

complish assignments. This in turn leads them to embrace their work and enjoy the endeavor and the success.

Organizational level. Personnel at different levels of the organization will have different training needs (Lawrence, 1985; Votruba, 1990). This applies not only to the skills they will be trained on, but also the techniques used for the training. Older workers who have been out of school for long periods of time (and tend to be at higher levels in organizations) tend to respond better to training that involves case studies and discussion and active learning.

In sum, opportunities for training, the nature of the work, flexibility, reward systems, and organization level all have an impact on career development behavior. While organizations and jobs vary widely along each of these parameters, the individual workers must navigate those parameters and manage their career growth. Not surprisingly, then, internal factors (those intrinsic to the individual) also have a significant impact on career development behavior.

Internal Factors Which Contribute to Career Development Behavior

In previous sections, several personality traits have already been presented, such as locus of control and need for achievement. Besides traits, attitudes also contribute to the desire to continue to work and to maintain the skills required to excel. These attitudes have been researched under the topic of organizational commitment.

Organizational commitment is a process of identification with the goals of an organization's multiple constituencies (Reichers, 1985). Randall (1987) speculates that commitment is an inverted-U function with the apex at a moderate commitment level. A healthy level of organizational commitment allows the balancing of work-related and personal responsibilities. Low levels of commitment generally are detrimental to both individual and organization. High levels are good for the organization, but hurt the individual's other responsibilities. Romzek (1989) found empirical support for Randall's suggestion.

Meyer and Allen (1984) distinguish between two dimensions of organizational commitment: con tinuance commitment and affective commitment. Continuance commitment is the perceived cost of leaving, exacerbated by a perceived lack of alternatives to replace or make up foregone investments. The longer one remains with an organization, the more "side bets" (Becker, 1960) one is likely to have. Examples of such side bets are social networks, organizations, clubs, and participation in family-related activities. Vacation time, vesting in retirement plans, and seniority-related perks are other examples. Clearly, side bets are important to older workers and their families and represent a major determinant of their continuance commitment.

Affective commitment is the emotional orientation to the organization and can be seen in two ways. One focuses on the attributions that are made to maintain consistency between one's behavior and attitudes (Mowday, Steers, & Porter, 1979). Simply becoming a member of an organization creates an affective commitment. The longer the tenure with that organization, the more likely it is for the worker's identity to become tied to that membership. While less common today than in the past, individuals can still work for many years for the same company. In the case of small business, it is also likely that commitment will be even stronger since the business is likely to dominate a person's time and attention.

The other version of affective commitment defines it as the congruence between individual and organizational goals. Commitment is strongest when workers identify with and extend efforts toward organizational goals and values. This version of affective commitment was operationalized in a survey by Steers (1977).

Evidence for the coexistence of affective and continuance commitment was provided by McGee and Ford (1987). Using factor analysis they found two uncorrelated factors, supporting Meyer and Allen's distinction. This is especially relevant to our discussion of older adults. As workers increase their tenure with an organization, they may feel increasing continuance commitment because they have established a home and friendships in the area, they have become specialized in a skill that they feel cannot be transferred, or they feel they could not get the same benefits if they moved to a new organization. On the other hand, affective commitment

gives the employee an emotional tie to the organization that motivates them to remain, not because they cannot afford to leave, but because they feel a sense of contribution and growth from and with the organization.

Organizational commitment has proven useful in predicting job performance (Sterns & McDaniel, 1994) and its role should be expanded in future career development models. However, it must be kept in mind that there is no simple relationship between age and continuance commitment on the one hand, and continuance commitment and job performance on the other. In fact, some research has shown a weak relationship between age and commitment (Mathieu & Zajac, 1990). Job characteristics (autonomy, scope, challenge) may overwhelm age. This suggests that the primary causal relationship is between job perceptions and commitment. Some evidence for reciprocal causation also exists. Mathieu (1991), using an exploratory structural analysis, found that the influence of satisfaction on commitment was stronger than the reverse effect. In this case, committed workers were more likely to be given opportunities that were satisfying.

Meyer, Paunonen, Gellatly, Goffin, and Jackson (1989) found affective commitment to be positively related to performance, and continuance commitment to be negatively related to performance. Individuals with higher affective commitment were less likely to leave an organization and more productive than individuals with low commitment. Individuals with high continuance commitment, in contrast, were also less likely to leave the organization but less productive.

Clearly, organizational commitment is driven to some extent by organizational characteristics (external factors). Organizations that encourage maintaining and improving the skills required to excel, and provide challenging work and the opportunity to inject new ideas will have employees with higher affective commitment, leading to reduced turnover and increased productivity. An organization can measure the success of its efforts by examining organizational-based self-esteem (OBSE).

OBSE has been operationalized as the degree to which organizational members believe they could satisfy their needs through their participation within the organizational context. Matheson (1991) explored age-related differences between OBSE and other work satisfaction and commitment measures and found that age was significantly and positively related to organizational satisfaction, continuance commitment, and self-esteem. However, after controlling for job and organizational tenure, two variables that have been found to co-vary with age, only self-esteem was significantly associated with age. Employees over age 50 had significantly higher self-esteem than did younger age groups. Employees who perceived that they were valuable as organizational members were more satisfied with their jobs and organizations, more committed to the organization (in terms of both affective and continuance commitment), and less likely to leave. These findings show the importance of understanding employees' perceptions and interpretations of organizational policies, procedures, and culture.

All in all, an overview of the research on career development behavior shows that this behavior is essentially shaped by two categories of influences: external factors and internal factors. For any increased understanding of career development behavior, future models must take into account all significant internal and external factors.

Recommendations

Recommendations for Research

Clearly, there is a need for more empirical research to investigate the role of both external and internal factors in the modeling of career development behavior. In the face of the aging of the workforce, it is imperative that career development models be age-neutral. Issues such as fairness and diversity may well be the very foundation upon which to build future research, so that equal opportunity and equal access apply to anyone, regardless of age, race, gender, or ethnicity.

In early career theory, career development models were based on the existence of large, stable organizations. However, the economic successes and failures of the start-ups of the 1990s, increasing percentages of small businesses as sources of new employment, increased globalization, health care and pension issues, the influx of technology, and of course the aging and diversification of the workforce, to name but a few recent trends, have impacted how we view and model career development. Late career decisions are much more dynamic than they have been in previous decades. New career development models must embrace this new reality and incorporate relevant factors – including roadblocks and hurdles that individuals encounter. Once the factors are modeled, strategies for recognizing and overcoming barriers can be examined. The detriments to both the individual and the organization can be researched and practical solutions to surmount or minimize them can be taught or institutionalized (Sterns, Junkins, & Bayer, 2001). The factors to be modeled can be divided into external and internal ones.

External factors. The external factors that new models should take into account include (but are not limited to) opportunities for training, flexibility, reward systems, job characteristics, and organizational size.

- Organizational support: The level of organizational support for career development activities can be conceptualized as a combination of opportunities for training, flexibility, and reward systems. Opportunities for training are easily determined. Participation rates are another important source of information and reflect the flexibility, or infrastructure, that exists inside the organization that actually allows employees to seize these opportunities. These rates should be broken down according to age, gender, racial, and ethnic variables in order to ascertain any disparate impact. Reward systems are another crucial element in determining the level of organizational support, as they show whether or not the organization literally puts its money where its mouth is.
- Job challenge: How challenging the work is can be measured through surveys of individuals, measured by competition in the field, or by using an index of the skills used in the job in comparison to others.
- Organization size: It will be important to test the robustness of emerging models in small and medium-sized organizations. Small businesses have become increasingly important to our economy, and it is likely that appropriate career development behaviors vary significantly between small and large organizations. These

differences need to be researched so that career development professionals can make appropriate recommendations.

Internal factors. Since attitudes are powerful predictors of performance, we believe that the concept of organizational commitment (both continuance commitment and affective commitment) will remain very important and needs to be included in future models. Another attitude needs to be researched that is of particular relevance to the older worker: self-perception. The older adult may have internalized the negative stereotype that one is too old to learn. This may be why older adults are least likely to volunteer for training (Peterson, 1983). This is a particularly important variable to include and further research, because without this variable, the impression is created that employers are solely responsible for their employees' career development behavior. This is antithetical to the concept of career self-management.

Recommendations for Practice

Regardless of whether the organization is large or small, the message of self-management must be emphasized from the earliest career interest programs and continuously throughout the career. This task is likely to become easier with increasing resources available on-line in both free and subscriber forms (London, 2002). Accelerating technologies and increasingly portable, flexible, and multifunctional electronic tools available to individuals make this job easier and more challenging at the same time.

By the same token, self-management does not absolve employers from their responsibility for career development. The following recommendations for human resources practitioners and career development practitioners may help them take that responsibility:

- Spread the message of career self-management. Educate employees on the new workplace and its consequences for career development activities.
- Concurrently, support employees in their self-management efforts by collecting and disseminating information about training opportunities

and resources inside and outside of the organization.
- Examine training policies, procedures, and practices that could be discriminatory in their impact on specific populations, particularly aging workers. Since all employees age 40 and up are protected by the Age Discrimination in Employment Act, there is a real business imperative to do this.
- Train both managers and employees on training. Ageist stereotypes are so pervasive that older workers themselves may have internalized that stereotype, which would prevent them from participating in training. Management needs to take responsibility for educating older workers on their own ability to learn, and in the process, they need to become sensitized to how these stereotypes manifest themselves. Such sensitivity trainings could easily be expanded to include race, gender, and ethnicity.
- Adjust reward systems to reflect a commitment to career development. Hold employees accountable for managing their own development efforts (for example, through individual development plans, which can be seen as an official agreement between employer and employee) while holding managers accountable for their employees' training utilization rates. Policies that do not reward older workers for acquiring new skills may actually encourage retirement by not using these productive workers (Cooperman & Keast, 1983).
- Maintain an appropriate balance between routine tasks and challenges in all jobs at all levels. Consider drawing on mentoring programs, cross-training, temporary assignments elsewhere, sabbaticals, or any other program that might stimulate learning and development.

Summary

The first career development theories, hailing back to the 1950s but still influential today, were characterized by an assumption of a linear career progression through time, culminating in stages of maintenance and decline when retirement age approached. The 1970s and 1980s yielded increased recognition that career behavior is essentially cyclical in nature, regardless of age. The layoffs, mergers, takeovers, and downsizing efforts all underscored the realization that lifetime employment was no longer feasible and that older workers are as much in need of career development as younger ones are. The 1990s embraced the new workplace reality, placing the responsibility for career development primarily with the individual employee. This was called the protean career or career self-management.

It is imperative that more research be conducted to more fully understand career self-management behavior, particularly for older workers. Future career development models must incorporate and quantify external and internal factors that predict career development behavior. The ultimate goal of a career development model should be to contribute to maximizing the potential of all workers – regardless of age, gender, race, or ethnicity – as they navigate their careers.

Chapter 9

Partnering Career Development and Human Resources

Martha M. Russell
Roemer M. S. Visser

To many people, career development means either one or both of the following: career advising upon entry into the workforce, or career counseling upon reentry into the workforce, usually after layoffs. Unfortunately, limiting career development to these activities has two major disadvantages. First of all, the strategic and long-term needs of the employer are not taken into account; services (which are often remedial, such as resume-writing workshops) stop once the employment contract has been signed. Secondly, the subsequent development that takes place on the job is ignored, implicitly assumed to be automatic if it happens at all.

Maintaining such a view of career development results in a lost opportunity for both employer and employee. This chapter builds on the previous one by arguing in favor of adopting a life span approach to (career) development, explicitly recognizing that older workers' careers develop much the same as younger workers' careers do. The main contention of this chapter is that an effective organizational career development program can provide an employer with a critical competitive edge in an increasingly competitive labor market. Implementing such a program within an organizational context is not easy, however, and much of this chapter is devoted to some of the issues that are likely to be encountered.

First, a brief historical overview of career development (CD) and organizational career development (OCD) is presented, along with a definition of OCD. Next, OCD's business case is argued: Why bother dealing with OCD? The following section presents some common barriers to a successful implementation, after which the chapter closes with recommendations for practice.

Organizational Career Development: A Brief Overview

The National Career Development Association

(NCDA), recognized as a leader in the profession, defines career development as a lifelong process, involving a continuous exploration and evaluation of skills, interests, values, life stages, and personal situations. It requires taking the time to build a foundation based on personal assessment and insight. It means examining the changing world of work and evaluating how personal needs can be met at the same time that the needs of work environments are being fulfilled. That often requires updating skills, adjusting career goals, and conceptualizing an individual career development plan - regardless of the employee's age.

Notice that the NCDA's definition takes into account the needs of the workplace. This was not always the case. For many years career development aligned strongly with school counseling, psychology, and education, and less with management, business, or human resources. In the late 1970s, a movement began to establish a link between career development and strategic business needs, and progressive companies added career development to human resource functions in the form of training programs and individual self-assessment. The 1970s were also the period of large, stable, and often bureaucratic companies that valued lifetime employment. Common conceptions of *career* were generally along those lines, with career development activities (e.g., career pathing, succession planning, and management development) being primarily the responsibility of the employer.

Then, in the 1980s, many such careers ended abruptly during periods of merging, acquiring, outsourcing, and downsizing. The primary career development activity that thrived in those times was outplacement. Outplacement involves assisting those whose jobs have been terminated to find other employment. Generally, it is offered as an employment benefit and services are often delivered outside of the company, either by a private outplacement firm or by a state employment agency. Because the terms *career development* and *outplacement* became interchangeable, it became difficult to promote a positive view of internal career programs.

In the 1990s, leaders in organizational career development started to push for alignment between individual career needs and organizational business strategies (Guterman & Holt, 1999; Simonsen, 1997). Many of these leaders came from a human resources and business perspective and promoted an OCD concept based on (a) the need for individuals to understand the new world of work and the emergence of *career self-management* and *career self-reliance*; (b) the organization's need to move from valuing lifelong employment to encouraging continued employability; and (c) the realization that restructuring will continue in organizations in order to keep competitive in the marketplace.

The term *career self-reliance* became a new paradigm for empowering workers when Harvard Business Review published an article by Waterman, Waterman, and Collard (1994). In many ways the article was a response to the fact that the implied promise (real or perceived) of lifetime employment was no longer viable. It pointed out that job security had been eroded by workplace practices often directed toward the older worker. The concept of career self-reliance involves individuals taking charge of their own careers, focusing on being proactive, being responsive to change, committing to continuous learning, and assessing skills, interests, and values on an ongoing basis. It means accepting that work is different than it has been for previous generations of employees, and that there will be no more immunity to change.

Along with the concept of career self-reliance, employees were also introduced to new ways of working with coworkers. Mirvis and Hall (1996) introduced the term *protean career*, making relationships one of the focal points. It emphasizes that people can change and grow in many ways. The new career profile offers individuals the opportunity to get their identity, satisfaction, and rewards from new kinds of relationships in the workplace. This workplace emphasizes collaboration, learning, meaning making, reflection, diversity, and community. Workers become self-directed individuals who manage their own careers while gaining respect for others and valuing differences. They learn to expect change and use transferable skills in increasingly popular models of work (such as part-time or contract employment) to meet the challenges of change.

Thus, from the downsizing rubble emerged a new social contract between employer and employee (Noer, 1993; Simonsen, 1997). Under this social contract, employers no longer guaranteed job security. Instead, they promised continued employability by providing challenging work. This left the employee totally responsible for the career direction taken and the skills acquired. Employers' responsibilities often stopped at offering a menu of training programs and posting internal job openings. Within a decade, responsibility for career development had shifted completely from the employer to the employee.

It is interesting to contrast this new reality with two definitions of OCD, proposed in the same period. In 1994, the Career Development Professional Practice Area of the American Society for Training and Development presented the following definition of career development (P. Simonsen, personal communication, April 16, 2003), which supported the NCDA definition and brought it into the workplace:

> Career development is an ongoing process of planning and directed action toward personal work and life goals. Development means growth, continuous acquisition and application of one's skills. Career development is the outcome of the individual's career planning and the organization's provision of support and opportunities, ideally a collaborative process.

This definition goes on to mention that the purpose of career development systems is to ensure the best fit possible between the individual's interests, skills, values, needs, and work preferences and the requirements of the position, work unit, and organization.

Along a similar vein, Gutteridge, Leibowitz, and Shore (1993) define organizational career development as a "planned effort to link the individual's career needs with the organization's workforce requirements" (p. 1). They describe the process as one of helping individuals plan their careers in concert with an organization's business requirements and strategic directions.

There is an apparent contradiction between these definitions (particularly their parts about collaboration between employer and employee) and the reality of the newly emerged social contract, which stressed the employee's own responsibility. This contradiction seems to instantly make *organizational* career development redundant. After all, if the employer carries no responsibility for career development, there is no more distinction between CD and OCD. This would be a premature conclusion, however. Under pressure from critiques of the career self-reliance concept, the responsibility pendulum seems to be swinging back from the employee in the direction of the employer.

One area of criticism concerns the concept's blindness to employees' need to belong (Byster, 1998). Byster draws attention to the singular dimension of career self-reliance, which ignores the importance of relationships, especially in permanent, full-time work. Another area of concern is that self-reliance is a way to support employers in their continuing downsizing efforts, again placing all responsibility for career success on the individual (Noer, 1993). Leana (2002) sums up the critiques as follows: "There are limits to the burden employers can shift to employees regarding career management" (p. 289).

While the concept of career self-reliance continues to be embraced today, it is becoming more and more clear that employers do carry some responsibility for career development initiatives (Moses, 2000; Simonsen, 1997). As a result, OCD is not redundant. On the contrary: OCD can be a key to the organization's continued success. In order to reduce ambiguity, a definition of OCD is offered next and will be the basis for the rest of this chapter.

Organizational Career Development: A Definition

Because of all the ambiguities surrounding the terms *career* and *career development* (Moses, 2000), a definition of OCD is called for. It is important to understand that an effective OCD program goes beyond the individual assessment and insight associated with traditional career development, beyond the training and resources provided in the context of traditional training and development, and certainly beyond job search activities that are undertaken primarily as a part of outplacement interventions. While an effective program may encompass all three, it does so in a way that identifies shared responsibility within the organization. It functions in an atmosphere of open and honest communication and is linked to business strategies.

Knowdell (1996) focuses on the roles of the manager as coach, information provider, guide, teacher, and developer. While human resources serves a support function, the employee should drive the CD process. Simonsen (1997) expands that model of shared roles and responsibilities. She argues that senior management's primary responsibility is to support and communicate the OCD process, while managers and supervisors are to support and provide opportunities for growth. Human resources is to provide information, resources, systems, and assistance to facilitate development. It is called upon to do this by establishing career centers and/or career processes in which staff can take part in a comprehensive program of assessment, decision making, goal setting, problem solving, and continuous development. Human resources is called upon to offer services and referrals that go beyond workshops and training and to include organizational information regarding business goals and strategies, staffing projections, performance measures, mentoring opportunities (either formal or informal), and development planning.

For the purpose of this chapter, we have synthesized the above into the following definition of organizational career development:

> Organizational career development is a collection of resources and processes aimed at optimally aligning the career needs of individual workers with the mission, vision, and goals of their employers. An effective organizational career development program is completely integrated in all relevant business processes, particularly those in the realm of human resources, and enjoys full commitment and support from senior management. Activities include, but are not

limited to: counseling and assessing; coaching; mentoring; training; hiring; and promoting. There is shared responsibility between the employee, HR staff, and management for delivering results in an atmosphere of openness and accountability.

This definition of OCD provides the basis for the rest of the chapter, starting with the business case for OCD.

Organization Career Development: Why Bother?

There are several compelling reasons why employers should consider implementing OCD. First, an organization that takes responsibility for its share in OCD financially supports its claim that people are the organization's most important resource. It also shows the organization's commitment to its part of the social contract regarding employability. Moreover, it is a way to create or restore trust: implementing a credible OCD program sends a message of "I care" (Moses, 2000, p. 155).

Second, and perhaps more important, OCD can serve as a powerful recruitment and retention tool. Waterman, Waterman, and Collard (1994) suggest that career-resilient workers are committed to continuous learning and that they are in charge of their own careers. If it is true that the pace of change in the workplace is likely to continue increasing, then these are the workers employers should be interested in. With their commitment to continuous learning and sensitivity to their own employability, career-resilient workers will be more likely to choose an employer where they can continue to develop.

This effect will be compounded in the next economic upturn. It is now well known that the workforce is aging and its growth is slowing to its lowest rate ever. Although there is no crisis due to a shortage of workers as yet, the next economic upturn may very well create one, and older workers will be in high demand. Many of them will need new skills. Others are comfortably retired and although they are willing to return to work, they have strong preferences with regard to the kind of work and environment they are willing to take on. An AARP survey of workers between 45 and 74 years

old showed that more than 80 percent said they would work even if they could financially afford not to work (Nicholson, 2002). Additionally, the survey unearthed a desire among older workers for continuous learning, development, and challenges that demonstrate the value of and respect for the older worker (Goldberg, 2000). Clearly, a successful OCD program that is geared toward older workers as much as it is toward younger ones is likely to attract educated, skilled, and experienced workers, and create a crucial competitive edge in an intensely competitive labor market.

Lastly, there is some empirical evidence supporting the usefulness OCD. Citing a study involving 250 Forbes 500 companies Stevens (1998) found that an effective career development system ranked fifth among 80 predictors for financial success.

In sum, organizations must recognize that a comprehensive career development process, supported by upper management and decision-makers, is as important as any of the other business processes, and can assist in improving (a) the retention of a workforce; (b) the recruitment of those who have chosen to leave the workforce but are needed because of skills, work ethic, and work history; and (c) the effectiveness of an organization in terms of restoring trust among employees, planning for succession, and remaining competitive and productive in a changing world.

Barriers to Successful Implementation

Implementing OCD successfully is not easy, however, and a multitude of barriers are encountered in practice. Consider the following example.

Several years ago, Jill was manager of the staff training and development department at the Central University system. The concept of career self-reliance motivated her to collaborate with George, the director of Human Resources, and move forward in communicating the need for redefining and expanding staff career services. A newly designed program resulted with the first steps being a staff development handbook and series of seminars that focused on the changing world of work. Strongly embracing the philosophy of career self-reliance, the terms for the employer/employee relationship were laid out as follows:

(a) The contract is between equals, which means the employees are to focus on developing and managing their own careers and accept responsibility for their career satisfaction, while the employer identifies organizational needs;

(b) There is a new, proactive partnership where responsibility for the employees' career development is shared, while the employees take responsibility for being responsive to change, continuous learning, and skills development;

(c) The expectation for the employer is to provide the employees with the tools, the open environment, and the opportunities for assessing and developing skills to be competitive.

The stage was set for implementing a comprehensive OCD program to support the needs of the Central University system and its employees, while outlining the responsibilities and roles of managers, supervisors, HR professionals, and employees.

However, translating the concept into practice met a serious challenge. The aim of the interventions had been to assist employees in interpreting changes in the world of work and the university's internal structures as a major staff development movement. However, many employees feared the underlying message was one of downsizing and job loss, and thus they were hesitant to self-select for the process. While implementing the program in staff development, an employee was unexpectedly laid off due to a departmental merger. The newly created staff development handbook was included in the lay-off package from HR with no discussion of what it was, how it could be used, or how to access the services it implied.

This lack of honest communication fed into employees' fear of job loss and the lack of trust so common in organizations today – trust that is needed if there is to be shared responsibility and a successful social contract between in employer and employee. The lack of communication between George's staffing professionals in Human Resources and Jill and her staff development employees jeopardized the entire OCD program.

Consistent with the above example, Goldberg

(2000) indicates that before employees can even hear the message regarding any new social contract, organizations must reduce workplace stress and anxiety, including the threat of losing a job or being forced into early retirement. Communication failures and lack of trust are by no means the only barriers to the successful design and implementation of an OCD program. Of all the barriers encountered in practice, the most prevalent are stereotyping and ageism; a lack of executive support and commitment; outdated career development theories; a lack of knowledge within the human resource profession regarding CD and OCD; and insufficient integration between HR and CD processes within the organization. They are discussed in more detail below.

Stereotyping and Ageism

Stereotyping and ageism are some of the most difficult barriers to deal with because often they are visible only to the sensitive eye and so many people, including older workers themselves, can be unaware of the practice and its impact. Moreover, stereotyping is often a systemic, even cultural issue, and as such needs to be tackled by means of an organizational development approach. Difficult as the challenges of intergenerational relations and ageism are, it is crucial that they be examined and dealt with. Otherwise, no OCD program, particularly any aimed at attracting, developing, and retaining older workers, will have a chance to succeed.

Lack of Executive Support and Commitment

In spite of all the business advantages of an effective OCD program, the current reality is that some employers are hesitant to implement such a program. The following are among the three most popular reasons not to engage in OCD:

1. We're a flat organization and our employees have no upward mobility. Why would we prepare them for something we can't deliver?
2. We have enough to do as it is and have no time to add "stuff" like career development.
3. Why would we make them more attractive to other employers? We're not in the philanthropy business!

Understandable as they may seem on the surface, these objections are based on misinformation, misinterpretation, and/or fear, and can be harmful to the organization.

Flatness and upward mobility. Of the three objections mentioned, this one appears to be most rational. However, as may be clear by now, it stems directly from an outdated view of "career" and "career mobility," since mobility is implicitly equated to *upward* mobility. OCD programs rooted in this tradition are archaic and doomed to failure. They also do not satisfy the requirements of the definition. When horizontal movement is included in career mobility, flat organizations often have surprising opportunities for OCD. Along these lines, Arnold and Jackson (1997) argue that new patterns of careers must be conceived. They claim that the changes taking place in the structure of employment opportunities mean a widening diversity of career patterns and experiences. Those patterns may include what Hakim (1994) refers to as a career lattice rather than movement "up a ladder." In a lattice, an employee may find new and creative ways to use skill sets by outsourcing to another department, taking a position at a lower level in order to gain experience, or focusing on projects as a way of aligning with the strategic goals of the organization. Hall and Associates (1996) suggest that careers increasingly will become a succession of "mainstages" (short, cyclical learning stages of exploration-training-mastery-exit), as workers move into and out of various product areas, technologies, functions, organizations, and other work environments (p. 33). Clearly, flat organizations often have plenty of opportunity for career development.

No time. This response is a particularly persistent one, especially given the aftermath of the downsizing in the 1980s which left fewer employees with larger work loads in its wake. Staff departments like human resources have been struck particularly hard. It is true that they can choose not to engage in OCD. What this boils down to is a choice of how they spend their precious time. Do they take the time *now* to improve employee trust, employee morale, and corporate image, with its possible benefits down the road (depending on the effectiveness of their efforts), or do they spend more time *later*, trying to fill positions while competing with other organizations who enjoy a more favorable reputation as employers? In the end, this dilemma is one between short-term and long-term thinking. In the case of OCD, those who claim to have no time appear to prefer the short term to the long term.

On philanthropy. This is a very tough argument to dispel because it is often rooted in a desire to stick with old organizational systems and employee practices, an unwillingness to change, and a misconception regarding OCD. As the definition above makes clear, OCD is about aligning employees' career needs with an organization's mission, vision and goals. This means that effective OCD programs create a win-win situation. The suggestion that they are philanthropy suggests that OCD creates a win-lose and this is patently wrong. This is not to say, however, that employees never adjust their career goals and leave the employer after taking part in an OCD program. In fact, this is to be expected in some cases and could be presented as a downside to OCD if solely viewed in terms of an employee loss. While there is a risk of employees leaving after participating in OCD, the following three arguments need to be kept in mind.

First, a happy, productive employee is unlikely to leave *because* of OCD. As a matter of fact, these employees are more likely to stay because of OCD as it fulfills a development need.

Second, an effective OCD program improves the (generally damaged) trust between the employee and employer. It enhances loyalty and satisfaction while increasing the knowledge and skills base in the organization and addressing employees' need to belong. OCD involvement increases the likelihood that the employee will know, support, and feel connected to the organizational goals and mission.

Third, while in some cases, OCD can lead directly to turnover (for example, a computer programmer who is recruited out of an organization that just invested in an expensive training), it must be emphasized that not all turnover is bad. Losing an employee on good terms often results in the ex-employee being an ambassador to the organization and subsequently, a source of good will, business revenue, and even new recruits. Moses (2000) comments as follows:

> Organizations may well bemoan investing time and resources to train and develop

people who then move to another organization. But what goes around comes around. Often these organizations will themselves benefit from hiring people who have been developed elsewhere – who may represent a better match than the people they lose to turnover. In the long run, the result is greater flexibility for individuals and organizations. (p. 108/109)

Outdated Career Development Theories

The previous chapter provides an excellent overview of the evolution of career development theory. Although it has long been accepted that development does not stop at age 18 but that it continues throughout the life span, much of contemporary career development theory still describes older adults in terms of decline and disengagement, as first established by Super (1957). Super's theory divided the career into different life stages, identified as growth, exploration, establishment, maintenance, and decline (Isaacson & Brown, 1999). According to this theory, people move through these stages in a linear way, arriving at the depressing stages of maintenance (holding the ropes) between the ages of 45-64 and decline (starting to withdraw from the workplace) after the age of 65.

Although the ageist assumptions underpinning the concepts of disengagement and decline are increasingly being challenged, in practice they are still in evidence as former workers adjust to diminished influence, income, health, energy, and other factors (Isaacson & Brown, 1999). Organizations often use this evidence to support their failure to adopt innovative and progressive OCD programs (Stevens, 1998). Whiston and Brecheisen (2002) point out that in the career literature, little attention has been paid to the older worker. In general, the midlife adult is associated with public agency employment assistance, while the meager amount of literature on older workers relegates them to struggles with unemployment or to the principles of decline and loss established in the early theories.

However, the reality of the current and future workforce is that individuals do not automatically find themselves in the decline mode when they reach the age of 65, nor do they meet the mainte-

nance expectations between ages 45-64. This type of theoretical framework discourages growth and development throughout the life span and diminishes the very definition of career development.

Ageist underpinnings are not the only concern in mainstream career development theory, however. Most theories in use today stem from the middle of the 20th century and speak to the career development of white, well-educated men – not that of women, persons of color, or those of lower socio-economic status (Herr, 2002). Alfred (2001) decries this as career development theories' generalization of "the White male developmental experience to that of minority groups" (p. 109).

Generally, CD theory has not been totally unresponsive to criticism, and improvements have been made as the previous chapter shows. However, insufficient attention is paid to the interconnectedness between CD theories and organizational and business-focused theories and practices.

There is a need for career development theories that apply to all workers, regardless of age, race, ethnicity, gender, or socio-economic status – especially in light of an aging and diversifying workforce. Moreover, they must somehow incorporate the workplace context. Herr's (2002) position is underscored: the failure of career development theories to encompass the interaction of the individual, corporate, and societal career development practices needs to be addressed. Advanced technology, international economic competition, accelerated change in the nature of work, declines of jobs in certain sectors and the growth of jobs in others, political factors, and a host of other influences on the world of work need to somehow be incorporated. In his terms, career development theory needs to be "contextualized." The previous chapter has charted promising new directions for CD theory.

Lack of Knowledge Within the Human Resource Profession Regarding OCD

A fourth barrier stems from a failure by human resources and staff development to fully understand OCD (or even CD). Some of the misunderstanding goes back to the educational schism between the career development profession (stemming from the psychology and counseling disciplines) and the human resource profession (stemming from business and industrial psychology). Organizational career development, then, may mean career counseling to the human resource professional, while meaning up-or-out succession planning to the career counselor. Interestingly, some of the most successful practitioners in OCD hail from an HR affiliation rather than career development.

Some of the misunderstanding also goes back to the concept of career self-reliance. If employees are supposed to manage their own careers, why would the organization get involved? CD continues to be viewed as an individual process with assessment and insight for the person, regardless of the context and needs of the organization.

Lack of Integration Between HR and CD Processes Within the Organization

As indicated previously, many OCD programs begin with, and are sometimes limited to, the introduction of a few training courses and perhaps the availability of some career resources. Managers, supervisors, and employees attend the programs but often fail to see any connection to the rest of the organization or to the work that is expected of them. There is a lack of what Senge (1990) calls systems thinking which would in turn promote a total learning and development organization. The lack of alignment and integration within the entire organization can take various forms. Here are some obvious examples. Many organizations do not use the information they had gathered from their new hires during the interview process as a starting point for a development plan. Often a valuable resource, that information remains mostly unused. Moreover, only rarely is there a link between performance appraisals and development plans – if there is such a thing as a development plan in the first place. Only the most forward-thinking organizations tie development plans to employee compensation. There are many more examples of such lack of integration, which inevitably slows the process of development of both the employee and the employer, and creates frustration for both parties (Laabs, 1996).

Guterman and Holt (1999) illustrate the case of a software company with three key issues that prompted the hiring of an external OCD consultant. The issues included difficulty identifying the talent needed in the organization, lack of a clear process for cultivating internal talent, and trouble retaining the most talented employees. Without involving all systems and assessing the organizational communication process, its mission, the goals of individual departments and units, compensation systems, staffing processes, and future organizational challenges, the career development effort would fail. Individual employees would go through assessment, would understand their talents and needs for development, but would have no process (or motivation) to align that knowledge with the needs of the organization. It is this kind of lack of integration that occurs most often, causing OCD to remain isolated from its organizational context. It is the integration of OCD with the other business processes that provides the professions of CD, HR, and management, as well as employees, with an opportunity to work together and become partners in the pursuit of a common goal.

Recommendations

It is tempting to compile a list of recommendations for practice that target each of the barriers identified above. However, tackling individual barriers would be ineffective (if implementing OCD is the goal), for three reasons. First, although some of the barriers are overcome quite easily (for example, lack of knowledge can be remedied by continuing education), others are much more complex. The barrier referred to as stereotyping and ageism is so complex that it defies a quick and easy solution and it may take years before noticeable success is booked on this front. Some organizations may not be able to afford putting off implementing an OCD program that long.

Second, there is the chain of causality. One may have the impression that removing the barriers will lead to successful OCD implementation (after all, that is what the term *barrier* implies). Instead, it may very well be that successful OCD implementation leads to decreased ageism, increased awareness of OCD among key stakeholders, and unequivocal executive support. In other words, the chain of causality can work in unexpected ways. Paradoxically, focusing on the removal of barriers before implementing OCD may in fact mean putting the cart before the horse.

The third reason for not tackling barriers individually is that they are interrelated. Ageist assumptions about older workers' capacity to learn and perform have a direct impact on the level of executive support for an OCD program. Moreover, even a well-intending HR department with supportive top management is not likely to succeed if the design of the program is based on outdated conceptions of career. This could then feed the common misperception that older workers are unwilling and unable to move, in turn diminishing management support. Therefore, to implement OCD successfully, a holistic approach needs to be taken.

This holistic approach, whatever it may be, needs to concentrate on achieving one overarching goal: a complete integration of OCD in all of the business processes in the organization, including the HR processes (e.g., staffing, performance appraisals, and training and development), the financial systems, and the IT infrastructure, to name but a few. As integration increases, barriers are likely to shrink.

Integration attempts ultimately depend on three pillars: education, awareness, and valuing. All stakeholders in the organization are likely to need some kind of education. The executives and HR professionals need to learn about the merits of OCD. The career development experts and consultants must learn to view their discipline from the organizational vantage point. And the employees need to be educated on the new social contract, set in the context of a changing world of work. Of course, education encompasses more than formal training programs. Other examples of education include organization-wide climate surveys, needs assessments, planning groups, and integrated involvement across the organization.

One intended outcome of educational interventions is increased awareness among organizational members. All parties need to be well aware of the mission and vision of the organization and how they can contribute to their achievement. They must also understand the harmful consequences for the organization of ageist stereotypes. Employees must realize that they share responsibility for continued employment, and that they must step up to the plate and volunteer, participate in meetings, ask for challenges, and make themselves available for cross-training. Managers must be aware of their part of

the deal in the social contract: asking employees to be vulnerable and take risks will not yield any results unless managers set the example by doing so themselves. They need to be aware that OCD needs an appropriate infrastructure (e.g., allowing employees to take time off for training sessions and allocating substantive budgets). And perhaps most importantly, HR professionals need to realize that they are the ones to initiate this process, to sell it to the entire organization and oversee its implementation. This involves advocacy, risk-taking, and constant communication. For many, it also means that they need to leave their HR office or cubicle and get to know the organization at all levels, including its products and processes, the environment and industry within which it operates, and all of the executive officers. HR needs to be a full-fledged business partner at the executive level.

What this eventually all boils down to is valuing, at all levels in the organization. If management truly values employees – *all* employees – policies and processes will be reviewed, stereotypes will start to dissolve, and trust will be restored. If OCD is valued, it will be well funded and the appropriate infrastructure will be created. If HR values OCD, it will drive the implementation and integration into the other business processes. If employees value their own development, and value contributing to the organization's continued success, they will participate in OCD programs.

This way, OCD indeed becomes a shared responsibility between employees, HR, and management. The success of an OCD program is not measured by its cost-benefit ratio or the extent to which it is integrated in the business processes, although admittedly these are important indicators. Ultimately, the most successful and effective OCD programs are those that help create a development culture. According to Simonsen (1997), a development culture is characterized by trust, openness, collaboration, conflict that is managed rather than avoided, risk taking, learning rather than training, and leadership that "walks the talk." Achieving a development culture ensures optimal adaptability and flexibility and, by extension, the organization's continued success in the future.

The following basic strategy is recommended for HR practitioners and managers interested in implementing OCD:

1. Get educated. Find out what OCD is and what it can do for the organization. Find out what OCD is not.
2. Look at the organization in terms of systems and develop an understanding of where OCD may best fit.
3. Advocate and take risks. Although it may appear safer to remain on the sidelines, the risk of not implementing OCD is at least as large as the risks taken when selling the organization on the idea.
4. Communicate consistently, clearly, and honestly.
5. Evaluate constantly.

Knowdell (1996) offers a nine-step strategy:

1. Define CD in the organization.
2. Assess the organization's need for CD.
3. Design a program for the organization.
4. Promote the program internally.
5. Acknowledge the individual employee's emotions.
6. Guide the employee's exploration process.
7. Facilitate the employee's exploration process.
8. Participate in the employee's goal setting and planning.
9. Coach the employee in implementing the career strategy.

The sequence of steps suggests that a continuous integration moves from the organization as a whole to the individuals within. Simonsen (1997) has a similar outline, but stresses the use of focus and advisory groups to assist in each step in her model as well as the need to continuously communicate and evaluate.

Career development and human resources have a unique opportunity to add value to American organizations in the upcoming 20 years (and beyond), especially in the face of rapid changes in the workplace and the aging of the workforce. A successful partnership can lead to the implementation of meaningful, relevant, and cost-effective OCD programs that keep the organization profitable, flexible, and staffed by productive, motivated, and employable workers – regardless of their age.

Summary

Effective organizational career development (OCD) programs can provide an employer and an employee with a critical competitive edge in an increasingly changing world. The partnership of career development (CD) and human resources (HR) is vital to the creation and support of such programs, which focus on continuously aligning the individual's career needs with the organization's strategic business plans and workforce requirements. OCD functions in an atmosphere of open and honest communication and requires all parties to share in a development culture and in the responsibilities that accompany it. A comprehensive OCD program is crucial for the recruitment and retention of an aging workforce. Some of the barriers to be overcome are stereotyping in organizations and ageist assumptions embedded in mainstream CD theories. Integration of OCD into the business processes is the goal, and hinges on education, awareness, and valuing at all levels in the organization. It means identifying needs and motivating all the players to become participants. It means working with the systems that are in place to build a culture of development. It means planning and designing a strategic program that can be evaluated in the context of business. Career development within the realm of human resources as a concept, as a practice, and as a business system is vital to the future workplace.

Synthesis

Career Development for Older Workers

An overview of Chapters 8 and 9 highlights three major observations related to career development.

First, many mainstream career development models and tools are outdated. Further, they are generally based on research conducted only on a subset of the American workforce (white, middle-class males). Moreover, they are based on the assumption that careers follow a relatively linear progression through time with only a very limited amount of employers. Current realities involving the aging and diversification of the workforce and increased changes in jobs, employers, and careers call for a thorough reconceptualization of the notions of career and career development. With the current gap between theory and practice wide, this poses a formidable challenge to both academicians and practitioners.

Second, career development programs, likely to become more and more critical over time, are a joint responsibility between employees and employers. Employers must realize that they cannot shift the entire burden of that responsibility to the employees. Creating an organizational infrastructure for a career development program, together with appropriate support systems, can yield big payoffs in future years. Simultaneously, workers must acknowledge and accept that they need to take charge of their own careers. In order to remain career-resilient, they must become used to self-managing their careers.

Third, this final observation closely echoes others made elsewhere. Career development is closely related to and intertwined with issues presented and discussed elsewhere in this book. Chapter 8 specifically lists training, reward systems, and management flexibility as critical predictors of career development behavior. Chapter 9 calls attention to the importance of combating ageism and creating a development culture.

Issues of intergenerational relations and organizational culture are discussed next.

ISSUE 4

ENHANCING INTERGENERATIONAL RELATIONS

Chapter 10

Intergenerational Issues Inside the Organization

Lisa M. Finkelstein

Throughout the last 30 years psychologists and industrial gerontologists have begun to amass a fairly substantial body of literature investigating the presence of and conditions under which access discrimination against older workers is likely to occur (e.g., Cleveland & Hollman, 1991; Finkelstein, Burke, & Raju, 1995; Perry, 1994, 1997; Perry & Finkelstein, 1999). By access discrimination I refer to situations whereby older workers are unfairly denied access to the organization itself (hiring) or to opportunities within that organization (training, promotion). Although continued research is certainly warranted to further unpack the complex package of cognitive and contextual factors that operate in instances of access discrimination (Perry & Finkelstein, 1999), there is a dearth of research looking at what happens between members of different age groups/generations once that access is achieved (O'Bannon, 2001). Access is an important hurdle, but a new host of issues abounds when individuals from different generations interact within the workplace.

The purpose of this chapter is to focus on a select set of organizational contexts (i.e., newcomer socialization, mentoring relationships, and work teams) where intergenerational expectations, perceptions, and communications may cause a rift in ideal functioning.

In this chapter I take a social-psychological perspective, considering generational groups as sociocultural groups from which individuals may garner social identity (Finkelstein, Gonnerman, & Johnson, 1999; Tsui, Xin, & Egan, 1995), and look into the focal contexts through a social-psychological lens. This chapter is by no means an attempt at a comprehensive literature review in the areas it covers, but rather an endeavor to tie together streams of literature to raise questions and spark interest in future empirical work designed to understand and improve intergenerational relationships in the workplace.

Generations as Social Groups

Generational groups consist of individuals born within the same time frame who share historical and social experiences at approximately the same life stages (Smola & Sutton, 2002). Although the specific birth-year boundaries that constitute any given generation have been up for debate (Zemke, Raines, & Filipczak, 2000), there exists a common notion that generations can be identified by a name (e.g., baby boomers, Gen X) and that they can be distinguished from one another by their attitudes, tastes, values, and even shared language of their members (Burke, 1994; Smola & Sutton, 2002; Williams & Nussbaum, 2001; Zemke et al., 2000; Zenger & Lawrence, 1989). Given this perspective, social identity theory (SIT) and stereotype matching theory are applicable grounding frameworks from where to examine intergenerational perceptions and behavior at work (Tajfel, 1978).

Briefly, SIT states that part of our self-concept, our definition of who we are, is derived from memberships in various social groups. Categorization of objects and people into similar groups is a natural cognitive process that allows us to deal with a multitude of information; social categorization of people into ingroups (of which the perceiver is a member) and outgroups (of which the perceiver is not a member) is a component of that process (Tajfel, 1978; Turner, 1982). The theory is thus not only one of cognition but also of motivation, as we define ourselves in part by our groups and are driven to positively distinguish our own group from others (Brewer & Kramer, 1985; Brewer, 1995; Hogg & Abrams, 1988). Social identity, then, is seen as multidimensional - having not only the cognitive component of awareness of group memberships, but also including emotional and value-laden components (Tajfel, 1978). Although a handful of differing versions of social identity theory have developed throughout the last 20 years (see Jackson, 2002, for a review), the essence of this set of theories is that we have a tendency to categorize into "us" and "them," and that our self-concept benefits to the degree to which being in the "us" group is valued and contributes to positive affect. Motivation to that end can contribute to bias toward the ingroup and against the outgroup.

Turning back now to generational groups as a source of group identity, the degree to which membership in these groups contributes to an individual's sense of identity affects the potential for intergenerational bias to occur. We may see ourselves as similar to others in our own generation, and see individuals from other generations as more similar to one another; similarity is highly predictive of attraction (Schneider, 1987). Moreover, we may hold expectations and stereotypes regarding members of other generations that allow us to distinguish ourselves from them, with the comparison often in our favor. Note that the context should always be considered; when we detect a mismatch between our expectations and beliefs about a generational group (possibly stereotype-based) and what is expected in a given context (due to age norms), unfair or disparate treatment toward a member representing that group may ensue (Perry & Finkelstein, 1999).

It is important to stress that merely encountering someone from another generation within the workplace is not a sufficient condition in and of itself for intergenerational conflict or misperceptions to occur. Many factors exacerbate the likelihood that this will happen. For example, generations as social groups need to be apparent to the perceiver, and the perceiver should have some sense of psychological identification to that generational group (Finkelstein & Burke, 1998; Nkomo, 1995). Merely chronologically being a member of a generation does not guarantee that an individual psychologically identifies with that generation. Additionally, as social identity is a multidimensional construct, one may categorize oneself into a generational group but still may not place much attachment or importance to that group membership (Jackson, 2002). Other factors that may influence intergroup bias include actual realistic conflicts over resources (e.g., political clout, monetary rewards) between groups, as well as power differentials between groups in a

given social structure (Jackson, 2002; Kelchner, 1999; McGrath, Berdahl, & Arrow, 1995; Triandis, 1995). One should keep mindful of these complexities when considering the likelihood of intergenerational bias in the work contexts discussed below.

A Selection of Work Contexts Where Generations Can Matter

Below I touch upon three work contexts, admittedly selective, where the generational membership of the individuals involved may affect what happens in that context, in turn impacting the individuals and quite possibly the organization. The literature base examining generations in some of these contexts is not yet widely developed; there is much empirical work yet to be done. Social identity theory and stereotype matching theory, as described above, can be used to develop testable propositions for research in all of these areas. These contexts were selected for inclusion as they appear to be particularly timely, as described in the sections below. It should be acknowledged that an intergenerational focus is quite applicable to other contexts as well, such as leadership and motivation, career development, and training. Some of these issues are tackled in other chapters in this book.

Newcomer Socialization

Newcomer socialization is a process that gets underway when a new employee enters an organization or takes a new position. Through socialization, employees learn both the skills explicitly needed to be effective as well as the more implicit cultural norms, attitudes, and politics that permeate an organization or a department (Bauer, Morrison, & Callister, 1998). Although organizations employ specific tactics in an attempt to ensure appropriate socialization of employees (Van Maanen & Schein, 1979), the employee is an active and important contributor to the process. Research has shown that newcomers may or may not choose to engage in proactive strategies such as developing relationships and seeking out information and feedback, and that these activities can be related to positive outcomes, such as role clarity and job satisfaction (e.g., Ashford & Black, 1996; Morrison, 1993a, b; Wanberg & Kammeyer-Mueller, 2000). In their review, Bauer and colleagues underscore the importance of understanding the socialization process, as it impacts the organization psychologically, culturally, and financially.

To date, the literature has both theoretically and empirically ignored the impact of the age or generational membership of the new employees as a potential driving factor in proactive newcomer socialization (Finkelstein, Kulas, & Dages, 2003). Much of the empirical literature in this area has focused on recent college graduates, where age is not often much of a variable. The assumption appears to be that newcomers are young people. However, this assumption should be challenged in today's workplace, where layoffs and midlife career changes are becoming more commonplace. It seems increasingly likely that more and more people from an older generation will find themselves in a position of starting over and learning new skills in a new organization and/or career.

Why should a new employee's age or generation group matter? It might largely be a matter of expectations. An older person in the position of newcomer, beginner, and learner may seem quite out of synch with commonly held age norms (Greller & Simpson, 1999; Lawrence, 1988). Although culturally there are many negative stereotypes that have been developed regarding workers from an older generation, one more positive stereotype ascribed to older individuals is that they are experienced; they have wisdom. Thus there may be a conflict and mismatch perceived when that older person is viewed in a position of inexperience - that of newcomer learning the ropes. It has been argued that although a newcomer may be driven to reduce uncertainty in a new situation, this drive may be tempered by perceptions of the social costs that could come from appearing unknowledgeable (Sias, Kramer, & Jenkins, 1997). Thus, it is possible that an older newcomer may avoid seeking information, or perhaps may take a more covert approach. For example, Miller and Jablin (1991) suggest that when newcomers sense social costs in seeking information, rather than directly asking questions they may more covertly test limits, casually observe others' behaviors and conversations, or disguise conversations to indirectly glean information. Although my colleagues and I (Finkelstein, Kulas, & Dages, 2003) attempted an initial empirical examination

of this idea, our study was hampered by a small age range (i.e., few people over 50) and sample, limiting our ability to provide an adequate test of the hypothesis. However, we found a small tendency for younger individuals to engage in more frequent acts of covert information seeking, clearly emphasizing the importance of context in determining what age groups might be more apt to feel a sense of social cost in obvious information-seeking attempts. Future examination of this idea should look at newcomers from different generations as well as the generational composition of the other newcomers and organizational incumbents. Also, as suggested by social identity theory, newcomers' generational identities should be considered; if newcomers are strongly identified with a generation, they should be more aware of perceived generational differences and expectations and perhaps more motivated to positively distinguish their generation from others.

As mentioned above, the forging of relationships at work is another valuable socialization activity. Here one's generation could largely impact one's willingness to engage in – and/or success at – relationship building, depending on the age composition of other newcomers and existing employees. Developmental psychologists have suggested that as people age they may be more focused on strengthening existing relationships with family and friends than forming new affiliative bonds (Bee, 2000; Lang & Carstensen, 1994). Similarity-attraction theory posits that people will prefer to associate with those they see as similar to themselves (Clark & Reis, 1988); social identity theory argues we are more likely to view ingroup members as similar. Indeed, Kelchner (1999) notes the difficulty younger individuals may have seeing members of older generations as similar to them. So, to the degree to which there are fewer individuals of an older generation with whom to associate, relationship building may be a less common behavior for older newcomers.

In sum, although individuals of an older generation may not be discriminated against at the door, once they enter the organization as newcomers they may be facing a qualitatively different challenge than more traditionally aged newcomers. Expectations held of members of the older generation by other generations, and perhaps even of themselves, could influence their socialization strategies. Clearly we are in need of much more empirical focus on older newcomers.

Mentoring Relationships

A classic conceptualization of a mentor is captured in the definition put forth by Noe (1988), who depicts a mentor as "a senior, experienced employee who serves as a role model, and provides support, direction, and feedback to the younger employee regarding career plans and interpersonal development . . ." (p. 458). Mentoring relationships have been the focus of a growing body of literature in the area of career development and industrial/organizational psychology; current energies have been directed toward trying to understand whether our traditional idea of mentoring still holds true, as our workforce has become more diversified in many ways (Ragins, 1997; 1999). Although the study of diversified mentoring relationships - their processes and their outcomes - is growing in popularity, little empirical work to date has focused on age diversity (Finkelstein, Allen, & Rhoton, 2003).

One may look at the more traditional definition of mentoring and conclude that by nature of the definition, age diversity has always been an inherent component in a mentorship; mentors have been the older, experienced employees commissioned to nurture younger employees in their careers. In other words, mentoring has typically been an intergenerational context. In that traditional pairing, however, the roles of each generational member in the pair are quite consistent with expectations and beliefs regarding age norms (Krueger, Heckhausen, & Hundertmark, 1995; Lawrence, 1987). Therefore, the generational members are fulfilling their expected roles. Tsui et al. (1995) suggest that under conditions where age differences concur with expected roles and status, the quality of a relationship between a supervisor and subordinate may be enhanced. The same logic can carry through to mentoring relationships.

Yet now we are faced with a world of work where people are less likely to continue along the same career path, no longer moving up the age ladder and career ladder in synchronized step. Members of an older generation may now be finding themselves in *need* of a mentor, and the experienced

individuals available to fill that role may well be from a younger generation (Allen, McManus, & Russell, 1999; Kram & Hall, 1996). This turns our expectations regarding age-appropriate roles on their head, and opens up the possibility for discomfort and intergenerational conflict. Cross-generational stereotypes may become particularly salient in this situation for members of both generations finding themselves in this unusual position. Younger mentors, for example, may see an older individual as resistant to change and harder to train, which would clearly mismatch their expectation about an ideal protégé. In turn, an older protégé may see a younger person as inexperienced, naïve, or immature (O'Bannon, 2001; Patel & Kleiner, 1995), and thus doubt that person's mentoring competence.

Finkelstein, Allen, and Rhoton (2003) conducted a content analysis of the reactions of 73 nonfaculty university employees to questions regarding potential advantages and disadvantages to reverse-age mentoring relationships. Most of the disadvantages suggested revolved around concerns an older protégé would have concerning the experience, knowledge, and maturity of a younger mentor, leading to the potential for disrespect and distrust. Advantages were noted as well; the potential for getting a fresh perspective, awareness of newer ideas, and an infusion of energy were suggested. Thus, a reverse-aged mentorship is not viewed as inherently disastrous; the challenge is to uncover strategies for success that overcome the negative effects of expectation violations and suspicion.

The few existing empirical examinations of the role of the age of the protégé in a mentoring relationship have found some differences in the style of mentoring received. For example, Whitely, Dougherty, and Dreher (1992) and Finkelstein, Allen, and Rhoton (2003) found less career-related mentoring (i.e., behaviors specifically enacted to help the protégés advance in their careers) with older protégés than younger protégés. Ragins and McFarlin (1990) found less role-modeling occurring with older protégés, whereas Finkelstein and associates did not find a difference in reports of role-modeling. They also found more psychosocial (friendship-related) mentoring occurring in pairs of younger mentors and older protégés than pairs of young mentors with young protégés. This was unexpected, but could underscore the idea that nontraditional pairings may need to take nontraditional forms; perhaps a younger mentor with an older protégé may not feel comfortable attempting to drive an older protégé's career, but could try a more friendship-based approach. Another finding that meshes with this idea is that older protégés reported more mutual learning occurring in the relationship. Perhaps if a mentorship is repackaged as a more mutual, power-balanced relationship, some of the discomfort regarding role and status incongruence can be alleviated. Indeed, this idea appears to have been adopted by several large corporations as a means for teaching computer skills to upper-level executives (Cook, 2002). Representatives from GE, for example, reported to Cook that in their mentoring program younger mentors are paired up with older executives to teach them technological skills, while in turn the executive shares corporate knowledge and career tips. This type of mutual learning and exchange relationship helps to curtail some of the discomfort that could be felt on both sides which could diminish its success. This emphasizes the idea of adjusting our expectations regarding different contexts so a perceptual mismatch between a group and a context is less likely to occur.

Work Teams

Work teams were selected as the third focus of discussion because much has been written in industrial/organizational psychology and management to indicate that teams are an increasingly common means for accomplishing tasks in an organization (De Dreu & Van Vianen, 2001; Guzzo & Shea, 1992). Issues regarding mixed-generation work teams have received more attention in the literature thus far than the formerly discussed contexts of newcomer socialization and mentoring relationships, as diversity of all types in work teams has been a hot topic for the past decade (Jackson, Brett, Sessa, Cooper, & Peyronnin, 1991; Jackson & Ruderman, 1995).

Studies that have focused on the effects of age dissimilarity within work teams have produced a mixed bag of findings. For example, Wagner, Pfeffer, and O'Reilly (1984) and Jackson et al. (1991) found evidence of greater turnover within teams with greater age heterogeneity; the actual processes within the team that drive this type of

finding are not clear (Smith et al., 1994). Communication and conflict among team members are logical process variables for investigation, as social identity theory would suggest that members of different social groups may evoke various stereotypes and expectations about outgroup members that could contribute to miscommunications and conflicts. Indeed, most of the research done thus far in this area has espoused this theoretical perspective. For example, Zenger and Lawrence (1989) found less technical communication between members of groups with more age dissimilarity. Jehn, Northcraft, and Neale (1999) found more relationship conflicts with age-diverse (and gender-diverse) groups, whereas Pelled, Eisenhardt, and Xin (1999) found more emotional conflict in groups with members closer in age. Rentsch and Klimoski (2001) expected age to be one variable predictive of team member schema agreement (i.e., the extent to which team members held similar mental frameworks for understanding their teamwork), but this was not supported in their findings. Finally, using an interesting and unusual team context of professional sports teams, Timmerman (2000) found lower performance in basketball teams with more age diversity than in those with less, but no effects of these variables on the less task-interdependent baseball teams. This set of investigations leaves one with the sense that age diversity seems to have a potential impact on teams, yet no consistent picture of the process and outcomes has quite emerged.

A major conundrum in regard to diversity (in general) in work teams is that on the one hand we expect diversity to have a negative impact on the relational aspects of a team as similarity between team members tends to breed attraction and cohesion. Conversely, however, diversity has been thought to infuse a team with multiple experiences and perspectives (Cox, 1995; 2001). Cox (1995) argues that the "core puzzle" (p. 235) we are faced with as researchers is to determine under what team conditions we can minimize potential problems and maximize potential benefits. One key component may indeed involve the social identity of group members, and particularly the salience of their particular social identities while engaged in team activities (Brewer, 1995; Cox 1995). To the degree that team members can recategorize their group members into a clear and salient ingroup and minimize viewing other members as part of demographically different outgroups, negative intergroup effects could be minimized (Brewer, 1995). Although this may be a theoretically sound strategy, in reality this is easier said than done for several reasons, such as real status/power differences among group members and real historical conflict (McGrath et al., 1995; Triandis, 1995). Furthermore, as pointed out earlier, some individuals may have stronger psychological ties to particular sources of social identity than others (Finkelstein et al., 1999; Jackson 2002), increasing the challenge of manipulating salient sources of identity within a team due to these individual differences. These challenges as well as others point us to the direction of future research needs, as discussed below.

Future Research: Where Do We Go?

Future research could take a multitude of directions to further our understanding of intergenerational issues in the workplace. I have selected three research themes that could be applicable to the specific contexts described in this chapter: generational identity, manipulation of contexts, and multiple sources of diversity.

Generational Identity

It has been discussed that generations can be considered to be sociocultural groups and therefore a source of social identity, but not much research attention has been given specifically to the generational identity construct, in terms of theory or measurement. Finkelstein et al. (1999) argue that because our age is a transient characteristic but our generation always remains the same, a generational group may be a more stable source of identity than an age group. My colleagues and I (Finkelstein et al., 1999; Finkelstein, Gonnerman, & Foxgrover, 2001) have presented an initial self-report scale to measure generational identification, based on the cognitive, emotional, and value components of social identity theory. This original measure has demonstrated some evidence of reliability and validity and revisions to further enhance the psychometric properties are currently underway. Attempting to measure generational identity as an individual

difference variable in a systematic fashion is recommended to try to help understand why intergenerational interactions may be more meaningful to some individuals than others, in all contexts mentioned above. For example, team group members more highly identified with their generation may experience more communication problems in mixed generation work groups than those who are not similarly identified. As a further example, newcomers from an older generation who do not identify with their generation may not approach the socialization process in a mixed-generation work environment in the same fashion as those who do. These questions should be put to systematic empirical scrutiny.

Manipulation of Contexts

Although intergenerational issues may be more salient among those who strongly psychologically identify with their generations, it has been suggested that contexts can be manipulated in such a way as to (a) make them less salient (by redefining the ingroup), or (b) make expectations regarding members of another generation less inconsistent with the context. First, as discussed above, attempting to make a work team, or a newcomer cohort, or a mentoring dyad a more salient ingroup identity could allow for recategorization of cross-generation individuals into the same ingroup (Brewer, 1995). It is not terribly clear, however, what needs to be done in a context to promote this type of recategorization. Future applied research aimed at designing or implementing team building, orientation, and training exercises to create contexts that are seen as ingroups would be extremely valuable.

Second, it was suggested above that if some contexts typically elicit a perceptual mismatch between expectations of a member of a generation and that context, a reframing of the context might lessen these effects. An example was provided of reframing mentoring relationships as more equal-exchange relationships so that a disconnect is not perceived between the age of the mentor (or a protégé) and the expected role. Quasi-experimental work could be done to see how this reframing is best accomplished in mentoring programs. Indeed this could also be expanded to see how the reframing of particular roles within teams, or roles of newcomers partaking in their socialization journey could also be put into play.

Multiple Sources of Diversity

I have alluded to the fact that social identity can come from many sources and obviously our generational group is only one of the groups to which anyone belongs. However, I have thus far ignored the importance of multiple sources of diversity (Cox, 1995) and how these sources can impact how we perceive others cross-generationally. Although a full-blown discussion of the meaning and role of generations for various demographic groups (e.g., racial groups, gender groups) is beyond the scope and purpose of the current chapter, I would be remiss to not suggest that this is a crucial issue for future research. Although the relational demography literature (e.g., Jackson et al., 1991; Smith et al., 1994) has often looked at demographic dissimilarity as a combination of many categories, there has been an absence of theoretical work specifically looking at if and, more importantly, why intergenerational perceptions and relations may differ due to identification with other demographic categories. Our different expectations of the proper roles for men and women at different ages, for example, make the general discussion of intergenerational perceptions, in the absence of other demographic qualifiers, seem somewhat simplistic. As an additional example, members of the younger generations may be more used to cultural diversity in the workplace than those of an older generation (Smola & Sutton, 2002), adding another degree of complexity to intergenerational relations. A framework for understanding what generations mean to people of all races, genders, and cultures of origin would add another piece to the puzzle, to be sure.

Recommendations

So how do we get there? It is imperative for both the building of theory and the advancement of applicable strategies for approaching intergenerational issues in the workplace that academic researchers and organizational practitioners develop collaborative partnerships. Morrison (1995) laments that without such efforts many theoretically sound ideas may not find their way into use. There are many challenges to overcome in creating these relationships; interestingly, these relationships in and of themselves are of the ingroup/outgroup sort. Just as with any other social categorization (like generations), academics and practitioners hold beliefs and expectations about one another. For example, academics may believe practitioners are not interested in theory-testing and doing scientifically sound (and sometimes painstaking) research. Practitioners may believe that academics don't have a handle on the real world. Recently, Rynes, Bartunek, and Daft (2001) cast doubt on whether our beliefs across these groups are backed by any empirical evidence. Yet the pervasiveness of these perceptions may be enough to discourage needed collaboration.

Mohrman, Gibson, and Mohrman (2001) and Amabile et al. (2001) note the importance of being aware of the possibility that academics and practitioners may have different goals and approaches to research and that taking the others' perspective and working jointly and closely on projects throughout all stages, with plenty of open communications, can help contribute to successful endeavors. Amabile and her academic and practitioner colleagues also note that providing social opportunities to form personal bonds between members of academic-practitioner teams can help tremendously in the face of task-related conflicts and disagreements.

These papers encourage us that successful partnerships are challenging yet can yield great rewards for all involved. However, how can we connect with each other in the first place? Morrison (1995) suggests such avenues as networking through consulting projects, symposia at conferences, and even miniconferences hosted by academics to bring local practitioners and academics together to discover mutual interests in organizational problems. I would also suggest perhaps an Internet-based service where academics and researchers could connect. A problem that remains, however, is a cautiousness and trepidation in becoming involved in diversity research. Diversity is a politically charged issue (McGrath et al., 1995) and one that many organizations may be wary of investigating, particularly in partnership with an outsider. Morrison heeds us all to be "proactive to remove the stigma" (p. 224) of diversity research. Until we overcome our discomfort, figure out ways to connect with one another, and discover ways to effectively collaborate, intergenerational research (as with any diversity research) is unlikely to advance at the pace needed to make a difference in our changing world of work.

Summary

In this chapter I conceptualized generations as groups that could be a source of social identity for individuals. Based on that assumption, theoretical knowledge regarding social identity and intergroup perceptions and behavior were applied to three select contexts that I believe may be the backdrop for intergenerational issues in our changing world of work: newcomer socialization, mentoring relationships, and work teams. Today and in the near future, organizational newcomers are likely to come from many generations, mentors may be younger than protégés, and work teams might often be intergenerational. These generational differences may be more salient for some individuals (with stronger generational identity) and in some contexts (where our beliefs and expectations about members of other generations do not cognitively match with our beliefs and expectations about roles). Understanding this, we can conduct research to attempt to minimize intergenerational misperceptions and conflicts and enhance the likelihood that intergenerational encounters will bring about positive outcomes. In order to do such research, academics and practitioners must eliminate barriers to collaboration and jointly approach intergenerational issues from both a theoretical and practical perspective.

Chapter 11

Building an Age-Friendly Workplace

Laura Markos

For a moment, picture yourself in today's workplace. Now fast forward: imagine yourself working 10, 20, or 30 years from now. What will the workplace look like? What, for that matter, will you look like? What role will you be playing in the organization? What kinds of work will you be doing? What skills, talent, and experience will you bring to the workplace, at that point in your career? Who will be your colleagues, your supervisors, and your customers? How do you think they will treat you? How do you think you will feel in that environment? Will you be successful? Included? Valued and rewarded for your work? If not, what's wrong in that picture? If so, how will you have achieved it?

The aging of the workforce is, for a change, a diversity issue with which we can all identify. Even the young, one would hope, will grow older, and most all of us are likely to want to remain engaged, contributing members of society. We may want more time for ourselves, for hobbies, travel, and leisure pursuits, but we are also likely to want to remain productive, whether in paid employment, entrepreneurial self-employment, volunteer service, teaching or mentoring, flexible, contingent or part-time work, or some combination thereof (AARP Public Policy Institute, 2002; Challenger, 2000; Drucker, 1999). We are likely to retire much later in life, owing to better health and longer life span, financial need, and the continuing desire for change and actualization (Bloch, 2000; Drucker, 2001; Dychtwald, 2000).

As our futures take shape in the mind's eye, the question becomes, what are organizations imagining and planning for us? How will we be received, managed, utilized, or put out to pasture in the workplaces of tomorrow? The increasing prevalence of an older workforce over the next several decades presents both evolutionary and revolutionary challenges, raising big questions for organizations:

- Are older workers different? If so, what are the key differences?
- How will increasingly prevalent older workers get along with younger workers?
- How does an organization best attract, retain, work with, fully utilize, and motivate older workers as part of its workforce?
- How can an organization create, build, and maintain a workplace that optimizes the environment for all workers, across age and other diversities, and avoids illegal discrimination and poor morale?

These questions prompt organizations to examine their successes, capacities, and shortfalls in engaging a diverse workforce (Bloch, 2000; Drucker, 2001). The answers reach across human resource development to organizational leadership, culture, systems, and processes, and may call upon organizations to reinvent themselves in terms of the fit between individual and organization (Argyris, 1964/1990; Ghoshal & Bartlett, 1997; Harrison, 1994).

Older Workers: Diversity Du Jour? Or Value-Driven Opportunity?

If organizations approach the aging workforce as just another diversity issue, like those of recent decades, they are likely to fail. They will find themselves no longer competitive, unable to attract, engage or retain the right people in a shrinking talent pool (Drucker, 1999). However, when organizations approach diversity in a values-driven, integrated manner, they can transform their cultures — and seize decisive business advantage for their efforts (Bennis, 1997; Ghoshal & Bartlett, 1997; Kanter,

1995; Kouzes & Posner, 1995; Pfeffer, 1998a; Waterman, 1994).

Changing organizational culture is difficult. But it is doable (Drucker, 1999; Kotter, 1996; Schein, 1992, 1999). The work entails a step-by-step process of unraveling organizational assumptions. Assumptions about diversity are the foundation of discriminatory bias, which becomes increasingly visible in organizational values, practices, structures and processes (Schein, 1992, 1999). Once underlying assumptions are uncovered, an organization's practices, structures and processes can be rebuilt or realigned to support and consistently sustain the desired culture — embracing the diversity of each member of the organization. To begin the deconstruction process, organizations may first want to look at recent diversity efforts, to understand why the results to date have been so disappointing (Carnevale & Stone, 1995; Fernandez, 1998; Lubove, 1997; Ritvo, Litwin, & Butler, 1995; Valian, 1998).

But We've Already Done Diversity!

Every U.S. organization has faced multiple diversity issues over the last several generations. Immigration increased radically in the latter third of the 20th century, heightening the visibility of race, ethnicity, national origin and religion. The women's movement, arising out of World War II female employment, and fueled by the civil discontent of the 1960s, engendered the battle against the glass ceiling, the invisible barrier to women reaching the highest roles in organizational leadership. The Civil Rights Act of 1964 sought to end employment discrimination on the basis of race, color, religion, or national origin, and promote voluntary action programs by employers. The color barrier in organizations was dubbed the cement ceiling (Fernandez, 1998).

Age and sex discrimination were added to the law in 1967; rehabilitation in 1973; Vietnam-era veterans in 1974; immigrants in 1986. The Americans with Disabilities Act of 1990 (ADA) sought to end employment discrimination against people with disabilities, requiring employers to establish the essential functions of a job, and make reasonable accommodations for the physical abilities of qualified persons that could perform those essential functions.

The increasing visibility of the gays, lesbians, bisexuals, and transsexuals, particularly as attractive targets for marketers, and the inclusion of HIV and AIDS as qualifying disabilities under ADA, have helped to expand awareness and interpretation of sex discrimination to include discrimination based upon sexual orientation as well. Sexual harassment claims in the 1990s added yet another dimension to awareness of gender-based discrimination. Yet compliance-based diversity efforts have produced little success. Discrimination continues, and employment status of these legally protected groups remains dismal (Carnevale & Stone, 1995; Fernandez, 1998; Lubove, 1997; Ritvo et al., 1995; Valian, 1998).

If organizations had addressed age discrimination adequately following the 1967, 1973, and 1990 laws, the aging of today's workforce might be a non-event. But most diversity efforts have been reactive to the letter rather than spirit of the law. While legislation and litigation are important motivators, mere compliance efforts fall far short of actually changing individual and organizational behavior. Heinous examples of failure still surface in the news and in the courts. Denny's restaurants' widespread pattern of racial discrimination resulted in a $54 million class action settlement with thousands of customers (Holden, 1994). Texaco agreed to a record-setting settlement for gender-based pay, and $140 million to settle a racial discrimination case (Bryant, 1997). Northwest Airlines' reputation and bottom line have been repeatedly battered in litigation over age, disability, and sexual harass-ment, and in a related 60 Minutes investigation ("Northwest Airlines," 2000). Even these huge global companies, with tens of thousands of employees, failed to direct their values, resources, and expertise against such bias.

Diversity is a controversial issue for organizations. Some view it as a "damned if you do, damned if you don't" dilemma: how to address various groups while avoiding claims of discrimination or reverse discrimination (Lubove, 1997). Some see diversity as a fad, the human resources bestseller of the early 1990s. Others view demographic groups, such as generation-defined age groups, as stereotypical factions among which management must mediate (Lancaster & Stillman, 2002; Moberg, 2001; Zemke, Raines, & Filipczak, 2000). And some see individual differences as insurmountable: how can an organization realistically cater to each and every group, persuasion, and cause, many of which should be left out of the workplace entirely? But each of these views compounds the assumption that stereotypified groups' concerns can be addressed en masse, rather than on a more individualized basis.

As a result, many organizations have not addressed diversity per se, whether by neglect or a sense of adequacy in the status quo. Their day-to-day practices and habits reflect the biases, prejudices, and attitudes of their diverse workers, managers, and leaders (Schein, 1992). Even if an organization has already addressed issues of diversity in the past, results are mixed at best (Carnevale & Stone, 1995; Lubove, 1997). Most organizations need and would welcome an approach that promises solid, articulated business advantage.

Diversity for Business Advantage

Valuing and engaging a diverse workforce, across age, tenure, physical ability, and other diversities, yields clear and decisive business advantage (Bennis, 1997; Ghoshal & Bartlett, 1997; Kanter, 1995; Kouzes & Posner, 1995; Pfeffer, 1998a; Waterman, 1994). As Peter Drucker (1999) eloquently and succinctly stated, the task is not to "'manage' people. The task is to lead people . . . to make productive the specific strengths and knowledge of each individual" (pp. 21-22). The payoff for doing so is enormous.

Revenue, Share Price, and Net Income Growth

Organizations that value workers as highly as customers and shareholders produce radically better results — by multiples over several decades — than those that put shareholders first (Collins & Porras, 1994/1997; Kotter & Heskett, 1992; Pfeffer, 1998a). Those that value workers as individuals also see increased productivity; people work harder, are more engaged and involved, and ultimately produce more than those in cultures that do not. Further, operating and administrative cost savings result when workers are empowered, given more information, and given more decision-making au-

thority, rather than solely relying on direction from superiors.

Innovation, Customer Satisfaction, and Competitiveness

Innovation flourishes in cultures in which people are encouraged to be open, to challenge the process (Kouzes & Posner, 1995), to bring new ideas to their work, and allowed to fail, regardless of age or tenure (Senge, 1998). As worker tenure increases, customer service and satisfaction are also enhanced (Pfeffer, 1998a). Employers that understand and embrace diversity also increase global competitiveness as both producers and marketers, able to think globally and act locally (Kanter, 1995).

Such clear business advantages also have internal appeal, making diversity more marketable to organizational leaders than tactics based upon legal compliance, liability fears, or efforts stamped with the dreaded "touchy-feely" label. These advantages repeat across industries, product and service firms, geography, and organizations large and small. What is consistent across such organizations is a values-driven commitment to employees as individuals across age, tenure, and other diversities. Thus the challenge for organizational leaders is not to try to address the latest diversity crisis, but how to become an employer of choice: to consistently include and engage workers across the range of individual differences presented by the increasingly diverse workforce (Carnevale & Stone, 1995; Levering & Moskowitz, 2002; Pfeffer, 1998a; Waterman, 1994).

A Diverse Approach to Diversity

The categories often mentioned in diversity programs — age, physical ability, race, gender, national origin — are only the most common and discernable labels applied to people, as protected classes under antidiscrimination legislation. Yet demographic labels belie individuality and mislead organizations in the mistaken belief that discussing stereotypified differences such as age or physical ability will somehow magically transform the fit between individual and organization. While such education may increase understanding, it may also solidify stereotypes, resentment, and prejudicial behavior. Such programs may actually do more harm than good, compounding stereotypes and leading organizations to believe that they have addressed diversity issues adequately (Carnevale & Stone, 1995; Young-Bruehl, 1996).

Ultimately, engaging diversity means engaging individuality. Each worker reflects a unique amalgam of experience, background, habits, approaches, talents, personality traits, multiple intelligences, phases in development across the life span, learning styles, motivators, family situations, education, and perspectives (Argyris, 1964/1990; Gardner, 1993; Ghoshal & Bartlett, 1997; Goleman, 1995; Keirsey & Bates, 1978/1984; Kegan, 1982; Merriam & Caffarella, 1999; Weisbord, 1987). Clearly this kaleidoscope of individuality factors does not simplify efforts to optimize the fit between individual and organization (Hattrup & Jackson, 1996). But it does help to explain why isolated diversity programs have not been more readily successful (Carnevale & Stone, 1995; Pfeffer, 1998a).

The goal is to build and maintain workplaces that reasonably accommodate a broad range of individual differences, including age and physical ability, for everyone qualified to do the work, work together, and achieve desired results. To successfully attract, retain, motivate, and fully utilize the talents and knowledge of all, including older workers, most organizations need to change. An age-friendly, diversity-engaged workplace requires a culture that embraces all workers, nourishes their success and diversity, and involves each member working together to achieve the organization's mission and objectives (Bloch, 2000; Collins & Porras, 1994/1997; Waterman, 1994). The process of building such a culture begins by identifying the assumptions underlying ageism and other prejudicial attitudes about differences (Schein, 1992).

Building an Age-Friendly Organizational Culture

At the root of ageism or any kind of discrimination are assumptions, attitudes, prejudices, and biases generalized into erroneous beliefs (Allport, 1979). Prejudices are themselves diverse, complex, and multifaceted, and cannot be attributed solely to social learning; to do so would normalize prejudice and imply that it can be unlearned. But all oppressed groups share the need and the desire to be understood and valued for themselves, as individuals, and to have hope of a future for such understanding and value (Young-Bruehl, 1996). By working toward shared understanding of the experience of oppression itself, rather than focusing on differences and the division they can promulgate, each of us can learn to see more, listen better, assume less, and become increasingly aware of our prejudices. Examining attitudes, beliefs, and assumptions is the starting point for untangling prejudices and the constructions they underlie (Carnevale & Stone, 1995; Schein, 1992; Young-Bruehl, 1996). These embedded organizational underpinnings reside in an organization's culture.

The culture of an organization is reflected in its espoused mission, vision and values, and its actual habits, values in practice, and behaviors. Every organization has a culture, but many management teams deliberately cultivate it. In the absence of such cultivation, an organization's culture is determined ad hoc, subject to the instincts, intentions, and accidental outcomes of its individual members. More intentional cultures actively manage systems to drive and sustain organizational behavior and outcomes, which are thus more consistent, predictable, and aligned with overall organizational goals (Deal & Kennedy, 1982; Schein, 1992).

Organizational cultures and the people within them are resistant to change and resilient to status quo (Maurer, 1996; Schein, 1992). Indeed, if an organization has a desirable culture, resistance and resiliency are assets. Changing even an undesirable organizational culture is thus another matter. It is fallacious to assume that an organization facing major demographic shifts will change as needed without leadership and concerted effort. Even orchestrated change efforts often fail, diversity programs being no exception (Kotter, 1995). Designing, implementing, and achieving planned change is not easy, and changing the culture of an organization is an even more subtle and daunting challenge. "In most organizations, valuing and managing diversity requires nothing less than cultural transformation" (Carnevale & Stone, 1995, p. 93). Cultural change involves leadership — including painstaking listening and learning — to build practices, structures, and processes that complement, fully support, and sustain the desired culture to achieve strategic goals (Kotter, 1996; Schein, 1992, 1999).

Facilitating an organizational culture that supports diversity requires skill and commitment across the organization and over time. Organizational culture exists on several levels, which are increasingly difficult to discern (Schein, 1992, 1999):

- Structures and processes — how work is done, assigned, and valued — are most visible.
- Values — as formally espoused and in actual practice — are less obvious.
- Underlying assumptions — determinants of behavior — are least discernable.

Building an age-friendly culture that embraces diversity requires organizational development on each of these levels.

Organizational and Individual Assumptions

An organizational culture's underlying assumptions are the "unconscious, taken-for-granted beliefs, perceptions, thoughts, and feelings" and its "ultimate source of values and action" (Schein, 1999, p. 16). These assumptions are the key to uncovering prejudices (Young-Bruehl, 1996) and thus facilitating a more egalitarian work environment, as assumptions drive overt behavior. Erroneous, prejudicial and/or mission-inconsistent assumptions can undermine an organization's diversity, and specifically its older workers. Thus, developing an age-friendly workplace begins with identifying and reevaluating these assumptions. Such assumptions may include the following.

Age and motivation. Assumptions about what motivates people are pivotal to how managers treat workers: whether people work because they have to or want to, whether managers lead or control, and whether they cajole and direct workers or facilitate their individuated success (McGregor, 1960). Age-based assumptions about work's importance to individuals may be wrong; workers from young to old vary in their views of work, its priority level in their lives, and its importance in defining their identities (Jensen, 1999). Worker motivation is not consistently predictable across age, personal values, lifestyle, family situation, income, and many other factors, and motivators change as individual

life and work situations change and evolve. Yet most people at all levels, regardless of age, just want to do their work, feel good about it, and get the job done well (McGregor, 1960; Weisbord, 1987). Thus motivation is not easily determinable, particularly by assumptions based upon demographics. Managers can better understand workers' motivations by eliciting them in interviews and ongoing discussion, to ensure shared expectations (Handy, 1993).

Age versus youth. The "younger is better" assumption is a myth (Lawrence, 1995). The true value of tenured workers is compounded across knowledge, expertise, productivity, continuity, experience, perspective, and turnover itself (Goldberg, 2000). Yet age discrimination, both subtle and legally actionable, continues to plague older workers in terms of obtaining employment, maintaining income levels when changing jobs, receiving involuntary early retirement, or being laid off (AARP Public Policy Institute, 2002). The assumption that older workers cost more is also a myth. Concerns such as higher salaries, injuries, and accommodations for physical ability are offset by increased productivity, effectiveness, knowledge, customer satisfaction, and savings in recruiting and training (Hays, 2001; Lawrence, 1995; Pfeffer, 1998a). Age-based assumptions about the ability to innovate are fallacious as well; creative ability continues across the lifespan (Jensen, 1999). Yet another misconception is that we become increasingly resistant to change with age; analysis of numerous studies does not bear out this bias (Baron, 1996).

Generational stereotypes. People in business and in the popular business press find it expedient to put labels on people: baby boomers, GenXers, Nexters, and the like (Lancaster & Stillman, 2002; Zemke et al., 2000). While convenient for discussion purposes, this perpetuates ageism with the myth that everyone in a generation (the dates of which are arbitrary) is alike, with values and workplace perspectives distinct from other generations. Yet even family-situation patterns no longer correlate to age. Thus assumptions about partners, parenting, caregiving, freedom to travel, and work schedules are dangerous (Jensen, 1999). Shared values across generations do indeed exist, yet these gross generalizations are found across the spectrum of age, in prejudices evidenced by young and old alike (Lawrence, 1995; Zemke et al., 2000).

Espoused Values Versus Attitudes and Values in Practice

Assumptions are interactive with more visible cultural elements evidenced in an organization's "strategies, goals and philosophies," its "espoused justifications" (Schein, 1999, p. 16). These elements of core ideology express what is authentically believed in an organization. They are designed to preserve and maintain core ideology, and are largely internal and independent of the external environment (Collins & Porras, 1994/1997). Attitudes and values in practice may be misaligned with espoused diversity-friendly values. These attitudes and actual practices provide the next level of cultural indicators to be examined in the process of building an age-friendly, diversity-engaged organization.

Espoused values are the explicit statements of what an organization believes in, and may include beliefs about an organization's products and services, its interface with the community, and its business partners and workers. While there is no right set of core values, the crucial question is how deeply these values run, particularly in times of crisis, decision, or action, and how consistently the values are executed or compromised (Collins & Porras, 1994/1997; Deal & Kennedy, 1982).

Organizational norms, attitudes, habits, metrics, and practices reflect the underlying assumptions, but not necessarily the espoused values of the organization (Schein, 1992, 1999). The gaps are usually well known to workers: Are the organization's espoused values meaningful? Do they resonate for workers? Are they obvious to customers and business partners as well? Or hollow, a water-cooler joke? Does organizational leadership walk the talk, modeling the way for all workers? Are workers at any level free to point out discrepancies without fear of retribution? The answers, comprising an organization's values in practice, provide clues as to how the organization really values and treats its people.

An organization's people-related values in practice reveal its underlying assumptions about groups and stereotypes. The knowledge economy has increased the value of workers along with their rec-ognition as individuals, rather than interchangeable, dispensable, mechanical parts (Drucker, 1999; Salopek, 2000), but many leaders have had difficulty letting go of command-and-control tactics and behaviors. Futurists predict that the knowledge economy will result in human capital being reflected on the balance sheet, giving workers bottom line impact in black and white (Jensen, 1999), and making those sometimes empty statements, e.g., "People are our most important asset," more tangible.

Values in practice reveal the efficacy of an organization's espoused culture, reflecting its deepest-level underlying assumptions in the actual atmosphere experienced by workers and business partners. Contradictions with espoused values, when identified, provide another step in the path toward cultural realignment supporting age-friendliness and diversity. An organization's assumptions and values become even more visible on the level of its culture-embedding structures and processes (Schein, 1992, 1999).

Organizational Structures and Processes

The most easily discernable cultural elements reflecting organizational beliefs and behaviors are its structures and processes (Schein, 1992), the contexts through which individuals must travel to be successful (Baron, 1994). These processes and structures reflect and interact with values in practice and ultimately the organization's underlying assumptions (Schein, 1992, 1999). Examples critical to supporting an age-diverse workforce include the following.

Hiring. Hiring practices reflect organizational assumptions and prejudices. Executives' demographic similarity has been the strongest initial determinant of social liking and coworker preference, only later in acquaintance time shifting to similarity of values as a predictor of both liking and preference for colleagues (Glaman, Jones, & Rozelle, 1996). Yet working beyond demographics, toward a determination of good fit and shared values, is crucial to hiring consistent with an organization's desired culture and avoiding social reproduction (Collins & Porras, 1994/1997; Deal & Kennedy, 1982).

Jobs versus roles. As the knowledge economy displaces the industrial economy (Drucker, 1999), jobs as we knew them are disappearing (Bridges, 1994). Work is changing rapidly, in shorter cycles, and is increasingly done by temporary, contingent, part-time, and contract workers, and outside vendors. Organizations are flatter, using cross-functional, self-managed teams. This all means change in who is hired or placed in a specific role, and what an organization looks for in an individual. Organizations and workers are taking a portfolio approach to work; specific knowledge, skills, and experience remain important, but competencies, aptitudes, capabilities, values, and fit take on greater importance. This transition can be facilitated by continuing education, development, and reexamination of outdated structures (e.g., pay-by-seniority versus performance and knowledge; entry-level nomenclature and treatment of otherwise experienced workers) (Bridges, 1994; Drucker, 1999; Handy, 1997; Kanter, 1995).

Hierarchy. Hierarchy also reflects organizational values and assumptions about power, responsibility, who's in command, and what latitude workers are given. Reduced hierarchy, in favor of more team-oriented, egalitarian worker/management relations, produces higher performance (Pfeffer, 1998a). It also means that ideas, as well as problems and constructive criticism, can come from anywhere, regardless of hierarchical status. This implies a culture that welcomes good news, or bad, from any source — young or old, tenured, experienced, new, or recently hired — particularly when institutional values are at issue (Senge, 1998).

Social reproduction or cloning. Diversity disrupts and threatens the power base in institutions, and is thus met with resistance. Ingroups tend to protect their insider status by affiliating with others like themselves (Bourdieu, 1977; DiMaggio, 1994; Strauss, 1971), perpetuating the so-called old boys' network. "[T]o move up in the ranks, the employee must not merely master his or her firm's spoken and unspoken rules, but actually adopt the style and behaviors of a prototypical employee of that firm" (Fernandez, 1998, p. 100). The irony of this orientation, in addition to its implicit pro-age bias, is that prejudicial exclusion assumes that everyone of a certain narrowly defined, insider-demographic group is alike. This behavior is still evident in terms of hiring and hegemonic maintenance of the status quo (Belliveau, O'Reilly, & Wade, 1996; Bird, 1996;

Burt, 1997; Carnevale & Stone, 1995; Kilduff & Mehra, 1996). The old boys' club ironically demonstrates that pro-ageism, like (anti-)ageism, is yet another form of discrimination.

Homosociality. Social reproduction often extends to exclusionary socializing within organizations. This habit of birds of a feather flocking together, also called homosociality (Louis Harris & Associates, 1997; Wharton & Bird, 1996) or collegial exclusion (Benokraitis, 1997), creates covert, institutionalized discrimination (Fernandez, 1998). It is much more subtle, difficult to detect and prove, and thus much more insidious than more blatant, overt forms of discrimination (Josefowitz, 1995). Working to expand organizational social environments toward more inclusion and cross-cultural experience is a path toward collegiality and the realization of shared values across demographic differences (Glaman et al., 1996).

Mentoring. Mentoring's recent resurgence reveals some very important differences from traditional programs: partnerships in which both parties learn from one another (Wasserman, Miller, & Johnson, 1995). Traditional mentor-protégé relationships were based on title, rank, or seniority: a top-down, senior-to-junior hierarchy based on who you know (the old boy network). The newer, age- and diversity-friendly approach is based on what you know: skills, expertise, knowledge, cultural or historical perspective (Jossi, 1997; Warner, 2002). This implies a culture in which sharing knowledge is the norm, and workers do not perceive that it will be used against them (Aeppel, 2002). With a mutual approach across age and generations, younger and older workers serve as both mentors and protégés, based not on age but on the specific knowledge and needs involved. In the process, crosscultural understanding is built, and assumptions and prejudices that undermine culture can be dispelled (Moberg, 2001; Warner, 2002; Wasserman et al., 1995).

The psychological contract. Job security is gone, and worker loyalty has thus become elusive. The new job security, per Rosabeth Moss Kanter (1995), is "employability" (p. 156). While presenting a worker flight risk, organizations can also improve retention by investing in training and valuing workers as human capital. By acknowledging workers' talents, skills, and value, and continuing to make them employable across change and turbulent times (Kanter, 1995), organizations can build worker tenure, particularly to counter discrimination against older workers (Lawrence, 1995).

The physical contract. Ergonomics and reasonable accommodation of physical abilities are issues not limited to older workers (Kupritz, 2000). Age is an unreliable predictor of safety or job performance (Stainaker, 1998). A good physical fit between worker and environment is crucial to worker effectiveness. Compliance-based organizations relying on largely reactive health and safety laws will continue to have injuries, illnesses, liability, absenteeism, and higher turnover. Work shouldn't hurt, and these are unneeded human and organizational costs. Organizations need to rethink compliance-based programs, which often assume a younger workforce, and build cultures that avoid and prevent injuries; those that do so eliminate unnecessary operating costs, and such cultures are fully consistent with high-performance workplaces, self-directed teams, continuous improvement, and total quality management (Fletcher & Harty, 1992; Hays, 2001; Krause, 1996; Stainaker, 1998).

The social contract. In a shrinking talent pool, flexibility and collaboration are increasingly important for both individuals and organizations. Workplaces that offer flexible roles, hours, methods, and work in teams — for balance, teamwork, optimal fit, and high performance — will reap the benefits of individual and collaborative success (Ghoshal & Bartlett, 1997; Katzenbach & Smith, 1993; Pfeffer, 1998a, b). Teambuilding should focus not on differences, but on inclusion, collaboration, synergy, and results. "Learning about differences may be fun. But learning about cooperation is useful" (Mieszkowski, 1999, p. 108).

Each of these structures and processes reflects the organization's assumptions about people and diversity. Once examined, adjusted, and aligned, these structures and processes strengthen the organization's culture, resiliently supporting its underlying values and reinforcing its commitment to an age- and diversity-friendly workplace.

Recommendations

This iterative process of examining and aligning culture to build an age- and diversity-friendly workplace can be summarized in its implications for overall policy, ongoing processes and actual practice. These implicit recommendations include the following.

Structures and Processes:
- Align organizational systems, structures, processes, and metrics with values.
- Identify and realign inconsistencies to reinforce organizational values.

Values:
- Put people first, valuing employees, customers, and shareholders equally.
- Value worker health and safety as well, by building a culture that avoids and prevents injuries and related costs.
- Reinforce values consistently and address discrepancies promptly.

Assumptions:
- Examine and align underlying beliefs, particularly regarding age, physical ability, experience, and tenure, in the hiring, placement, socialization, development, and advancement processes.

Hiring and Placement:
- Define essential work functions, competencies, and physical requirements.
- Target shared values, motivators, interpersonal skills, capabilities, and fit.
- Focus on task, talent, and role over experience or job structures as defined.
- Provide flexibility in roles, hours, methods, and so on, where possible.

Conduct:
- Outline a code of conduct consistent with organizational values.
- Establish processes that allow, encourage, and make it safe for workers to address discrepancies between espoused values and values in practice.
- Ensure follow-through to align conduct and systems accordingly.

Hierarchy:
- Decrease hierarchy wherever possible.
- Share information and authority with workers.
- Suspend hierarchy when values are at issue.

Teams:
- Engage self-managed, high-performance, cross-functional teams across age, tenure, experience,

and other diversities.

- Use teams for work processes, problem solving, innovation, cross-training, and organizational issues.

Development:

- Acknowledge workers' talents, competencies, value, and individuality.
- Invest in training and development to build retention, resources, and tenure.
- Build, expand, and flex workers' roles based on aptitudes and capabilities.

Mentoring:

- Partner people based on competency, not on age, status, or tenure.
- Engage workers as both mentors and protégés in different contexts.
- Encourage information sharing as the norm, without repercussions.

Socialization:

- Build an egalitarian workplace, friendly to all workers, united on values while diverse in talents, experience, age, backgrounds, and abilities.
- Foster an inclusive, collegial social environment that draws upon, pools, and encourages cross-functional and cross-cultural collaboration.

Modeling:

- Lead by example.
- Ensure that leaders and workers alike walk the talk.

Summary

The emergence of an aging workforce presents organizations with both challenge and opportunity. The opportunity is a systemic approach to diversity — where many legal compliance-based efforts have understandably failed — and to individuality, for definitive organizational advantage. Engaging the workforce across age and other differences has proven impact in human relations and in markedly improved revenue, stock price, income, innovation, productivity, customer relations, and competitiveness over time.

The challenge is engaging individuality across a diverse workforce, which for most organizations means reappraising their organizational cultures. The process involves deconstructing, evaluating, realigning, and rebuilding to consistently reinforce the organization's values in daily practice. Organizational culture is most discernable in its structures and processes, which in turn evidence values, ultimately founded upon organizational assumptions. These interactive cultural elements reflect the biases and beliefs that influence behavior and results.

The work of examining and realigning organizational culture is not simple. Cultural change confronts the embedded resistance and resiliency of the status quo and the prejudices underlying organizational structure and process. Change requires an open, egalitarian, non-hierarchical learning environment. Each member is ideally mentor and protégé, and each has the freedom and responsibility to address discrepancies between values and practice.

When attitudes, values, structure, and practices are aligned, self-reinforcing culture results. Each individual is valued, and all build upon shared values to achieve the organization's mission. The reward of such cultures is radically improved organizational performance and individual motivational fulfillment. These business advantages occur in cultures in which all workers can flourish across age, physical abilities, tenure, and a wide range of individual differences.

Synthesis

Enhancing Intergenerational Relations

Chapters 10 and 11 complement each other in two different ways. First, Chapter 10 views the intergenerational relations issue through a social-psychological lens. As such, these relations manifest in behavior between people as members of different social groups. In contrast, Chapter 11 views intergenerational relations as an expression of organizational culture. Ageist biases, therefore, are visible not only at the behavioral level in interactions between individuals or groups, but also at the level of organizational policies and processes. If ageism is embedded in culture, rather than merely a manifestation of individual prejudice, then overcoming it demands a systemic, holistic approach.

The second difference that stands out between the two chapters centers around the relative importance of age groups or generations. Chapter 10 argues that people tend to identify with social groups and that generations may very well be a powerful, underestimated predictor of behavior. If true, this would provide insights into how to better serve the cohort of older workers. In fact, this entire book is based on the premise that older workers have different needs than younger ones and that these needs will have to be met if older workers are to be successfully recruited and retained.

Chapter 11, in contrast, points out the dangers of placing too much emphasis on social groups, whether they be race, generation, gender, or anything else. The main danger, of course, is the perpetuation of stereotypes because of an underlying assumption that groups are relatively homogeneous. The result would be the opposite of what is intended in the first place. One of Chapter 11's core arguments is that embracing diversity (which includes age) means embracing individuality. The two stories of Dot and Thanh in Chapter 5 are good illustrations of the individual nature of older workers' needs.

This is not to say, of course, that talking in terms of groups is counterproductive. There appears to be consensus that there are indeed meaningful differences between groups. Therefore, viewing individuals as members of particular social groups can yield very enlightening insights. However, it must also be kept in mind that the differences within groups may be more substantial than the differences between them. When seen from this perspective, Chapters 10 and 11 each highlight different aspects of the complex nature of human behavior in the context of prejudice. In effect, these chapters both offer most valuable tools for workers, human resource practitioners, managers, and academicians to help them identify and address ageist prejudice in organizations.

ISSUE 5

HEALTH AND OLDER WORKERS

Chapter 12

Balancing Work and Caregiving

Jennifer Reid Keene

In a recent *Newsweek* article, writer Elizabeth Cohen (2002) talks about her experiences as an "extreme mom" as she simultaneously provides care for her preschooler and her elderly mother while working full-time. As sympathetic readers, we are exhausted as she describes returning home from a full day at work to dress, feed, and care for her 80-year-old mother as well as her 3-year-old daughter. Although controversy exists about the pervasiveness of Cohen's situation, the popular press has given increasing attention to the experiences of the "Sandwiched Generation." Now, academics are also investigating the issue. The Sandwiched Generation refers to the cohort of people who are "sandwiched" between caring for their children and their aging parents. As greater numbers of workers take on eldercare responsibilities in the context of other family and paid work obligations, the Sandwiched Generation has implications for work-family social policies as well as caregivers' and care-receivers' well-being.

Discussions of the Sandwiched Generation have evolved in response to increasing concerns about the long-term care needs of our aging population (Spillman & Pezzin, 2000). Families have long been responsible for the majority of informal eldercare. However, the "graying of America" raises questions about whether families can continue to provide such care (Himes, 1994; Spillman & Pezzin, 2000). Recent macro-societal trends have been central to academic and popular discussions of the Sandwiched Generation and have important implications for both those in need of long-term care as well as potential caregivers.

This chapter begins with a discussion of the demographic, economic, and social trends that suggest an impending crisis of care and dramatically increased caregiving demands for the Sandwiched Generation. Next, this chapter turns to the literature on family caregiving and women's multiple

roles and outlines the research in this area in recent years. This chapter then examines the debates regarding the potential versus actual experiences of the "beleaguered Sandwiched Generation." Finally, this chapter discusses the implications of work-family social policies for workers with caregiving responsibilities and offers suggestions for policy, human resource (HR) practitioners, and researchers.

Trends Suggesting a Crisis in Care

Underlying the discussions of the Sandwiched Generation are the demographic, economic, and social trends that influence both the future demand for eldercare as well as the availability of potential informal caregivers. The general concern regarding the Sandwiched Generation is that as the population ages, it is increasingly likely that midlife adults will become multigenerational caregivers (Price & Rose, 2000), simultaneously caring for their own children as well as assuming informal eldercare responsibilities. The potential to be sandwiched between generations is most common between the ages of 45 and 60 (Himes, 1994; Hogan & Eggebeen, 1995).

First, consider the potential demand for eldercare. As a result of lower fertility and lower mortality rates, the proportion of older people in the overall population is increasing, a process termed *population aging* (Kinsella, 1996). Life expectancy for the U.S. population has increased throughout the last century and is now close to 77 years (Centers for Disease Control and Prevention, 2001b). Between 1999 and 2050, the population age 65 and over is expected to grow from 34.6 milion to 82.0 milion, a 137 percent increase (United States Bureau of the Census, 2000a).

Related changes in the incidence and types of morbidity and disability among elders also affect population aging. Shifts in morbidity, from acute to chronic impairments and disabilities, suggest that the elderly will require increasing assistance with activities of daily living such as eating, dressing, bathing, and toileting (Jette, 1996; Kinsella, 1996). Furthermore, delayed morbidity into the last years of life suggests that elders may require care for chronic illnesses and disabilities that may last for extended periods of time (Manton & Stallard, 1996). Combined with the increase in the overall number of elderly, these trends suggest a growing demand for informal elder-caregivers in decades to come.

A second issue is the availability of potential informal caregivers for the frail elderly. Longer life expectancy and lower fertility rates have significantly changed the generational structure of families. Whereas it used to be uncommon to have more than two family generations alive at the same time, family structures are becoming increasingly vertical (Bengtson, Rosenthal, & Burton, 1990; Kinsella, 1996). Over the past century, the number of living generations within a lineage has increased while the number of members in each generation has decreased (Bengtson et al., 1990). These changes in family structure imply that as parents live longer, there is a greater likelihood that adult children will be involved in their care, and that there will be fewer children within families available to provide such care (Uhlenberg, 1996). Furthermore, other changes in family forms – resulting from divorce and remarriage, for example – have the potential to affect the availability of caregivers (Bengtson, Rosenthal, & Burton, 1996).

Researchers have established that the majority of informal caregivers for the elderly are women (Brody, 1985; Lee, 1992; Mellor, 2000; National Alliance for Caregiving, 1997). Women's increased labor force participation is a central factor affecting the availability of potential caregivers. Currently, 60 percent of women are in the labor force and women comprise almost half (46 percent) of the paid labor force (Bureau of Labor Statistics, 2001). Numerous studies document women's struggles to combine paid work and family obligations (Hochschild, 1989; Keene & Quadagno, 2002; Moen, 1992). Furthermore, as more women have entered the labor force, an accompanying trend has been a delay in childbearing (Spillman & Pezzin, 2000).

Many studies focus on the competing demands of paid work and childcare responsibilities. However, social gerontologists and family scholars have also considered the impact of informal eldercare demands on employed women. Since women continue to shoulder most caregiving responsibilities, and because more women are in the labor force than ever before, there is increasing concern about the availability and ability of women workers to perform informal eldercare as they manage the responsibilities to their employers (Boyd & Treas, 1996).

Family Caregiving and Long-Term Care

Long-term care is defined as the wide range of services designed to help people with chronic conditions compensate for limitations in their ability to function independently (Quadagno, 2002). Informal caregiving to the frail elderly is defined as *unpaid* assistance provided by family in areas of everyday activities that elders can no longer perform for themselves (Hooyman, 1992). Families provide the majority of long-term care to elderly relatives. Indeed, family members provide as much as 80 percent of in-home care for elder relatives with chronic impairments (Dwyer, 1995; Dwyer, Folts, & Rosenberg, 1994). The National Academy on an Aging Society (2000a) states that 75 percent of elders with a chronic disability rely on adult children for assistance with basic activities of daily living. Demographic projections suggest that the potential for informal elder-caregiving at some point in a person's life is becoming increasingly likely (Himes, 1994; Rosenthal, Matthews, & Marshall, 1989).

The political and social context surrounding these trends has been one that favors an increasing shift of caregiving responsibilities from the state to the private sphere, and specifically to families (Dwyer, 1995; Hooyman, 1990). Indeed, care provided by families relieves the formal long-term care system of a substantial social and economic burden (Himes, 1994; Rice, Fox, & Max, 1993). The question remains, however, whether families will be able to provide such care considering the gendered nature of care work and the number of workers who find themselves in multigenerational caregiving situations.

Gender and Family Caregiving

Scholars have demonstrated that caregiving across the life course remains primarily women's responsibility, despite their increased labor force participation (Allen & Barber, 1994; Ferree, 1990; O'Connor, 1996). Women perform the majority of informal eldercare (Brody, 1985; Lee, 1992; Mellor, 2000; National Alliance for Caregiving, 1997), often in addition to engaging in childcare and paid work (Dwyer & Coward, 1992). Scholars offer a variety of explanations for women's apparent propensity for care work, including the persistent gender inequality due to the gender division of paid and unpaid labor and traditional gender norms, expectations, and stereotypes (Ferree, 1990; Guberman, Maheu, & Maille, 1992; O'Connor, 1996). Others emphasize the reciprocal nature of intergenerational relationships over the life course and adult children's desire to "give back" to their parents (AARP, 2001; Bengtson et al., 1996). Research has found evidence that the traditional gender division of labor outside of the home is changing somewhat, as women enter more male occupations (Reskin & Padavic, 1994). However, changes in the gendered division of labor in the home are slower in coming (Hochschild, 1989; O'Connor, 1996).

Since women are the caregivers in society and in the family, there is concern regarding the availability of women to provide care to the increasing numbers of impaired elderly (Boyd & Treas, 1996). Although women's responsibilities as caregivers to children and elders are not a new trend in and of itself, the combination of paid work and caregiving responsibilities for such a large proportion of women constitutes a relatively new phenomenon. Nichols and Junk (1997) found that 23 percent of the women caregivers in their sample had children under 18 at home and 65 percent were employed full-time. In light of projections for future need for caregivers, Mellins, Blum, Boyd-Davis, and Gatz (1993) predict that the average American woman will spend 18 years of her life helping an elderly parent. The question may be raised regarding how eldercare fits with the rest of women's work and family responsibilities.

Eldercare in the Context of Women's Multiple Roles

As Cohen's description in *Newsweek* demonstrates, the idea of being "sandwiched" between anything has negative implications. Our vision of those women sandwiched between parents and children is one of exhaustion, frustration, and potential burnout. Indeed, most discussions of the Sandwiched Generation implicitly assume that multigenerational caregiving is inherently stressful, as caregivers balance their roles as parents and adult children (Ward & Spitze, 1998).

Much of the research on eldercare examines the issue from a role theory perspective and focuses on either negative or positive aspects of women caregivers engaging in multiple roles (Reid & Hardy, 1999). At its inception, the research literature on eldercare focused on the negative implications for women caregivers of managing caregiving and competing family, marital, and paid work demands, arguing that the competing demands associated with individuals' multiple role commitments lead to negative consequences, such as mental and physical exhaustion and increased stress (Brody, 1981, 1985; Goode, 1960; Mui, 1992, 1995; Pearlin, 1989). By contrast, role enhancement theorists argue that individuals' multiple role involvements can have positive outcomes for well-being such as increased emotional and economic resources, self-esteem, and heightened social integration. They emphasize the interrelatedness of work and family roles and the ways in which positive experiences in one role may spill over and positively affect experiences in another (Barnett, 1999; Baruch & Barnett, 1986; Crosby, 1991; Lambert, 1990; Moen, Robison, & Dempster-McClain, 1995; Stephens & Franks, 1995).

In support of role enhancement theories, researchers emphasize the potential benefits of eldercare (Barnett, 1999; Baruch & Barnett, 1986; Crosby, 1991; Ingersoll-Dayton, Neal, & Hammer, 2001; Moen et al., 1995). In a study of employed middle-aged women and men, Marks (1998) found that when differences in work and family conflict between caregivers and non-caregivers were eliminated, the caregiving role tended to lead to positive rather than negative well-being. Indeed, some studies have demonstrated that multiple roles, particularly employment, are actually beneficial for caregivers and that women who are stay-at-home elder-caregivers experience the greatest levels of stress (Scharlach, 1994; Stoller & Pugliesi, 1989). Other research indicates that employees facing competing work and family demands may actually find work to be a useful respite from caregiving responsibilities. Hochschild (1997) posits that lacking substantial organizational changes in family life, employees actually enjoy the formality of paid work as well as the system of rewards and feelings of accomplishment in comparison to their family responsibilities.

Studies of multiple roles and well-being often focus on the number of roles an individual assumes and the demands associated with those roles. More recently, research has emphasized the quality of or satisfaction with work and family roles (Barnett, 1994; Baruch & Barnett, 1986; Marks & MacDermid, 1996; Reid & Hardy, 1999; Stephens & Franks, 1995) and the subjective meaning assigned to particular roles (Penning, 1998). While role conflict may result when the demands of multiple roles are competing, individuals' subjective perceptions of the roles may have a greater effect on well-being than simply the number and demand associated with those roles (Baruch & Barnett, 1986; Reid & Hardy, 1999). In addition, emotional support from significant others also contributes to women's successful combination of multiple roles (Epstein, 1987). From a life course perspective, the duration and timing of caregiving in women's lives is also important for their well-being (Moen et al., 1995).

Bologna Sandwich?

While demographic and social trends discussed suggest an imminent surge in the number of sandwiched caregivers, empirical evidence on the extent of the reality of the Sandwiched Generation is mixed. Recently, scholars have identified a number of shortcomings in the empirical literature investigating the prevalence of the Sandwiched Generation. First, many studies use convenience samples of caregivers, which tend to be biased toward a negative view of the caregiving situation. Second, the literature tends to overemphasize the negative aspects of multiple roles and ignore the potential

benefits of multiple roles and intergenerational relationships. Third, the literature often fails to distinguish between degrees of sandwiched status—that is, the potential for multigenerational caregiving versus those who are actively engaged in simultaneously caring for children and parents (Bengtson et al., 1996; Logan & Spitze, 1996; Price & Rose, 2000; Ward & Spitze, 1998).

Population aging raises the concern about the potential for more middle-aged people to become responsible for eldercare at some point over the life course. A recent national AARP survey of over 2,300 baby boomers reports that 70 percent of Americans between 45 and 55 have aging parents or parents-in-law as well as children under 21 years of age. However, 70 percent report that they feel comfortable handling their family responsibilities, and although they may feel "squeezed," they do not feel "stressed" (AARP, 2001). However, the analysis does not distinguish between potential and actual caregiving behavior.

At issue is the notion that simply having elderly parents alive may indicate the potential need for adult children to undertake eldercare responsibilities. However, this does not automatically translate into actual, active caregiving responsibilities and behaviors. In fact, the experience of simultaneously caring for one's aging parents and children is *not* typical. Empirical studies using probability samples show that only a small proportion of caregivers are *actively* engaged in both roles simultaneously (Bengtson et al., 1996; Hogan & Eggebeen, 1995; Logan & Spitze, 1996; Loomis & Booth, 1995; Martin-Matthews & Rosenthal, 1993; Spitze & Logan, 1990; Ward & Spitze, 1998).

One reason for the rarity of the fully engaged sandwiched caregiver is that, although changes in mortality and morbidity may increase the likelihood of becoming a caregiver to an elderly parent during one's lifetime, these changes also increase the age at which caregiving is likely to start (Himes, 1994). The peak demand for caregiving by adult children occurs between ages 45 and 54, and by this age most women have raised their own children beyond childhood and into young adulthood (Cantor, 1995). Additionally, the onset of eldercare needs should continue to occur later in life, further reducing the potential for simultaneously caring for children and elders.

Although some adult children have returned to their parents' home as part of a phenomenon called the "crowded nest" (Schnaiberg & Goldenberg, 1989), research demonstrates that young adult children can actually mediate the eldercare situation for the caregiver and play a strong supportive role to women caregivers (Raphael & Schlesinger, 1994; Stull, Bowman, & Smerglia, 1994). Furthermore, young adult children can connect caregivers to kin and nonkin who may also provide informal care (Gallagher & Gerstel, 2001). Thus, the assumption that simultaneous responsibility to children and parents is inherently stressful ignores the potential role of grandchildren in helping to care for their grandparents.

Do these findings completely negate popular and academic concerns about the Sandwiched Generation? Hardly. While the sandwiched experience may not be normative for all women as it was once assumed to be (Brody, 1981, 1985), demographic trends do imply that it will become more common in the future (Boyd & Treas, 1996). Indeed, in a nationally representative survey of persons providing informal care for a friend or family member over age 50, 41 percent reported having a child under age 18 in the household (National Alliance for Caregiving, 1997). Thus, for those American households in which people are actively caring for older relatives and their own children, we can hardly dismiss the issue.

Responses to Balancing Work and Caregiving

If the pervasiveness of the Sandwiched Generation is actually more myth than reality, perhaps the larger issue is how workers in general balance obligations to employers as well as family caregiving responsibilities. Indeed, studies find that the work-family balancing act is largely left up to individuals who find ways to accommodate caregiving responsibilities. The lack of substantial organizational change at home and in the workplace has meant that many informal caregivers have been innovative and found alternative ways of accomplishing caregiving tasks (Stull, Bowman, & Smerglia, 1994) or made informal arrangements with their employers (Metlife, 1999). In response to competing demands, caregivers may leave the labor force altogether,

make changes at work by cutting back hours, or make changes at home (Boyd & Treas, 1996; Pavalko & Artis, 1997). Individuals and families adopt a variety of work-family adaptive strategies such as making changes in work or family roles, obtaining support from spouses, and using family-oriented policies and programs (when available) in order to reduce the role strain associated with work-family role conflict (Gornick & Meyers, 2001; Moen & Wethington, 1992; Voydanoff, 2002).

At work, eldercare responsibilities are related to greater absenteeism, health-related stress, and difficulty with work-family balance (Metlife, 1999; Neal, Chapman, Ingersoll-Dayton, & Emlen, 1993). To investigate these issues, Gottlieb, Kelloway, and Fraboni (1994) examined a sample of eldercaregivers and identified aspects of eldercare that place employees at risk for adverse job-related consequences. The authors found that assistance with activities of daily living, eldercare management activities, and the number of eldercare crises to which the employee responded significantly predicted a decreased ability to meet job responsibilities and less opportunity to advance at work. Another study of the costs involved with balancing paid work and caregiving found that eldercare had a long-term effect on workers' earnings, and affected workers' prospects for career advancement and worker productivity (Metlife, 1999). Despite the financial losses for both caregivers and employers, only 23 percent of firms with more than 100 employees have support programs for caregivers (Galinsky & Bond, 1998; Metlife, 1999).

Implications for Work-Family Social Policy

The issue of work-family balance for the Sandwiched Generation has implications for work-family social policy and should be of concern to policy makers and employers. Despite women's increased labor force participation, the majority of jobs remain organized according to a traditional male work model, as if workers had no family responsibilities (Acker, 1990; Gerson, 1998; Moen, 1994). Furthermore, women continue to shoulder responsibility for the majority of housework, childcare, and eldercare (Gager, 1998; Moen, 1992), despite a modest (but incommensurate) rise in men's time spent caregiving (Bianchi, 2000).

Employers' Responses—Flextime and the FMLA

The feminization of the workforce in recent decades has forced some employers, including the federal government, to recognize the link between work and family life (Ezra & Deckman, 1996; Glass & Estes, 1997). Although it would be unfair to ignore the changes that some employers have made in response to women's influx into the labor market, much progress is still yet to be made. Flexible work scheduling is one of the most useful "family-friendly" benefits for workers with childcare or eldercare responsibilities. Indeed, 90 percent of workers with parental responsibilities report that they want access to compressed workweeks, flextime, job-sharing, and part-time work benefits (Hewlett & West, 1998). Recent research suggests that employers are beginning to recognize the need for flexible work schedules and that more workers are taking advantage of this option. The proportion of wage and salary workers with flexible job schedules grew from about 13 percent in 1985 to about 25 percent in 1997 (Beers, 2000).

Flexible work arrangements are growing in popularity, yet these benefits are unequally distributed throughout the labor force and benefit the working affluent more often than the working poor (Employee Benefit Research Institute, 1992; Kimball, 1999; Polatnick, 2000). Flexible work schedules are most common in occupations with higher pay and greater autonomy such as executive, managerial, and administrative occupations, with 42 percent of workers in such occupations taking advantage of flexible scheduling arrangements (Beers, 2000). Thus, workers in the lower rungs of the labor force are the least likely to have flexible scheduling arrangements, although these workers may stand to benefit the most from scheduling flexibility. Work-family social policies should focus on providing workers with flexible work arrangements across jobs.

In 1993, Congress passed the Family and Medical Leave Act (FMLA), currently the only family-leave social policy in the United States. The FMLA allows 12 weeks of *unpaid* leave for workers with caregiving (childcare or eldercare) responsibilities

who are employed in workplaces with at least 50 employees (Polatnick, 2000). The FMLA is an important first step in U.S. family-leave policy; however much progress is yet to be made. The primary shortcomings of the FMLA are that it is unpaid leave and applies only to larger firms and therefore benefits only workers who can afford to take leave and whose companies are large enough. Because the FMLA is unpaid leave and the majority of U.S. firms are smaller than 50 employees, many workers do not use or are not eligible for this leave option. Indeed, in 1996, 64 percent of workers who could have benefited from the FMLA, but did not take it, reported that they couldn't afford the loss of income during the 12 weeks (Polatnick, 2000).

An additional weakness of the FMLA is that the majority of workers who do take the leave are women. This trend is likely due both to gendered expectations about caregiving and women's paid work, as well as women's lower wages (O'Connor, 1996). Furthermore, research demonstrates that many workplace cultures discourage men from taking leave (Fried, 1998). Thus, the FMLA does little to challenge the gendered distribution of care work in home or society.

Feminist scholars argue that substantial changes in work-family policies require extensive government intervention into work organizations (both private firms and government agencies) as well as welfare state expansion in order to achieve gender equity and solve the work-family dilemma (O'Connor, 1996). As the most extensive U.S. government intervention into the work-family debate, the FMLA is our first and, so far, only attempt to mandate that employers recognize workers' family responsibilities.

Some evidence suggests that the FMLA has been successful in increasing the number of workers eligible for family leave (Waldfogel, 1999). However, critics of the FMLA argue that the program is difficult for employers to implement, and therefore its administration is virtually untenable (Papa, Kopelman, & Flynn, 1998). Nonetheless, while some groups do not favor expanded government intervention into work and family life, in order to sufficiently resolve the work-family dilemma for caregivers, it appears that government incentives are necessary. Policymakers have been increasingly concerned about those caregivers who cannot afford to take unpaid leave and the impact this will have on other social welfare programs such as social assistance programs and Medicaid. Some have suggested using existing state insurance systems as a source of income during family leaves and allowing federal employees to use accrued paid sick leave during family leaves (Family Caregiver Alliance, 2000). In the late 1990s legislators began proposing revisions to the FMLA in order to expand benefits to cover 13 million workers by including employees in firms of 25 or more. An additional measure proposes allowing workers to take up to 24 hours intermittent leave to attend to children's school activities or to accompany elderly relatives to medical appointments (Papa et al., 1998). In light of recent research, these proposed amendments to the FMLA would be positive changes.

Recommendations

Policy Directions

Since some employers argue that implementing the FMLA is too difficult and time-consuming, policymakers and employers should consider how job flexibility and paid parental leave will not only benefit workers (Hill, Hawkins, Ferris, & Weitzman, 2001), but also companies' bottom lines due to more balanced workers (Landauer, 1997; Metlife, 1999). One nationally representative study of caregivers demonstrated that caregiving had a negative effect on worker productivity, including replacement costs for employees who quit due to caregiving responsibilities; absenteeism costs; costs due to partial absenteeism, workday interruptions, and unanticipated eldercare crises; and costs associated with supervising and emotionally supporting employed caregivers (Metlife, 1997).

An overall weakness of the FMLA and similar policy orientations is that they do not focus on the long-term caregiving project. That is, the short-term family and parental leave policies ignore the responsibilities that accompany child-rearing and elder-caregiving across the life course. Workers and their families need the latitude and ability to balance their work-family responsibilities on a daily basis. Workers need to be able to make changes in how and when they meet the demands of employers and fami-

lies at their own discretion throughout the life course and not only in the weeks following a birth or the months leading up to an elder's death.

We must also continue to strive for gender equity in the home – in terms of housework and childcare arrangements – by continuing to encourage men to undertake caregiving responsibilities for children and elderly relatives. Research demonstrates that men can be loving and effective caregivers (Parke, 1996; Price & Rose, 2000). In order to achieve gender equity in the home and work, men will have to continue to increase their participation in all aspects of family caregiving.

Suggestions for Human Resource Practitioners

Within work organizations HR practitioners can help ameliorate the potentially negative aspects of combining paid work and eldercare. The most useful strategy to help caregivers is to institutionalize flexible work arrangements and scheduling. Although informal arrangements between workers and supervisors offer a quick fix for caregivers, it is imperative that workplaces move toward implementing formal institutional arrangements for workers with caregiving responsibilities. Formal, recognized interventions are necessary in order to impact workplace cultures and create workplaces that recognize workers' family needs and obligations.

Furthermore, caregivers would clearly benefit greatly from paid family leave as well as unscheduled family illness days to allow caregivers to respond to unanticipated caregiving demands. The Family Caregiver Alliance, a national organization for informal caregivers, suggests that employers offer benefits that allow employees to select supplemental dependent care coverage that would reimburse families for costs for in-home care or adult day care (1999).

In addition, the FCA suggests that HR practitioners can provide employees with information about Internet resources as well as local services available to caregivers. As workplaces increasingly recognize employees' caregiving responsibilities, employers may consider holding a "caregiver fair" or brownbag seminars to introduce employees to issues such as home care support services (Family Caregiver Alliance, 1999). One study of employee awareness of family leave benefits found that work situations such as job tenure and firm size actually affect workers' awareness of benefits more than family situational factors (Baird & Reynolds, 2002). Thus, HR practitioners are in the position to impact employees' awareness benefits such as the FMLA and other institutionalized supports.

Suggestions for Future Research

Although the empirical research demonstrates that the impending crisis for the Sandwiched Generation is not as prevalent as we once believed, researchers should continue to examine the implications of elder-caregiving for workers, families, and the long-term care system. This review of the scholarly literature suggests both methodological and conceptual directions for future research.

First, to further distinguish between potential and actual caregiving responsibilities, empirical research should draw on a variety of methods. Survey data with large, representative samples can further elucidate the prevalence of the Sandwiched Generation and identify those who are sandwiched between older and younger generations. Such analyses may provide a demographic description of the Sandwiched Generation and differences in well-being across different groups of caregivers.

On the other hand, qualitative accounts, like that of Elizabeth Cohen (2002), can explain the objective versus subjective aspects of what it means for individuals to be sandwiched. Qualitative methods may also help to explain and distinguish the relationship between potential and actual caregiving responsibilities, and whether the potential caregiving role necessarily precipitates an active caregiving role. While some scholars have argued that we have oversold demography and created the myth of the beleaguered Sandwiched Generation, researchers should investigate the experiences of those Americans who are indeed engaged in multigenerational caregiving. Qualitative methodologies may help elucidate the existing strategies that individuals use in order to manage their competing responsibilities of home and work on a daily basis.

Second, the research literature would benefit from a life course perspective that emphasizes the timing of caregiving over the life course as well as the interrelatedness of caregivers and care-receivers' lives. Caregivers' experiences may depend on the nature of the relationship between caregiver and care receiver as well as the history and reciprocity characteristic of that relationship. A related issue is the importance of intergenerational exchanges over time and the reciprocal nature of parent-child relationships. Bengtson et al. (1996) contend that care tends to flow from parents to children until parents are in old age and begin to find themselves in need. Without acknowledging the intergenerational flow of resources over time, the literature tends to overemphasize the dependency of elderly parents and the construction of the caregiving situation as unavoidably burdensome.

Finally, researchers should continue to investigate ways in which employers and policymakers can ameliorate the caregiving situation for all workers. Areas of interest include public laws, healthcare benefits, workplace policies as well as gender equity in the home. Scholars, policymakers, activists, and individuals must continue to push in order to further disseminate work-family benefits throughout all sectors of the labor force. Although the prevalence of the Sandwiched Generation may have been a case of the "overselling of demography" (Martin-Matthews, 2000; Rosenthal, 2000), the larger of issues of who should provide long-term care and how workers manage the caregiving situation remain of vital concern to scholars and policymakers.

Summary

The Sandwiched Generation refers to the cohort of people who are "sandwiched" between caring for their children and their aging parents. Societal trends in fertility, mortality, chronic illness, and delayed morbidity suggest that more workers will be involved in unpaid eldercare. As more people take on eldercare responsibilities in the context of other family and paid work obligations, the prevalence of the Sandwiched Generation has implications for work-family social policies as well as caregivers' and care-receivers' well-being.

Although eldercare is becoming increasingly likely at some point in the life course, empirical research demonstrates that the impending "crisis" for the Sandwiched Generation is not as grave as once predicted. Studies show that although workers have both their own children and elderly parents alive, this "sandwiched" situation does not necessarily precipitate active multigenerational caregiving. Thus, the occurrence of actively caregiving for both children and parents is relatively rare. Nonetheless, the issue of work-family balance for caregivers remains of great concern for families, employers, and the long-term care system.

The Family and Medical Leave Act (FMLA) of 1993 is the only federally mandated family benefit in the United States. Although it has impacted caregiving situations of some workers, it is unpaid leave and eligibility is unequally distributed throughout the labor force. Employers and policy-makers should strive to make family leave paid and available to workers in all levels of the labor force. Furthermore, HR practitioners can work to implement formal caregiver supports within organizations as well as disseminate information about benefits to workers. Suggestions for future research are discussed.

The author would like to thank Jill Quadagno, Lori Parham, and Jarret Keene for their helpful comments on earlier versions of this chapter.

Chapter 13

Rising Health Care Costs and the Aging Workforce

Paul Fronstin
Dallas L. Salisbury

The cost of providing health benefits to employees has been increasing. Annual increases in the cost of providing health benefits have been increasingly outpacing the consumer price index (CPI) and the medical portion of the CPI since 1998. While the factors accounting for rising health benefit costs are the subject of debate, a number of studies provide some evidence of the relative magnitudes of selected cost determinants. Newhouse (1992) and Cutler (1995) discuss how a number of factors have contributed to increased spending on health care services. They include the aging of the population, the comprehensiveness of insurance, increased income of employees, differential productivity growth from medical care, avoidable administrative expense, provider-induced demand, and technological innovation. Ultimately, the rising cost of providing health benefits will drive employer decisions regarding the provision of those benefits to both employees and retirees, and employee and retiree decisions regarding the take-up of those benefits.

Today, 21 percent of the population is age 55 and older, a figure that has not changed since 1980, though the percentage of the population age 65 and older has increased slightly (U.S. Bureau of the Census, 2002). According to Newhouse (1992) and Cutler (1995), the aging population accounted for a *tiny* fraction of the increase in spending through 1987. While the aging population has had little effect on national health spending so far, it likely will have a major impact in the not too distant future. The percentage of the population 55 and older will increase from 21 percent today to roughly 30 percent over the next 20 years, and the percentage age 65 and older will increase from 13 percent to 19 percent.

As the population ages, the working population will age too. Inevitably this will increase the cost of providing health benefits. Unless population demographics change, the cost of providing health benefits will increase as the age of the working population increases because an older population will be competing for the same amount of health care resources. Even if the age of the working population did not change, new technologies will continue to be developed. As long as new technologies become available, Americans in need of those technologies will likely demand those benefits. To the degree that new technologies become accepted as part of the standard practice of medicine, insurers and employers will be under pressure to cover them under existing health benefits. Since older Americans use more health care services than younger Americans, older Americans will likely drive medical innovations, which will continue to increase the cost of providing health care services.

The purpose of this chapter is to discuss several trends in employment-based health benefits, including some recent innovative changes that are taking place. Much of the focus is on retirees because when a worker retires, access to health benefits changes radically.

This chapter is organized as follows. First, it presents current insurance options for older workers, including some cost considerations. The next section discusses trends in retiree health benefits. The following section discusses the outlook for active worker health benefits and retiree health benefits. The final sections include our recommendations and summary.

Insurance Options and Cost Considerations

Older workers have several options when it comes to health insurance. The most popular ones are employment-based health benefits and the individual market. Other options include COBRA, Medicaid, and Medicare. All are discussed below.

Group Market: Employment-Based Health Benefits

The most prevalent form of health insurance is employment-based. In 2000, 67 percent of the 55-64 year olds were covered by employment-based health benefits. Nearly 9 percent purchased health insurance directly from an insurer, over 16 percent were covered by some form of public health insurance, and 14.5 percent were uninsured (Employee Benefit Research Institute [EBRI], 2001d). Aside from being the most prevalent form of health insurance, employment-based health benefits usually represent the most attractive option for older Americans. For workers, employers typically offer a comprehensive benefits package that is likely to be significantly less costly than a similar plan in the individual market. In 2001, employee-only coverage cost on average $2,650 per year, of which employees paid an average of $360 through payroll deduction (Levitt, Holve, & Wang, 2001). Moreover, employer and employee contributions to health benefits are generally not counted in taxable income, and employees also typically pay only a portion of the full cost of coverage, although Pauly (1997) would argue that they pay the full cost in the form of lower wages. Older workers benefit even more than younger workers because the employee share of the premium for health benefits through an employment-based plan does not vary with age or health status. So, regardless of age, employees generally pay the same amount for the same benefits, despite the fact that on average, the cost of providing health benefits for older workers is much higher than it is for young workers. Actual costs vary by age because older workers are less healthy than younger workers and because older workers use more health care services than younger workers. According to the Agency for Health Care Research and Quality (2002), men ages 55-64 used an average of $3,402 in health care services in 1998, while women ages 55-64 used an average of $3,306 (see Table 13.1). This compares with $1,339 for men ages 35-44 and $1,912 for women. It is clear that the cross subsidies from young healthy workers to older less healthy workers can be enormous, making employment-based health benefits a highly valued benefit to older workers.

Table 13.1
Health Care Spending, by
Age and Gender 1998

	Men	Women
Under 18	$ 1,003	$ 1,512
18-24	$ 785	$ 1,244
25-34	$ 795	$ 1,607
35-44	$ 1,339	$ 1,912
45-54	$ 1,793	$ 2,451
55-64	$ 3,402	$ 3,306
65 or older	$ 4,736	$ 5,629

The employment-based health benefits system has some important advantages: the risk of adverse selection is relatively low; the existence of economies of scale in the purchase of group health benefits results in lower average premiums; and the value of health benefits is not included in taxable income. Workers generally, and older workers more specifically, share in these advantages when comparing the employment-based system to the individual market.

Individual Market

Older workers and retirees sometimes choose to purchase health insurance in the individual market. They will often purchase this coverage when they do not have access to an employment-based health plan. According to data provided by the Commonwealth Fund (2002), premiums in the individual market are roughly double group-based premiums for older individuals. Older individuals may experience other significant differences between the group market and the individual market. In the individual market, individuals may be denied coverage, may have certain conditions or body parts excluded from coverage, and may pay premiums that are not only higher on average than the group market, but also vary with demographic conditions and health status. Unlike the group market, the individual market may offer older workers and retirees a greater choice among health insurers and insurance products. As a result, individuals will be able to lower their premium if they are willing to assume greater financial risk through higher deductibles, high coinsurance, and less comprehensive benefits.

States in large part regulate the provision of insurance in the individual market. They determine whether or not they will regulate premium rates and whether they will regulate availability of health insurance. In 1996, the federal government passed legislation that adds additional requirements for insurers offering products in the individual market to comply with. The Health Insurance Portability and Accountability Act of 1996 (HIPAA) requires insurers in the individual health insurance market to guarantee issue and prohibits the insurer from applying preexisting conditions exclusions for the following:

- Individuals who have had coverage for at least 18 months, most recently with an employment-based group health plan, governmental plan, or church plan (*not an individual plan*).
- Individuals who have exhausted COBRA coverage.
- Individuals who are not eligible under a group plan, Medicare or Medicaid.
- Individuals who have no other health insurance coverage.

The insurer must offer at least two plan options. This may include either the two most popular policy options for that individual market, or two options that are representative of health insurance coverage offered in the state.

Besides the cost of insurance, older workers and retirees can expect to incur significant out-of-pocket health care expenses. People age 65 with average life expectancy and average health care costs can currently expect to need $160,000 to cover expenses associated with medical care after they have stopped receiving employment-based health insurance (Fidelity Workplace Services, 2002). Someone leaving the labor force at age 55 without employment-based health insurance would need $260,000. This is where COBRA, Medicare, and Medicare may provide some relief.

COBRA. Older workers who leave a job have very few options when it comes to continuing health insurance coverage. One option is to continue to participate in the health insurance they already had on their job through so-called COBRA benefits. Under the Consolidated Omnibus Budget Recon-

ciliation Act of 1985 (COBRA), workers are assured access to health insurance after job termination. COBRA requires employers with health insurance plans to offer continued access to group health insurance to qualified beneficiaries if they lose coverage as a result of a qualifying event. COBRA requires continued access for 18 months (or 29 months if the qualified beneficiary is disabled) for covered employees, and dependents, and can be a useful means for providing coverage for individuals age 63½ and older to bridge the gap between employment and Medicare eligibility. Employers with fewer than 20 employees are excluded from these provisions, as are plans offered by churches, the District of Columbia, or any territory, possession, or agency of the United States.

COBRA beneficiaries can be required to pay up to 102 percent of the premium. As a result, while individuals have access to coverage through their former employer, affordability of that coverage is often a huge concern as job change or retirement is often associated with a decline in income.

Medicaid. Medicaid is a jointly funded state-federal health insurance program for certain low-income and disabled people. The federal government provides general guidelines for the program, though specifics are determined at the state level. Older adults with no children will generally qualify for Medicaid benefits if they qualify for Supplemental Security Income (SSI). Others who may qualify are certain disabled persons with income below the poverty level; certain institutionalized persons; persons who may have too much income to qualify but who could "spend down" to Medicaid eligibility by incurring medical and/or remedial care expenses to offset their excess income; and Medicare beneficiaries who have low income.

Medicare. Medicare is a health insurance program for people 65 years of age and older, some disabled people under 65 years of age, and people with End-Stage Renal Disease (permanent kidney failure treated with dialysis or a transplant). Generally, individuals will automatically be enrolled in Medicare after they have received Social Security disability benefits for 24 months. As a means for bridging the gap to Medicare coverage for the disabled under age 65, disabled individuals are allowed to keep COBRA coverage for 29 months.

Trends in Retiree Health Benefits

To understand the current state of retiree health benefits in the United States, it is necessary to understand how financial accounting dramatically changed for most American companies in December 1990. That is when the Financial Accounting Standards Board (FASB), a private-sector organization that establishes standards for financial accounting and reporting, approved Financial Accounting Statement No. 106 (FAS 106), "Employers' Accounting for Postretirement Benefits Other Than Pensions." FAS 106 dramatically impacts a company's calculation of its profit and losses. Not-for-profits and governmental entities have similar accounting requirements under the Government Accounting Standards Board.

As a result of FAS 106, and the increasing cost of providing retiree health benefits in general, many employers began a major overhaul of their retiree health benefit programs. Some employers placed caps on what they were willing to spend on retiree health benefits. Some added age and service requirements, while others moved to defined contribution health benefits. Some completely dropped retiree health benefits for future retirees, while others dropped benefits for current retirees, although this happened less frequently than other changes. While these changes do not appear to be having much impact on current retirees, they are more likely to be felt most by future retirees who are not yet or may never become eligible for retiree health benefits because the courts have ruled that an employer has a right to terminate or amend retiree health benefits only if it has proved that such a right has been reserved or stated in specific language and on a widely known basis (EBRI, 1991). In all probability, these changes will continue in the near future (Levitt, Holve, & Wang, 2001).

These changes can be summarized in the following seven trends: (1) fewer employers offer retiree benefits; (2) changed retiree benefits packages; (3) tightened eligibility requirements; (4) spending caps; (5) increased co-pay; (6) reduced benefits for those hired after a certain date; and (7) consumer-driven approaches.

The first six are discussed below, while two consumer-driven approaches are the subject of the next section.

Fewer Employers Offer Retiree Benefits

In general, the percentage of employers offering health benefits to future retirees seems to be declining. An annual survey of employers with 500 or more workers shows that the percentage of employers expecting to continue offering health benefits to future early retirees declined from 46 percent in 1993 to 31 percent in 2000 (William M. Mercer, 2001). The percentage of employers offering health benefits to Medicare eligible retirees today and planning to offer them to future Medicare eligible retirees is also declining.

Another survey of larger employers (most with 1,000 or more employees) also showed that the percentage offering retiree health benefits declined. The likelihood of offering retiree health benefits to early retirees declined from 88 percent in 1991 to 73 percent in 2000 (Hewitt Associates, 1999b; Coppock & Zebrak, 2001). The decline is mainly due to two factors: (1) some employers are terminating existing benefits, and (2) new organizations are choosing not to offer retiree health benefits at all.

Changed Retiree Benefits Packages

Most employers continuing to offer retiree health benefits have made changes in the benefit package. Modifications to cost-sharing provisions are a common change, with employers asking retirees to pick up a greater share of the cost of coverage. In 2000, 39 percent of employers with 500 or more workers offering retiree health benefits required retirees to pay 100 percent of the premium for coverage, up from 31 percent of employers in 1997 (William M. Mercer, 2001). See Figure 13.1.

The observant reader will notice a small decline in the percentage of employers who require retirees to pay the full cost of health benefits between 1999 and 2000. However, this apparent decline is not statistically significant. Moreover, the survey used in Figure 13.1 includes public sector employers, which are more likely than private sector for-profit employers to require retirees to pay the full cost.

Similarly, as Figure 13.2 shows, a survey conducted for the Henry J. Kaiser Family Foundation and the Health Research and Educational Trust (Levitt, Holve, & Wang, 2001) revealed that large employers intend to ask retirees to cover an increas-

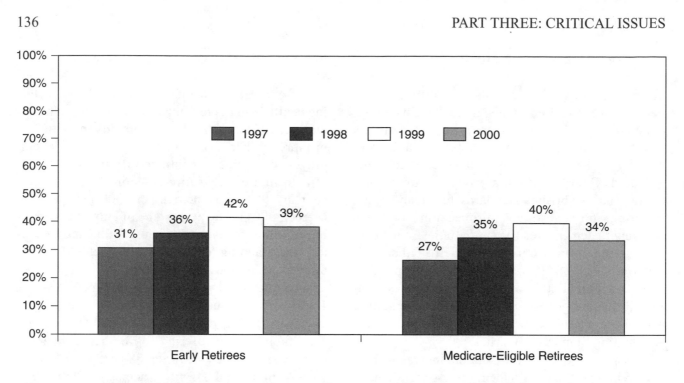

Figure 13.1 Percentage of large employers requiring retiree to pay full cost of retiree health benefits, employers with 500+ employees, 1997-2000

ing share of the cost of their health insurance coverage (see Figure 13.2).

Tightened Eligibility Requirements

Employers do not have to change the benefits package to control spending on retiree health benefits. Instead, they can tighten eligibility require-

ments such as requiring workers to attain a certain age and/or tenure with the company before they can receive any retiree health benefits. Overall, the percentage of employers requiring an age of 55 and a service requirement of 5 years increased from 30 percent in 1996 to 38 percent in 2000 (Hewitt Associates, 1999b, 2000). At the same time, some employers instituted a requirement of age 55 and

Table 13.2
Eligibility Requirements for Retiree Health Benefits, Employers with 1,000 or more Employees, 1996 & 2000

	1996 %	2000 %
Age 50 + 10 years service	1	2
Age 50 + 15 years service	1	1
Age 55 + 5 years service	9	10
Age 55 + 10 years service	30	38
Age 55 + 15 years service	5	8
Age 55 + 20 years service	0	2
Age 60 + 10 years service	0	1
Based on age/service points	1	5
Based on age and/or service plus age/service points	6	3
Two or more alternatives	35	19
Other (e.g., age only or service only)	11	11

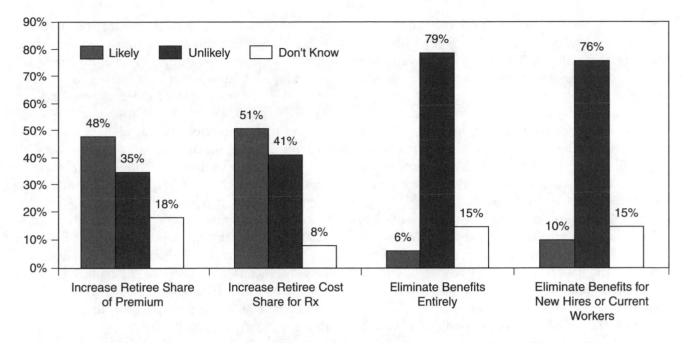

Figure 13.2 Likelihood of making various changes to retiree health benefits in the next two years, among large firms offering retiree health benefits in 2001

20 years service or age 60 and 10 years service for the first time (see Table 13.2).

Spending Caps

Employers have also instituted caps on the total amount of money they are willing to spend on retiree health benefits. These caps could work on a total aggregate spending basis or on a per-retiree basis. In 1993, 72 percent of employers with 1,000 or more employees did not have any type of cap on their total contributions, compared to 55 percent in 2000. Only 4 percent of those with a defined dollar cap on the employer subsidy have indexed it for inflation (Hewitt Associates, 1993, 2000).

Increased Co-pay

Employers also are continuing to consider more changes to retiree health benefits. Nearly 50 percent of firms with 200 or more workers are likely to increase the amount retirees are asked to pay, and 51 percent are likely to ask retirees to pay more for prescription drugs (Figure 13.2). Only 6-10 percent are likely to eliminate retiree health benefits either for new hires, current employees, or current retirees.

Reduced Benefits for Those Hired After a Certain Date

One aspect of changes some employers have made to retiree health benefits is the degree to which benefits have been reduced for workers hired (or retiring) after a specific date. Some employers have reduced the subsidy for workers hired after a certain date, while some employers have eliminated benefits altogether for workers hired after a certain date. Data from William M. Mercer (2001) and the General Accounting Office (2001b) show that about 16 percent of employers with 500 or more employees offering retiree health benefits only offer them to current retirees or those hired before a specific year.

Outlook for Health Benefits: Consumer-Driven Approaches

A number of health policy analysts have suggested that employers are rethinking their entire approach to managing employee health benefits (EBRI, 2001c; Milliman & Robertson, 2001; Salisbury, 1998, 1999; National Center for Policy Analysis, 2000). The terms *defined contribution* and *consumer-driven* have been used to describe a range of potential health benefit options available to employers that would allow them to change their approach to providing health benefits for both active workers and retirees. These terms generally connote programs in which employees are intended to be treated more as *direct purchasers* of health coverage and health care services rather than the *indirect beneficiaries* of purchases made by the employer, so that they will be more careful purchasers and will be more satisfied with the choices they make on their own, rather than having someone else make those choices for them.

Employers are interested in these health benefits for a number of reasons. First, employers continually look for more cost-effective ways to provide health benefits for their workers, and are concerned about future cost increases. These arrangements would allow them to set a monetary contribution for health benefits regardless of cost increase. Second, many employers sponsoring health plans are concerned that the public and political backlash against managed care will result in new restrictions or laws that will entangle them in litigation. Employers could distance themselves from health care coverage decisions by limiting their involvement only to the contribution amount for health benefits and not to the actual coverage or delivery of the health care services. Third, employers may be able to provide workers and retirees more choice, control, and flexibility through these arrangements.

The defined contribution and consumer-driven approaches typically expose active workers and retirees to more of the costs of their health benefits and the cost of the health care services they use. All strategies to increase consumer involvement in health care spending decisions have a common theme: to shift decision-making responsibility regarding some aspect of health care or delivery from employers to employees and retirees. While only a handful of employers have implemented these types of programs, we expect more employers will in the future. The remainder of this section discusses how these plans may work, first for active workers, then for retirees.

Health Reimbursement Accounts for Active Workers

Although there is a wide range of approaches that can be taken in providing more consumerism in health benefits, this section limits the discussion to a specific benefit design that some employers are using and many others are interested in (for a more detailed treatment of the available options, see EBRI, 2002a). These employers have moved toward high-deductible health plans but are also providing other means to assist employees with out-of-pocket expenses that they incur prior to reaching their deductible. As an example, an employer may provide a comprehensive health insurance plan that has a high deductible, say $2,000. In order to help employees pay for expenses incurred before the deductible is reached, the employer would also provide a health reimbursement account (HRA) with, say, $1,000. The employee would use the money in the account to pay for the first $1,000 of health care services. While the actual deductible is $2,000, in this example, because the employer provides $1,000 to an account, employees are subject only to the $1,000 deductible gap. After the employee's expenses reach the deductible, comprehensive health insurance would take effect. The Internal Revenue Service (IRS) recently released Revenue Ruling 2002-41 and Notice 2002-45 (2002a, b) to provide guidance clarifying the general tax treatment of HRAs, the benefits offered under an HRA, the interaction between HRAs and cafeteria plans, FSAs, and COBRA coverage, and other matters.

Generally, employers have a tremendous amount of flexibility in designing health plans that incorporate an HRA. For example, the amount of money that is placed in the account, the level of the deductible, and the comprehensiveness of the health insurance are all subject to variation. Employers can offer comprehensive health insurance that covers 100 percent of health care costs after the deductible has been met or they may offer coverage with 80 percent co-insurance (or some other portion of costs) after the deductible is met. If employers choose to pay less than 100 percent of health care expenses after the deductible has been met, they then have the option of designing the plan with or without a maximum out-of-pocket limit.

Employers can also vary employee cost sharing based on in-network visits and out-of-network visits. Employers may choose to pay 100 percent of health care consumed after the deductible has been met for employees who use network providers, but pay only 70 percent or 80 percent if employees use an out-of-network provider.

HRAs can be thought of as providing "first-dollar" coverage until funds in the account are exhausted. Leftover funds at the end of each year can be carried over to the following year, allowing employees to accumulate funds over time, and, in principle, creating the key incentive for individuals to make health care purchases responsibly. Employers can place restrictions on the amount that can be carried over. One feature of HRAs is that when unused funds are carried over each year, employees may be able to accumulate enough funds in their accounts to satisfy their deductible in future years. In addition, as employees build account balances, they may be more likely to switch to higher deductible health plans in the future. However, employees may also choose to forgo necessary health care in order to accumulate funds in the account. Ultimately, the amount of money in the account will be a function of how long persons have had an account, usage of health care, and the size of the annual contribution.

Employers also have used a design option based on paying for certain health care expenses in full before an employee would be asked to pay for services from the funds accumulated in their account. Some employers, for instance, will cover preventive services in full. This addresses one of the most contentious issues regarding high-deductible health plans: that low-income families will be tempted to economize by avoiding preventive health care services and early treatment, only to be faced with more serious and costly health care problems later.

Perhaps the biggest difference between the health plan many employees are enrolled in today and a health plan with an HRA is that under the latter, employees would face a much larger deductible, and would be responsible for paying the full cost of health care services until they reach their deductible. Instead of paying $10 or $20 to visit a doctor, employees may pay $100 or $150. Instead of paying $5 or $10 for a prescription drug, employees may pay $30, $125, for example, or even $300, depending on the price of the drug. One goal of these plans is that the knowledge that employees

will gain on the actual cost of providing health care will turn them into more cost-conscious and efficient users of care.

Health benefits with an HRA can also incorporate features of managed care. Incentives are often provided for employees to use network providers, and employers and insurers typically negotiate a discounted fee schedule with doctors, hospitals, and retail pharmaceutical providers. Hence, employees would not be negotiating prices with health care providers.

One disadvantage of HRAs is that accumulation of accounts over time will effectively reduce some employees' cost-sharing responsibilities to zero. This could work to induce demand, especially when an employee is nearing job termination, if account balances are not portable. The ability to access real dollars upon termination will temper the induced demand effect. The question is whether employees will become more cost-conscious and efficient users of health care, thereby offsetting any induced demand arising from large account accumulations.

Defined Contribution Health Benefits for Retirees

Defined contribution (DC) health benefits may apply to active workers as well as retirees, and it is important to understand the difference. For active workers, a DC health benefit would be used to fund their current health insurance and/or health care services. While DC health benefits could be provided under a number of different scenarios, under all scenarios employers would generally provide a fixed contribution that employees would then use to buy health insurance and/or health care services. In contrast, DC health benefits for retirees are similar to DC retirement benefits, such as 401(k) plans. Like a DC retirement plan, under a DC health plan for retiree health benefits, active employees would typically accumulate funds in an account to prefund retiree health benefits during their working lives. Upon retirement, the funds in the account could then be used to purchase health insurance from the former employer or union, or directly from an insurer.

Employers are interested in these accounts for retiree health benefits for a number of reasons. Pre-funding an account could reduce future employer costs for retiree health benefits. By pre-funding an account, an employer decides how much to contribute to retiree health benefits while a person is working. Contributions to the account may accumulate interest and the value of the contribution could grow over time or could vary with age or years of service, but it is possible that the value of the account would not grow as fast as the anticipated cost of providing retiree health benefits. Essentially, in this type of model the risk of unpredictable health benefit cost inflation is borne by employees. While the risk of health care cost inflation is transferred to employees under both types of DC arrangements, the risk for retirees may be greater because of the longer time frame between the accumulation of assets to pay for health insurance and the actual purchase of insurance. Moreover, the retiree bears the risk of assets being insufficient to keep up with the cost of health insurance increases.

Issues to Consider When Designing a DC Health Plan

Who contributes? While working, each employee would have an account. The account might be funded or unfunded. Both employer and employees can contribute to the value of account balances. Employer contributions to the value of the account can be unfunded. If only employer contributions were made to the account, the employer could set up the account on paper, and can amend, modify, or even terminate the plan at any time for current and/or future retirees. If employee contributions were made to the account, an actual account would have to be established as the employees would "own" their contributions (i.e., such amounts would be fully funded), though they would not own the employer contributions.

Another issue to consider when deciding who could contribute to the account is the tax treatment of contribution sources. Employer contributions to the account can be designed so as to not be treated as taxable income to the employee, either during working years or during retirement upon payout of insurance benefits. Active employee contributions, however, cannot be treated on a pre-tax basis.

Eligibility requirements. Another issue to con-

sider in designing a plan is how to treat new employees who are older than the plan's entry age when they join the employer. A lump-sum or opening balance could be provided to employees to join the plan if they commence participation after entry age into the plan has passed. The opening balance also could be tied to age and/or years of service.

Employers may still require that employees meet an age and/or service requirement before being allowed to use the funds in the account to buy insurance in retirement. They may also vary their contribution to the account based on age and/or service requirements. Age requirements are common in defined benefit pension plans, where employees do not qualify for retirement benefits until they reach a minimum age. They are also increasingly common for qualifying for retiree health benefits.

Employer involvement. After retirement, retirees could use the funds accumulated in the account to buy health insurance. The insurance could be provided by the employer – meaning, the employer would continue to decide what benefits to offer and at what price or the employer could allow retirees to buy insurance on their own and pay an insurer of the retiree's choice directly.

Use of the account. Employers must also design how the account is to be used upon the employee's retirement. They could continue to provide the health benefit. This means retirees would be purchasing health insurance from their former employer using funds accumulated in the account. In contrast, employers might allow retirees to use the funds to purchase any health insurance, including policies sold directly by insurers. Account balances also could be used to pay out-of-pocket expenses, and health care services not covered by the benefit plan.

Annuities. Because the DC health account could be depleted before the death of a retiree, employers could consider allowing retirees to convert their account balance to an annuity. While the annuity may not provide enough funds to cover the full cost of health insurance, retirees would be guaranteed a stream of funds until their (or their spouse's) death. The annuity also could allow for different payouts before and after age 65 when the cost of health insurance falls substantially for retirees because they become eligible for Medicare. Annuities, however, may be taxable upon payout if the retiree has a choice of receiving money or health insurance coverage.

Other considerations. Whether or not retirees are allowed to use the funds accumulated in the account to purchase insurance on their own or as a spending account, retirees run the risk of depleting the assets in the account while money is still needed to purchase insurance. As a result, employers run the risk of losing a tool to manage the retirement process. If employees think that the balance of their account is not large enough to pay for retiree health benefits they may postpone their retirement date until they are closer to being eligible for Medicare. Research already shows that there is a strong link between a worker's decision to retire and the availability of retiree health benefits (Fronstin, 1999).

Hence, it will be an important exercise for retirees to predict how much it will cost them to purchase health insurance during retirement, and whether there will be enough assets accumulated in the account to purchase health insurance throughout retirement. If a shortfall is expected, retirees may want to start saving additional funds for later years. They also may want to use some of their own money up front, rather than the funds in the account, if they expect the cost of insurance to increase faster than the gains on the assets accumulated in the account, or because health care cost inflation is typically higher than overall inflation and may be higher than the amount of money the account may earn over time. The decision to use personal assets, rather than the assets accumulated in an un-funded account, is highly complex, and involves predicting the cost of health insurance, the composition of the benefits package, the rate of return on personal assets, the rate of return on the assets in the paper account, life expectancy, future income, other budget needs, and the ability of the plan sponsor to make good on its promise to fund the liability.

Recommendations

Before implementing defined contribution or consumer-driven health plans for active workers and retirees, there are a number of things that employers need to think about that can affect their decision to offer a new plan and the design of that plan. First, employers need to consider the administrative capability needed in switching to and running

a consumer-driven health care plan. They will also need a communication and education strategy. It would be desirable if employers and policymakers started thinking now about outreach initiatives that educate workers, starting at a young age, about the need to start saving early for retirement, and to factor in the cost of everyday health expenses as well as unpredictable expenses, such as long-term care. (For an example, see www.choosetosave.org.) Such initiatives to educate the American population regarding saving and investing for the future have started, but have in large part ignored the role that spending on medical care will play in retirement.

Employers will need to understand the marketability issues with different employee sectors, the impact on employer costs, the impact on employee costs, and the impact on employee satisfaction. Decisions will need to be made on how to handle new hires, terminations, and family status changes. Finally, employers will need to decide if they want to fully replace their current health plan with a consumer-driven health plan, or if they are going to add it as an additional choice to the existing plan.

The decisions that employers will need to make for retiree health benefits are similar but different. Employers will need to decide how the account is funded. They will also have to decide how to transition older workers into the plan. Presumably, older employees will not have had a lot of time to accumulate assets. Employers will need to decide what type of health plans will be offered to retirees and how those plans will be priced. Finally, employers could consider allowing retirees to convert their account balance to an annuity.

Under both arrangements individuals may have to use some of their own money to buy insurance and/or services, but the issues of how much money and when it is used differ. For example, under a DC health benefits arrangement for active workers, employers may provide a fixed contribution that covers only 90 percent of the cost of health insurance. In order to buy insurance, employees would then have to pay the difference each month. Under a DC health benefits arrangement for retirees, it is likely that the retirees will have accumulated enough assets in the account to buy health insurance without having to use their own funds for at least a few years, or they could apportion their funds so that all of the assets accumulated in the account are not used all at once. However, once the assets in the fund are depleted, the retirees will then need to purchase health insurance with their own funds.

Summary

The cost of providing health benefits to workers and retirees is increasing and is expected to continue increasing. In addition, employers continue to be concerned about how FAS 106 liabilities appear on their balance sheets. While employers are unable to increase the cost of health benefits for older workers any more than they can for younger workers, they have been cutting back on retiree health benefits by either making it more costly for workers to have health benefits during retirement, or by making it more difficult for workers to qualify for retiree health benefits. As a result, workers' access to health benefits will be an issue once they retire, and workers will also bear a greater burden of the cost of health benefits during retirement.

Public policymakers face the difficult task of trying to provide policy solutions for a system that is largely voluntary. By law, employers are under no obligation to provide health benefits to active workers, nor are they legally required to provide retiree health benefits, except to current retirees who can prove that they were promised a specific benefit. The issue of voluntary or mandatory employer sponsorship of benefits is central to the cost of providing those benefits. It is likely that employers will continue to make changes to health benefits for workers and retirees, and policymakers will continue to grapple with the issue of health security while dealing with a voluntary benefit. Consumer-driven and defined contribution approaches for health benefits will likely play a greater role for both active workers and retirees in the future. Ultimately, it is up to health policy researchers, employers, and policymakers to examine the impact on older workers and retirees and to recommend sound policies that first do no harm.

Synthesis

Health and Older Workers

Chapters 12 and 13 address two different substrands that were visible in the panel's responses placed under the heading of health. While Chapter 13 focuses on health care, Chapter 12 emphasizes the need for institutional infrastructures that would allow the flexibility many workers need to appropriately balance the responsibilities placed on them by their families and in their jobs.

What emerges from superimposing the chapters on each other is the realization that unless both physical and mental needs of the aging older are met, it will be impossible to speak of a healthy aging workforce. An aging worker who never calls in sick may in fact be suffering from tremendous stress caused by an inability to care for an ill parent. Another aging worker may have struck an ideal balance between work and family, but may still be worried about reductions in health care coverage. Needless to say, both of these employees are likely to exhibit suboptimal performance, resulting in a potentially large opportunity cost for employers. At the very least, they will start exploring options to change employment, either to work in a more flexible environment, or to work with an employer with more comprehensive health care benefits.

One other observation is warranted. As was said in the training chapters, health-related interventions to accommodate older workers' needs benefit all workers, regardless of their age. In the case of training, using larger fonts, scaling back on reading loads and lectures, and increasing collaborative learning and discussion benefit both younger and older workers. Similarly, increasing job flexibility for older workers to allow them to care for aging parents also benefits younger workers who may need to take care of a sick child. It also allows men to more easily carry their share of the caregiving burden in either case, in turn facilitating increased gender equity in the workplace.

There is one snake in the grass, however, and it is unclear how this will play out. Chapter 13 shows that health care is generally more costly for older workers than it is for younger workers. Obviously, the burden of health care cost is not evenly distributed across the age spectrum or across other variables such as the amount of dependents in households. The consequence is that on the whole, younger workers pay relatively more for health care than older workers. As the workforce becomes progressively older, this trend is likely to continue. Unless this is addressed at some point in the future, it could set the stage for future conflict, negating any efforts that may have been taken to improve intergenerational relations in the workplace.

ISSUE 6
PENSIONS AND OLDER WORKERS

Chapter 14

Adapting Pensions to Demographic Change

Rudolph G. Penner

Baby boomers have had a profound impact on American life. There are so many of them that they overwhelm the rest of the population, economically and politically. When they were young, it was in their interest to have a retirement system that encouraged early retirement. That was a way to make room on the career ladder for this huge bulge in the population.

Now the boomers are themselves on the verge of retirement. It is neither in their own interest nor in the interest of a healthy economy to continue to encourage early retirement. Yet, the old system has become calcified and numerous laws and institutions make it a challenge to change (Committee for Economic Development, 1999).

This chapter will describe barriers to change and suggest means of overcoming them. Some of the barriers result from private employment practices and it will require some innovative thinking by human resource professionals to adapt the workplace to new demographic realities. Other barriers are created by legislation and the article will suggest changes in the legal environment that could be helpful in developing more flexible work arrangements. As new arrangements are developed, it is necessary to keep in mind that Social Security will eventually have to be reformed. Unfortunately, we are not making much progress on this issue and that creates considerable uncertainty. However, it will be surprising if the retirement income provided by Social Security is not eventually reduced somewhat relative to wages. The chapter will examine the implications of Social Security reform for private pension policy.

The possibility of changes in private and public pensions immediately creates a conflict. Many laws and regulations have the good intent of protecting workers from abrupt changes in their pension rights. But those same laws make it difficult to adapt the system to new demographic conditions.

Adaptation is important for the sake of the whole economy. The nation will lose an enormous store of skills and experience as the baby boomers leave the labor force. The problem is not so much that the baby boomers will be leaving. It is that there won't be many young people to replace them. The rate of growth of the labor force will slow from 1.1 percent annually in the 1990s to less than 0.4 percent between 2010 and 2020, because baby boomers and the generation Xers that followed have not been very fertile. Indeed, were it not for immigrants and their relatively high birth rates, the labor force would be virtually constant by the second decade of the new millenium.

Some professions will be affected more than others by the wave of retirements. A disproportionate number of nurses and teachers are nearing retirement while blue collar workers tend to be younger, because so many work their way into white collar jobs as they age.

In a recent report financed by the Sloan Foundation, Penner, Perun, and Steuerle (2002) argue that the situation could be mitigated if older workers could be persuaded to work longer. They are certainly able to work longer as health at older ages has improved and the proportion of jobs that are physically arduous has declined (Steuerle, Spiro, & Johnson, 1999). That does not mean, of course, that huge numbers would choose to work longer if given better opportunities. Many like retirement and could not be induced to work longer, regardless of the incentives provided. Many others would find it difficult to work because of poor health and disability.

The Health and Retirement Survey (HRS) reports that proportionately more younger retirees, aged 51 to 54, say that they retired for health reasons (67%) than do older retirees, aged 62 to 64 (42%). This counterintuitively hints that if one is looking for people to work longer, it may be more profitable to look in the direction of older rather than younger retirees. Also, as the age of retirement rises, fewer say that they were forced to retire and more say that they retired voluntarily.

It is extremely unlikely that removing disincentives for longer work could completely counter the deceleration of labor force growth discussed above, but it could help. More important, there would be a significant improvement in the welfare of those individual older workers who would choose to work longer if they were given the opportunity.

One way to encourage longer work is to offer more flexible employment arrangements. In particular, many older workers say that they would be interested in part-time work or full-time work with longer vacations. Unfortunately, the combination of the Employment Retirement Income Security Act of 1974 (ERISA), the Age Discrimination in Employment Act of 1967 (ADEA), and the tax laws and regulations affecting pensions — all written without reference to one another — create a complex barrier to flexible arrangements that only the bravest of employers tries to conquer.

While ADEA prevents discrimination in employment for people above the age of 40, ERISA defines employee rights and employer obligations under various types of retirement plans. Employers do not have to offer plans, but if they do, they must satisfy specific requirements and employers may not arbitrarily reduce pension benefits. Insurance is also provided for defined benefit retirement plans offered by employers who have gone out of business or who are in a state of bankruptcy. Tax laws and regulations determine whether contributions to specific plans are deductible from taxable income and the conditions under which funds can be withdrawn from plans. They also prevent plans from discriminating against low-paid employees.

It is not so much that the problems created by the combination of laws are insurmountable. Rather, the sheer complexity of the laws and their many ambiguities create a justifiable fear of litigation. Even if an employer is brave enough to break through the barriers, there may not be any takers, because the incentives provided by defined benefit pension plans may make it foolish to work into one's 60s. Health insurance problems and the desire to integrate private pension plans with Social Security also limit the flexibility of employment arrangements. Ironically, the combination of legal and institutional barriers makes it very much easier to hire an older worker from outside a firm than it is to persuade a long-time employee to work longer. These problems will now be described in more detail.

Legal and Institutional Barriers

Defined Benefit Pension Plans

A typical defined benefit plan provides a pension determined by the worker's income in the last few years of work and by the number of years that the worker has been with the employer. It is the employer's responsibility to maintain funding to cover the promises made by such plans. A defined benefit plan often defines the normal retirement age as 65. However, it generally creates a powerful incentive to retire much earlier, because after a certain point, long-term employees find that the addition to the annual pension earned by working one year more does not compensate them for the fact that they will be receiving the pension one year less.

Penner, Perun, and Steuerle (2002) examined a number of public pension plans for Federal employees and teachers. Typically, the expected present value of the pension grows most rapidly between ages 51 and 55 for a worker who started at age 25 and between 56 and 60 for one starting at age 30. While the increase in the expected value of the pension is peaking, it is becoming most costly to the employer relative to wages and most rewarding to the employee. The employer, therefore, has an incentive to shed the employee and the employee may find it propitious to leave before the relative value of the pension begins to decline.

Defined benefit plans in the private sector often have the same characteristics as public plans, but few are now being started as the private sector is turning to defined contribution plans. A defined contribution plan is financed by employee contributions, often supplemented by employer contributions of cash or of equity in the employer's company. The employee usually has considerable discretion in investing these funds in either equity or bond funds or cash. Thus, defined contribution plans tend to be inherently more risky to the employee than are defined benefit plans in which benefits are determined by an explicit formula.

Defined contribution plans tend to cost the employer a similar amount relative to wages as an employee ages, and the pension benefit tends to accrue at a constant rate. Consequently, such plans do not create the same strong incentive to retire early as do typical defined benefit plans. Cash balance plans are technically considered to be defined benefit plans, although they have many of the characteristics of defined contribution plans. Cash balance plans are financed by contributions to a fund and eventual benefits are determined by the cumulated balance at the time of retirement. Such plans are called defined benefit plans, because the rate of return on the fund is specified by the employer. However, cash balance plans generally provide the same work incentives as defined contribution plans.

Companies shifting to cash benefit plans have often done so to save money and the plans have acquired a bad reputation among workers. As of late 2002, a moratorium is in effect against converting to cash balance plans. It is likely, however, that the moratorium will soon be lifted. Even a cost-neutral shift will tend to benefit younger workers more than older workers, because benefits are easier to move from job to job. Therefore, it is not easy to shift from a traditional defined benefit plan to a cash balance plan in an equitable manner. But the structure of cash balance plans and the associated work incentives are very appealing.

Health Benefits

An employer offering health insurance has an added incentive to shed older workers, because the cost of such insurance rises rapidly with age. When combined with the rising cost of defined benefit plans for workers in their 50s, the incentive to encourage early retirement becomes very powerful indeed. Unfortunately, the problem has been exacerbated by a law that requires private insurance to cover health costs before Medicare will pay. This only affects workers eligible for Medicare, that is workers 65 and older, but the cost of employing such workers could be lowered considerably if Medicare were made the first payer. The cost to the government would be modest, because so few now

work beyond age 64 and only a portion of those working are covered by private insurance.

ERISA, ADEA, and Tax Laws and Regulations Governing Pensions

These laws and regulations have the good intent of protecting workers against abrupt changes in pension plans and against discrimination based on age. They also prohibit plans from discriminating against lower-paid employees. However, the laws are incredibly complex individually, and in combination, they create a maze that is extremely difficult for employers and employees to navigate.

Suppose that an employer and employee wish to agree to a deal that would provide the employee a partial pension while continuing to work part-time. There are numerous restrictions on what is legally possible. In tax-favored plans, such as 401(k)s, distributions before 59½ would have a tax penalty applied (though profit-sharing plans can make penalty-free distributions before age 59½). In defined benefit plans, pension withdrawals are not allowed before the normal retirement age while the employee is still drawing pay. If the defined benefit depends on income in the last years of work, part-time work could dramatically reduce the benefit. Such rules usually cannot easily be changed under ERISA.

Since older workers often are paid more than the average worker in a firm, the new arrangement would also have to satisfy prohibitions on discriminating against low-paid employees. Most difficult of all, the deal could not violate the ADEA. That law was written vaguely and is only gradually being fleshed out by the courts. Employees may willingly agree to a special deal, but if they eventually become disgruntled, the employer must worry about litigation regarding age discrimination.

One approach is to hire a retiring employee as a consultant. However, the IRS then may be concerned that the consultant is, in fact, a regular employee. Another common approach has the employee separate from the firm for a time and then be rehired in a special category of employees with a special fringe package. Remarkably, the IRS has never provided precise guidance on what constitutes a real separation. Brave employers might define it as being as short as one day. Others may require as much as a year's separation.

In general, it is much safer to hire someone from the outside than to create a special deal for a long-time employee. It is also easier to offer special arrangements to a very limited number of employees. The key is whether the special arrangement is sufficiently widespread to be considered a benefit "plan." If it is, it becomes restricted by a myriad of rules.

ERISA does not apply to public employees and this has allowed much more flexibility in developing special arrangements in the public sector. Public employers are also less restricted by various IRS rules. State and local governments have developed Deferred Retirement Option Plans (DROP plans) in which employees are able to shift to part-time work for a stated period while drawing benefits from their pension plans. In a typical plan, new benefits are not accrued after the employee shifts to part-time and the pension is deposited in an account that earns interest. The deposit can be withdrawn in a lump sum when the employee fully retires. Some legal questions have arisen with regard to particular DROP plans, but for the most part they have functioned without legal challenge for over 20 years.

In 1998, the ADEA was amended to allow special phased retirement plans for academics. These have also functioned well and give universities considerable flexibility in creating phased retirement plans for professors.

Major advantages would accrue if ordinary employers and employees in the private sector were allowed to negotiate special arrangements similar to DROP plans and the phased retirement arrangements for academics. It would be necessary to amend ERISA, ADEA, and the tax law to provide employers a "safe harbor" against litigation and tax penalties if they developed specified phased retirement plans. The law would have to require full disclosure to employees of the implications of the new plans. There is a precedent in that all three laws were earlier amended to allow the offer of specified early retirement packages.

With the new law being drafted and debated, it would be useful to promulgate new regulations to clarify some of the ambiguities in existing law. In particular, the IRS should clarify how long employees must be separated before they can be rehired under a new employment arrangement.

The Role of Social Security

The median elderly household, ranked by income, receives considerably more income from Social Security than from private or civil service pensions. Therefore, private and civil service pension plans must take Social Security's benefits and rules into account. Most important, Social Security has probably been the dominant force in setting the cultural norm as to when it is appropriate to retire. Its so-called normal or full retirement age is now being increased as the result of reforms enacted in 1983. The increase is gradual – only two months per year starting with the cohort reaching age 62 in 2000. It will eventually reach 67 for those born after 1959. Not many private employers have been changing their plans in response to the increase in the normal retirement age.

As the normal retirement age increases, the actuarial reduction for early retirees will become more and more significant. Employers will eventually have to take this reduction into account, if early retirement is common among their employees.

There has been an important recent reform that has significantly changed the role of Social Security. Benefits used to be reduced and could be eliminated entirely for people aged 65 to 69 as their earned income increased. Now the "earnings test" has been eliminated for this age group and people can draw full benefits while continuing to work full or part-time. This should make phased retirement much more attractive after 64 and would make the type of pension delay involved in most DROP plans less painful. A stringent earnings test is still applied to beneficiaries aged 62 to 64.

Social Security is a pay-as-you-go system. That is to say, about 80 percent of the payroll tax paid by employers and employees is immediately used to pay benefits to retirees, survivors, and disabled individuals. Such a system's generosity is limited by the number of workers paying in, their earnings, their payroll tax burden, and by the number of retirees that they must finance. The future reduction in the growth of the labor force just as the retired population will burgeon means that the system is in trouble. There are about three workers for every beneficiary today. By 2030, there will only be two.

The system must be reformed. Private and civil service pension plans should be designed to take account of this reality, but there is great uncertainty about how reform will proceed. The political debate is cantankerous and misleading. Antireform demagogues frighten older people into believing that reform will be extremely painful, while young people, seeing no reform, do not believe that the system will last until they retire.

The reality of the situation is very different than that portrayed by the current debate. Even though the rate of growth of the labor force will slow, wages can be expected to rise continually because of productivity increases. Projections based on reasonable economic and demographic assumptions indicate that there will be sufficient growth in tax revenues using current tax rates to provide for an increase in average real benefits of about 9½ percent between 2000 and 2030 (United States Board of Trustees of the Federal Old-Age and Survivors Insurance and Disability Insurance Trust Funds, 2002). No one need worry that the elderly of the future will have a lower absolute living standard than the elderly living today, and younger workers need not worry about a complete collapse of the system.

The need for reform arises because current law promises average benefit increases much greater than 9½ percent between 2000 and 2030. It promises that initial benefits will keep up with average wages and that implies a real benefit increase of more than 30 percent.

It is the promise that replacement rates will remain constant that makes the system so expensive to maintain. Even that challenge would not be too demanding except that the rise in the future cost of Social Security will coincide with much greater increases in the cost of Medicare and Medicaid, if those programs are not reformed. Projections of the Congressional Budget Office (2002) indicate that Social Security, Medicare, and Medicaid will absorb 6 percentage points more of the GDP in 2030 than they do today. If the cost increases were to be financed entirely with tax increases, every Federal tax in the system would have to be increased by about one-third – a politically implausible result. Conversely, if the increased costs are financed by borrowing, the national debt will explode toward infinity – a mathematically implausible result.

Clearly, there will have to be reforms on the spending side and that will probably lower the So-

cial Security replacement rate below what is now promised. Serious analysts on both the right and the left of the political spectrum would like to mitigate the Social Security problem by reducing our reliance on the pay-as-you-go approach and moving toward a funded system where the financial health of Social Security depends on the rate of return to capital and not on the whims of demographics. However, the left and right disagree on how this should be done.

The left would like to do it through government action. General revenues would be transferred into the Social Security trust fund and the budget outside Social Security would be balanced, thus converting the trust fund surplus into real national saving. The right does not believe that politicians have the discipline to balance the budget outside Social Security and they prefer to fund part of the system through individual accounts. In the Bush approach, the individual accounts would be funded by diverting some payroll tax revenues from the traditional Social Security system. The diversion would, in turn, be financed by reductions in the growth of traditional benefits, but the benefit reduction would be gradual and general revenues would be needed to subsidize the system until the individual accounts built up enough to replace the cuts in traditional benefits.

In other words, both the left and right use general revenues to subsidize the system. This implies that benefits can be as generous as society desires and there is no absolute need for a reduction in the replacement rate. But general revenues have to be financed and that will be painful. Given the demographics and the fact that the traditional system starts with a deficit, some reduction in replacement rates will be difficult to avoid.

But until more political progress is made toward reform, it is difficult to say precisely what design changes are needed in private pensions in order to adapt. The design changes should take account of a possible reduction in the replacement rate provided by the government program. It should also be noted that risks faced by the retiree will increase as the private sector moves away from defined benefit and toward defined contribution approaches and Social Security possibly moves toward individual accounts.

However, most proposals for individual accounts

in this country and almost all individual account plans implemented around the world take considerable risk away from the individual investor and give it to the government. There is an enormous variety of approaches. At a minimum, an enhanced safety net is provided for investors who do very badly. A few countries guarantee a minimum rate of return on the individual account. Some American proposals make the rate of reduction of traditional benefits depend on the return to the individual account. In other words, if investments in the individual account do poorly, traditional benefits are not cut as much. That, of course, implies that costs to government rise if investment performance falters.

We have known that significant changes in Social Security will be necessary ever since birth rates plummeted in the 1960s. It is tragic that we have waited so long to act, because the necessary changes become ever more painful the longer reform is delayed. Recent events in Europe suggest that democracies have grave difficulty reforming a public retirement system until they face a budget crisis. Dramatic reforms have occurred as a result of crises in Sweden and Italy. Admittedly, the crisis in the latter was somewhat artificial in that it was caused by the Maastricht restraints on fiscal deficits necessitated by the move to the Euro. Let us hope that we do not have to await a crisis to provoke action. A really big budget crisis is unlikely before the early 2020s.

Recommendations

For Human Resource Professionals

As baby boomers retire in greater numbers, there will be growing shortages of experienced workers and specific skills. Human resource professionals must begin thinking about arrangements for partial retirement that would suit their firm and that could induce skilled and experienced workers to stay on the job longer. Currently, the details of such arrangements are constrained by the many laws and regulations described above. However, legislators are slowly becoming interested in the problem and may eventually make room for more flexible arrangements.

For full-time employees, it is necessary to consider gradually departing from defined benefit plans

that strongly encourage retirement at an early age. Plans must either be restructured to reduce the disincentive to remain employed, or the move toward cash balance and defined contribution plans must be continued. Employees may be subject to more risk as a result, but it is worth it to remove incentives for very early retirement and to reduce the cost of employing older workers.

I would stick with this recommendation even if Social Security evolves into something that has some of the characteristics of a defined contribution plan and so increases risks further. Employees will have to adapt to greater risk by saving more for retirement on their own and by planning for the possibility of working a bit longer.

In designing pension plans, employers will have to consider the possibility that the replacement rate under Social Security will be lowered below that implied by current law. Private plans do, however, tend to be slow in adjusting to Social Security reforms. Not many private plans have made any adjustment for the gradual increase in the full retirement age that has been scheduled since 1983. The increase implies that the replacement rate will gradually decline for an employee retiring at a specific age, such as 65.

For Legislators

ERISA, ADEA, and tax laws and regulations should be amended simultaneously to allow clearly described partial retirement arrangements, such as those now enjoyed by academics and many state and local employees. Such amendments would provide a "safe harbor" for employers that shields them from litigation. The law should, of course, require that employers provide employees with full information regarding the characteristics of new plans.

It would be useful for the IRS to issue regulations clarifying some of the ambiguities in current law. It would be particularly useful to precisely define what constitutes a real separation from a previous job.

Moreover, it would be extremely beneficial to amend Medicare law to make Medicare be the primary insurer for employees enjoying employer-provided health insurance. This would reduce the cost of employing people aged 65 and over.

It may seem politically implausible to hope for

an early resolution of the Social Security problem, but great benefit could come from quick action. Uncertainty regarding future benefits would be reduced and the benefit adjustments necessary to restore the financial viability of the system would be smaller and less abrupt.

It is important to add a funding component to today's pay-as-you-go system. I do not believe that government is disciplined enough to eschew using government funding for purposes other than Social Security, and therefore, I believe that some variant involving President Bush's individual account approach is appropriate. It is important to reemphasize that benefits can be whatever society wants them to be regardless of the approach to funding, and that there are numerous options for spreading risk between government and the individual in a system of individual accounts.

However, demographic realities suggest that a huge and growing burden will be imposed on the working population if replacement rates promised by current law are maintained. That implies that planners of private plans must consider the real possibility that Social Security replacement rates will be reduced. It should also be noted that any risk related to individual accounts that is absorbed by government is ultimately borne by individuals in the form of more uncertain future tax rates and benefits. Government risk sharing simply makes it less clear which individuals in which generations will absorb the cost if investments go bad.

Summary

As the baby boomers contemplate retirement, there are powerful arguments for redesigning defined benefit plans to reduce incentives for early retirement and for continuing the move toward defined contribution and cash balance plans that are more neutral toward the time of retirement. It is also important to reform private practices and public laws to allow for flexible work arrangements that might persuade people to work a bit longer. This will not be easy, because the permissible nature of such reforms is restricted by an array of complex and ambiguous laws and regulations that attempt to protect worker's rights. However, these barriers can be overcome by simultaneously amending ERISA, ADEA, and tax laws and regulations to protect employers from litigation if they offer specifically approved plans for partial retirement.

Designers of reforms will have to keep one eye on Social Security which is so important to the retirement income of most Americans. Unfortunately, there is enormous uncertainty how it might be reformed and when. The only certainty is that it is not now sustainable.

These private and public pension issues are more important than most Americans realize. The American psyche has not yet absorbed the size of the demographic shock that is about to hit us. The United States has never before experienced a stagnant labor force. When a stagnant labor force is combined with an exploding retired population, it is not clear how we shall cope. It is true that our aging problem is much less severe than that of Japan, Italy, or many other European countries, but it is even less clear how they will cope.

The author is grateful to the Alfred P. Sloan Foundation for financial assistance. The views expressed are those of the author and should not be attributed to the Urban Institute, its trustees, or its funders.

Chapter 15

Retirement Security in a Post-Enron Environment

Susan J. Stabile

One cannot discuss the aging of the American workforce without discussing pensions and the need to increase retirement income security, especially in light of the experience of plan participants in the wake of the bankruptcy of companies such as Enron Corporation. Although Americans are living longer, they still tend to retire by age 65. According to a report from the Congressional Research Service, the labor force participation rate for men age 65 and up is 17.7 percent, compared to 68.1 percent for men age 55-64 and 91.3 percent for men age 25-54. For women, the figures are even lower, with a labor force participation rate of 9.7 percent for women age 65 and up, compared to 53 percent for women age 55-64 and 76.4 percent for women age 25-54 (Congressional Research Service, 2002a). These findings are consistent with findings that workers are commencing receiving Social Security benefits at earlier ages. The average age for commencement of Social Security benefits has decreased from 68.7 years to 63.6 years from 1940 to 1965 (Forman, 1999). In 1995, almost 60 percent of workers chose to commence these benefits at age 62 (Moore, 2001). Longer life spans combined with continued retirement at or before age 65 means that whatever amounts workers have accumulated in pension benefits and personal savings (supplemented by Social Security) must last for a longer period of time.

In addition, the increasing life span in this country has been accompanied by a declining birth rate, with the result that the number of active employees in relation to retired employees has declined. For example, although in a healthy population pyramid the number of active workers exceeds the number of nonworkers, it is expected that by 2030 the state of California will have more persons over the age of 50 and under the age of 20 than persons between age 20 and 50 (Torres-Gil, 2002). Nationwide, it is expected that almost 20 percent of the population will be age 65 or older (Congressional Research Service, 2002b). This population shift puts more stress on the Social Security system. As Torres-Gil (2002) observes,

> [A]lthough Social Security is running big surpluses today and can cover the forty-five million disabled and retired persons now living in the United States, those surpluses will disappear and turn into annual deficits after 2038, when all of the baby boomers will have retired. Those future deficits . . . could require cutbacks in benefits, increases in payroll taxes, an increase in the eligibility age, or all of the above (p. 97).

Thus, the question of how to best promote retirement income security is a crucial one. How can we ensure that increasing numbers of retirees who are living longer have sufficient resources to finance their retirement in a manner that allows them to maintain a reasonable standard of living?

The problem with ensuring adequate retirement income security is not simply an individual problem for those retirees themselves. If employees retire with insufficient assets to support themselves during their retirement, the government will be forced to step in and meet their needs. Thus, in the final analysis, the public as a whole will bear the consequences, putting the blame for their suffering on employers.

This chapter discusses the effects of the shift from defined benefit plans to defined contribution plans as the primary means of providing retirement income to employees. It argues that the 401(k) plan, the form of defined contribution plan that has proliferated over the last quarter of a century, is too unreliable a vehicle to achieve the goal of retirement income security and suggests that employers consider steps to reduce the risks that employees retire with insufficient retirement income.

The Move to Defined Contribution Plans

In the 25 years since the passage of the Employee Retirement Income Security Act of 1974 (ERISA), the principal piece of federal legislation that regulates the pension plans of private employers, there has been a marked shift in how employers provide for the retirement security of their employees. At the time ERISA was enacted, defined benefit pension plans were the dominant means of providing pension benefits. In the traditional defined benefit plan, the employer promises to pay participants an annual pension benefit for life, in an amount determined by a preestablished formula that typically takes into account both compensation and years of service.

Today, however, defined contribution plans have replaced the traditional defined benefit plan as the primary retirement vehicle for a significant and increasing number of employees. Whereas in 1975, 72 percent of pension plan assets were held in defined benefit plans, by 1998, less than half of all pension plan assets were in defined benefit plans. More significantly in trend terms, in 1998, 83 percent of the total assets contributed to pension plans were contributed to defined contribution plans (Congressional Research Service, 2002a), which had 50.3 million participants, compared to 23 million participants in defined benefit plans (Congressional Research Service, 2002b). Specifically, 401(k) plans, a form of defined contribution plan in which participants direct the investment of their personal account balances, and in which the participant's pension benefit is determined solely by the value of the participant's account balance at retirement, have become the norm. For example, 401(k) plans account for 48 percent of active employees and 65 percent of new plan contributions (Employee Benefit Research Institute [EBRI], 2002b), with currently almost 40 million employees participating in such plans (EBRI, 2001a).

Many reasons have been proffered for this shift, including a perceived preference on the part of workers for defined contribution plans over defined benefit plans. The sustained bull market that preceded the last couple of years may have fueled that preference, by making defined contribution plans appear to be a guaranteed means of ensuring much higher benefits than those offered by defined benefit plans.

The shift to defined contribution plans responded to a very real need for pension portability. The traditional defined benefit pension plan typically calculates benefits based on a participant's final pay. That works well in a world where workers begin and end their careers with a single employer. It however works less well in the face of a mobile work force. The final pay plan seriously disadvantages employees who do not spend their entire careers with a single employer, since a disproportionately higher portion of an employee's total retirement benefit is earned during the last few years of employment. However, in attempting to address the mobility problem, the shift to defined contribution plans has created other problems.

The Danger of Reliance on 401(k) Plans to Provide Retirement Security

There are some fundamental problems with relying on 401(k) plans as the sole or primary means of providing pension benefits. The first problem is that in a 401(k) plan the decision whether to participate in the plan and the decision how much to contribute to the plan are made by the employee. In contrast to a defined benefit plan, in which eligible employees are automatically enrolled as plan participants, in most 401(k) plans employees need to make the choice. Not only do many workers not participate at all in their employer's 401(k) plan – participation rates vary between 50 and 90 percent – but many do not contribute the maximum amount permitted by the plan (Stabile, 2002). Older workers tend to contribute a higher percentage of their income to plans than younger workers (EBRI, 2001b; 2000b). The problem, of course, is that dollars contributed later in one's working year have less years to accumulate earnings than contributions made earlier.

A second major problem is that 401(k) pension plans place investment risk squarely on the shoulders of plan participants. At the same time, investment decisions are made, not by professional asset managers subject to fiduciary standards of prudence, loyalty and diversification (as in defined benefit plans), but by participants themselves. Not only are participants subject to no fiduciary standards, but also a substantial number of participants are financially illiterate. They lack knowledge and understanding of financial concepts and common financial instruments and their general knowledge of retirement planning and savings issues is inadequate. Surveys have found that participants lack knowledge of their plan's investment options and, indeed, knowledge of how their own plan accounts are allocated among the plan's options (Stabile, 2002).

This is an issue particularly for women, whose life expectancy has increased even more than that of men. Whereas the average life expectancy in the year 2000 for men was 74, for women, it was 80 (Centers for Disease Control and Prevention, 2001a). Thus, women have even greater retirement income than men, yet their financial and investment knowledge tends to be less sophisticated than that of men. While the gap between men and women's pension plans has decreased slightly for women between the ages of 45 and 53, it has widened for all other age groups (EBRI, 2000b).

The experience of the last several years has underscored the seriousness of both of these problems, highlighting the dangers of overreliance on a 401(k) plan structure. To some extent, one may suggest these problems are self-inflicted, in the sense that many employees choose not to participate in a 401(k) plan and others choose to contribute too little. However, asking low-income employees to choose between very real current consumption needs and providing for their future needs is asking a lot. Moreover, problems of poor investment decisions are often not an issue of volition, but rather of ability. More importantly, the effects of those choices are not felt by employees alone, but have spillover effects that make the problem one for society as a whole – and therefore, for employers.

Overinvestments in Employer Securities

It has become very common for 401(k) plans of large public companies to include an employer security stock fund, thus allowing plan participants to invest their retirement assets in company stock. More than half of all 401(k) plans, covering almost 75 percent of all 401(k) plan participants, include an employer security stock fund.

Employees take advantage of the ability to invest 401(k) plans in company stock. Those participating in plans that have an employer security stock fund invest 30 to 40 percent of their account balances into that fund. Approximately one in four 401(k) plans has more than 50 percent of its assets in employer securities and in many companies the percentage of assets devoted to company stock exceeds 75 percent (Francis, 2001).

The experience with Enron provides a graphic illustration of the dangers of such heavy accumulations of employer stock in 401(k) plan accounts. During the late 1990s, the company experienced tremendous growth and by 2000, it was the darling of the business community, with an annual revenue approaching $100 billion. In that year, it was the seventh largest company in revenue terms, and its stock reached a peak of $90 per share. In February 2001, employees were promised by the new CEO that Enron stock would be trading at $120 per share by year-end.

Employees responded enthusiastically to the prospects of enormous growth of their retirement savings. By the end of 2000, more than 60 percent of the company's 401(k) plan assets – approximately $1.3 billion - were invested in Enron stock. As employees later testified, the culture at Enron was one of investing in company stock.

As we all know by now, however, the ending of this story was anything but a happy one. On December 2, 2001, Enron Corporation filed for bankruptcy. It did so after taking a third-quarter loss of $618 million and a reduction in shareholder equity of $1.2 billion and then disclosing that its profits for each of the previous four years had been vastly overstated. The effect on plan participants was devastating. Many lost between 70 and 90 percent of their retirement funds.

Enron presents a particularly horrific illustration of the problem of overconcentration of 401(k) plan assets in company stock because it was accompanied by tales of corporate mismanagement and of corporate officers and directors selling off their own shares of company stock even while they told employees the stock was a good investment. However, it is by no means an isolated instance of 401(k) plan loss. Between 1999 and 2001, the stock of Lucent Technologies fell approximately 90 percent, which caused devastating losses to employees, many of whom had 70 or 80 percent of their plan account balances invested in company stock. When Polaroid Corporation filed for bankruptcy in October 2001, almost 40 percent of the company's 401(k) plan was invested in company stock, resulting in enormous losses to plan participants. Newspaper reports over the last year have highlighted plan losses resulting from the fall of companies like Global Crossing and WorldCom.

As a general matter, investment advisors advocate putting no more than 5 to 10 percent of assets in the stock of a single company. With respect to retirement funds, some would argue that no 401(k) plan assets should be invested in employer securities because one's human capital is already invested in that one company. Despite these general rules of thumb, and in spite of the extensive publicity surrounding the fall of companies like Enron, employees continue to invest large proportions of their 401(k) plan assets in company stock. In many cases, this is because of employees' own feelings of loyalty to their employers or an overly optimistic view of their employers' financial prospects. Other times, it is due to employer pressure or overaggressive encouragements to employees about the expected future value of company stock. However, whatever the cause, overinvestment in company stock should be a cause of significant concern, particularly because older workers tend to invest more heavily in company stock than do younger workers (VanDerhei & Holden, 2001). In fact, one-third of employees over the age of 60 have 75 percent or more of their 401(k) funds invested in employer securities ("Our Opinions," 2002).

Defined contribution plans proceed under the assumption that funds contributed to the plan will grow, albeit at higher or lower rates depending on investment returns. Any Enron employee would be willing to testify as to the folly of that assumption.

Effects of Market Downturns

Many of the employees who have grown to love the 401(k) plan structure, did so in the belief that the market moves in only one direction. As the experience of the last two years has demonstrated, and as investment professionals always knew, that is not the case.

Apart from the negative effect on 401(k) account balances of declining stock prices, another adverse consequence is the effect on plan participation and contribution levels. According to recent survey findings, about 6 percent fewer employees participated in 401(k) plans in 2002 than in prior years and almost 3 percent stopped contributing to plans altogether (Coombes, 2002). The survey found that employees fear that contributing to a 401(k) plan means losing money rather than saving for retirement. Thus, a period of sustained market decline will mean even less savings for retirement.

For all of the reasons discussed, the assumption that 401(k) plans generate steady growth until retirement is a flawed one. Not only that, but the supposed advantage of defined contribution plans over defined benefit plans in the face of a mobile work force is exaggerated. The superiority of a defined contribution plan structure for employees who switch jobs assumes that each time a worker changes employment, the worker's account balance remains with the former employer or is rolled over to a new plan. In fact, however, many participants fail to do either. A study performed by Hewitt Associates (1999a) found that 68 percent of 401(k) plan participants who switch jobs between the ages of 20 and 59 take cash distributions from their plans. This early cash out has a tremendously adverse effect on account balances of such employees, particularly employees at the low end of the compensation range. Although there is empirical evidence to suggest that older workers who switch jobs are more likely to rollover than are younger employees (EBRI, 2000a; National Bureau of Economic Research, 1999), the damage in terms of years of lost savings has already be done by that point.

The bottom line is that the 401(k) account balances of many employees are woefully inadequate. Although half of all employees between the ages of 55 and 64 owned at least one retirement account in 2000, the median value of those accounts was $33,000 (Congressional Research Service, 2002b). When you add to that the value of retirement accounts owned by members of the families of those workers, the median value rises to $56,000, an amount that would purchase a joint-and-survivor annuity of $332 per month – hardly a princely sum from one of the major components of retirement income. These are disturbingly low figures for workers with not many more years to contribute to plans prior to retirement and do not represent amounts sufficient to guarantee a reasonable standard of living in retirement, especially when one considers that personal savings rates outside of pension plans have been falling. Given longer life expectancies, the gap between what workers save and what they will need during their retirement is potentially very large. This is likely to put a severe strain on social welfare programs. The strain is especially likely to be severe because of the need to provide for the needs of workers without any pension coverage. The sober reality is that almost 41 million workers between the ages of 25 and 64 work for companies that offer no retirement plan at all and 12 million more are not eligible to participate in plans offered by the companies for which they work (Congressional Research Service, 2002b).

Recommendations

I return to the question which forms the basis of this chapter: How can we ensure that increasing number of retirees who are living longer have sufficient resources to finance their retirement in a manner that allows them to maintain a reasonable standard of living?

Some suggest the answer is to find ways to encourage workers to work for longer periods of time. This may be appealing to some and certainly the regulatory system should not be such as to discourage those who would wish to work longer from doing so. However, from a policy prospective, the notion that those who have labored throughout their lifetimes should be forced by economic circumstances to work for longer periods rather than having the retirement they spent their working lives believing they would have is not an appealing one. Most developed countries have a concept of forced retirement; the United States is one of the only developed nations to expect its elderly to work for pay.

Moreover, from an employer's standpoint, the prospect of employees of retirement age remaining in the workforce for the sole reason that they lack the financial wherewithal to retire is similarly undesirable. The result is retention of less motivated employees, a loss of job opportunities for new employees, and limited prospects for advancement of other employees. While there may be some older workers an employer is desirous of retaining, that objective can be better accomplished through individual negotiation.

This is an important point because it means that it is in the best interest of employers to take steps to help assure that employees have sufficient means to support themselves in retirement. If any added incentive is needed for employers to take a serious look at how well their retirement plans are functioning, the prospect of an impending social welfare crisis may lead the government to step in and regulate in ways that are more restrictive than businesses would like to see. It thus makes sense for companies to act on their own now to better ensure the needs of their workers, before the government decides to act.

A defined benefit plan structure is arguably the surest way to guarantee adequate retirement security. To meet the needs of today's mobile workforce, however, benefits must be portable, making a return to the traditional defined benefit plan less than optimal. A defined benefit plan that does provide for portability is the cash balance plan, a hybrid form of plan in which a retirement benefit is guaranteed, based on an account balance that grows by a specified amount. In a typical cash balance plan, each participant has an account, which is credited with an annual contribution based on salary as well as with an interest credit. Employers who have not discussed a cash balance structure with their advisers should consider whether it is a structure that would work for them. One cautionary note: care must be taken when converting an existing defined benefit plan to a cash balance structure to ensure that older workers are not adversely affected. Many companies who have converted to a cash balance structure have included grandfathering provisions to ensure that the conversion does not have an adverse impact on the pensions promised to older workers.

Those employers who determine to continue providing benefits through a defined contribution plan structure should examine their plans to determine whether changes are desirable to better ensure adequate retirement security. Let me offer several suggestions for consideration.

First, 401(k) plan participants currently make plan investment decisions on their own and subject to no standards. Although the law does not require employers to provide any education or advice to plan participants, employers who do not currently provide any education should consider doing so. Fear of fiduciary liability for participant investment choices should not be a deterrent, since the Department of Labor's Interpretive Bulletin on this subject provides guidance to employers as to the types of investment-related educational information employers may offer to participants without being considered to be giving investment advice (United States Department of Labor, 1999). Although there are some participant biases that are not likely to be amenable to change through education, a number of participants will benefit from the effort. Still, general investment information and asset allocation models are insufficient; what many participants need is advice regarding how to best invest their assets in a way to promote meaningful account growth. Thus, employers should be aware that Congress is currently considering legislation that would substantially broaden their ability to provide investment advice to participants and should track the progress of that legislation.

Second, employers should consider taking direct action regarding heavy participant accumulations of employer securities. Because participants often invest heavily in employer stock because of loyalty to their employer and because of other psychological biases that have little to do with lack of investment sophistication, no amount of advice or education about the value of diversification is likely to have a significant affect on 401(k) plan employer stock concentrations.

As I have testified during congressional hearings, I believe Congress should act to limit the percentage of a participant's account balance that can be invested in employer securities. Having decided to grant pensions tax-favored status in order to achieve the goal of pension security, Congress is justified in taking steps to prevent participants in 401(k) plans from acting contrary to that goal. However, Congress is not likely to take such a step, viewing it a limitation on an individuals' freedom of choice, despite the fact that the pension system in this country is paternalistic at its core. After all, the reason for giving pension savings a tax-favored status is precisely that we do not believe individuals will save sufficiently for their own retirement.

Nonetheless, employers should recognize the dangers of allowing participants to invest 80 to 90 percent of their retirement savings in the stock of a single company. Indeed, many have. In the wake of all of the publicity surrounding the fall of Enron, Global Crossing, WorldCom and others – including widespread publicity about the effect of such falls on employees' 401(k) plan account balances – some employers have moved to impose limits on the amount participants can invest in company stock through the employer's 401(k) plan. Those that have not should consider doing so, recognizing that there are other means by which employers can provide incentives for employees and ensure their loyalty.

A third suggestion is aimed not only at participant investment decisions but also at participation and contribution levels. Although most 401(k) plans require that employees affirmatively elect to participate in the plan and make an affirmative election regarding contribution levels and investment decisions, some employers have opted for automatic enrollment of participants in plans. Interestingly, there are studies finding that the effect of automatic enrollment is to increase plan participation. In the case of one large U.S. company that switched to automatic enrollment, 86 percent of employees hired after automatic enrollment participated in the plan, compared to a 72 percent participation rate prior to the plan change (Madrian & Shea, 2001). These findings suggest that participation rates could be increased if employers shifted to automatic enrollment, thus solving one of the basic problems with the 401(k) plan structure.

Automatic enrollment also helps with investment decisions. Employers could establish a default investment allocation for participants selected by a professional asset manager, giving employees the ability to affirmatively elect to modify the default allocation. Whether through inertia or otherwise, many plan participations will stick with the professionally selected investment decisions, representing an improvement over decisions made by most plan participants. Given the potential of automatic enrollment to improve both participation levels and investment decisions, those employers who have not investigated the possibility of switching their plans to that structure should do so.

Employers should not sit passively. Large numbers of employees with 401(k) account balances that will not provide adequate retirement security not only harms those employees. Not only will the inability of such employees to retire have potentially adverse effects on the rest of an employer's workforce, but also fears about an impending social crisis may result in government action far more intrusive than any steps an employer may adopt on its own.

None of this is to suggest that the law does not need to change to better accommodate the needs of our aging workforce and a population with an increasing life span. It is important for policymakers to focus on a more flexible approach to retirement, for example, considering options for partial retirement, and more generally on ways to improve the lives of the aging. Nonetheless, the steps I have suggested here offer some means for employers to improve the retirement security of their workers, which is an important step in the right direction.

Summary

The pension landscape has changed drastically in the last 25 years. Whereas most employers once promised employees an annual pension based on a predetermined formula that took both compensation and years of service into consideration, most employees today are offered a 401(k) plan as their primary means of saving for retirement. However, because of limitations on participants' ability to invest their own pension assets and other weaknesses, the 401(k) plan is an unreliable vehicle to achieve the goal of retirement income security. As this chapter has discussed, overreliance on 401(k) plans is dangerous. Employers would be wise to consider to taking steps to reduce the risk that employees will approach retirement age with insufficient retirement income.

Synthesis

Pensions and Older Workers

The picture that emerges from Chapters 14 and 15 is rather bleak for those organizations that offer defined benefit pension plans and would like their workers to remain employed upon becoming eligible for retirement. Essentially, there are four options: delaying retirement; partial retirement; re-hiring workers as consultants upon retirement; and changing pension plans.

1. Delaying retirement: This is not really an option because defined benefit plans provide a powerful financial incentive for employees to retire early, as the limited added value to the pension does not weigh up against the fact that they will be receiving the benefits over a shorter period of time. Moreover, employers are reluctant to pursue this because these plans are relatively expensive to employers once workers reach their 50s. When the rising costs of health care are also taken into consideration, employers are faced with a compelling incentive to induce retirement.

2. Partial retirement: Special arrangements to allow for partial retirement are hardly more attractive. These deals must satisfy ADEA and other laws, such as those prohibiting discrimination against lower-paid employees. Since these laws are often ambiguous, employers are at increased risk for litigation. Moreover, any such deal can only be available for a limited number of workers as otherwise the arrangement could be considered a benefit plan.

3. Consulting: Hiring a retiree as a consultant is an option, provided there has been a real separation between the time of retirement and the time of rehiring. Since it is insufficiently clear what constitutes a real separation, the IRS may consider the consultant a regular employee, which would have adverse consequences for both the employer and the retiree.

4. Changing pension plans: This is a cumbersome process because of the extent to which these plans are protected by ERISA and ADEA. Therefore, they must be carried out carefully and systematically, and are unlikely to have significant effect in the short term. To make the picture complete, the Social Security system is not sustainable in the long run and will have to be reformed. How this reform will take place in the future will have a significant impact on pension plans.

Still, both Chapters 14 and 15 identify a shift away from defined benefit plans toward defined contribution plans. These plans remove some of the most powerful incentives to retire and they also address the additional drawback of pension portability. However, as Chapter 15 demonstrates, defined contribution plans shift the risk and responsibility for retirement income from the employer to the employee. This has potentially disastrous consequences that may well end up dominating the political agenda. First, participation rates and levels among eligible workers have dropped. Second, these workers have a tendency to overinvest in their employer's stock. Enron is of course a vivid example of what can happen. Third, the portability of defined contribution plans – a distinct advantage over defined benefit plans – appears to lead in practice to workers cashing out their balances rather than rolling them over into new accounts. When we add to this mix the fifty-plus million workers who are not eligible for pension plans at all and the recent increases in life expectancy, it becomes clear that dramatic change will be needed in the future.

ISSUE 7

REDEFINING RETIREMENT

Chapter 16

New Models for Post-Retirement Employment

Scott A. Bass

Retirement as We Have Come to Know It

Since the end of the Great Depression nearly 70 years ago and the advent of Social Security in America, retirement has been pegged at the age of 65. While many people leave work at younger ages, 65 has been the age most commonly associated with full-blown exit from the labor force. The selection of 65 as the age of retirement was determined back in 1935 as a reasonable benchmark to provide respite with economic security after many years in the workforce. However, it may no longer fully serve its intended purpose.

For most laborers in the early to mid-20th century, the ravages of illness, disability, and poor general health were sufficient conditions to drive older people from the workplace. During that time, much of the labor was physical and demanding, and workers were often exposed to harmful or hazardous environmental conditions. In addition to the nature of work in industrialized America, other factors such as the lack of a public health system, lack of regular medical and dental care, poor sanitary conditions, low standards of living, poor dietary habits, and tobacco use for men or women born in the 1860s or 1870s helped to chisel the aging individual in ways that are quite different today.

While numerous occupations were not included in the original Social Security Act, resulting in many individuals not being eligible for Social Security, by 1974 nearly all Americans who had worked a sufficient number of quarters and had paid into the system were eligible for Social Security (Achenbaum, 1994). Within one generation, the concept of retirement shifted from being an aspiration to that of being perceived as a right. Not only did retirement become a right that afforded older people an opportunity to live their later years with basic economic security free of the obligations of work, but it became part of the societal expecta-

tions. The introduction of Social Security freed many people who no longer could work, or wanted to stop working, from that obligation and moved thousands of older people out of the clutches of destitution and poverty.

No longer an option limited to a fortunate, financially independent few, retirement became a universal social expectation: families expect their elders to retire, company executives plan on waves of retirements, and younger workers count on the systematic vacating of positions in order to move up the career ladder.

The establishment of retirement as part of the normal life course became as common as the expectation of going to school or learning to drive. Massive exits from the workforce by people age 65 and older caused a decline in the workforce so steady and so dramatic that few could have anticipated the kind of cultural shift that ensued. According to data from the U.S. Department of Labor's Bureau of Labor Statistics (United States Senate Special Committee on Aging, AARP, the Federal Council on Aging, & the United States Administration on Aging, 1991), from 1950 (the rebuilding of the domestic economy just after World War II) to 1985, the labor force participation rate for men age 55 to 64 dropped from 86.9 percent to 67.9 percent, near to where it is today. During the same period, the labor force participation rate for men age 65 and older dropped from 45.8 percent down to 15.8 percent around where it hovers today. In the 10-year period from 1950 to 1960, the labor force participation rate for men age 65 and older dropped from 45.8 percent to 39.6 percent; in the next decade it fell another 11.5 percent (United States Senate Special Committee on Aging et al., 1991). For a man born in 1885, the likelihood of working until the mid-to-late 60s was just under one out of every two. For a man born in 1920 who lived through the Great Depression, the likelihood of working beyond his mid-to-late 60s dropped to just below one out of every six.

The story for women is more complex in that women were historically less prevalent than men in the labor force. While women age 55 to 64 have demonstrated relatively steady labor force participation from 1950 to now, there has been some decline over time in the labor force participation of women age 65 and older. In 1950, 26.7 percent of women age 65 and older were in the labor force. This dropped in 1985 to its lowest point where only 10.8 percent of women age 65 and older were active in the labor force (United States Senate Special Committee on Aging et al., 1991). As larger cohorts of these working women age, indications are that they are likely to participate in the labor force in a pattern more akin to that of older men. Further, the data indicate that the decline in labor force participation for men stemmed in the mid-1980s and that it will remain stable or show some very modest increase in the near future (Quinn, 1999).

From the vantage point of social and cultural change, this type of shift in older adult working behavior must be viewed as dramatic. In this case, the advent of Social Security and the desire to extricate oneself from the world of paid work were in harmony. Riley, Kahn, and Foner (1994) have argued that there is constant interplay and interaction between individual choice and societal structures. In the case of retirement, there was a genuine individual need for relief from a lifetime of hard work. The interplay between societal structures afforded the development of pension and Social Security programs to provide some measure of economic security. With the development of these new structures, not only was retirement an option, it became an expectation for the older worker and the individuals around them. These social structures and norms exerted pressures on the individual to conform and to behave in certain anticipated ways. Paradoxically, neither individuals nor social structures remain static. Over time, each influences the other, forcing a constant process of change and adjustment.

Riley and Riley (1994) point out that social structures often lag behind the desires of individuals. In the case of older people, the retirement expectations developed for past generations may be insufficient for, and insensitive to, the desires,

needs, and capacities of today's and tomorrow's elderly. We know that older people are living longer and are healthier than ever before. While most elect to retire before age 65, there is growing recognition that 65-year-olds on average are likely to live another 18 years or more (Federal Interagency Forum on Aging Related Statistics, 2000) in part due to quality public medical and dental care. Moreover, the nature of work has shifted from an industrial base to that of a service economy (Hinterlong, Morrow-Howell, & Sherraden, 2001), leading to safer, better work environments. For many older Americans, if not most, these later years will be quality years, both intellectually and physically.

Currently, the role that older people play in retirement has been left open. For some, it has been left blank – what Rosow (1976) calls a "roleless role." That is, the social structure of retirement has cut the older person off from the responsibilities, needs, and social exchanges associated with employment. For them, finding other structures to replace those roles associated with employment has proven to be difficult. So, we ask, do we have a case of structural lag on our hands? Does the life path envisioned for previous generations – who studied in their youth, worked jobs throughout their early and middle adult years, and retired in their later adult years – make sense for a healthy baby boom generation, born between 1946 and 1964, in an advanced economy?

Structural Lag

To answer these questions, we can look at the following factors: the desire of older workers to remain working or return to work; changes in perspectives on older workers; employment opportunities for older workers; and career services for older workers.

Older Workers' Desire to Work

Evidence indicates that among current retirees there is a significant constituency interested in "unretiring" (Achenbaum & Morrison, 1993). At least three sources of data address this issue. The first was drawn from a national stratified random sample of 2,999 noninstitutionalized older Americans aged 55 and older conducted by Louis Harris and Associates in 1991, known as the Common-wealth Fund Productive Aging Survey (Bass, 1995a). It found that a relatively small percentage, but a large number of older retired people, were eager to return to work. Barth, McNaught, and Rizzi (1995) estimated that of those 52.4 million individuals age 55 and older, 14.3 million wanted to remain in the workforce, a much larger 38.1 million were not working, and 26.4 million people did not want to work again (6.3 million are not able to work due to some disability). Nevertheless, 8 percent of those age 55 and older, or 5.4 million Americans, indicated that they were willing and able to work. These were not just the youngest of the retirees: of these 5.4 million people, 2 million (37 percent) were age 55 to 64, 2.3 million (43 percent) were age 65 to 74, and 1.1 million (20 percent) were age 75 and older. The fact that this many retirees were considering reentering the workforce as early as 1991 suggests that the institution of retirement, identified by Riley and Riley as lagging behind the preferences and capabilities of older people, is beginning to show signs of its lack of universal appeal.

The second source of data relevant to the discussion of current and future retirees is the National Institute on Aging's Health and Retirement Survey (HRS). According to the results from a 1998 longitudinal study of older Americans, 73 percent of the respondents age 51 to 61 indicated that after they retired from their career job, they "would like to continue some work" (AARP Public Policy Institute, 1998). Paralleling this finding, and representing a third data source, is a national survey of baby boomers conducted in 1997 by the AARP Research Group called the Retirement Confidence Survey. Although most baby boomers indicated that they "plan to retire before the age 65, a large majority of boomers expects to continue working at least on a part-time basis after retirement" (AARP Public Policy Institute, 1998). In fact, more than 75 percent of those born between 1956 and 1964 indicated that they would work at least part-time after retirement and 72 percent of those born between 1946 and 1955 indicated the same. This shows that baby boomers have a very different approach to retirement than previous generations did.

Of course, while these are important findings, the eventual decision to retire or continue working depends on more than just a desire to continue working. Older workers face peer, family, and cultural pressures, and they may also be given substantial economic incentives to retire. Of course, there are those older individuals who do not have sufficient income from Social Security to meet their lifestyle needs. For these individuals, work is not merely a choice; it is a necessity.

Sometimes, these incentives are simply too good an opportunity to pass up. For example, to encourage early retirement as a state savings strategy in 2002, Massachusetts offered professors age 55 or older in public universities some combination of an additional five years of service or calculating their benefits based on someone five years their senior. For a 57 year-old professor with 30 years service, the pension would be increased from 51 percent of the most recent salary to 66 percent. In addition, the university added a one-time cash bonus of 1.65 percent of the current annual salary for each year of work. A professor earning $75,000 per year would receive an additional lump sum award of over $37,000 (Fogg, 2002).

Employers have the option to create incentives for retirement even if the individual is fully capable or talented at carrying out job responsibilities. Such incentive plans are blunt tools, often causing employers to lose some excellent workers. After all, as we consider the performance and capability of older workers, significant variability exists across the age span, causing age to be a factor but not the salient predictor (Sterns & Sterns, 1995a).

The choice to retire may be an individual one, but it is strongly influenced by economic incentives combined with considerations of pension, savings, health, work satisfaction, health insurance, and family obligations. Barth et al. (1995) report that about half of the older workers indicating a desire to return to work do so because of the social exchange and stimulation afforded by the workplace. For the other half, income is the main reason.

Changing Perspectives

So, if surveys reveal that there is a viable and interested supply of older workers, will there be a demand? If there is interest in returning to work or remaining at the workplace beyond traditional retirement years, do employers want to hire and retain older workers?

Much has changed regarding employer attitudes toward older workers and the tales of employment discrimination against them. A 1999 survey of 774 human resource directors by Harris Interactive revealed rather widely held positive views of older workers (those aged 55 or older) compared to younger workers. Human resource directors interviewed in the study indicated that in their opinion older workers have less turnover, are more committed, are more reliable, are able to acquire new skills, and are more motivated than their younger counterparts (Taylor, 2000). In general, the stereotypical attitudes that viewed older workers as deadwood have been replaced by an attitude that views them as meaningful assets. This is not to say that older workers are viewed favorably by all human resource directors, but it does show that they have recognized that many older workers bring a set of work habits and experiences that can benefit the workplace. It appears that in the case of a job opening, an older worker would have a real chance of landing the position. The question is, will there be positions available?

Employment Opportunities

The job market is responsive to the economy. In lean economic times, older workers are often the first to be let go and the last to be rehired. In a flush economy, these surplus workers become needed. A Hudson Institute report, *Workforce 2020*, identifies selected skilled-labor shortages as we look to the future, placing older workers with strong technical skills in great demand (Judy & D'Amico, 1997). Growth in the economy, even with greater productivity increases, will result in increased employment in selected industries.

Demands for an expanded workforce can be met through young people, immigrants, or special populations. Demographics over the next 20 years, however, point to a smaller number of younger workers entering the labor force (Judy & D'Amico, 1997; Zinke & Tattershall, 2000). Moreover, the nation has demonstrated a reluctance to expand the number of immigrants, and it has already attracted large numbers of women into the labor force. Based on the responses of human resource directors cited earlier, the only untapped pool of highly skilled labor is that of older workers. The combination of projected skilled-labor shortages with an untapped labor pool suggests that there will indeed be many employment opportunities for older workers who are willing to be retained, retrained, or attracted back to the workforce.

Career Services

When we think of careers for young people, we have a panoply of programs, thousands of educational institutions, hundreds of internships, and many different training activities that provide bridges to a desired area of interest. For the best and brightest, summer programs exist in federal laboratories, university research centers, the private sector, and government agencies that offer young people an opportunity to become acclimated to a profession or field of study. Colleges and universities market their baccalaureate degree programs to young people. Often these programs have work-study opportunities in industry, internships off-campus, and career counseling designed to assist tomorrow's educated workforce with job options. In spite of an aging undergraduate population – average age is around 25, because many take time off from college to work, travel, or begin a family (Eurich, 1990) – the emphasis of these institutions remains on younger, traditional students (whereas a nontraditional student is considered someone age 25 or older).

Corporations frequently offer their own training programs. In fact, the American Society for Training and Development estimates that 14 million workers are enrolled in workforce training programs, more than are enrolled in all the baccalaureate programs in America. The vast majority of those enrolled in corporate training programs are age 25-45 (Eurich, 1990). These workers are given opportunities to receive specialized training, career counseling, and advising to move effectively into the labor market and rise in the sector of their choice.

The support system for younger people, defined as 45 or younger, is so common and so pervasive that we do not even give it much thought. Career planning, career counseling, career placement, and career training are extensive in American institutions. The concept has reached down to the elementary school level where young people are given career exposure and to the high school level where, in addition to traditional work-study programs, there are internship programs in agencies, government offices, and companies for some of the schools' most promising students. More recently, colleges and universities have developed specialized programs for executives and midcareer professionals who are seeking to enhance their knowledge or hone new skills.

Clearly, there is a career ladder (or multiple ladders) that depends on academic success and begins in elementary school and stretches to middle age. But what about career services for people beyond middle age? For an older worker or an older person wanting to return to work, these structures are remarkably silent and distant.

What happens when a person reaches the age of 60, 65, 70, or older and seeks career mobility? Where are the career counseling centers? What internship programs exist to provide career mobility? What prestigious fellowship programs exist like those for early or midcareer aspirants? What organizational structures specialize in training and retooling mature workers, akin to those that compete for the dollars provided by younger customers? Indeed, there are a few federal programs that seek to assist displaced homemakers and unemployed older workers, but where is the rung of the ladder for the majority of ordinary, able-bodied people? If the research evidence shows that older people are capable of doing complex, intellectually demanding work just as well as those who are younger, where is the human resource industry to support this capability?

Given older Americans' desire to work beyond retirement age, their increased popularity among employers, and the projected increase in employment opportunities, the absence of career services targeted specifically toward this population leads to the conclusion that there is a structural lag between our institutional services and programs and the aging population in America.

New Models

If we accept the notion that structures often lag behind the desires of the population, we should expect the opening of new kinds of organizations and the expansion of existing organizations to service an aging workforce. These innovative and new organizations will begin to build the rungs on the ladder so that able, elderly people will, in all likelihood, have support systems and organizational structures to support their career interests far beyond age 55.

One could imagine career programs, like the one in gerontology at the University of Massachusetts Boston, designed for those age 60 and older to provide careers in the human services field or social welfare causes (Morris & Bass, 1986). Career programs for older individuals interested in monitoring the environment, in helping infants and children, in teaching in the public school classroom, or in a myriad of capacities dictated by the market place and public need, are easily envisioned. Experienced older workers can be an enormous asset, but they will need support and training to make full use of their potential.

Certainly there are those older individuals who will cross the invisible age barriers and enter college, serve in the Peace Corps, or run for elected office. But for most older people, the array of career options shrinks rather than expands after middle age. Organizational structures that help individuals find new opportunities and challenges later in life are essential to opening the doors to a floodgate of talent. While these structures have largely not been established as yet, they will be.

Imagine the establishment of the equivalent of a Rhodes Scholarship for older people where they could spend a year abroad, the equivalent of a Guggenheim for the older person who now is ready to pen the book he or she always wanted to write, or a corporate internship for those 65 and older seeking to spend six months or a year in an allied but different industry or company. Philanthropists and foundations looking for new niches will be attracted to this highly visible population that can provide good public relations. Through these efforts, we will begin building additional rungs on the career ladder for older people.

While little opportunity currently exists in the United States that is comparable to what is available for younger people, new structures are emerging here and elsewhere. For example, the popularity and rapid growth of Elderhostel dramatize the kind of structure that did not exist 30 years ago, but now serves thousands of older people. Elderhostel offers education and travel for personal enrichment and has stayed away from career-related education. Nevertheless, it is a widely acclaimed institution that has grown quickly and serves a specific need among older people. It would not be too difficult to think of an "Elderopportunity" organization that would provide older people with training and career placements.

Japan, a country that values work much like the United States, has a rapidly aging population. The Japanese have established a number of organizational structures to assist older people with jobs after traditional retirement. One such program, involving over 642,000 older retired Japanese, is the Silver Human Resource Centers (SHRC) of Japan. This program began in 1974 as a single center dedicated to helping older Japanese with paid work after mandatory retirement. The centers provide service through contracts with the government or private sector. These services are provided by older people who receive an hourly wage. The centers receive some overhead, manage the placement of workers, and pay them an hourly wage. According to the website of the National SHRC Association (www.sjc.ne.jp/zsk dir/toukei/toukei.html), there were 1,577 SHRCs in Japan by Fiscal Year 2000.

The SHRC is quite different from any program in the United States and more closely resembles a sheltered workshop than a senior center. SHRCs are well-financed, nonprofit companies with start-up funds from the national government. They customarily have a fleet of vehicles, high quality equipment, attractive uniforms, and an infrastructure appropriate to a small successful company. SHRC gardeners, for example, have late-model trucks with ladders, pruning equipment, landscape materials, and the like. Whenever possible, SHRCs try to find contracts for services that do not compete with the private sector. For example, bicycles are used by many adults and children in Japan as a primary form of transportation. Old, abandoned bicycles are commonly found. With so many bicycles, an SHRC decided to establish a bicycle repair center to collect them and repair them for resale. Soon the SHRC found itself competing with local merchants for the sale of the used bicycles. To resolve the situation, the SHRC decided to continue its program, but to export the bikes to China for resale so as not to compete with the local bicycle businesses.

Some SHRC services include proofreading, translating, tutoring, gardening, carpentry, clerical duties, caretaking services, canvassing jobs, light manual labor, and home-helper services (Bass, 1995c). This innovative model designed to foster economic development among retirees should be considered elsewhere including variations on its theme in the United States (Bass, 1995c; Campbell, 1992).

Another model that merits attention is a new business entity being designed and developed by a prominent American entrepreneur, William Zinke, that will serve older executives, those age 55 and older, who have left their regular career jobs, but want to continue working. Zinke, a mature worker himself at age 75, organized his consulting firm, Human Resource Services, Inc., in 1969 to focus on issues relating to human resource management. With close ties to a broad group of business leaders and gerontologists, Zinke asserts that demographic changes will require substantially increased utilization of people aged 55+ in productive activities. With an aging workforce growing at a negligible rate, labor shortages projected for the next 30 years, and a growing need for talent, companies will need to tap this large and growing pool of experienced workers to sustain the growth of the nation's economy. Although the focus in his new company is primarily on older people who have terminated jobs at the midmanagement level and up, he makes clear that this model applies to people at all work levels.

Zinke's new venture is among the first to carve out a business niche designed to help older Americans continue working and to provide them with employment-related services. It is particularly appropriate to the Zinke model that the initiative comes from a successful older businessperson who is passionate about serving the needs of a target group that includes himself. This is the wave of the future where visionaries, young and old, begin to respond to the lag that exists between current institutional structures and the increasing impact of demographic change. As these new institutions take hold, they will serve an important but often overlooked segment of our population and will clearly add value.

Implementing Change

There are essentially three key players for the creation of new programs designed to engage or re-engage the able, older worker: (1) the government, either state or federal, (2) the philanthropic community, or (3) the private sector – or some combination of these three. At this time, the likelihood of new national programs emanating from the Department of Labor or the Administration on Aging, designed for productive economic roles of the traditionally retired, seems quite low. Each of the agencies mentioned has a culture which, out of necessity, has focused on society's most vulnerable populations – those at most economic or social/health risk. Therefore, large amounts of older Americans – those who are quite able and have some financial security – are unlikely to be served. Saddled with serious economic and labor considerations for at-risk younger populations and faced with a growing very old and frail population, federal agencies are less likely to become concerned with creating programs for able, older people who want to make career transitions. The SHRC model in Japan is a public-private partnership in a nation that is concerned with the meaning older people have in later life (after retirement) and a nation that links its security with its economic development. In contrast, the United States government is far less concerned with issues of meaning in later life and derives much of its confidence in security through its military prowess. The cultural differences are significant, leading one to anticipate little from federal or state governments in fostering new models of productive engagement. With very visible issues such as the stabilization of Social Security and the financing of Medicare looming before Congress, issues of productive aging have received little attention in the public policy arena.

One public organization, however, that might selectively become involved in the (re)training of older workers is the higher education community. Always seeking new markets, community colleges and continuing education programs might be interested in offering market-responsive programs designed for mature workers or new retirees. Many of these institutions receive subsidies from the state and could be seen as a place to provide career enrichment to this special segment of the labor force.

Major foundations such as Sloan, Carnegie, Ford, or Kellogg, could create programs and options for productive aging. These initiatives are not limited to existing foundations, but also could emerge from the establishment of new philanthropic organizations seeking to find new areas of high visibility. As mentioned earlier, sooner or later, the equivalent of a Rhodes Scholarship for someone age 60 or older will emerge. While they will be prestigious, they will not have the wide impact that programs like the SHRCs do in Japan. One could envision, however, new nonprofits being created at the neighborhood level that could seek a combination of funding from individuals and foundations to fill the niche of community-based, fee-for-service organizations fully staffed and run by older people. A nonprofit organization designed to provide contracted services like our existing sheltered workshops could raise money from wealthy individuals, foundations, or corporations, charge an individual membership fee, and contract for services that include overhead to assist in the operation of the organization. The organization would provide part-time or full-time jobs for older people in the services provided as well as in the management of the organization.

The area that may hold most promise for the developing new models is the private sector. Companies established by older entrepreneurs designed to assist with job retraining or placement may find fertile ground in terms of clients seeking placement and companies needing skilled labor. While there are many companies that may provide temporary laborers or career counseling and placement, companies that specialize in such services will find a following. These boutique companies will find an older population willing to purchase services designed to enhance their career options and employers seeking to purchase a service that is capable of screening and identifying qualified, mature talent.

From a public policy perspective, market forces will dominate this sector. Employment and career industries that exist for the majority of the population can be tailored to targeted audiences. Market forces and opportunities like those being considered by Zinke reflect the risks and rewards as the consumer and market populations become further defined and segmented. Opportunities await future pioneers and entrepreneurs. It is difficult to predict the way these new industries will emerge, just as it was difficult to imagine the growth of the fast food industry, the success of the natural foods movement, or the proliferation of SUVs. But one can be assured that we will see new companies, new policies within existing companies, new programs, new services, new fellowships, new kinds of awards, new scholarships, redesigned academic programs, redesigned career training programs, and new career counseling programs configured explicitly to service an able and interested group of older pioneers. It is anticipated that the market of innovative options will move into full bloom until around 2011-2015 when larger groups of the baby boom generation confront retirement as we know it today. The models and industries of the future will be more responsive to, and conscious of, older workers' needs and capabilities.

The older-worker revolution is just beginning. As witnessed in past cultural transitions, institutions lag behind the public sentiment, but because of opportunity and social change, they catch up quickly. Although we have not yet reached that moment in America, we are beginning to experience a shift in the tide.

Recommendations:
Strategies for the Post-Retirement Era

Multiple strategies can be exercised now to tap into and cultivate the available talented pool of older workers. They involve individual strategies for government, philanthropy, and the private sector, but a collective collaboration among them is needed to maximize economic potential.

Recommendations for Government

- Provide targeted training and retraining programs for unemployed workers interested in learning skills needed in growth industries (such as applied information technologies, biotechnology laboratory skills, or service industry jobs).
- Encourage retirees with strong science and mathematics backgrounds to attend university programs aimed at reducing current labor shortages in nursing and education by offering state tuition wavers or interest-free loans.
- Encourage community colleges to offer career-related and age-neutral educational programs targeted at local economic development and employment needs of the region.
- Under the auspices of the Older Americans Act, encourage local Area Agencies on Aging to include employment issues as one of the areas under their periodic community assessment of the needs of older Americans.
- At the community level, encourage programs sponsored by the Department of Labor, the Administration on Aging, and the community colleges that target and engage older people in training and economic development.
- Encourage the Small Business Administration, state, county, and regional economic development councils, private industry councils, and angel investors to examine the market potential for niche organizations that target products and services to the growing older population and are managed and owned by older people themselves.
- Develop tax credits and tax deductions for individuals age 50 and older to assist with payment for career-related educational programs.
- Encourage colleges and universities to offer continuing education programs, targeted at human resource managers, and designed to highlight nontraditional skilled labor and career-related issues for an aging society.

Recommendations for the Philanthropic Community

- Initiate local programs that provide grants, scholarships, travel/study tours, and enrichment to active, older people seeking to continue career development.
- Provide funding to senior centers, community-based organizations, and community colleges interested in developing entrepreneurship programs for older people.
- Support research and documentation of innovative work models involving the unretired and dissemination of the information nationwide.
- Pilot-test an SHRC-type program in one of America's metropolitan areas and seek new organizational models of elder productivity.

- Assist in bringing community organizations and leaders together to examine the labor resources available and fund mechanisms to better engage older people in service to the community.

Recommendations for Private Industry

- Assess the consumer market and the role older consumers play and will continue to play over the next decade.
- Recognize that older workers are a valuable and perhaps irreplaceable asset to the organization by (re)training older workers.
- Begin formal mentoring programs where older workers pass on tradition to younger workers.
- Consider rehiring retired employees or competitors' retired employees to service the organization during peak demand times.
- Develop a list of recent retirees interested in temporary work and circulate the list throughout the company.
- Develop a phased-retirement program where older workers can work part-time hours.
- Consider establishing divisions within human resource firms or new companies that specialize in mature workers and mature executives seeking work or late-life job changes.
- Establish private, for-profit, business training programs for retired executives and middle managers. Niche programs for older female managers who delayed climbing the corporate ladder are particularly needed.
- Partner with local colleges and universities and clarify existing and future training needs.
- Establish career counseling centers designed to assist the able retired with job reentry. These centers could make referrals to specific career training programs and human resource personnel.

Summary

In a relatively short period of time, retirement has become a popular and accepted notion. The idea of leaving a lifetime of hard labor with economic security has served an important social and economic need in industrialized nations. Nevertheless, with increasing life expectancy, improved preventive health, a workforce that will soon stop growing, and a growing service economy, many of the expectations and structures which served previous cohorts of older workers may not apply to the majority of those now entering early retirement years.

Social structures such as retirement often lag behind the needs of individuals. That is, retirement as an institution lagged behind the needs of workers prior and during the Great Depression. It was established to respond to the prevailing social and economic needs. In the current economy, the social structure of retirement may now lag behind the desire of some older people to be engaged in paid work. As a result of this lag, innovators and pioneers have begun forging new models and approaches to work and career enhancement well beyond the traditional ages of retirement.

This article identifies some new models and ideas that are emerging regarding career options and alternatives for adults between the ages of 55 and 85. In many cases these new models are just at the incubation stage, but structural lag suggests that the demand for these services will grow as the baby boom generation enters the retirement years.

Chapter 17

How to Become Employer of Choice for the Working Retired

Beverly Goldberg

In mid-2002, worrying about labor shortages seemed a bit like bringing coal to Newcastle or air conditioners to Siberia. Layoffs and downsizings were the name of the game in the struggling American economy. Most organizations, however, continue to believe that economic cycles are a constant and look to a future marked by a return to growth. In fact, "at the end of 2002, the jobless rate was still relatively low in comparison to the rates reached during the labor market downturns of recent decades" (McMenamin, Krantz, & Krolik, 2003, p. 10).

The difficult economic situation in the first years of the new century, however, had an unintended consequence. It made it easier for organizations to continue to overlook a major demographic change, one that has been on the horizon, and written about extensively but mostly ignored, for more than a decade – the coming retirement of the baby boom generation. In the second decade of this century, the baby boomers, the 76 million people born between the close of World War II and 1964, will begin to retire in force, and the generation that follows is far smaller.

For example, the General Accounting Office (2001a) warns that "from 1950 to 1990, the labor force under 55 grew at an average annual rate of 1.9 percent. From 1990 to 2000, the average annual growth rate for this group was 1.0 percent, and [the Bureau of Labor Statistics] projects that from 2000 to 2025 labor force growth will slow to an annual rate of 0.3 percent" (p. 5). The result, when these numbers are combined with the potential retirement of older workers, according to the Organization for Economic Cooperation and Development (1998), is that labor force participation by those over 55 will have to increase by about 25 percent to maintain a constant total employment-to-population ratio from 2005 onward.

Another change this will bring is an older workforce. The median age of Americans in the workforce (which is higher than the median age of the population because of the number of nonworking youth) will reach 40 in 2005; in 1979, it was 34.7. Moreover, starting in 2011, when the first of the boomers reach 65, half of all prime age workers will be over 45. These data should serve as a clarion call to all employers, and especially human resource professionals, to rethink their attitudes and actions when it comes to defining the parameters of jobs. It also should drive business leaders and policy-makers to put in place programs and policies for addressing the issues involved in recruiting and retaining older workers.

If there remain naysayers, those who think that too much is being made of something that really is not going to be a problem, the difficulties emerging in the public sector may serve as a lesson. The aging of the boomers already is having an impact on federal, state, and local governments where, because of work rules, employees can retire after completing a given number of years of service, usually 25 to 30. In fact, many of the first of the boomers, who are now just inching past 55 and have served as firefighters, police, teachers, or in some other capacity within government for the requisite number of years, have declared their intent to leave. Samuel Ehrenhalt, a senior fellow at the Rockefeller Institute of Government, calculated in 1999 that "two-fifths of state and local government employees will be eligible to retire in the next 15 years, raising the specter of the most significant talent and brain drain ever experienced by government" (Walters, 2000, p. 36).

There is increasing awareness of this problem in some areas, especially when it comes to teachers. For example, surveys in Worcester, Massachusetts, have discovered that "about one-quarter of the state's teachers, about 23,000, will be eligible for retirement in the next five years," ("Exodus Begins," 2001) and many have indicated that they will take advantage of this opportunity. The situation is much the same across the nation:

> The teacher shortage is squeezing Connecticut and other states while student enrollments continue to rise. A U.S. Department of Education report says the nation will need as many as 2.7 million new teachers by 2008. In Connecticut, officials predict that 40 percent of the state's teaching force will retire over the next decade, worsening the shortage. (Frahm, 2002, p. B7)

While those in charge of civil service human resource departments are aware of the situation, most admit "that so far there's been no comprehensive or long-range plan put in place to address it" (Walters, 2000, p. 36). It is no wonder that private sector employers feel safer; first, since they are not bound by the salary constraints of the public sector, they tend to believe that solutions can be found in the area of increased pay if such a problem does eventually become real. Second, many express the opinion that because the boomers were hit hard by the stock market collapse, they are less likely to have enough in their 401(k)s to retire early. In fact, the retirement age of 62, which was rapidly becoming a new norm, has leveled off to 63 (Smart, 2001). For the most short-sighted, that offers great comfort. After all, many of those in charge, who have the authority to heed the warnings of their human resource directors, are themselves older and do not anticipate having to deal with the problem. Those who are younger rationalize that since the problem will occur some 10 years in the future, they still have plenty of time to address it.

Such short-term thinking is extremely dangerous. For example, house values have not been affected by current economic conditions, and those houses in prime locations (that is, located near or in driving distance of centers of commerce) can be sold to finance the purchase of smaller, less expensive homes in areas farther out. Selling those homes will provide money to ease the financial needs of retirement. In addition, with their children grown, older individuals' income needs are lower. Finally, an economic rebound that restored pension-fund losses would allow even more workers to leave their jobs – jobs they have stayed with only for economic reasons.

The unpleasant reality is that many older Americans eagerly anticipate retiring because they find the restrictions and the boredom of their jobs overwhelming. As they enter what is now described as the third stage of life, they want to do new and different things, things that will bring them satisfaction, growth, and rewards that are more than monetary. They are tired of doing the same things at work that they have done for years. In addition, as the years went by, they noticed that they were receiving fewer opportunities for growth because employers rarely offer older workers training. The reason for this lack of training is that employers do not believe they will be able to amortize the costs of investing in workers close to retirement, which was the case under the economic model that dominated in the post-World War II era.

At that time, limiting major investments in training to those 25 to 44 years of age made sense. After all, average job tenure was 15 to 20 years, and systems and processes changed infrequently. In the new world of work, people switch jobs most frequently in the very years they receive the most training (older employees who have a more difficult time finding new positions tend to stay put), and technology brings changes in systems and processes every 2 to 3 years (training in some areas is necessary across the board anyway) (Goldberg, 2000).

If employers can design new patterns of employment, models that do not limit employees' growth and that meet the other needs of employees as they age, they should be able to work around the coming labor shortage of prime age workers. They will be helped by an interesting development: the recent change in intentions of those nearing retirement. In 1998, only 75 percent of workers aged 55 to 64 said that they planned to work after 65. Around 95 percent indicated that they plan to work once retired, according to a Harris Interactive poll taken in 2002 (Wallace, 2002). Far less hopeful, given the current structure of work in most organizations, is that the 95 percent qualify their intentions with the phrase "in some capacity." The key to understanding what is happening is the fact that they plan to work "once retired." Most do not envision their post-retirement employment as the job they now have – and if it is, they want a very different schedule.

Before exploring the kinds of alternatives to current work arrangements that retirees will find attractive, it is important to examine the reasons for this new vision of life in the third age. Indeed, those who want to build a workplace that will be attractive to older workers when labor shortages once again take place will need to have a broader understanding about the older workforce, and that includes those approaching retirement as well as post-retirement workers, a group that will represent a substantial percentage of employees over the coming decades.

The Third Age

The years after 65 have changed dramatically. First, there are many more of them than there once were, which affects the way people think about spending those years. Second, many people just do not feel as old physically (particularly when they compare themselves with their mental pictures of people from earlier generations) as the calendar tells them they are. At the same time, they do begin to experience more chronic conditions with age although many of those conditions are, with the advances that have taken place in medical care, now more a nuisance than a hindrance. Third, through stories in the media and discussions with others, those nearing retirement have become aware of social and psychological needs and expectations that surface in later life, which are causing them to rethink their idea that the retirement model of their parents' generation is the one that will work for them. Fourth, economic factors come into play, especially as a result of longer life expectancy. Each of these factors has effects on pre- and post-retirement decision making.

The Rise in Life Expectancy

When Social Security legislation was passed in the late 1930s, those who had reached the age of eligibility – and there were not many who reached the lofty age of 65 since average life expectancy at the time was 61 – could expect to spend about 5 years in retirement. Today, 20 years spent retired is not unusual (United States House of Representatives, Committee on Ways and Means, 1998). Thus,

where once retirement was a few years at the end of life spent resting (after years of a job that probably involved hard physical labor), those facing retirement now are looking at a period as long as their pre-work lives. The realization that life after retirement is likely to be long enough to accomplish things one never had time for is, for many, an awakening. This third stage of life is long enough to pursue – and then take advantage of – a college degree; to start a business based on a hobby; to travel; to take part in politics; or to do volunteer work in an area of interest. Then, after some 15 or 20 years of working retired, there will be time to spend a few years resting and contemplating one's life.

Improvements in Health

Advances in health care have brought vast improvements in people's health status at all ages. People are coming to see that they are far healthier than they expected to be as they age, and the ailments that do afflict them can be alleviated if not eliminated. In fact, a majority of those over 55 are as healthy as people 10 years younger were a decade ago. For example, "the rate of disability among older Americans . . . dropped from 26.2 percent in 1982 to 19.7 percent in 1999" (Wellner, 2002, p. 28). However, there are some problems with an older workforce that human resource departments will have to address. For example, Walter Maher of DaimlerChrysler Corporation notes that "it has become very clear that there is a priority in designing jobs in a way to reduce the risk of injury." He also points out that "standardized work practices are critical to injury prevention" (Rappaport, 2001b, p. 60).

Aging introduces a number of problems that often make work harder and more tiring. For example, eyesight declines with increasing age, although this can be overcome by proper glasses for the unusual distance of a computer (between far vision and reading) and attention to ergonomics. Further, stiff joints tend to decrease mobility, although this can usually be mitigated by proper medication. Overall, however, the physical condition of today's retirees is remarkable compared to that of earlier generations: today's retirees travel to rugged areas and explore new venues, they learn to scuba dive, and they participate in senior sports. These activities are far more physically demanding than most jobs in today's economy, which is more information- and service-oriented and far less involved in manufacturing.

In addition, when it comes to health, particularly mental abilities, it is hard to avoid information about how important it is to stay challenged. Biologist Alexander Spence (1995) notes that "memory seems to be retained better in older persons who continue working or otherwise keep busy after retirement. . . . [I]t seems as if 'exercising' the brain helps maintain its normal functioning" far longer (pp. 85-86).

Social and Psychological Conditions

For many people, retirement results in a loss of identity. We are a members of a society in which people tend to define themselves by what they do: "Oh, I work for GE." "I'm a teacher." "I sell cars." It also can result in a sense of isolation and loneliness because so many Americans in our mobile society are less connected than ever before. Often with family and friends at a distance, they depend on work for socializing.

As they get older, many people suffer a sense of sadness at no longer being important, not being listened to for advice, not contributing to the world in some way. The result can be depression, which in turn leads to inactivity, often exacerbating minor health problems. Fortunately, depression in older people is now recognized by physicians, who have medications to offer that alleviate many of the symptoms. Once treated pharmacologically, it is easier for doctors and families to encourage sufferers to take action. For example, part-time jobs, even low-paid ones such as those offered by places like Wal-Mart and Publix that hire a lot of part-time help, get people out of the house, keep them active, and connect them to others.

Economic Concerns

Many of those who are close to retirement have become aware that the pensions they are entitled to will not support them at the level they wish to live. Although some have savings that they thought would be enough to augment their pensions, they now are confronting the fact that the amount they have saved will never stretch out over the long number of years they may spend in retirement. At the same time, they realize that they will be fine if they spend 5 to 10 years post-retirement earning enough to augment their pensions without touching their savings.

Experts such as Robert Friedland, director of the National Academy on an Aging Society in Washington, D.C., say that many boomers will "reconcile a dream of early retirement with their meager retirement savings. They'll compromise by trading in full-time, high-powered careers for less-stressful, part-time jobs" (McCune, 1998, p. 15).

Designing New Models of Work

As a result of these forces, those retiring are looking for new ways to continue to work without totally abandoning some of the goals they have set for retirement, such as taking some courses, doing some traveling, or taking some time to enjoy grandchildren. Aware of this, human resource professionals are trying to wake their organizations up to the need to change. Bringing about change, however, is never easy, so management resists making any changes until the moment comes when it cannot avoid doing so. Cynthia Winder, president of the South Puget Sound Chapter of the Northwest Society for Human Resource Management, says that in trying to get recognition for the looming problem, many professionals in the field are emphasizing the numbers. She notes that in her area of the country, "[W]e are looking at demographics saying we have a potential of losing about a third of our workforce in the next five to seven years" (Carson, 2002, p. SL1). And yet, despite the urging of those in charge of human resources, more than half of the companies surveyed by William M. Mercer said that they have not put formal programs in place, particularly when it comes to older workers (Rappaport, 2001a).

Forward-looking human resource managers can begin to prepare for the problem by promoting new work arrangements as necessary, for example, to meet the demands of valuable younger employees who may want work arrangements that allow them to continue their education and spend more time with their families. When shortages occur because of retirements, those companies that have such flexible arrangements in place will find that those who want to work retired will make them their employer of choice.

Some companies already have developed flexible work arrangements as a result of the move to the lean organization in the aftermath of the downsizings of the late 1980s and early 1990s. These arrangements – which often involve temporary, consulting, and contract work – allow them to avoid the trap of expanding their workforces only to have to reduce them later through massive layoffs that often involve costly severance packages. Today, other kinds of accommodations are creeping into most organizations. In some cases, job descriptions have begun to be tailored to individuals; in others, new forms of employment used in moments of crisis have become permanent. These models need to be examined for their effects on the bottom line as well as their relevance to the likely demands of those who would like to work retired.

Work Models that Can Be Adapted to Retirees

Full-time permanent work with a twist. Although full-time permanent work is still the norm, more than 25 percent of the full-time workforce had made flexible scheduling arrangements in 1997 – more than double the number in 1991. The higher the position, the higher the percentage with flexible arrangements. The most common flexible arrangements for full-time workers are flextime (people choose to start their day at a time of their choosing between 8:00 a.m. and 10:00 a.m. and leave eight hours later) or compression (these arrangements tend to involve either working nine days every two weeks with shorter lunch hours or four 10-hour days a week).

Part-time permanent work. These jobs are for less than 40 hours a week. They may call for two or three full-time days, five half-time days, or any other combination, but they are not limited in duration. Included in this category is the somewhat new concept of shared jobs, a development that was pushed by new mothers who wanted to reduce their time at work for a few years without exiting the workforce. Some companies are very good about providing prorated benefits for those who work under these arrangements, and there are rules in place to ensure that people in this category who work more than a certain number of hours a week receive the same benefits as full-time workers. (See below for a discussion of job-sharing as a retirement strategy.)

Full-time and part-time temporary work. There has been some confusion over the labeling of these jobs. Contingent work, which is usually defined as full-time work that is not expected to last, accounts for about 5 percent of the workforce. Although most of these jobs are in the service industry, particularly in sales, about 20 percent of these workers are ranked as professional. Today, the majority of people in these jobs are under 35; in the future, older workers are likely to make up the largest group in this category.

A significant development in this area is the use of former employees who temporarily return to the organizations from which they have retired. A pioneer in this area is Travelers Corporation, which set up such a service for retired workers some two decades ago and has had such success with it that other companies have adopted similar programs. This approach is extremely beneficial to an organization because former employees understand the organization's culture and know the ways things work.

Contract or consulting work. There are few standards for these arrangements. Some involve individuals who consult with organizations in the hope that the quality of their work will eventually result in full-time employment. Others consult for a number of companies at once in order to earn the equivalent of full-time pay; they choose this road because they have areas of expertise that no single company needs on a full-time basis. While many consultants are self-employed, consulting is also an industry, and some consultants work for large consulting organizations. In some fields, there is a tradition of having people ease out gradually when retirement draws close by serving as consultants in areas in which they have very specific expertise that would be expensive to replace. New hires are brought in to take over most of the work and to learn how to do the more specialized work from them over time. Since the downsizings of the late 1980s, however, many people have been called back to their old organizations on a consulting basis, which means they do the same work they did in the past for about the same salary – but without benefits and with the understanding that the arrangement may be terminated at any time.

Organizations like these arrangements because they allow them to add workers temporarily for specific projects while providing more stability than would be the case with temporary workers from agencies. This is particularly important when companies need to add people to teams that are set up to handle large, short-term projects. In these situations, companies often entice retired workers to return for the life of the project because they understand the corporate culture, making things run far more smoothly.

Telecommuting. Working at home has been gaining in popularity: 5.4 million people worked at home at least three days a month in 1993; in 1998, 9.9 million did. Companies react very differently to telecommuting. For example, about 55 percent of managers at AT&T telecommute, but only 2 percent of Aetna employees do. At Leisure Co./America West, where 16 percent telecommute, potluck team dinners are held to make sure people keep in touch (Dunkin, 1998).

These arrangements, which are made possible by technology, are still taking shape, but it has become clear that they offer advantages and disadvantages. New "rules of the road," especially performance measurement and managerial training, will have to be developed to ensure that telecommuters are successful. In addition, for some older employees, at-home work can make life easier if money is the major reason for returning to work. Working at home, however, does not bring the social interaction that makes work so attractive to other older workers.

On-call work. The terms of on-call work often involve a guaranteed minimum number of hours. Organizations that must be fully staffed at all times in certain areas, such as hospitals, tend to make these arrangements. For the organization, it ensures that backup personnel is available at relatively low cost whenever needed. For workers, it eliminates some of the uncertainty involved in finding temporary work. Since on-call work usually involves varying shifts, it is ideal for older workers who have few specific demands on their time. In many hospitals, it often serves as a partial retirement strategy.

Retirement Options

Some companies have already developed programs aimed at easing the transition to retirement for both older workers and the organization itself. These firms tend to be concerned with losing institutional memory and specialized skill sets. Among the programs they have developed are phased retirement, work-sharing arrangements, bridge jobs, seasonal employment, and mentoring assignments.

Phased retirement. Under phased retirement, older employees work out a plan for withdrawing from the company. They reduce the number of days they work each week by, say, a day the first three months, then two days for the next three months, and so on until they reach full retirement. This benefits the organization because it allows for a transfer of the expertise and institutional knowledge of the retiring worker to the person who will eventually take over the job. The younger worker may actually share a job with more than one person or have other responsibilities to fill the week. Neuville Industries of Hildebran, North Carolina, set up a job-sharing program for employees over the age of 62. The program, which was initiated in the early 1990s, is aimed at employees with at least five years of experience, and allows employees to work as long as they want for 20 hours a week and provides benefits (Challenger, 1997).

Job-sharing. A company facing the loss of a large number of older workers can offer the opportunity for them to stay on half-time, sharing their jobs with other older workers who choose to work retired but also prefer a less hectic schedule. A department with six people, four of whom are ready for retirement, could end up having to hire only two new people, if two can be persuaded to job-share. The result would be a far smoother transition.

Bridge employment. In bridge employment, an older worker is often given special assignments, such as serving on a disaster recovery project or representing the company in a community project. It also includes assignments that would disrupt younger workers' lives. For example, Whirlpool Corp. finds it is less expensive to hire retired workers for short-term assignments abroad than to relocate full-time workers, Quaker Oats has tapped retirees for a project in Shanghai, and GTE also has tested this approach and plans to expand it.

Seasonal work. Seasonal work takes a number of forms. Sometimes it can involve asking retired workers to come back during the summer when so many younger workers with children choose to take vacation time. Other times, it can provide opportunities for workers to choose to work in different areas of the country during different seasons, for example, in Florida in winter when tourists swarm there.

Mentoring. When organizations are concerned about maintaining their institutional history and values, and even some older skills and techniques, they often turn to older workers, who can answer such questions as: Why were certain decisions about processes made? Why don't we do business with company X (and who has to leave before we can try to get in the door again)? This is information that does not get captured in memos or expert systems; it is the stuff of history, stored in memory, recounted as conversation. One of the ways companies can capture this knowledge is to ask older workers to become mentors, training younger employees so that the expertise and experience they have acquired over long years are passed on rather than lost.

Becoming the First Choice of the Working Retired

Putting new models of work in place is just a first step. Companies that want to attract the working retired will have to develop programs that solve some of the problems of early retirees, particularly in terms of pensions and health care coverage. They will have to address possible health-related issues that affect productivity. They will have to train managers and trainers to deal with older employees. Finally, companies should stimulate the development of creative, unusual, and attractive programs for retirees. This will ensure that they become employers of choice when labor markets tighten as the boomers leave the workforce.

When it comes to pensions, companies that have plans in place that penalize people for staying will have to adjust the rules. Sometimes all it takes is having the person leave for a period of time and then be rehired. Governments are putting in place programs that increase benefits to those who work longer, similar to the increase in Social Security that comes from putting off collecting benefits.

When it comes to health insurance, older workers do raise the cost of insurance. On the other hand, insurance costs on an individual basis are extremely high. Therefore, it may be a worthwhile trade-off to ask part-time employees for copayments that are higher than usual, yet lower than they would otherwise be on the private market.

When it comes to health issues, awareness and increased scrutiny are critical, but the line between care and perceived discrimination is a delicate one. For example, a manager might notice that an older employee has developed hearing problems. Instead of telling that person to have a hearing evaluation, an offer can be made to provide anyone who is interested with phone headsets that have special volume controls. Another way to discover such problems among older workers is mandatory company physicals for all employees. With an overall older workforce, early diagnosis of hypertension, heart disease, and diabetes alone would amortize the cost of such a preventive plan.

Training managers to deal with older workers is critical. With the adoption of flexible work arrangements, managers will have to learn how to assess productivity in terms of hours worked in relation to tasks completed, not days worked, for example. If someone on flextime is in four days a week, for six hours a day, and someone else is working three 10-hour days, how should productivity be measured? There are also problems inherent in younger workers managing those old enough to be their parents. The discomfort on both sides can bring about great dissatisfaction. Workshops for managers, similar to other kinds of diversity training, are a key to success when older workers become a large part of the workforce.

Training departments also need to find ways around the problem of teaching people of different ages. For example, testing is a very different experience to someone just out of school than it is to someone who has not been in a classroom setting for 30 years. People also learn differently at different ages, and they react differently to displaying a lack of knowledge or difficulty learning a specific skill.

When it comes to imaginative offerings, companies would do well to have brainstorming sessions with older employees who have approached the human resource department to talk about retirement. Such sessions can provide solutions to problems that companies may not even realize they have. For example, a utility company in Omaha discovered through a facilitated session, designed to uncover the reasons for poor attendance, that older employees did not like to drive to work in the severe winter weather typical of that part of the country. It turned out that it was not just a fear of driving, but problems like shoveling out a car from high snow drifts. Most of those who admitted to the problem were older, but not all, which made the "confession" less difficult. The company set up a van trans-port service that brought people door-to-door for a small fee, and attendance improved substantially.

A second example (observed in the course of consulting assignments) relates to the proximity of bathrooms to the workstations. This proximity turned out to be an issue in an insurance company in a suburb of Hartford that occupied a huge low building. The problem developed when the company, which was making a push to hire the disabled, began reassigning workspaces to place the disabled close to the exits. Some of the people being displaced were upset and complained. When the human resource manager investigated the problem, it turned out that the complaints were not, as originally thought, because the company was hiring the disabled, but because those being reassigned were senior workers who had over time managed to relocate themselves to those areas because the bathrooms in the building were located near the exits.

In other words, an older workforce can present issues, but they are usually issues that can be resolved fairly easily. Those organizations that are interested in long-term planning can look ahead and discover what they need to do now to be "employers of choice" when the day comes that workers are scarce.

Recommendations

The following are critical concrete steps for human resources departments to take in order to ensure that they will be prepared to deal with this issue before it becomes a major problem:

- Conduct careful analyses of the demographics of your organization's workforce. You must ex-amine the ages of workers by job description and department to see whether there might be a number of simultaneous departures that could create problems. You also must analyze the area in which each division of your organization is located to determine how difficult it might be to find replacements. You need to know whether possible replacements exist. Is the education in the area good? Is a division in a region that is losing younger people to other areas of the country? Have new industries that pay better moved in?

- Institute a company-wide policy (stated in the employee handbook) of conducting preretirement interviews with all employees when they reach a given age, say, 60. The handbook must explain that this is not being done to encourage older employees to leave, but rather is a way of determining succession planning and working out arrangements that will help employees understand their retirement options.

- An analysis to determine the average age at which past employees doing similar work in the company in similar locations retired will help determine what age should be set for these interviews. For example, if the company has a division in Florida and another in Minnesota, the results of such a breakdown are likely to be very different, yet the age set to start such interviews must be the same to avoid any implication of unfairness.

- Conduct periodic ergonomic analyses in conjunction with tracking health issues that arise in unusual numbers. Also do a breakdown to determine if there is an age differential in relation to these ailments. For example, are an unusual number of employees in sedentary jobs being treated by chiropractors because of back problems? Are the instances of tendinitis among employees rising? An ergonomics specialist will be able to determine whether workstations need redesigning.

- Develop economically feasible and psychologically beneficial strategies for partial retirement. The costs and benefits of the various arrangements discussed earlier in the chapter, ranging from job-sharing to phased retirement to an internal "temp" agency, need to be calculated so a set of choices can be presented to employees for consideration at their preretirement interviews.

- Advise trainers on the ages of those who will be in their classes and, where necessary, work with them to ensure age-appropriate training methods are offered.

- Work with those who are in charge of pension plans to ensure that when the time comes that the retention of older workers is necessary, those who want to work after a certain age are not penalized for it. Penalties for working after a certain age that were enacted when the company was looking for ways to encourage retirement need to be changed in time to help retain members of the baby boom generation when the inevitable shortfall of trained workers occurs.

Summary

No matter what happens to the American economy over the next few years, barring another Great Depression, starting in 2011 the workforce will essentially stop growing – and it will get older. No matter how many babies are born now or how many immigrants we admit to this country, people ready to take over the skilled jobs that will be vacated by those in the large post-World War II baby boom will not be easy to find in numbers sufficient to maintain productivity.

Our notion of retirement, both the age at which people retire and what retirement means, has to change. Our nation's legislators have already taken a step in this direction, raising the age at which people can collect full Social Security benefits when they retire and relaxing the reductions in benefits for those who work after retirement. Now it is time for business to take action.

Individuals clearly do not expect to spend their last 20 or 30 years doing nothing but sitting on their front porches in rockers. Many plan to learn something new, perhaps even earn a degree; some plan to open their own business; others contemplate pursuing an avocation and perhaps making some profit out of doing so. Surveys show that the description of what people plan to do when they retire can best be described as working retired.

Most people looking at retirement, however, do indicate a strong desire for more free time than they now have. Many just want to escape from a job that has become tedious, from a workplace that does not seem to value them and offers too little opportunity for growth. The challenge human resource personnel face is bringing about change in the way older workers are perceived and treated. They must develop policies and programs that will encourage older workers to stay at work in some capacity after retirement, and they must especially ensure that older workers are offered training in order to keep their jobs interesting, even exciting.

Synthesis

Redefining Retirement

Chapters 16 and 17 are appropriate final chapters in Part Three because they show how the retirement transition is integrally linked to the other issues. While Chapter 16 zooms in on the importance of career services for older worers, Chapter 17 specifically mentions the importance of pensions, health, training, and intergenerational relations. Of course, both of the chapters base their recommendations on the recognition that older workers must be recruited and retained more successfully upon their retirement. Therefore, it seems that the book has come full circle.

If there is one thing that has become clear in these and other chapters, it is that many older workers wish to continue employment in some form upon retirement. To accommodate these preferences, it would behoove American organizations to become much more flexible in their work arrangements. Chapter 17 discusses at length specific structures for employing the retired.

Chapter 16 views retirement through a public policy lens. The existence of a structural lag is signaled, suggesting that many baby boomers' needs and expectations regarding retirement are different than what is currently the norm. In other words, the need to reconceptualize retirement is currently insufficiently being met. We are already seeing the first innovative businesses offering services to meet these needs – many of which are run by older workers themselves. We can expect many more to follow.

This leads to an important observation: aging workers are perfectly capable of taking care of themselves. In our discussions of the aging workforce, we need to be careful in our choice of words. In this book, we have effectively suggested that the aging of the workforce is an impending storm to which organizations must adapt – or else. Though not untrue, this could have adverse side effects: it may inadvertently perpetuate stereotypes that portray older Americans as somehow inferior to younger ones. After all, who says that the aging of the workforce is a bad thing? It should be kept in mind that it is the older Americans who are running many corporations today, changing legislation, and not to forget, buying products and voting. Clearly, they themselves have significant ability to continue adjusting society to meet their needs as they have done thus far.

The demand for workers in times of growth and the supply of retired workers willing to remain employed will over time combine to usher in a new chapter in the employment of older Americans. The only question is: How long can your organization afford to wait?

PART FOUR

SYNTHESIS

Chapter 18

Achieving Organizational and Systemic Change

Roemer M. S. Visser
Paulette T. Beatty

Julie is Vice President for Human Resources at a small hospital that is the biggest employer in the county. She has been with the hospital now for more than 23 years after starting as an emergency room nurse and switching to the human resources profession 10 years later. Well-connected and well-respected in the hospital, Julie has overseen a slow workforce growth that kept pace with the growth of the surrounding rural community. However, times are changing. The rural environment, the easygoing pace of life, and the moderate climate have combined to make her community one of the more popular retirement locations in the state. This has resulted in an accelerated growth of the town, an increase in its average age, and as a result, a disproportionate increase in demand for services.

While in itself this would hardly be a problem, Julie faces another challenge. As nationwide shortages of nurses are increasing, the hospital is expecting major turnover among its nurses within the next five years. By that time, more than one-third of the nurses will be eligible for retirement, and many of them have indicated their intention to retire when that time comes.

Julie knows that action must be taken now to prevent a crisis five years down the road and decides that preventing this crisis is her top priority. Hiring nurses from outside the county is not a strategy she would like to depend on. Past experience has taught her that she cannot compete with big-city hospitals that pay higher wages. On the other hand, enticing all the current nurses to stay employed upon becoming eligible for retirement would still not allow the hospital meet the projected need for health care services. She knows she must hire more nurses.

Intuitively, she knows that major changes need to be made soon in order to continue to meet the demand for services in the future. These changes will involve both the hospital and the local community. She becomes dizzy at the daunting complexity of the task that lies ahead. But the questions that haunt her most are: Where to start? How to proceed?

Chapter 1 describes how this book came to be. It is our attempt to meet the need for a comprehensive exploration of future consequences of the aging workforce for U.S. organizations. In order to get a grasp of some of these consequences and not be limited by our own personal and professional affiliations, we created a panel of nationwide experts hailing from a variety of backgrounds and representing multiple perspectives. We asked them what they believed were the five most critical issues that U.S. organizations will be confronted within the next 20 years because of the aging of the workforce. The panel yielded a total of 171 answers that showed remarkable consistency and fit into nine major themes, which we then subdivided into two trends and seven critical issues.

The two trends, workforce demographics and workplace trends, are discussed in Chapters 2 and 3. They are two phenomena that will continue to play out at national and global levels, beyond the influence of any single economy. Chapters 2 and 3 together form Part Two of this book and describe five trends that will continue to make their influence felt across the nation: the workforce is aging; the workforce is diversifying; the economy will continue to shift to one based on information and services; technological innovations will transform the workplace; and globalization will continue.

These developments form the backdrop against which the seven critical issues identified by the panel will play out. In contrast to the workforce and workplace trends, these issues can indeed be influenced to some degree at organizational, community, and government levels. These seven critical issues are: recruitment and retention; training; career development; intergenerational relations; health; pensions; and redefining retirement. Part Three of this book devotes two chapters to each of these critical issues, with each of the paired chapters representing a particular perspective. Still, every chapter in Part Three ends with concrete, specific recommendations for proactively addressing the issue at hand.

Upon soaking up the perspectives, analyses, and recommendations contained within this volume, it became clear to us that the following two related conclusions can be drawn regarding the seven issues discussed in Part Two:

1. Each issue is complex and multifaceted, requiring multiple actions by multiple actors.
2. The issues are to an important degree interrelated with each other.

The next two sections present evidence from the preceding chapters that we believe supports these two conclusions.

Conclusion One: Complexity and Multiple Actors

Recruitment and retention is one of the more complex issues treated in this volume, as it is to some extent a result of each of the other six issues. For example, health benefits can have a strong effect on recruitment and retention success, while pensions can provide a strong incentive for workers of a certain age to retire. Similarly, training and career development can be seen as retention tools and some of the authors framed their chapters that way.

Clearly, there is no single, magic determinant that is to be changed in order to increase recruitment and retention rates among older workers. Thus, it follows that there is no single group of stakeholders that can achieve success on its own: government regulations affect recruitment and retention rates much the same as organizational policies and workers' individual attitudes do. Consequently, there are many stakeholders who can exert influence on recruitment and retention in many ways.

Although on the surface less dependent on external forces than recruitment and retention, the

training of older workers is by no means a simple issue. Not only do delivery methods need to be adjusted to accommodate a variety of learning preferences, but training participation rates of older workers often need to be increased as well. These lower rates are in part explained by the myths and stereotypes that surfaced so often throughout this book. Increasing these participation rates and facilitating transfer of training in turn depend on the organizational infrastructure, including – but not limited to – performance appraisals, compensation mechanisms, and time off for classes.

Again, the conclusion that multiple actors may exert influence in multiple ways is equally clear. Some of the key players invoked in the book include researchers, trainers, HR professionals, managers, community colleges, and government. Researchers are called upon to increase our knowledge base regarding informal training. Trainers are to adjust their curricula and delivery methods to make sure they are age-neutral. To create and sustain an appropriate training infrastructure, HR professionals and management must be involved. Of course, much of the training cannot be done in-house and needs to be done by external experts, such as training consultants and community colleges. It has also been suggested that government provide incentives for organizations to continue upgrading older workers' skills. In sum, there are many actors who exert their influences on training practices.

Career development to a large extent takes place through employee training. Therefore, the intricacies of the training issue carry over to career development. Yet, while training programs are often limited to skills that are needed on the job or in the near future, career development programs have a significantly wider scope. This means that there are many more factors that influence career development behavior. For example, fluctuations in job markets and industries have a clear impact. The transition to career self-management also introduces complexities of its own.

Much like the training issue, the key players have been identified as academicians, trainers, HR professionals (HRM and HRD), and line and executive management. Moreover, there is an important role for individual employees as they are increasingly inheriting primary responsibility for managing their own careers. Academics are called upon to adjust or replace outdated models and theories to reflect the current economic reality that life-long employment is of the past. HR professionals have been identified as critical in initiating the process of building a career development program and getting support from the entire organization, particularly senior management. Moreover, there are players outside the context of the organization, such as higher education institutions, career counselors, and the career development and human resource professionals, who have an important role to play in facilitating the successful creation of career development programs for older workers.

Closely related to training and career development, the **intergenerational relations** issue is also multifaceted. For the purpose of this book, intergenerational relations emcompasses interactions within groups, between groups, and generally within the organizational context. A focal point here is the organizational culture, which expresses itself in shared practices, values, and assumptions. Of course, an age bias may also exist in the broader cultural context within which organizations function, as evidenced by the existence of the Age Discrimination in Employment Act. Improving intergenerational relations in organizations therefore involves interventions in structures, policies, practices, attitudes, and assumptions.

As with the two aforementioned issues, the individual employees, supervisors, managers, and HR professionals – in particular organization development practitioners – are among the most important players for a successful intervention. Researchers can support this effort by providing more insight into how membership in a particular generational group plays out in interactions with members of a different generation. Finally, as ageism is not an isolated organizational phenomenon, but appears to pervade American organizations, government, advocacy groups, think tanks, and researchers all have important parts to play in debunking ageist myths at this broader, national level.

Health may very well be the most elusive and complex issue at hand, particularly when conceptualized as encompassing both physical and mental well-being. Older workers' mental health at work depends on a host of factors. While individual attributes may be important, work-life balance is certainly a crucial aspect as well since older work-

ers are more likely to have eldercare responsibilities for their parents or spouses than are younger workers. On top of that, there is the problem of health insurance: costs are on the rise, causing more and more workers to be at risk for having their coverage reduced and, upon retirement, even canceled. Complicating this issue further are the many different kinds of coverage, including variations of defined benefit and defined contribution plans, all of which interact with tax laws and regulations that are seldom left unchanged. The many causes of rising health insurance costs add yet another layer to the complexity of the health issue for older workers, implicating legislation pertaining to Medicare and the Family and Medical Leave Act, among others.

Already it is clear that government is a key stakeholder in tackling the health issue for older workers. This means that advocacy organizations, think tanks, researchers, professional associations, and any other group that influences public policy need to participate in the nationwide conversation. While change at the national level may be slow in coming, our authors show that managers and HR executives can still take the initiative to have a significant impact on employee health within their organizations.

The same holds true for the issue of **pensions**. The timing of workers' retirement depends on eligibility criteria, Social Security, tax laws and regulations, and health insurance coverage, among other things. Moreover, a wide variety of pension programs, both public and private, exist including defined benefit and defined contribution plans. While both defined benefit and defined contribution plans have distinct advantages and drawbacks, the shift to defined contribution benefit plans appears to continue.

As with the health issue, this leads to the immediate observation that many stakeholders need to be involved in pension reform. Government is a crucial partner, in turn informed by those who influence public policy. In the absence of legislative reform, company executives still have an opportunity to make changes to the way their pension programs are administered to increase participation rates and help improve employees' fiscal responsibility. In turn, this calls for significant training and awareness initiatives for employees.

Finally, the extent to which **retirement** will be

successfully redefined to meet individual and generational needs will to an important degree depend on changes made in Social Security, Medicare, and other relevant legislation; changes in pension plan design; and changes in health care policies. Moreover, training and career development programs are critical in making the transition to more flexible retirement arrangements. Clearly, this is another issue that requires multiple stakeholders to take multiple courses of action in order to achieve meaningful change.

Conclusion Two: Interrelatedness of Issues

The second conclusion is that when seen as a whole, the seven critical issues, embedded in the context of demographic shifts and workplace trends, are to an important degree interrelated. Any intervention designed to address a particular issue will more than likely spill over and influence another one. Rather than treating each of the issues separately and presenting evidence of interrelatedness for each based on the preceding chapters, we will illustrate this interrelatedness by examining the hypothetical (and admittedly oversimplified) situation described at the beginning of this chapter.

Julie realizes that one of the problems providing an impetus to retire is the nurses' feelings of inadequacy in working with emerging technologies. Most comfortable with hand-drawn patient charts, many are having difficulty navigating screens on desktop computers and entering data in handheld computers. Julie contacts an expert on training older learners and the local community college to address this issue. Together, they design a training program for this population of nurses that assumes no prior knowledge of computers and is based on adult learning principles.

After running a pilot with some volunteers and improving the program in several areas, the first batch of nurses attends the training, held on the premises during working hours. The results are significant. Many of the nurses commit fewer errors, and they report increased feelings of competence and improved job satisfaction. Word of this training program spreads and more nurses volunteer to register for the course.

An unanticipated by-product is also reported, however. The nurses who have attended the training also report being treated differently by the doctors, who are mostly younger males. Whereas doctors' interactions with the nurses appeared at times to be sexist, ageist, even elitist, the nurses now report being taken seriously as a conversation partner, further increasing their sense of competence, improving their job satisfaction, and enhancing intergenerational and intergender relations within the hospital.

For their part, the doctors also report a change in attitude. They informally express their pleasant surprise at the ability of these mature workers to master these new technologies in such a short time period. The decrease in patient errors has made their jobs easier and has made them look better to their peers and their patients. The first ever doctor-nurse social is announced.

The success of the training program spills over into yet other areas. With a critical mass of nurses being comfortable with and literate in emerging technology, some of the nurses take over the delivery of the training program, becoming trainers themselves. For these nurses, becoming a trainer amounts to a career move. Some transfer their new knowledge of computers to the home computer, where they successfully navigate the Internet and stay abreast of professional developments in their field at their own pace. Yet others take up e-mail, improving communications with distant relatives, or use their computer skills for pursuing hobbies.

Most importantly, the nurses who completed the training now report a desire to remain employed past retirement age, albeit not on a full-time basis. Citing a desire for more leisure time to spend with family members or for pursuing a hobby, they provide Julie with a crucial clue to the next area of intervention: flexible work arrangements.

A Strategy for Implementing Change

The two conclusions derived from a study of the seven critical issues provide two important clues as to where and how to begin in implementing change. As for where to start, the above example suggests that the exact starting point is not critically important since any meaningful intervention to address one issue will most likely have consequences for other issues as well. Any meaningful starting point, therefore, will do.

As for how to proceed, however, our overarching recommendation is clear. *In order to affect significant, lasting change, it is imperative that a collaborative, holistic approach be taken, involving multiple stakeholder groups.*

Combining this with the use of a tried-and-true approach to change management may be the key to success, and Lewin's force field model for social change is one of those approaches. We present it here as an illustration of a viable tool among others.

Lewin's Force Field Analysis

According to Lewin (1997), social phenomena take place within a particular, unique context. He calls this context the force field, and for our purposes, we can consider an organization to be an example of such a force field. The idea of a unique force field highlights the reality that each organization is unique, discouraging a one-size-fits-all approach to achieving systemic change.

As an example of an organization as force field, we can look at Julie's situation. One of the problems facing Julie is that her nurses are expressing a desire to retire upon becoming eligible. If possible, she would therefore like to increase the average retirement age of her nursing staff. If currently the average retirement age of nurses in that hospital is 62, then according to Lewin, the situation can be graphically depicted as a collection of forces acting on the average retirement age; some pushing it up, others pushing it down.

Forces pushing the retirement age down may include financial incentives embedded in defined benefit pension plans, pay inequities vis-à-vis younger workers, poor work relationships with younger, mostly male doctors, deficiencies in working with computers, and insufficient opportunities for flexible work arrangements.

Forces pushing the retirement age up, conversely, are continued health insurance coverage, continuation of current income levels, an opportunity to continue contributing to the community, and membership in a tight-knit professional community. Collectively, these forces are in a dynamic equilib-

rium with each other. This is depicted in Figure 18.1.

In essence, the average retirement age for nurses is a resultant of the totality of the forces that are acting on it. The forces that are pushing the turnover rates up are in equilibrium with those that are pushing it down (the thickness of the arrows represents the strength of the force). Thus, the force field model stimulates a systemic analysis of the issue at hand and a thorough exploration of its determinants. In Lewin's own words:

> For changing a social equilibrium, too, one has to consider the total social field: the groups and subgroups involved, their relations, their value systems, etc. The constellation of the social field as a whole has to be studied and so reorganized that social events flow differently. (p. 327)

Figure 18.1 suggests that Julie thus has two courses of action: either reduce the forces pushing the average retirement age up, or increase the forces pushing it down (or both). Budget constraints may reduce the feasibility of immediately reducing pay equities, while legal constraints may prevent an easy intervention in the defined benefit pension plans. However, much can be done to improve intergenerational relations in the hospital and to increase the amount of available options for work arrangements. The idea, of course, is that only the major forces in either direction should get attention. Focusing on increasing job flexibility would not be a wise way to spend time and energy if its influence is limited.

Julie's situation is an example of an organization in need of intervention. Lewin's tool is equally applicable to larger systems, including those with a nationwide scope. Take the average retirement age in the United States as an example. Assuming that the current average age is 62, this could be graphically depicted as in Figure 18.2.

In this hypothical example, the forces pushing the average retirement age up are insufficient retirement savings, higher life expectancy, improved health at older age, a decrease in the amount of young workers entering the workforce, the prospect of losing health care coverage, and increased job flexibility (e.g., telecommuting). On the other hand, the forces keeping the retirement age down

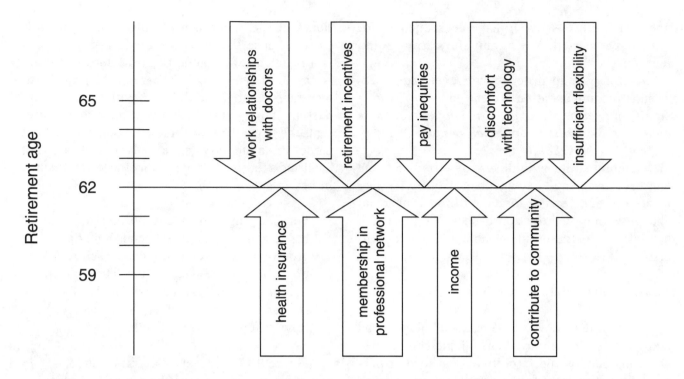

Figure 18.1 Average retirement age for nurses at Julie's hospital as a function of multiple forces.

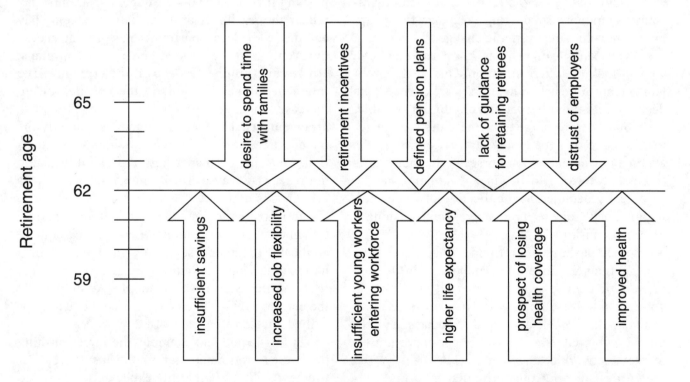

Figure 18.2 National average retirement age as a function of societal forces (hypothetical).

may be distrust of employers, a desire to spend significantly more time with family, lack of guidance for employers with respect to retaining retired workers, intricacies involving Medicare, and defined benefit pension plans.

If, as a nation, the United States is serious about retaining older workers in the labor force longer, a host of issues will have to be addressed, as this force field suggests. Employers need to have guidelines for safely reinstating their retired employees on company payroll. Financial incentives embedded in defined benefit pension plans need to be addressed. The interactions of pension plans with Medicare should also be examined. At the same time, Americans need to start saving more wisely for their retirement, trust needs to be restored, and job flexibility maximized. From this example, it becomes clear that employers must partner with employees, government, and other stakeholder groups (public policy groups, professional associations, and advocacy groups) because no single group can achieve success on its own.

Lewin's force field model can quickly make a complex and inherently dynamic situation transparent, allowing for prioritization and effective interventions. Moreover, it can be applied again when interventions are made in one of the forces. In the example in Figure 18.1, it could very well be that intergenerational relations is the strongest factor over which the hospital can exert some influence in the timing of nurses' retirement. In that case, intergenerational relations itself can be conceptualized as an outcome of a host of different forces. The example above already suggested that these relations may in turn be rooted in doctors' assumptions regarding nurses' capability to work with new technologies as well as in the nurses' sense of competency. It is likely, of course, that there are many other forces that contribute to these workplace relations, some being more amenable to change than others. In turn, the doctors' age- and gender-biased assumptions can be seen as a resultant of yet other forces. And so on. Conceptualizing such forces as resultants of yet other forces stimulates us to explore root causes, preventing us from merely addressing symptoms.

So, how did Julie get from signaling a future crisis to deciding that a training program on technology in health care was time and energy well spent?

Julie realized that any plan of action would take resources, both human and financial. Thus, her first action point was to present her concerns to the hospital's management team and request the formation of a task force to help ward off this crisis. She requested – and was granted – the reassignment of two of her current full-time HR staff, a budget reallocation, and adequate compensation for any hospital employees who would volunteer to serve on this task force.

Julie's next step was to assemble that task force. Besides herself and the two HR staff, Julie recruited a nurse and a supervisor for one day per week. Moreover, she established contact with the local community college, the county's workforce development office, and a representative of the recently opened senior center. As a VP, she represented the hospital administration.

After several meetings, having mapped the crisis and explored various plans of action, Julie's task force decided to pursue two separate tracks. The first focuses on the longer term (more than four years) and consists of the creation of a partnership between the community college, the senior center, and the hospital to recruit and train community members to become nurses as well as recruiting retired physicians to unretire on a part-time basis.

The second track intends to yield payoffs in less than two years and focuses on stemming the brain drain by enticing currently employed nurses to remain employed past retirement age. To this end, a second team was created, consisting of HR staff, nurses, doctors, hospital administration officials, and patients. Based on surveys and interviews with nursing staff, this team analyzed the situation and concluded that the decision to retire is a function of a variety of factors. First, there are the incentives to stay employed. Such incentives include health insurance, an opportunity to continue contributing to the community, continuation of current income levels, and membership in a tight-knit professional community. Second, there are incentives to retire. These include: pay inequities vis-à-vis younger workers; defined benefit retirement plans; inappropriate ageist, sexist, and elitist attitudes among the younger, urban, and mostly male doctors in their interactions with the older, mostly female nurses; insufficient comfort levels in working with emerging technologies; and inadequate opportunities for more flexible work arrangements.

Julie and her team decided to pursue interventions to reduce the incentives to retire, as the incentives to stay employed were not perceived as very amenable to change. Of these incentives to retire, the first two were left alone: reducing pay inequities was not an option because of budgetary complications, and changing pension plans would only start paying off after 10 years or so. The ageist and sexist attitudes of the doctors, problematic as they were, did not seem to be easy to change in a direct manner either. Although increased flexibility in work arrangements was certainly something to work on, the team chose to start by increasing the nurses' comfort level with desktop and handheld computers.

So, how did Julie get there? Although this example is hypothetical and admittedly oversimplified, our answer is that her key to success was that she took *a proactive, collaborative, holistic approach, involving multiple stakeholder groups* from the outset.

Of course, not every organization is headed for a crisis as urgent as Julie's hospital. Many, if not most American organizations are not headed for one – that is, not in a distinct, identifiable way. To them, the aging of the workforce is akin to a distant thundercloud, and since it is unclear when or if that cloud will ever make its presence felt, they continue to proceed with their daily business, increasing shareholder value quarter by quarter.

Yet other organizations take a different approach: the thundercloud is real, but its distance prevents them from seeing a clear sequence of steps to take. If there is no imminent crisis, why move? And if there is reason to move, what should be the first steps?

To answer those questions indirectly, we ask you to fast forward to 2020 and read the following descriptions of two different Internet companies.

Frank is CEO of one of the few Internet startup companies that survived the industry's collapse in the late 1990s. He founded the company as a college student at the age of 19, in 1996. Currently employing 56 full-time employees, he values youthful energy and ambition. It is to these attributes that he owes the very survival of the company. During the crisis of the late 1990s, he and his cofounders were able to consistently put in 80+ hour workweeks and thus outperform their competitors. Over time, his cofounders have left the company. In most cases, the constant pressures to perform took their toll on the early employees, in spite of more-than-competitive levels of compensation.

Currently, Frank is in a bit of a quagmire. He is noticing that turnover rates have gone up in his company. Until now, turnover was always essentially good. When an employee left, it allowed him to hire a young, ambitious college graduate. He could pay less while expecting more and avoid costly training. At the same time, he could keep his company young and aggressive.

The current reality is quite different, however. College graduates are no longer available in the quantities he was used to. On the one hand, it has become harder to replace workers with recent college graduates when they leave. On the other hand, it has also become harder to keep them from leaving in the first place – including his high performers. They are no longer responding to incentives to work harder and they are increasingly citing family pressures as reasons to leave. In spite of the pay cuts they are taking, they are opting for more family-friendly work environments.

At age 43, he has noticed that it is becoming more and more difficult for him to keep that pace and continue to set that example for his employees. As a result, Frank has started to question his management approach, not in the least because his costs have gone up significantly. He increasingly relies on independent contractors, many of whom are retired, and temp agencies to get the job done.

With his company facing increased competition from much cheaper and equally ambitious firms located primarily in India, China, and Russia, Frank realizes that the current work pace is not sustainable in the long term. He recognizes that the sole source of sustainable competitive advantage over his competitors lies in his human resources, particularly those who have intimate knowledge of the business and those who maintain relationships with customers. Therefore, if Frank is to survive another crisis, he must stem the brain drain, in particular among his older, long-term employees. However, he has no idea where or how to start.

✦ ✦ ✦ ✦

Chris is founder and CEO of a market-leading firm in Internet-based financial services. In 2003, at the age of 29, she left the company she had co-founded in 1996 because of a mismatch, as she puts it, between the organizational values and her own. While that organization, wildly successful at first and still in existence, rewarded hard work, she noticed that her recent marriage was already under pressure from prolonged working hours. The burst of the tech bubble in the late 1990s was cause for reflection for her.

At the end of the 20th century, the software industry was notorious for systematically excluding older workers from employment. It was also responsible for its own demise, she felt. Although she could not prove it, she had a hunch that perhaps the tech bubble had burst because of the exclusion of older workers. She had an epiphany that older workers are probably much more valuable to employers than had been suspected. She tried something new in the industry and founded a firm that specifically targets older workers for employment.

At age 46, Chris is younger than most of her 2,200 employees, who are, on average, 55 years old. According to industry analysts, one of the main strengths of Chris's firm, and a critical competitive advantage, is superior customer service. The call center, where 90 percent of customer service transactions are made, employs a total of 500 workers with an average age of 65. The vast majority of them work part-time, and the sheer amount of workers on the payroll ensures sufficient flexibility for all because it is easy to swap shifts with someone else.

"I can train anyone on the specifics of the products we offer," Chris says about the call center. "But it is much more difficult to teach someone customer service skills. I have found that older workers generally outperform younger ones in this area. They are more balanced, they are better listeners, and they do not take it personally when a customer gets upset at them. They are very good relationship builders and relationship menders."

So what is Chris's secret to her success? "In our company, older workers are spread out across the company and across hierarchical levels. The success we've had with our call center and the critical edge it has given us in the market could lead one to think that we only employ older workers in the call center. But we are careful to avoid that." The average age of workers outside the call center is 39, much lower than in the call center. The reason for the difference is that the vast majority of jobs outside the call center are regular, full-time jobs that are not yet available for part-time or job-sharing arrangements. "In the call center, we just have employment contracts where employees commit to working a certain number of hours a month, and it is up to the individual employees, their co-workers, and their managers and supervisors to sort out when those hours are worked," Chris explains. "For many retirees, and for us, this is an ideal arrangement. But for the other jobs, we are now also increasing flexibility in arrangements. Although there are costs in the short term, the call center has taught us that the payoff in the longer term is enormous. Plus, if we don't follow through with increasing this flexibility, what will eventually happen is that we limit the late careers of these workers to call center positions. Some of our workers may get restless in that position after some time, and when they do, I want to make sure we can offer some attractive alternatives. That would also help us avoid the perception of a class system where the older workers are relegated to the call center, as if they were second-class employees. Given the critical importance of our call center, that would seriously jeopardize our market position in the long run. So we clearly have enough of an incentive to continue increasing flexibility and accommodating older employees. As we speak, we are actually considering a job-sharing arrangement for the Chief Financial Officer position. You see, this is not philanthropy, although I do believe it is the right thing to do. It is a strategy that just makes good business sense."

But what about younger employees? Do they perceive preferential treatment toward the older employees? "No. They too benefit from increased flexibility. Whether our workers have eldercare or childcare responsibilities, job flexibility will help them meet those demands. Although sometimes this causes some managerial stress, overall our work-ers are more satisfied, more productive, and more committed. And that is something we cannot put a price tag on. It all contributes to a healthy work environment for everyone who works here, but it takes a while to get to this point. In our case, it has taken consistent, public support from me and my management team, and intense and constant communication up and down. Of course, there were additional challenges: to walk the talk and make our performance appraisals, promotion criteria, and other HR processes consistent with these values."

The result? Chris beams when she reports that turnover rates are 50 percent below the industry average for call centers, so worker retention is not an issue. Moreover, recruitment is hardly a prob-lem either: "Whenever workers leave, potential re-cruits are referred by other workers or attracted by word-of-mouth."

We hope you will agree that Chris is in a more enviable position than Frank. Chris recognized long ago that older workers can yield a competitive edge for her company and she calibrated all her HR strat-egies and processes to that premise. Over time, she has built a healthy company that acts in accordance with its espoused values. Frank, on the other hand, followed a strategy that may appear to have been dictated by market forces but his hiring practices really were based on fallacious assumptions regard-ing older workers. Almost 25 years later, he real-izes that things are going wrong and senses that substantive change is going to be needed if his com-pany is going to be sustainable in the future.

This brings up the parable of the frog and the hot water. As legend has it, when a frog is thrown into boiling water, it will immediately jump out, minimizing injury. However, when it is placed in cool water, and the heat is gradually increased, the frog will be unable to move by the time it realizes that it is being boiled. Julie was thrown into boiling water: the consequences of inaction were immedi-ately very clear to her. She jumped out and mini-mized injury. Frank was initially very comfortable in the cool water. He either did not notice the water warming, or he chose to ignore it. The price he pays is that he is metaphorically almost dead in the wa-ter. It may take some desperate moves to create the kind of changes that his company needs to survive. Chris is in the best shape because she was more proactive than Frank or even Julie. She moved even before the water got warmer.

We now return to the two questions posed ear-lier. We hope that we have answered the question, "Why move?" by contrasting Frank's and Chris's situations and relating them to the parable of the frog.

The question, "Where to start in the absence of an imminent crisis?" remains. Our conclusion that all issues are interrelated, and that an intervention in one area will spill over in another, suggests that it really does not matter where to start. Those look-ing for a specific action plan with steps that will guide a change process from point A to point B will be quickly overwhelmed because of the sheer complexity of the issues and the many viable start-ing points. Moreover, the local, contextualized par-ticularities of each organization prevent any kind of one-size-fits-all approach that we could recom-mend. What matters is not how to get there as much as *that* the process is started. Since all roads lead to Rome, all that is needed is a compass and a broadly supported willingness to travel. Rather than worry about what exit to take next on the road to this some-what elusive destination, it might be better to speak, act, and think as though you are already there. De-scribe your organization in 2020 as specifically as possible. Are you Chris? Or Frank?

This visioning will expose gaps and weaknesses that need to be addressed and the road map, unique to each organization, will become clear along the way. The only recommendation that holds true, re-gardless of the characteristics of any particular or-ganization, is that in order to affect significant, last-ing change, it is imperative that a collaborative, holistic approach be taken, involving multiple stakeholder groups.

References

AARP. (1993a). *How to recruit older workers*. Washington, DC: AARP.

AARP. (1993b). *How to train older workers*. Washington, DC: AARP Workforce Programs Department. (ERIC Document Reprodution Service No. ED 392893).

AARP. (1998). *Boomers look forward toward retirement*. Washington, DC: AARP.

AARP. (1999). *A profile of older Americans: 1999*. Washington, DC: AARP.

AARP. (2000a). *American business and older employees: A summary of findings*. Washington, DC: AARP.

AARP. (2000b, September/October). Tips for employers: How to attract and retain older workers. *Working Age, 16*(3), 2-3.

AARP. (2001, July). *In the middle: A report on multicultural boomers coping with family and aging issues*. Washington, DC: Belden, Russonello & Stewart, & Great Falls, VA: Research/Strategy/Management. Retrieved March 30, 2003, from http://research.aarp.org/il/in the middle.pdf.

AARP Public Policy Institute. (1998). *Boomers approaching midlife: How secure a future?* Washington, DC: AARP.

AARP Public Policy Institute. (2002). *Update on the older worker: 2001*. Washington, DC: S. E. Rix. Retrieved March 30, 2003, from http://research.aarp.org/econ/dd69 worker.pdf.

Achenbaum, W. A. (1994). U.S. retirement in historical context. In A. Monk (Ed.), *The Columbia retirement handbook* (pp.12-28). New York: Columbia University Press.

Achenbaum, W. A., & Morrison, M. H. (1993). *Is unretirement unprecedented?* In S. A. Bass, F. G. Caro, and Y. P. Chen (Eds.), *Achieving a productive aging society* (pp. 97-116). Westport, CT: Auburn House.

Acker, J. (1990). Hierarchies, jobs, bodies: A theory of gendered organizations. *Gender & Society, 4*(2),139-159.

Adams, G. A., & Beehr, T. A. (1998). Turnover and retirement: A comparison of their similarities and differences. *Personnel Psychology, 51*(3), 643-665.

Adams, G. A., & Lax, G. A. (2002, April). Job seeking among retirees seeking bridge employment. In K. S. Shultz (Chair), *Addressing projected workforce shortages by recruiting and retaining older workers*. Symposium conducted at the 17th annual meeting of the Society for Industrial and Organizational Psychology (SIOP), Toronto, Canada.

Aeppel, T. (2002, July 1). Tricks of the trade: On factory floors, top workers hide secrets to success. *Wall Street Journal*, p. A1.

Agency for Healthcare Research and Quality. (2002, June). *1998 Medical expenditure panel survey: Table compendium*. Rockville, MD: Agency for Healthcare Research and Quality. Retrieved March 30, 2003, from http://www.meps.ahrq.govCompendium Tables/98Ch1/TC98Ch1 TOC.htm.

Alfred, M. V. (2001). Expanding theories of career development: Adding the voices of African American women in the white academy. *Adult Education Quarterly, 51*(2), 108-127.

Allen, K. R., & Barber, K.M. (1994). Issues of gender. In P. C. McKenry & S. J. Price (Eds.), *Familes and change* (pp. 21-39). Thousand Oaks, CA: Sage.

Allen, T. D., McManus, S. E., & Russell, J. E. A. (1999). Newcomer socialization and stress: Formal peer relationships as a source of support. *Journal of Vocational Behavior, 54*(3), 453-470.

Allport, G. W. (1979). *The nature of prejudice* (25th anniversary ed.). Reading, MA: Addison-Wesley.

Amabile, T. M., Patterson, C., Mueller, J., Wojcik, T., Odomirok, P. W, Marsh, M., & Kramer, S. (2001). Academic-practitioner collaboration in management research: A case of cross-profession collaboration. *Academy of Management Journal, 44*(2), 418-431.

Ancona, D. G., Kochan, T., Scully, M., Van Maanen, J., & Westney, D. E. (1999). *Managing for the future: Organizational behavior and processes*. Boston: South-Western College.

Andrisani, P., & Daymont, T. (1987). Age changes in productivity and earnings among managers and professionals. In S. H. Sandell (Ed.), *The problem isn't age: Work and older Americans* (pp. 52-70). New York: Praeger.

Argyris, C. (1964/1990). *Integrating the individual and the organization*. New Brunswick, NJ: Transaction Publishers.

Arnold, J., & Jackson, C. (1997). The new career: Issues and challenges. *British Journal of Guidance and Counselling, 2*(4), 427-434.

Arthur, D. (1998). *Recruiting, interviewing, selecting & orienting new employees* (3rd ed.). New York: AMACOM.

Arthur, W., Fuentes, R., & Doverspike, D. (1990). Relationships among personnel tests, age, and job performance. *Experimental Aging Research, 16*(1), 11-16.

Ashford, S.J., & Black, J.S. (1996). Proactivity during organizational entry: The role of desire for control. *Journal of Applied Psychology, 81*(2), 199-214.

Auerbach, J. A., & Welsh, J. C. (Eds.). (1994). *Aging and competition: Rebuilding the U.S. workforce*. Washington, DC: National Council On the Aging, Inc., & the National Planning Association.

Baird, C. L., & Reynolds, J. R. (2002). *The 1993 Family and Medical Leave Act: Employee awareness of family leave benefits*. Unpublished manuscript.

Baldi, R. A. (1997). Training older adults to use the computer: Issues related to the workplace, attitudes, and training. *Educational Gerontology, 23*(5), 453-465.

Baltes, P. B., & Lindenberger, U. (1997). Emergence of a powerful connection between sensory and cognitive functions across the adult life span: A new window in the study of cognitive aging? *Psychology and Aging, 12*(1), 12-21.

Baltes, P. B., Reese, H. W., & Lipsitt, L. P. (1980). Life-span developmental psychology. *Annual Review of Psychology, 31*, 65-110.

Barber, A. E. (1998). *Recruiting employees: Individual and organizational perspectives*. Thousand Oaks, CA: Sage.

Barber, G. M., Crouch, R. T., & Merker, S. L. (1992). Implications of an aging labor force for human resource development policy. *Educational Gerontology 18*(1), 99-110.

Barkin, S. (1970). Retraining and job redesign: Positive approaches to the continued employment of older persons. In H. L. Sheppard (Ed.), *Toward an industrial gerontology: An introduction to a new field of applied research and service* (pp. 17-30). Cambridge, MA: Schenkman.

Barnett, R. C. (1994). Home to work spillover revisited: A study of full-time employed women in dual-earner couples. *Journal of Marriage and the Family 56*(3), 647-656.

Barnett, R. C. (1999). A new work-life model for the twenty-first century. *The annals of the American Academy of Political and Social Science, 562*, 143-158.

Baron, J. N. (1994). Reflections on recent generations of mobility research. In D. B. Grusky (Ed.), *Social stratification: Class, race, and gender in sociological perspective* (pp. 384-393). Boulder, CO: Westview Press.

Baron, R. A. (1996). Interpersonal relations in organizations. In K. R. Murphy (Ed.), *Individual difference and behavior in organizations* (pp. 334-370). San Francisco: Jossey-Bass.

Bartel, A., & Sicherman, N. (1993). Technological change and retirement decisions of older workers. *Journal of Labor Economics 11*(1), 162-183.

Barth, M. C., McNaught, W., & Rizzi, P. (1993). Corporations and the aging workforce. In P. H. Mirvis (Ed.), *Building the competitive workforce: Investing in human capital for corporate success* (pp. 156-200). New York: Wiley.

Barth, M. C., McNaught, W., & Rizzi, P. (1995). Older Americans as workers. In S. A. Bass (Ed.), *Older and active: How Americans over 55 are contributing to society* (pp. 35-70). New Haven, CT: Yale University Press.

Baruch, G. K., & Barnett, R. (1986). Role quality, multiple role involvement, and psychological well-being in midlife women. *Journal of Personality and Social Psychology, 51*, 578-585.

Bass, S. A. (1995a). Older and active. In S. A. Bass (Ed.), *Older and active: How Americans over 55 are contributing to society* (pp. 1-9). New Haven, CT: Yale University Press.

Bass, S. A. (Ed.). (1995b). *Older and active: How Americans over 55 are contributing to society.* New Haven: Yale University Press.

Bass, S. A. (1995c). *Productive aging and the role of older people in Japan: New approaches for the United States.* New York: Japan Society, Inc. and International Leadership Center on Longevity and Society.

Bass, S. A., Caro, F. G., & Chen, Y. P. (Eds.). (1993). *Achieving a productive aging society.* Westport, CT: Auburn House.

Bauer, T. N., Morrison, E. W., & Callister, R. R. (1998). Organizational socialization: A review and directions for future research. *Research in Personnel and Human Resource Management, 16*, 149-214.

Becker, G. (1964). *Human capital.* New York: Columbia University Press.

Becker, H. S. (1960). Notes on the concept of commitment. *American Journal of Sociology, 66*, 32-40.

Bee, H. L. (2000). *The journey of adulthood* (4th ed.). New Jersey: Prentice Hall.

Beehr, T. A., Taber, T. D., & Walsh, J. T. (1980). Perceived mobility channels: Criteria for intraorganizational job mobility. *Organizational Behavior & Human Decision Processes, 26*(2), 250-264.

Beers, T. M. (2000, June). Flexible schedules and shift work: Replacing the '9-to-5' workday? *Monthly Labor Review, 123*(6), 33-40.

Belliveau, M. A., O'Reilly, C. A. I., & Wade, J. B. (1996). Social capital at the top: Effects of social similarity and status on CEO compensation. *Academy of Management Journal, 39*(6), 1568-1593.

Bengtson, V., Rosenthal, C., & Burton, L. (1990). Families and aging: Diversity and heterogeneity. In R. Binstock & L. George (Eds.), *Handbook of aging and the social sciences* (3rd ed., pp. 263-287). San Diego, CA: Academic Press.

Bengtson, V., Rosenthal, C., & Burton, L. (1996). Paradoxes of families and aging. In R. Binstock & L. George (Eds.), *Handbook of aging and the social sciences* (4th ed., pp. 253-283). San Diego, CA: Academic Press.

Bennett-Alexander, D. D., & Pincus, L. B. (1998). *Employment law for business* (2nd ed.). San Francisco: McGraw-Hill.

Bennis, W. (1997). *Managing people is like herding cats.* Provo, UT: Executive Excellence.

Benokraitis, N. V. (1997). Sex discrimination in the 21st century. In N. V. Benokraitis (Ed.), *Subtle sexism: Current practice and prospects for change* (pp. 5-33). Thousand Oaks, CA: Sage.

Bianchi, S. M. (2000). Maternal employment and time with children: Dramatic change or surprising continuity? *Demography, 37*(4), 401-414.

Bird, S. R. (1996). Welcome to the men's club: Homosociality and the maintenance of hegemonic masculinity. *Gender & Society, 10*(2), 120-132.

Bloch, M. (2000). The changing face of the workforce. *Training, 37*(12), 72-78.

Blumental, A. J., Cober, R. T., & Doverspike, D. (2000). Appreciating differences in work ethic: Comparing techno-savvy Generation Xers to Baby Boomers. *Journal of e.Commerce and Psychology, 1*, 60-77.

Booth, A. L. (1993). Private sector training and graduate earnings. *The Review of Economics and Statistics, 75*(1), 164-170.

Bourdieu, P. (1977). *Reproduction: In education, society, and culture.* Beverly Hills, CA: Sage.

Bové, R. (1987). Retraining the older worker. *Training and Development Journal, 41*(3), 76-78.

Boyd, S. A., & Treas, J. (1996). Family care of the frail elderly: A new look at women in the middle. In J. Quadagno & D. Street (Eds.), *Aging for the twenty-first century* (pp. 262-268). New York: St. Martin's Press.

Brewer, M. B. (1995). Managing diversity: The role of social identities. In S. E. Jackson & M. N. Ruderman (Eds.), *Diversity in work teams: Research paradigms for a changing workplace* (pp. 47-68). Washington, DC: American Psychological Association.

Brewer, M. B., & Kramer, R. M. (1985). The psychology of intergroup attitudes and behavior. *Annual Review of Psychology, 36*, 219-243.

Bridges, W. (1994). *JobShift.* Reading, MA: Addison-Wesley.

Brody, E. M. (1981). 'Women in the middle' and family help to older people. *The Gerontologist, 21*(5), 472-479.

Brody, E. M. (1985). Parent care as a normative family stress. *The Gerontologist, 25*(1), 19-29.

Brotherton, P. (2000, March/April). Tapping into an older workforce. *Mosaics*, pp. 1-4.

Brubaker, T. H., & Powers, E. A. (1976). The stereotype of "old": A review and alternative approach. *Journal of Gerontology, 31*(4), 441-447.

Bryant, A. (1997, November 2). How much has Texaco changed? *The New York Times*, pp. C1, C16, C17.

Bureau of Labor Statistics. (1967). *Occupational mobility of employed workers.* (Special Labor Force Report No. 84) Washington, DC: S. Saben.

Bureau of Labor Statistics. (1975). *Occupational mobility of workers.* (Special Labor Force, Report No. 176). Washington, DC: J. J. Byrne.

Bureau of Labor Statistics. (2001). Labor Force. *Occupational Outlook Quarterly, 45*(4), 36-41. Retrieved March 30, 2003, from http://www.bls.gov/opub/ooq/2001/winter/art06.pdf.

Burke, R. J. (1994). Generation X: Measures, sex and age differences. *Psychological Reports, 74*(2), 555-562.

Burt, R. S. (1997). The contingent value of social capital. *Administrative Science Quarterly, 42*(2), 339-365.

Byster, D. (1998). A critique of career self-reliance. *Career Planning and Adult Development Journal, 14*(2), 17-28.

Caffarella, R. S., & Barnett, B. G. (1994). Characteristics of adult learners and foundations for experiential learning. In L. Jackson & R. S. Caffarella (Eds.), *Experiential learning: A new approach* (pp. 29-42). New directions for adult and continuing education, no. 62. San Francisco: Jossey-Bass.

Campbell, J. C. (1992). *How policies change.* Princeton, NJ: Princeton University Press.

Cantor, M. H. (1995). Families and caregiving in an aging society. In L. Burton (Ed.), *Families and Aging* (pp. 135-144). Amityville, NY: Baywood.

Carnevale, A. P., & Stone, S. C. (1994). Developing the new competitive workforce. In J. A. Auerbach & J. C. Welsh (Eds.), *Aging and competition: Rebuilding the U.S. workforce* (pp. 94-144). Washington, DC: The National Council on the Aging, Inc., & the National Planning Association.

Carnevale, A. P., & Stone, S. C. (1995). *The American mosaic: An in-depth report on the future of diversity at work.* New York: McGraw-Hill.

Carson, R. (2002, March 6). Increasing numbers of workers decide to return to work after retirement, *The News Tribune,* p. SL1.

Caudron, S. (1997). Boomers rock the system. *Workforce, 76*(12), 42-47.

Centers for Disease Control & Prevention (2001a, October 9). Deaths: Preliminary data for 2000. *National Vital Statistics Reports, 49*(12). Atlanta, GA: A. M. Minino & B. L. Smith. Retrieved March 23, 2003, from http://www.cdc.gov/nchs/data/nvsr/nvsr49/nvsr49 12.pdf.

Centers for Disease Control & Prevention (2001b, February 7). United States life tables, 1998. Deaths: Preliminary Data for 2000. *National Vital Statistics Reports, 48*(18). Atlanta, GA: R. N. Anderson. Retrieved March 30, 2003, from http://www.cdc.gov/nchs/data/nvsr/nvsr48/nvs48 18.pdf.

Cerella, J., Poon, L. W., & Williams, D. M. (1980). Age and the complexity hypothesis. In L. W. Poon (Ed.), *Aging in the nineteen-eighties: Psychological Issues* (pp. 332-340). Washington, DC: American Psychological Association.

Challenger, J. A. (2000). 24 Trends reshaping the workplace. *The Futurist, 34*(5), 35-41.

Challenger, J. E. (1997, January 6). Wise employers plan "soft landing" for retirees. *Houston Business Journal.* Retrieved April 3, 2003, from http://www.amcity.com/houston/stories/010697/editorial5.html.

Charness, N., Schumann, C. E., & Boritz, G. M. (1992). Training older adults in word processing: Effects of age, training technique, and computer anxiety. *International Journal of Technology & Aging, 5*(1), 79-106.

Clark, M. S., & Reis, H. T. (1988). Interpersonal processes in close relationships. *Annual Review of Psychology, 39,* 609-672.

Clark, S. K. (1994). Training implications for our graying work force. *Performance & Instruction, 33*(1), 30-32.

Cleveland, J. N., & Hollman, G. (1991). Context and discrimination in personnel decisions: Direct and mediated approaches. In J. R. Meindl (Ed.), *Advances in Information Processing in Organizations* (Vol. 4, pp. 223-237). Greenwich, CT: JAI Press.

Cleveland, J. N., Shore, L. M., & Murphy, K. R. (1997). Person- and context-oriented perceptual age measures: Additional evidence of distinctiveness and usefulness. *Journal of Organizational Behavior* (UK), *18*(3), 239-251.

Cober, R. T., Brown, D. J., Blumental, A. J., Doverspike, D., & Levy, P. (2000). The quest for the qualified job surfer: It's time the public sector catches the wave. *Public Personnel Management, 29*(4), 479-496.

Cohen, E. (2002, March 4). The life and times of an extreme mom. *Newsweek,* p. 12.

Collins, J. C., & Porras, J. (1994/1997). *Built to last: Successful habits of visionary companies.* New York: HarperBusiness.

Committee for Economic Development (1999). *New opportunities for older workers.* New York: Committee for Economic Development. Retrieved April 15, 2003, from http://www.ced.org/docs/report/report_older.pdf.

Commonwealth Fund (2002, May). *Are tax credits alone the solution to affordable health insurance? Comparing individual and group insurance costs in 17 U.S. markets* (Pub. No. 527). J. R. Gabel, K. Dhont, & J. Pickreign. Retrieved March 30, 2003, from http://www.cmwf.org/programs/insurance/gabel taxcredits 527.pdf.

Congressional Budget Office (2002). *The budget and economic outlook: Fiscal years 2003-2012.* Washington, DC: U.S. Government Printing Office. Retrieved March 20, 2003, from http://www.cbo.gov/showdoc.cfm?index=3277&sequence=0.

Congressional Research Service (2002a, October 7). *Pensions and retirement savings plans: Sponsorship and participation.* Washington, DC: P. J. Purcell.

Congressional Research Service (2002b, December 12). *Retirement savings and household wealth in 2000: Analysis of Census Bureau data.* Washington, DC: P. J. Purcell.

Cook, J. (2002, March 20). Junior Instructors. *Human Resource Executive, 16*(4), 33-35.

Coombes, A. (2002, November 14). *Fewer workers contributing to 401(k)'s, survey finds.* Retrieved March 23, 2003, from http://cbs.marketwatch.com/news/newsfinder/default.asp?Property=mktwissue&siteid=mktw&value=Personal+Finance&hidProp=mktw-issue&doctype=2005&Button=Go&scid=3&source=&dtmToMonth=11&dtmToDate=14&dtmToYear=2002&selCount=20

Cooperman, L. F., & Keast, F. D. (1983). *Adjusting to an older workforce.* New York: Van Nostrand Reinhold.

Coppock, S., & Zebrak, A. (2001, April 24). Finding the right fit: Medicare, prescription drugs and current coverage options. *Testimony before the United States Senate, Committee on Finance.*

Corso, J. F. (1987). Sensory-perceptual processes and aging. In K. W. Schaie & C. Eisdorfer (Eds.), *Annual review of gerontology* (Vol. 7; p. 29-55). New York: Springer.

Costello, C. (1997). *Training older workers for the future.* Cambridge, MA: Radcliffe Public Policy Institute.

Cox, T. J. (1995). The complexity of diversity: Challenges and directions for future research. In S. E. Jackson & M. N. Ruderman (Eds.), *Diversity in work teams: Research paradigms for a changing workplace* (pp. 235-246). Washington, DC: American Psychological Association.

Cox, T. J. (2001). *Creating the multicultural organization: A strategy for capturing the power of diversity.* San Francisco: Jossey-Bass.

Crosby, F. J. (1991). *Juggling.* New York: Free Press.

Crown, W. H. (Ed.). (1996). *Handbook on employment and the elderly.* Westport, CT: Greenwood.

Cutler, D. M. (1995, September). *Technology, health costs, and the NIH.* Paper prepared for the National Institutes of Health Economics roundtable on biomedical research, Cambridge, MA.

Czaja, S. J. (1995). Aging and work performance. *Review of Public Personnel Administration, 15*(2), 46-61.

Czaja, S. J., & Drury, C. G. (1981). Aging and pretraining in industrial inspection. *Human Factors, 23*(4), 485-494.

Czaja, S. J., & Sharit, J. (1998). Age differences in attitudes toward computers. *The Journals of Gerontology, 53B*(5), 329-340.

Dailey, N. (1998). *When baby boomer women retire.* Westport, CT: Praeger.

Deal, T., & Kennedy, A. (1982). *Corporate culture.* Reading, MA: Addison-Wesley.

De Dreu, C. K. W., & Van Vianen, A. E. M. (2001). Managing relationship conflict and the effectiveness of organizational teams. *Journal of Organizational Behavior, 22*(3), 309-328.

Dennis, H. (1988). *Fourteen steps in maintaining an aging work force.* Lexington, MA: Lexington Books.

DiMaggio, P. (1994). Social stratification, life-style, and social cognition. In D. B. Grusky (Ed.), *Social stratification: Class, race, and gender in sociological perspective* (pp. 458-465). Boulder, CO: Westview Press.

Dixon, N. M. (1990). *Evaluation: A tool for improving HRD quality.* San Diego, CA: University Associates.

Dobbs, A. R., & Rule, B. G. (1989). Adult differences in working memory. *Psychology and Aging, 4*(4), 500-503.

Doeringer, P. B. (Ed.). (1990). *Bridges to retirement: Older workers in a changing labor market.* Ithaca, NY: Cornell University Press.

Doeringer, P. B., & Terkla, D. G. (1990). Business necessity, bridge jobs, and the nonbureaucratic firm. In P. B. Doeringer (Ed.), *Bridges to retirement: Older workers in a changing labor market* (pp. 146-171). Ithaca, NY: Cornell University Press.

Doverspike, D., Taylor, M. A., Shultz, K. S. & McKay, P. F. (2000). Responding to the challenge of a changing workforce: Recruiting nontraditional demographic groups. *Public Personnel Management, 29*(4), 445-460.

Doverspike, D., & Tuel, R. C. (2000). *The difficult hire: Seven recruitment and selection principles for hard to fill positions.* Manassas Park, VA: Impact.

Driver, M. J. (1994). Workforce personality and the new information age workplace. In J. A. Auerbach & J. C. Welsh (Eds.), *Aging and competition: Rebuilding the U.S. workforce* (pp. 185-204). Washington, DC: The National Council on the Aging, Inc., & the National Planning Association.

Drucker, P. F. (1999). *Management challenges for the 21st century.* New York: HarperCollins.

Drucker, P. F. (2001, November 3). The next society: A survey of the near future. *The Economist,* 3-20.

Duncan, G., & Hoffman, S. (1979). On the job training and earnings differences by race and sex. *The Review of Economics and Statistics, 61*(4), 594-603.

Dunkin, A. (1998, October 12). Saying adios to the office. *Business Week,* 152-156.

Dwyer, J. W. (1995). The effects of illness on the family. In R. Blieszner & V. Bedford (Eds.), *Handbook of aging and the family* (pp. 401-421). Westport, CT: Greenwood.

Dwyer, J. W., & Coward, R. T. (Eds.). (1992). *Gender, families, and eldercare.* Newbury Park, CA: Sage.

Dwyer, J. W., Folts, W. E., & Rosenberg, E. (1994). Caregiving in a social context. *Educational Gerontology 20*(7), 615-631.

Dychtwald, K. (1990). *Age wave: How the most important trend of our time will change your future.* New York: Bantam Books.

Dychtwald, K. (2000). *Age power: How the 21st century will be ruled by the new old.* Los Angeles: J. P. Tarcher.

Elias, P., Elias, M., Robbins, M., & Gage, P. (1987). Acquisition of 'word processing skills by younger, middle-age, and older adults. *Psychology and Aging, 2*(4), 340-348.

Elliot, R. H. (1995). Human resource management's role in the future aging of the workforce. *Review of Public Personnel Administration, 15*(2), 5-17.

Elman, C. (1998). Adult education: Bringing in a sociological perspective. *Research on Aging, 20*(4), 379-388.

Elman, C., & O'Rand, A. (1998). Midlife entry into vocational training: A mobility model. *Social Science Research 27*(2), 128–158.

Employee Benefit Research Institute. (1991, March). *Retiree health benefits: Issues of structure, financing, and coverage* (Issue Brief no. 112). Washington, DC: J. Davis.

Employee Benefit Research Institute. (1992, October). *The distribution of family oriented benefits* (Issue Brief No. 130). Washington, DC: B. Miller

Employee Benefit Research Institute. (1997). *Increased saving, but little planning: Results of the '97 retirement confidence survey* (Policy Brief No. 191). Washington, DC: P. Yakoboski & J. Dickemper.

Employee Benefit Research Institute. (1999). *Retirement patterns and bridge jobs in the 1990's* (Policy Brief No. 206). Washington, DC: J. Quinn.

Employee Benefit Research Institute. (2000a, March). Rollover rates. *Facts from EBRI.* Retrieved March 19, 2003, from http://www.ebri.org/facts/0300fact1.htm.

Employee Benefit Research Institute. (2000b, November). *Women and pensions: A decade of progress?* (Issue Brief 227). Washington, DC: V. L. Bajtelsmit & N. A. Jianakoplos.

Employee Benefit Research Institute. (2001a, February). *401(k) Plan asset allocation, account balances, and loan activity in 1999.* (Issue Brief 230). Washington, DC: J. VanDerhei & S. Holden.

Employee Benefit Research Institute. (2001b, October). *Contribution behavior of 401(k) plan participants* (Issue Brief 238). Washington, DC: S. Holden & J. L. VanDerhei.

Employee Benefit Research Institute. (2001c, March). *Defined contribution health benefits* (Issue Brief no. 231). Washington, DC: P. Fronstin.

Employee Benefit Research Institute. (2001d, August). *Retiree health benefits: Trends and outlook* (Issue Brief No. 236). Washington, DC: P. Fronstin.

Employee Benefit Research Institute. (2002a, July). *Can 'consumerism' slow the rate of health benefit cost increases?* (Issue Brief no. 247). Washington, DC: P. Fronstin.

Employee Benefit Research Institute. (2002b, January). *Company stock in 401(k) plans; results of a survey of ISCEBS members* (Special Report). Washington, DC: J. L. VanDerhei.

Employment Policy Foundation (2000, February 2). Temporary workers – no longer growing. Retrieved March 20, 2003, from http://www.epf.org/etrend/02feb2000/et02feb2000pg1.htm.

Encyclopedia of associations (2001). Detroit, MI: Gale Research Co.

Epstein, C. F. (1987). Multiple demands and multiple roles: The conditions of successful management. In F. Crosby (Ed.), *Spouse, parent, worker: On gender and multiple roles* (pp. 25-35). New Haven, CT: Yale University Press.

Eurich, N. P. (1990). *The learning industry.* Princeton, NJ: Carnegie Foundation for the Advancement of Teaching.

Exodus begins: Early educator retirements haunt schools (2001, July 9). *Worcester Telegram & Gazette,* p. A6.

Ezra, M., & Deckman, M. (1996). Balancing work and family responsibilities: Flextime and childcare in the federal government. *Public Administration Review 56*(2), 174-176.

Family Caregiver Alliance. (1999). *Fact sheet: Work and eldercare.* San Francisco, CA: Family Caregiver Alliance.

Family Caregiver Alliance. (2000). *Interview with Donna R. Lenhoff.* San Francisco, CA: Family Caregiver Alliance. Retrieved March 30, 2003, from http://www.caregiver.org/interviewsdlenhoffC.html.

Farr, J. L., & Middlebrooks, C. L., (1990). Enhancing motivation to participate in professional development. In S. L. Willis & S. S. Dubin (Eds.), *Maintaining professional competence: Approaches to career enhancement, vitality, and success throughout a work life* (pp. 195-213). San Francisco: Jossey-Bass.

Farr, J. L., Tesluk, P. E., & Klein, S. R. (1998). Organizational structure of the workplace and the older worker. In K. W. Schaie & C. Schooler (Eds.), *Impact of work on older adults,* (pp. 143-185). New York: Springer.

Federal Interagency Forum on Aging Related Statistics. (2000). *Older Americans 2000: Key indicators of well-being.* Washington, DC: U.S. Government Printing Office.

Feldman, D. C. (1988). *Managing careers in organizations.* Boston, MA: Scott, Foresman.

Feldman, D. C. (1994). The decision to retire early: A review and conceptualization. *Academy of Management Review, 19*(2), 285-311.

Feldman, D. C. (2002). Stability in the midst of change: A developmental perspective on the study of careers. In D. C. Feldman (Ed.), *Work careers: A developmental perspective* (pp. 3-26). San Francisco: Jossey-Bass.

Feldman, D. C., & Kim, S. (2000). Bridge employment during retirement: A field study of individual and organizational experiences with post-retirement employment. *Human Resource Planning, 23*(1), 14-25.

Fernandez, J. P. (1998). *Race, gender, and rhetoric: The true state of race and gender relations in corporate America.* New York: McGraw-Hill.

Ferree, M. M. (1990). Beyond separate spheres: Feminism and family research. *Journal of Marriage and the Family, 52*(4), 866-884.

Fidelity Workplace Services (2002, September). *Retiree health care costs: Addressing the growing gap* (Health and Welfare Report). Retrieved March 30, 2003, from http://www.fidelity.com/work place/PublicSites/DCL/UploadedFiles/325879 retiree whitepaper 2724.pdf.

Finkelstein, L. M., Allen, T. D., & Rhoton, L. (2003). Examining the role of age in mentoring relationships. *Group and Organization Management, 28*(2), 249-281.

Finkelstein, L. M., & Burke, M. J. (1998). Age stereotyping at work: The role of rater and contextual factors on evaluations of job applicants. *The Journal of General Psychology, 125*(4), 317-345.

Finkelstein, L. M., Burke, M. J., & Raju, N. S. (1995). Age discrimination in simulated employment contexts: An integrative analysis. *Journal of Applied Psychology, 80*(6), 652-663.

Finkelstein, L. M., Gonnerman, M. E. J., & Foxgrover, S. K. (2001). The stability of generation identification over time and across contexts. *Experimental Aging Research, 27*(4), 377-397.

Finkelstein, L. M., Gonnerman, M. E., & Johnson, B. A. (1999, April). *The development of measures of age and generation identity.* Paper presented at the 14th annual meeting of the Society for Industrial and Organizational Psychology, Atlanta, GA.

Finkelstein, L. M., Kulas, J. T., & Dages, K. (2003). Age differences in proactive socialization in two populations. *Journal of Business and Psychology, 17*(4), 473-502.

Fletcher, M., & Harty, S. J. (1992, July 13). How doing the right thing is paying off. *Business Insurance*, p. 25.

Flynn, G. (1997). Aging baby boomers may mean more lawsuits. *Workforce, 76*(12), 105-106.

Fogg, P. (2002, July 21). Early exit. *The Chronicle of Higher Education, 48*(41), pp. A11-12.

Forman, J. B. (1999). Federal tax policy in the new milennium: Universal pensions. *Chapman Law Review, 2*(1), 95-131.

Forteza, J. A. & Prieto, J. M. (1994). Aging and work behavior. In H. C. Triandis, M. D. Dunnette and L. M. Hough (Eds.), *Handbook of industrial organizational psychology* (2nd ed., Vol. 4, pp. 447-483). Palo Alto, CA: Consulting Psychological Press.

Fossum, J. A., & Arvey, R. D. (1990). Market place and organizational factors that contribute to obsolescence. In S. L. Willis & S. S. Dubin (Eds.), *Maintaining professional competence: Approaches to career enhancement, vitality, and success throughout a work life* (pp. 44-63). San Francisco: Jossey-Bass.

Fozard, J. L. (1990). Vision and hearing in aging. In J. E. Birren & K. W. Schaie (Eds.), *Handbook of the psychology of aging* (pp. 150-171). New York: Academic Press.

Frahm, R. A. (2002, January 31). Shortage of educators called a 'crisis': Problem will be grist for legislative session. *The Hartford Courant*, p. B7.

Francis, T. (2001, September 11). Company stock fills many retirement plans despite the potential risks to employees. *Wall Street Journal*, p. C1.

Frazis, H., Gittleman, M., & Joyce, M. (1998). *Determinants of training: An analysis using both employer and employee characteristics.* Washington, DC: Bureau of Labor Statistics. Retrieved April 15, 2003, from http://www.bls.gov/ore/pdf/ec980010.pdf.

Fried, M. (1998). *Taking time: Parental leave and corporate culture.* Philadelphia: Temple University Press.

Friedberg, L. (2001). *The impact of technological change on older workers: Evidence from data on computer use* (Working Paper No. W8297). Cambridge, MA: National Bureau of Economic Research.

Fronstin, P. (1999). Retirement patterns and employee benefits: Do benefits matter? *The Gerontologist, 39*(1), 37-47.

Fullerton, H. N. (1999a). Labor force participation: 75 years of change, 1950-98 and 1998-2025. *Monthly Labor Review, 122*(2), 3-12.

Fullerton, H. N. (1999b). Labor force projections to 2008: Steady growth and changing composition. *Monthly Labor Review, 122*(11), 19-32.

Fullerton, H. N., & Toossi, M. (2001). Labor force projections to 2010: Steady growth and changing composition. *Monthly Labor Review, 124*(11), 21-38.

Fyock, C. D. (1990). *America's work force is coming of age.* Lexington, MA: Lexington Books.

Fyock, C. D. (1991). Teaching older workers new tricks. *Training & Development Journal, 45*(4), 21-23.

Fyock, C. D., & Dorton, A. M. (1994). *A career guide for the retired...the soon-to-be retired...the never-want-to-be retired.* New York: AMACOM.

Gager, C. T. (1998). The role of valued outcomes, justifications, and comparison referents in perceptions of fairness among dual--earner couples. *Journal of Family Issues 19*(5), 622-648.

Galagan, P. A., & Cummins, T. W. (1993). Trading places at Monsanto: Special report of the ASTD board of governors symposium held in October, 1992. *Training & Development, 47*(4), 28-60.

Galinsky, E., & Bond, J. T. (1998). *The 1998 business work-life study.* New York: Families and Work Institute.

Gallagher, S. K., & Gerstel, N. (2001). Connections and constraints: The effects of children on caregiving. *Journal of Marriage and the Family, 63*(1), 265-275.

Gardner, H. (1993). *Multiple intelligences: The theory in practice.* New York: Basic Books.

Garfein, A. J., Schaie, K. W., & Willis, S. L. (1988). Microcomputer proficiency in later-middle-aged and older adults: Teaching old dogs new tricks. *Social Behavior, 3*(2), 131-148.

Geary, J. (1997, July 7). Sowing the seeds of speech. *Time* (Canadian ed.), *150*(1), 41.

General Accounting Office. (2000, June 30). *Contingent workers: Incomes and benefits lag behind those of rest of workforce* (HEHS-00-76). Washington, DC: GAO.

General Accounting Office. (2001a, November 16). *Older workers: Demographic trends pose challenges for employers and workers* (GAO-02-85). Washington, DC: GAO.

General Accounting Office. (2001b, May). *Retiree health benefits: Employer-sponsored benefits may be vulnerable to further erosion* (GAO-01-374). Washington, DC: GAO.

Gerson, K. (1998). Gender and the future of the family: Implications for the postindustrial workplace. In D. Vannoy & P. J. Dubeck (Eds.), *Challenges for work and family in the twenty-first century* (pp. 11-22). New York: Aldine de Gruyter.

Ghoshal, S., & Bartlett, C. A. (1997). *The individualized corporation: A fundamentally new approach to management.* New York: HarperCollins.

Gilsdorf, J. W. (1992). The new generation: Older workers. *Training & Development, 46*(3), 77-79.

Gist, M., Rosen, B., & Schwoerer, C. (1988). The influence of training method and trainee age on the acquisition of computer skills. *Personnel Psychology, 41*(2), 255-265.

Glaman, J. M., Jones, A. P., & Rozelle, R. M. (1996). The effects of co-worker similarity on the emergence of affect in work teams. *Group and Organization Management, 21*(2), 192-215.

Glass, J. L., and Estes, S. B. (1997). The family responsive workplace. *Annual Review of Sociology, 23*, 289-313.

Goddard, R. W. (1987). How to harness America's gray power. *Personnel Journal, 66*(5), 33-40.

Goldberg, B. (2000). *Age works: What corporate America must do to survive the graying of the workforce.* New York: Free Press.

Goleman, D. (1995). *Emotional intelligence: Why it can matter more than IQ.* New York: Bantam.

Goode, W. J. (1960). A theory of role strain. *American Sociological Review, 25*, 483-496.

Gornick, J. C., & Meyers, M. K. (2001). Support for working families. *The American Prospect, 12*(1), 1-10.

Gottlieb, B. H., Kelloway, E. K., & Fraboni, M. (1994). Aspects of eldercare that place employees at risk. *The Gerontologist, 34*(6), 815-821.

Gould, S. (1979). Characteristics of career planners in upwardly mobile occupations. *Academy of Management Journal, 22,* 539-550.

Gray, J. H., Boyce, C. A., Hall, R. J., & McDaniel, M. A. (1996, April) *Age differences in training: Less pre-training mastery or less learning?* Poster presented at the 11th annual conference of the Society for Industrial and Organizational Psychology, San Diego, CA.

Greenhaus, J. H., & Sklarew, N. D. (1981). Some sources and consequences of career exploration. *Journal of Vocational Behavior, 18*(1), 1-12.

Greller, M. M., & Simpson, P. (1999). In search of late career: A review of contemporary social science research applicable to the understanding of late career. *Human Resource Management Review, 9*(3), 309-347.

Griffeth, R. W., & Hom, P. W. (2001). *Retaining valued employees.* Thousand Oaks, CA: Sage.

Guberman, N., Maheu, P., & Maille, C. (1992). Women as family caregivers: Why do they care? *The Gerontologist, 32*(5), 607-617.

Gustman, A. L., & Steinmeier, T. L. (1985). The effect of partial retirement on the wage profiles of older workers. *Industrial Relations, 24*(2), 257-265.

Guterman, M., & Holt, R. (1999, November). *Aligning individual and organizational aspirations.* Paper presented at the 16th annual meeting of the California Career Development Association, Long Beach, CA.

Gutteridge, T., Leibowitz, Z., & Shore, J. (1993). *Organizational career development: Benchmarks for building a world-class workforce.* San Francisco: Jossey-Bass.

Guzzo, R. A., & Shea, G. P. (1992). Group performance and inter-group relations in organizations. In M. D. Dunnette & L. M. Hough (Eds.), *Handbook of industrial and organizational psychology* (2nd ed., Vol. 3, pp. 269-314). Palo Alto, CA: Consulting Psychologists Press.

Haefner, J. E. (1977). Race, age, sex, and competence as factors in employer selection of the disadvantaged. *Journal of Applied Psychology, 62*(2), 199-202.

Hakim, C. (1994). *We are all self-employed: The new social contract for working in a changing world.* San Francisco: Berrett-Kuehler Publishers.

Hale, N. (1990). *The older worker: Effective strategies for management and human resource development.* San Francisco: Jossey-Bass.

Hall, D. T. (1971). Potential for career growth. *Personnel Administration, 34*(3), 18-30.

Hall, D. T., & Associates (Eds.). (1996). *The career is dead, long live the career: A relational approach to careers.* San Francisco: Jossey-Bass.

Hall, D. T., & Mirvis, P. H. (1994). The new workplace and older workers. In J. A. Auerbach & J. C. Welsh (Eds.), *Aging and competition: Rebuilding the U.S. workforce* (pp. 58-93). Washington, DC: National Council on the Aging, & the National Planning Association.

Hall, D. T., & Nougiam, K. (1968). An examination of Maslow's need hierarchy in an organizational setting. *Organizational Behavior and Human Decision Processes, 3*(1), 12-35.

Handy, C. (1993). *Understanding organizations.* New York: Oxford University Press.

Handy, C. (1997). Finding sense in uncertainty. In R. Gibson (Ed.), *Rethinking the future* (pp. 16-33). London: Nicholas Brealey.

Hansson, R. O., DeKoekkoek, P. D., Neece, W. M., & Patterson, D. W. (1997). Successful aging at work: Annual review, 1992-1996: The older worker and transitions to retirement. *Journal of Vocational Behavior, 51*(2), 202-233.

Harkness, H. (1999). *Don't stop the career clock: Rejecting the myths of aging for a new way to work in the 21st century.* Palo-Alto, CA: Davies-Black.

Harrison, M. I. (1994). *Diagnosing organizations: Methods, models and processes* (2nd ed.). Thousand Oaks, CA: Sage.

Hartley, A. A. (1992). Attention. In F. I. M. Craik & T. A. Salthouse (Eds.), *The handbook of aging and cognition* (pp. 3-49). Hillsdale, NJ: Erlbaum.

Hasher, L., & Zacks, R. T. (1988). Working memory, comprehension, and aging: A review and new view. In G. H. Bower (Ed.), *The psychology of learning and motivation* (Vol. 22, pp. 193-225). San Diego, CA: Academic Press.

Hassell, B. L., & Perrewe, P. L. (1995). An examination of beliefs about older workers: Do stereotypes still exist? *Journal of Organizational Behavior, 16*(5), 457-468.

Hattrup, K., & Jackson, S. E. (1996). Learning about individual differences by taking situations seriously. In K. R. Murphy (Ed.), *Individual difference and behavior in organizations* (pp. 507-547). San Francisco: Jossey-Bass.

Havighurst, R. J. (1982). The world of work. In B. B. Wolman (Ed.), *Handbook of developmental psychology* (pp. 771-787). Englewood Cliffs, NJ: Prentice Hall.

Hays, D. (2001, April 30). Risk managers cope with aging workforce. *National Underwriter (Property & Casualty), 105*(18), 16-39.

Hayslip, B., Miller, C., Beyerlein, M. M., Johnson, D., Metheny, W., & Yeatts, D. (1996). Employee age and perceptions of work in self-managing and traditional work groups. *International Journal on Aging and Human Development, 42*(4), 291-312.

Hecker, D. E. (2001). Occupational employment projections to 2010. *Monthly Labor Review, 124*(11), 57-84. Retrieved April 15, 2003, from http://www.bls.gov/opub/mlr/2001/11/art4full.pdf.

Heindel, R. A., Adams, G. A., & Lepisto, L. (1999, April). *Predicting bridge employment: A test of Feldman's (1994) hypotheses.* Poster presented at the 14th annual meeting of the Society for Industrial and Organizational Psychology, Atlanta, GA.

Herr, E. L. (2002). Adult career development: Some perspectives on the future. In S. G. Niles (Ed.), *Adult career development: Concepts, issues and practices* (pp. 389-396). Alexandria, VA: National Career Development Association.

Herz, D. E. (1995). Work after early retirement: An increasing trend among men. *Monthly Labor Review, 118*(4), 13-20.

Hewitt Associates. (1993). *Salaried employee benefits provided by major U.S. employers in 1993.* Lincolnshire, IL: Hewitt Associates.

Hewitt Associates. (1999a). *Hewitt study shows more than half of 401(k) plan participants in U.S. opt for cash when changing jobs.* Press release, September 13. Retrieved March 19, 2003, from http://www.businesswire.com/webbox/bw.091399/1925 61563.htm.

Hewitt Associates. (1999b, October). Retiree health coverage: Recent trends and employer perspectives on future benefits. Menlo Park, CA: The Henry J. Kaiser Family Foundation. Retrieved March 30, 2003, from http://www.kff.org/content/1999/1540/Retiree.pdf.

Hewitt Associates. (2000). *Salaried employee benefits provided by major U.S. employers, 2000-2001.* Lincolnshire, IL: Hewitt Associates.

Hewlett, S. A., & West, C. (1998). *The war against parents: What we can do for America's beleaguered moms and dads.* New York: Houghton Mifflin.

Hill, E. J., Hawkins, A. J., Ferris, M., & Weitzman, M. (2001). Finding an extra day a week: The positive influence of perceived job flexibility on work and family life balance. *Family Relations, 50*(1), 49-58.

Himes, C. L. (1994). Parental caregiving by adult women: A demographic perspective. *Research on Aging, 16*(2), 191-211.

Hinterlong, J., Morrow-Howell, N., & Sherraden, M. (2001). *Productive aging: Concepts and challenges.* Baltimore: Johns Hopkins University Press.

Hipple, S. (1998). Contingent work: Results from the second survey. *Monthly Labor Review, 121*(11). Retrieved March 20, 2003, from http://www.bls.gov/opub/mlr/1998/11/art2full.pdf.

Hochschild, A. (with Machung, A.) (1989). *The second shift.* New York: Avon Books.

Hochschild, A. (1997). *The time bind*. New York: Metropolitan Books.

Hogan, D., & Eggebeen, D. (1995). Sources of emergency help and routine assistance. *Social Forces, 73*(3), 917-936.

Hogarth, T., & Barth, M. C. (1991). Costs and benefits of hiring older workers: A case study of B&Q. *International Journal of Manpower, 12*(8), 5-17.

Hogg, M. A., & Abrams, D. (1988). *Social identifications*. London: Routledge.

Holden, B. (1994, May 24). Denny's chain settles suits by minorities. *Wall Street Journal*, p. A3.

Holland, J. L. (1959). A theory of vocational choice. *Journal of Counseling Psychology, 6*, 35-45.

Holland, J. L. (1962). Some explorations of a theory of vocational choice: One and two year longitudinal studies. *Psychological Monographs, 76*(26, Whole No. 545).

Hooyman, N. R. (1990). Women as caregivers to the elderly. In D. E. Biegel & A. Blum (Eds.), *Social support networks and the care of the elderly* (pp. 67-92). New York: Springer.

Hooyman, N. R. (1992). Social policy and gender inequities in caregiving. In J. W. Dwyer & R. T. Coward (Eds.), *Gender, families, and eldercare* (pp. 181-201). Newbury Park, CA: Sage.

Howard, P. J. (1994). *The owner's manual for the brain: Everyday applications from mind-brain research*. Austin, TX: Leornian Press.

Ingersoll-Dayton, B., Neal, M. B., & Hammer, L. B. (2001). Aging parents helping adult children: The experience of the sandwiched generation. *Family Relations, 50*(3), 263-271.

Institute for Policy Studies. (2000, December). *The top 200: The rise of corporate global power*. Washington, DC: S. Anderson & J. Cavanagh. Retrieved March 20, 2003, from http://www.ips-dc.org/downloads/Top_200.pdf.

Internal Revenue Service. (2002a, June 27). *IRS Notice 2002-45*. Retrieved March 30, 2003, from http://www.tog-usa.com/resource files/1088.pdf.

Internal Revenue Service. (2002b, October 15). *Internal Revenue Bulletin 2002-41*. Retrieved March 30, 2003, from http://www.irs.gov/pub/irs-irbs/irb02-41.pdf.

International Telework Association and Council (2001, October 3). *Number of teleworkers increases by 17 percent*. Washington, DC: ITAC. Retrieved March 20, 2003, from http://www.working fromanywhere.org/news/2001newsrelease.htm.

Isaacson, L. E., & Brown, D. (1999). *Career information, career counseling, and career development*. Needham Heights, MA: Allyn & Bacon.

Jackson, J. W. (2002). Intergroup attitudes as a function of different dimensions of group identification and perceived intergroup conflict. *Self and Identity, 1*(1), 11-33.

Jackson, S. E., Brett, J. B., Sessa, V. I., Cooper, J. A., & Peyronnin, K. (1991). Some differences make a difference: Individual dissimilarity and group heterogeneity as correlates of recruitment, promotions, and turnover. *Journal of Applied Psychology, 76*(5), 675-689.

Jackson, S. E., & Ruderman, M. N. (Eds.). (1995). *Diversity in work teams: Research paradigms for a changing workplace*. Washington, DC: American Psychological Association.

Jacobsen, B. (1980). *Young programs for older workers*. New York: Van Nostrand Reinhold.

Jehn, K. A., Northcraft, G. B., & Neale, M. A. (1999). Why differences make a difference: A field study of diversity, conflict, and performance in workgroups. *Administrative Science Quarterly, 44*(4), 741-763.

Jensen, R. (1999). *The dream society: How the coming shift from information to imagination will transform your business*. New York: McGraw-Hill.

Jette, A. M. (1996). Disability trends and transitions. In R. E. Binstock & L. K. George (Eds.), *Handbook of aging and the social sciences* (4th ed., pp. 94-116). San Diego, CA: Academic Press.

Johnson, J. J. (1994). Cognition and aging: A practical analysis. *Performance & Instruction, 33*(1), 33-35.

Jones, B. D., & Bayen, U. J. (1998). Teaching older adults to use computers: Recommendations based on cognitive aging research. *Educational Gerontology, 24*(7), 675-689.

Jones, E. E., Jr. (1984). Nine tips for training older workers. *Training and Development Journal, 38*(3), 12-13.

Josefowitz, N. (1995). The clonal effect in organizations. In R. A. Ritvo, A. H. Litwin, & L. Butler (Eds.), *Managing in the age of change: Essential skills to manage today's diverse workforce* (pp. 181-187). Burr Ridge, IL: NTL Institute/Irwin.

Jossi, F. (1997, August). Mentoring in changing times. *Training, 34*(8), 50-54.

Judy, R. W., & D'Amico, C. D. (1997). *Workforce 2020: Work and Workers in the 21st Century*. Indianapolis: Hudson Institute.

Kaeter, M. (1995). Age-old myths. *Training, 32*(1), 61-64.

Kanter, R. M. (1989). *When giants learn to dance*. New York: Simon & Schuster.

Kanter, R. M. (1995). *World class: Thriving locally in the global economy*. New York: Simon & Schuster.

Karp, H. B., & Sutton, N. (1993). Where diversity training goes wrong. *Training, 30*(7), 30-34.

Katz, R. (1978). The influence of job longevity on employee reactions to task characteristics. *Human Relations, 31*(8), 703-725.

Katzenbach, J. R., & Smith, D. K. (1993). The discipline of teams. *Harvard Business Review, 71*(2), 111-120.

Kaufman, H. G. (1990). Management techniques for maintaining a competent professional workforce. In S. L. Willis & S. S. Dubin (Eds.), *Maintaining professional competence: Approaches to career enhancement, vitality, and success throughout a work life* (pp. 249-261). San Francisco: Jossey-Bass.

Kausler, D. H., & Kausler, B. C. (1996). *The graying of America: An encyclopedia of aging, health, mind and behavior*. Urbana, IL: University of Illinois Press.

Keene, J. R., & Quadagno, J. (2002, February). Beyond role models: Institutional structures and workers' perceptions of work-family balance. Paper presented at the Persons, Processes, and Places: Research on Families, Workplaces and Communities conference, San Francisco, CA.

Kegan, R. (1982). *The evolving self: Problem and process in human development*. Cambridge, MA: Harvard University Press.

Keirsey, D., & Bates, M. (1978/1984). *Please understand me: Character and temperament types*. Del Mar, CA: Prometheus.

Kelchner, E. S. (1999). Ageism's impact and effect on society: Not just a concern for the old. *Journal of Gerontological Social Work, 32*(4), 85-100.

Kilduff, M., & Mehra, A. (1996). Hegemonic masculinity among the elite: Power, identity, and homophily in social networks. In C. Cheng (Ed.), *Masculinities in organizations* (pp. 115-129). Thousand Oaks, CA: Sage.

Kim, S., & Feldman, D. C. (1998). Healthy, wealthy, or wise: Predicting actual acceptances of early retirement incentives at three points in time. *Personnel Psychology, 51*(3), 623-642.

Kim, S., & Feldman, D. C. (2000). Working in retirement: The antecedents of bridge employment and its consequences for quality of life in retirement. *Academy of Management Journal, 43*(6), 1195-1210.

Kimball, G. (1999). *21st century families*. Chico, CA: Equality Press.

Kinsella, K. (1996). Aging and the family: Present and future demographic trends. In R. Blieszner & V. Bedford (Eds.), *Handbook of aging and the family* (pp. 32-56). Westport, CT: Greenwood.

Knowdell, R. (1996). *Building a career development program: Nine steps for effective implementation*. Palo Alto: Davies-Black.

Knowles, M. (1987). Adult learning. In R. Craig (Ed.), *Training and development handbook* (pp. 168-179). New York: McGraw-Hill.

Kotter, J. P. (1995, March/April). Leading change: Why transformation efforts fail. *Harvard Business Review*, 59-67.

Kotter, J. P. (1996). *Leading change: An eight-step action plan for leaders.* Cambridge MA: Harvard Business School Press.

Kotter, J. P., & Heskett, J. L. (1992). *Corporate culture and performance.* New York: Free Press.

Kouzes, J. M., & Posner, B. Z. (1995). *The leadership challenge* (2nd ed.). San Francisco: Jossey-Bass.

Kram, K. E., & Hall, D. T. (1996). Mentoring in a context of diversity and turbulence. In S. Lobel & E. Kossek (Eds.), *Human resource strategies for managing diversity* (pp. 108-136). London: Blackwell.

Krause, T. R. (1996). *The behavior-based safety process: Managing involvement for an injury-free culture* (2nd ed.). New York: Wiley.

Krueger, J., Heckhausen, J., & Hundertmark, J. (1995). Perceiving middle-aged adults: Effects of stereotype-congruent and incongruent information. *The Journals of Gerontology, 50B*(2), 82-93.

Kubeck, J. E., Delp, N. D., Haslett, T. K, & McDaniel, M. A. (1996). Does job-related training performance decline with age? *Psychology and Aging, 11*(1), 92-107.

Kupritz, V. W. (2000). The role of the physical environment in maximizing opportunities for the aging workforce. *Journal of Industrial Teacher Education, 37*(2), 66-68.

Kurzweil, R. (1992). *The age of intelligent machines.* Cambridge, MA: MIT Press.

Laabs, J. J. (1996, July). Expert advice on how to move forward with change. *Personnel Journal, 75*(7), 54-63.

Lambert, S. (1990). Processes linking work and family: A critical review and research agenda. *Human Relations, 43*(3), 239-257.

Lancaster, L. C., & Stillman, D. (2002). *When generations collide.* New York: HarperCollins.

Landauer, J. (1997). Bottom-line benefits of work/life programs. *HR Focus, 74*(4), 3-4.

Lang, F. R., & Carstensen, L. L. (1994). Close emotional relationships later in life: Further support for proactive aging in the social domain. *Psychology and Aging, 9*(2), 315-324.

Lawrence, B. S. (1987). An organizational theory of age effects. In S. Bacharach & N. DiTomaso (Eds.), *Research in the sociology of organizations,* (Vol. 5, pp. 37-71). Greenwich, CT: JAI press.

Lawrence, B. S. (1988). New wrinkles in the theory of age: Demography, norms, and performance ratings. *Academy of Management Journal, 31*(2), 309-337.

Lawrence, J. H. (1985). Developmental needs as intrinsic incentives. In R. G. Baldwin (Ed.), *Incentives for faculty vitality.* San Francisco: Jossey-Bass.

Lawrence, L. A. (1995). Older workers. In A. P. Carnevale & S. C. Stone (Eds.), *The American mosaic: An in-depth report on the future of diversity at work* (pp. 435-491). New York: McGraw-Hill.

League for Innovation in the Community College (2000). *Learning outcomes for the 21st century: Report of a community college study.* Phoenix, AZ: C. D. Wilson, C. L. Miles, R. L. Baker, & R. L. Schoenberger.

Leana, C. R. (2002). The changing organizational context of careers. In D. C. Feldman (Ed.), *Work careers: A developmental perspective* (pp. 274-293). San Francisco: Jossey-Bass.

Lee, G. R. (1992). Gender differences in family caregiving: A fact in search of a theory. In J. W. Dwyer and R. T. Coward (Eds.), *Gender, families, and eldercare* (pp. 120-31). Newbury Park, CA: Sage.

Lefkovich, L. L. (1992) Older workers: Why and how to capitalize on their powers. *Employment Relations Today, 19*(1), 63-80.

Lei, D., Slocum, J. W., Jr., & Pitts, R. A. (1999). Designing organizations for competitive advantage: The power of learning and unlearning. *Organizational Dynamics, 27*(3), 24-28.

Levering, R., & Moskowitz, M. (2002, February 4). The best in the worst of times: The 100 best companies to work for. *Fortune, 145*(3), 60-90.

Levinson, D. J., Darrow, C. N., Klein, E. B., Levinson, M. L., & McKee, B. (1978). *The seasons of a man's life.* New York: Knopf.

Levinson, H., & Wofford, J. C. (2000). Approaching retirement as the flexibility phase. *Academy of Management Executive, 14*(2), 84-95.

Levitt, L., Holve, E., & Wang, J. (2001). *Employer health benefits: 2001 Annual survey.* Menlo Park, CA: The Henry J. Kaiser Family Foundation, and Chicago, IL: Health Research and Educational Trust.

Lewin, K. (1997). *Resolving social conflicts: Field theory in social science.* Washington, DC: American Psychological Association.

Lillard, L. A., & Tan, H. W. (1986). *Private sector training: Who gets it and what are its effects?* (R-3331-00L/RC). Santa Monica, CA: Rand Corporation.

Lindbo, T. L., & Shultz, K. S. (1998). The role of organizational culture and mentoring on mature worker socialization toward retirement. *Public Productivity and Management Review, 22*(1), 49-59.

Litwin, G. H. (1970). Achievement motivation and the older worker. In H. L. Sheppard (Ed.), *Toward an industrial gerontology: An introduction to a new field of applied research and service* (pp. 61-70). Cambridge, MA: Schenkman.

Logan, J. R., & Spitze, G. D. (1996). *Family Ties.* Philadelphia: Temple University Press.

Loi, J. L. P., & Shultz, K. S. (2002, April). Why older adults seek employment: Differing motivations among subgroups. In K. S. Shultz (Chair), *Addressing projected workforce shortages by recruiting and retaining older workers.* Symposium conducted at the 17th annual meeting of the Society for Industrial and Organizational Psychology, Toronto, Canada.

London, M. (2002). Organizational assistance in career development. In D. C. Feldman (Ed.), *Work careers: A developmental perspective* (pp. 323-345). San Francisco: Wiley.

Loomis, L. S., & Booth, A. (1995). Multigenerational caregiving and wellbeing: The myth of the beleaguered sandwich generation. *Journal of Family Issues 16*(2), 131-148.

Lord, R. G., & Maher, K. J. (1993). *Executive leadership and information processing: Linking perceptions and organizational performance.* New York: Routledge.

Louis Harris & Associates. (1997). *Survey results from our groundbreaking study about the differences in working styles between men and women .* New York: Louis Harris.

Lubove, S. (1997, December 15). Damned if you do, damned if you don't. *Forbes, 160*(13), 122-134.

Luttropp, N. (1993). *The business and aging information packet.* San Francisco: National Eldercare Institute on Business and Aging.

Lynch, L. (1992). Private sector training and the earnings of young workers. *American Economic Review, 82*(1), 299-312.

Madrian, B. C., & Shea, D. F. (2001). The power of suggestion: Inertia in 401(k) participation and savings behavior. *The Quarterly Journal of Economics, 116*(4), 1149-1187.

Manton, K., & Stallard, E. (1996). Changes in health, mortality, and disability and their impact on long term care needs. *Journal of Aging and Social Policy, 7*(3-4), 25-51.

Marks, N. (1998). Does it hurt to care? Caregiving, work-family conflict, and midlife well-being. *Journal of Marriage and the Family, 60*(4), 951-966.

Marks, S. R., & MacDermid, S. M. (1996). Multiple roles and the self: A theory of role balance. *Journal of Marriage and the Family, 58*(2), 417-432.

Martin-Matthews, A. (2000). Intergenerational caregiving: How apocalyptic and dominant demographics frame the questions and shape the answers. In E. M. Gee & G. M. Guttman (Eds.), *The overselling of population aging: Apocalyptic demography, intergenerational challenges, and social policy* (pp. 80-89). Toronto, Canada: Oxford University Press.

Martin-Matthews, A., & Rosenthal, C. J. (1993). Balancing work and family in an aging society: The Canadian experience. In G. L. Maddox & M. P. Lawton (Eds.), *Focus on kinship, aging, and social change: Annual review of gerontology and geriatrics* (Vol. 13, pp. 96-119). New York: Springer.

Massey, D. S., Arango, J., Hugo, G., Kouaouci, A., Pellegrino, A., & Taylor, J. E. (1993). Theories of international migration: A review and appraisal. *Population and Development Review, 19*(3), 431–66.

Matheson, N. S. (1991). The influence of organization-based self--esteem on organizational commitment: An analysis of age differences (Doctoral dissertation, The University of Akron, 1991). *Dissertation Abstracts International, 52(3-B),* 1762.

Mathieu, J. E. (1991). A cross-level nonrecursive model of the antecedents of organizational commitment and satisfaction. *Journal of Applied Psychology, 76*(5), 607-618.

Mathieu, J. E., & Zajac, D. M. (1990). A review and meta-analysis of the antecedents, correlates, and consequences of organizational commitment. *Psychological Bulletin, 108*(2), 171-194.

Maurer, R. (1996). *Beyond the wall of resistance: Unconventional strategies that build support for change.* Austin, TX: Bard Press.

McCune, J. C. (1998, April). The future of retirement. *Management Review,* p. 15.

McEvoy, G., & Cascio, W. (1989). Cumulative evidence of the relationship between employee age and job performance. *Journal of Applied Psychology, 74*(1), 11-17.

McGee, G. W., & Ford, R. C. (1987). Two (or more?) dimensions of organizational commitment: Reexamination of the affective and continuance commitment scales. *Journal of Applied Psychology, 72*(4), 638-642.

McGrath, J. E., Berdahl, J. L., & Arrow, H. (1995). Traits, expectations, culture, and clout: The dynamics of diversity in work groups. In S. E. Jackson & M. N. Ruderman (Eds.), *Diversity in work teams: Research paradigms for a changing workplace* (pp. 17-45). Washington, DC: American Psychological Association.

McGregor, D. (1960). *The human side of enterprise.* New York: McGraw-Hill.

McMenamin, T. M., Krantz, R., & Krolik, T. J. (2003). U.S. labor market in 2002: Continued weakness. *Monthly Labor Review, 126*(2), 3-25. Retrieved April 3, 2003, from http://www.bls.gov/opub/mlr/2003/02/art1full.pdf.

McNaught, W., & Barth, M. C. (1992). Are older workers "good buys"? A case study of Days Inns of America. *Sloan Management Review, 33*(3), 53-63.

Mellins, C., Blum, M., Boyd-Davis, S., & Gatz, M. (1993). Family network perspectives on caregiving. *Generations 17*(1), 21-24.

Mellor, J. (2000). Filling the gaps in long-term care insurance. In M. H. Meyer (Ed.), *Care work* (pp. 202-216). New York: Routledge.

Merriam, S. B., & Caffarella, R. S. (1999). *Learning in adulthood: A comprehensive guide* (2nd ed.). San Francisco: Jossey-Bass.

MetLife. (1997, June). *MetLife Study of Employer Costs for Working Caregivers.* Westport, CT: MetLife Mature Market Institute/National Alliance for Caregiving. Retrieved March 30, 2003, from http://www.metlife.com/WPSAssets/88881768001015600333V1F5.1.066.pdf.

MetLife. (1999, November). *The MetLife juggling act study: Balancing caregiving with work and the costs involved.* Westport, CT: MetLife Mature Market Institute/National Alliance for Caregiving/National Center on Women and Aging. Retrieved March 30, 2003, from http://www.metlife.com/WPSAssets29227611101027365764V1FPDF8.pdf.

Meyer, J. P., & Allen, N. J. (1984). Testing the "side bet" theory of organizational commitment: Some methodological considerations. *Journal of Applied Psychology, 69*(3), 372-378.

Meyer, J. P., Paunonen, S. V., Gellatly, I. R., Goffin, R. D., & Jackson, D. N. (1989). Organizational commitment and job performance: It's the nature of the commitment that counts. *Journal of Applied Psychology, 74*(1), 152-156.

Mieszkowski, K. (1999, October). Generation *##@**##@!! *Fast Company, #28,* 106-108.

Miller, V. D., & Jablin, F. M. (1991). Information seeking during organizational entry: Influences, tactics, and a model of the process. *Academy of Management Review, 16*(1), 92-120.

Milliman & Robertson (2001, Spring). *Defined contribution health plans: The shape of things to come?* (Benefits Perspective). D. F. Ogden & M. G. Strum. Retrieved March 30, 2003, from http://www.milliman.com/eb/publications/benefits perspectives/spring 01 final.pdf.

Mintz, F. (1986). Retraining: Graying of the training room. *Personnel, 63*(10), 69-71.

Mirvis, P. H., & Hall, D. T. (1996). The new protean career: Psychological success and the path with a heart. In D. T. Hall & Associates (Eds.), *The career is dead, long live the career: A relational approach to careers* (pp. 15-45). San Francisco: Jossey-Bass.

Mitchell, O. S. (Ed.). (1993). *As the workforce ages: Costs, benefits, and policy challenges.* Ithaca, NY: ILR Press.

Moberg, D. J. (2001). The aging workforce: Implications for ethical practice. *Business and Society Review, 106*(4), 314-329.

Moen, P. (1992). *Women's two roles.* Westport, CT: Auburn House.

Moen, P. (1994). Women, work, and family: A sociological perspective on changing roles. In M. R. Riley, R. L. Kahn, & A. Foner (Eds.), *Age and structural lag: Societies failure to provide meaningful opportunities in work, family, and leisure* (pp. 151-170). New York: Wiley.

Moen, P., Robison, J., & Dempster-McClain, D. (1995). Caregiving and women's well-being: A life course perspective. *Journal of Health and Social Behavior, 36*(3), 259-273.

Moen, P., & Wethington, E. (1992). The concept of family adaptive strategies. *Annual Review of Sociology, 18,* 233-251.

Mohrman, S. A., Gibson, C. B., & Mohrman, A. M. (2001). Doing research that is useful to practice: A model and empirical exploration. *Academy of Management Journal, 44*(2), 357-375.

Moore, K. L. (2001). Raising the Social Security retirement ages: Weighing the costs and benefits. *Arizona Law Review, 33*(2), 543-612.

Mor-Barak, M. E. (1995). The meaning of work for older adults seeking employment: The generativity factor. *International Journal of Aging and Human Development, 41*(4), 325-344.

Morris, R., & Bass, S. A. (1986). The elderly as surplus people: Is there a role for higher education? *The Gerontologist, 26*(1), 12-18.

Morrison, A. M. (1995). Closing the gap between research and practice. In S. E. Jackson & M. N. Ruderman (Eds.), *Diversity in work teams: Research paradigms for a changing workplace* (pp. 219-224). Washington, DC: American Psychological Association.

Morrison, E. W. (1993a). Longitudinal study of the effects of information seeking on newcomer socialization. *Journal of Applied Psychology, 78*(2), 173-183.

Morrison, E. W. (1993b). Newcomer information seeking: Exploring types, modes, sources, and outcomes. *Academy of Management Journal, 36*(3), 557-589.

Moses, B. (2000). *The good news about careers: How you'll be working in the next decade.* San Francisco: Jossey-Bass.

Mowday, R. T., Steers, R. M., & Porter, L. W. (1979). The measurement of organizational commitment. *Journal of Vocational Behavior, 14*(2), 224-247.

Mui, A. C. (1992). Caregiver strain among black and white daughter caregivers: A role theory perspective. *The Gerontologist, 32*(2), 203-212.

Mui, A. C. (1995). Caring for frail elderly parents: A comparison of adult sons and daughters. *The Gerontologist, 35*(1), 86-93.

Mullan, C., & Gorman, L. (1972, Fall). Facilitating adaptation and change: A case study in retraining middle-aged and older workers in Aer Lingus. *Industrial Gerontology,* 20-39.

Murphy, C. (2002, April 15). The Fortune 500: Now that Wal-Mart is America's largest corporation, the service economy wears the crown. *Fortune,* 94-98.

National Academy on an Aging Society. (2000a, May). Helping the elderly with activity limitations. *Caregiving,* (No.7). Washington, DC: National Academy on an Aging Society.

National Academy on an Aging Society. (2000b). *Who are young retirees and older workers?* Washington, DC: National Academy on an Aging Society. Retrieved April 16, 2003, from http://www.agingsociety.org/agingsociety/pdf/aarp1.pdf.

National Alliance for Caregiving. (1997). *Family caregiving in the U.S.: Findings from a national survey.* Bethesda, MD: NAC & AARP.

National Bureau of Economic Research. (1999, August). *Pre-retirement cashouts and foregone retirement savings: Implications for 401(k) asset accumulation* (NBER Working Paper No. 7314). Cambridge, MA: J. M. Poterba, S. F. Venti, & D. A. Wise. Retrieved March 19, 2003, from http://papers.nber.org/papers/w7314.pdf.

National Center for Education Statistics. (2002, August). *Projections of education statistics to 2012* (NCES 2002-030). Washington, DC: U.S Department of Education. Retrieved March 20, 2003, from http://nces.ed.gov/pubs2002/2002030.pdf.

National Center for Policy Analysis. (2000, October 26). *Defined contribution health insurance* (Policy Backgrounder No. 154). Washington, DC: G. Scandlen. Retrieved March 30, 2003, from http://www.ncpa.org/bg/bg154/bg154.html.

National Committee on Careers for Older Americans. (1979). *Older Americans: An untapped resource.* Washington, DC: Academy for Educational Development.

National Institute on Aging. (1993). *Health and retirement study.* Press release, June 17. Washington, DC: National Institute on Aging.

Neal, M. B., Chapman, N. J., Ingersoll-Dayton, B., & Emlen, A. C. (1993). *Balancing work and caregiving for children, adults, and elders.* Newbury Park, CA: Sage.

Neapolitan, J. (1980). Occupational change in mid-career: An exploratory investigation. *Journal of Vocational Behavior, 16*(2), 212-225.

Newhouse, J. P. (1992, Summer). Medical care costs: How much welfare loss? *Journal of Economic Perspectives 6*(3), 3-22.

Nichols, L. S., & Junk, V. W. (1997). The sandwich generation: Dependency, proximity, and task assistance needs of parents. *Journal of Family and Economic Issues, 18*(3), 299-326.

Nicholson, T. (2002, November 7). What do older workers want? AARP Bulletin, p. 7. Retrieved November 7, 2002, from http://www.aarp.org/bulletin/.

Nkomo, S. M. (1995). Identities and the complexity of diversity. In S. E. Jackson & M. N. Ruderman (Eds.), *Diversity in work teams: Research paradigms for a changing workplace* (pp. 247-253). Washington, DC: American Psychological Association.

Noe, R. A. (1988). An investigation of the determinants of successful assigned mentoring relationships. *Personnel Psychology, 41*(3), 457-479.

Noer, D. (1993). *Healing the wounds: Overcoming the trauma of layoffs and revitalizing downsized organizations.* San Francisco: Jossey-Bass.

Northwest Airlines loses decision in complaint alleging handicap bias. (2000, May 3). *Wall Street Journal,* pp. B8.

O'Bannon, G. (2001). Managing our future: The Generation X factor. *Public Personnel Management, 30*(1), 95-109.

O'Brien, F. P., Robinson, J. F., & Taylor, G. S. (1986). The effects of supervisor sex and work environment on attitude toward older employees. *Public Personnel Management, 15*(2), 119-130.

O'Connor, J. S. (1996). Caring work: A gendered activity. *Current Sociology, 44*, 13-29.

Office of Technology Assessment. (1986). *Technology and structural unemployment: Reemploying displaced adults.* Washington, DC: U.S. Government Printing Office.

O'Rand, A., & Henretta, J. (1999). *Age and inequality: Diverse path ways through later life.* Boulder, CO: Westview Press.

Organization for Economic Cooperation and Development (1998). *Maintaining prosperity in an ageing society.* Paris, France: OECD.

Our opinions: Workers need to invest wisely (2002, August 30). *Atlanta Journal and Constitution,* p. 21A.

Papa, J. R., Kopelman, R. E., & Flynn, G. (1998). Sizing up the FMLA. *Workforce, 77*(8), 38-44.

Parke, R. D. (1996). *Fatherhood.* Cambridge, MA: Harvard University Press.

Patchett, M. B., & Sterns, H. L. (1984, February). Career progression in middle and later adulthood. In *Industrial gerontological psychology: Current issues for the curriculum and research,* symposium conducted at the 10th annual meeting of the Association for Gerontology in Higher Education, Indianapolis.

Patel, B., & Kleiner, B. H. (1995). New developments in age discrimination. *Equal Opportunities International, 14*, 69-79.

Pauly, M. V. (1997). *Health benefits at work: An economic and political analysis of employment-based health insurance.* Ann Arbor: University of Michigan Press.

Pavalko, E., & Artis, J. E. (1997). Women's caregiving and paid work: Causal relationships in midlife. *Journal of Gerontology: Social Sciences, 52B*(4), S170-S179.

Pearlin, L. I. (1989). The sociological study of stress. *Journal of Health and Social Behavior, 30*(3), 241-256.

Pelled, L. H., Eisenhardt, K. M., & Xin, K. R. (1999). Exploring the black box: An analysis of work group diversity, conflict, and performance. *Administrative Science Quarterly, 44*(1), 1-28.

Penner, R. G. (1998, June 18). *The economic impact of trends in retirement and expected life.* Statement submitted to the Senate Finance Committee.

Penner, R. G., Perun, P., & Steuerle, C. E. (2002). *Legal and institutional impediments to partial retirement and part-time work by older workers.* Washington, DC: Urban Institute.

Penning, M. J. (1998). In the middle: Parental caregiving in the context of other roles. *Journal of Gerontology: Social Sciences, 53B*(4), S188-S197.

Perry, E. L. (1994). A prototype matching approach to understanding the role of applicant gender and age in the evaluation of job applicants. *Journal of Applied Social Psychology, 24*(16), 1433-1473.

Perry, E. L. (1997). A cognitive approach to understanding discrimination: A closer look at applicant gender and age. In G. R. Ferris (Ed.), *Research in personnel and human resources management* (Vol. 15, pp. 175-240). Greenwich, CT: JAI Press.

Perry, E. L., & Finkelstein, L. M. (1999). Toward a broader view of age discrimination in employment-related decisions: A joint consideration of organizational factors and cognitive processes. *Human Resource Management Review, 9*(1), 21-49.

Peterson, D. A. (1983). *Facilitating education for older learners.* San Francisco: Jossey-Bass.

Peterson, D. A., & Wendt, P. F. (1995). Training and education of older americans as workers and volunteers. In S. A. Bass (Ed.), *Older and active: How Americans over 55 are contributing to society* (pp. 217-236). New Haven, CT: Yale University Press.

Pfeffer, J. (1998a). *The human equation: Building profits by putting people first.* Boston MA: Harvard Business School Press.

Pfeffer, J. (1998b, Spring). The real keys to high performance. *Leader to Leader* (No. 8), 23-29.

Phillips, J. J. (1991). *Handbook of training, evaluation and measurement methods* (2nd ed.). Houston, TX: Gulf.

Phillips, J. J. (1996). Measuring the results of training. In R. L. Craig (Ed.), *The ASTD training and development handbook: A guide to human resource development* (4th ed., pp. 313-341). New York: McGraw-Hill.

Pink, D. H. (2002). *Free agent nation: The future of working for yourself.* New York: Warner Business Books.

Pogson, C., Cober, A., Doverspike, D., & Rogers, J. (2003). Differences in self-reported work ethic across three career stages. *Journal of Vocational Behavior, 62*(1), 189-201.

Polachek, S. W. (1981). Occupational self-selection: A human capital approach to sex differences in occupational structure. *The Review of Economics and Statistics 63*(1), 60–69.

Polatnick, M. R. (2000). Working parents: Issues for the next decades. *National Forum, 80*(3), 1-4.

Pollan, S. M., & Levine, M. (1995, December/January). The rise and fall of retirement. *Worth, 5*(2), 64-74.

Ponds, R. W. H. M, Jolles, J., & van Boxtel, M. P. J. (2000). Age-related changes in subjective cognitive functioning. *Educational Gerontology, 26*(1), 67-81.

Pressley, S. A. (2001, May 11). The South's new car smell. *Washington Post*, p. A1.

Price, C. A., & Rose, H. A. (2000). Caregiving over the life course of families. In S. Price, P. McKenry, & M. J. Murphy (Eds.), *Families across time: A life course perspective* (pp. 145-159). Los Angeles, CA: Roxbury.

Public Policy Institute of California (2002, April). *Local and global networks of immigrant professionals in Silicon Valley*. San Francisco: A. Saxenian.

Quadagno, J. S. (2002). *Aging and the life course*. New York: McGraw-Hill.

Quinn, J. F. (1999). *Has the early retirement trend reversed?* (Social Security Administration Working Paper 424). Washington, DC: U.S. Government Printing Office.

Quinn, J. F. (2000). New paths to retirement. In O. S. Mitchell, P. B. Hammond, and A. M. Rappaport (Eds.), *Forecasting retirement needs and retirement wealth* (pp. 13-32). Philadelphia: University of Pennsylvania Press.

Quinn, J. F., & Kozy, M. (1996). The role of bridge jobs in the retirement transition: Gender, race and ethnicity. *The Gerontologist, 36*(3), 363-372.

Ragins, B. R. (1997). Diversified mentoring relationships in organizations: A power perspective. *Academy of Management Review, 22*(2), 482-521.

Ragins, B. R. (1999). Where do we go from here, and how do we get there? Methodological issues in conducting research on diversity and mentoring relationships. In A. J. Murrell, F. J. Crosby, & R. J. Ely (Eds.), *Mentoring dilemmas: Developmental relationships within multicultural organizations* (pp. 227-246). Mahwah, NJ: Lawrence Erlbaum.

Ragins, B. R., & McFarlin, D. B. (1990). Perceptions of mentor roles in cross-gender mentoring relationships. *Journal of Vocational Behavior, 37*(3), 321-339.

Randall, D. M. (1987). Commitment and the organization: The organization man revisited. *Academy of Management Review, 12*(3), 460-471.

Raphael, D., & Schlesinger, B. (1994). Women in the sandwich generation: Do adult children living at home help? *Journal of Women and Aging, 6*, 21-45.

Rappaport, A. M. (2001a). Employer strategies for a changing workforce: Phased retirement and other options. *Benefits Quarterly, 17*(4), 58-64.

Rappaport, A. M. (2001b, Summer). Postemployment benefits: Ensuring health and income security for an aging workforce. *Compensation & Benefits Management 17*(3), 59-61.

Reichers, A. E. (1985). A review and reconceptualization of organizational commitment. *Academy of Management Review, 10*(3), 465-476.

Reid, J., & Hardy, M. A. (1999). Multiple roles and well-being among midlife women: Testing role strain and role enhancement theories. *Journal of Gerontology: Social Sciences, 54B*(6), S329-S338.

Reio, T. G., & Sanders, J. (1999). Combating workplace ageism. *Adult Learning, 11*(1), 10-14.

Rentsch, J. R., & Klimoski, R. J. (2001). Why do 'great minds' think alike? Antecedents of team member schema agreement. *Journal of Organizational Behavior, 22*(2), 107-120.

Reskin, B., & Padavic, I. (1994). *Women and men at work*. Thousand Oaks, CA: Pine Forge Press.

Rice, D., Fox, P. J., & Max, W. (1993). The economic burden of Alzheimer's disease care. *Health Affairs 12*, 164-176.

Richardson, V., & Kilty, K. M. (1992). Retirement intentions among black professionals: Implications for practice with older black adults. *Gerontologist, 32*(1), 7-16.

Riley, M. W., Kahn, R. L., & Foner, A. (Eds.). (1994). *Age and structural lag*. New York: Wiley.

Riley, M. W., & Riley, J. W., Jr. (1994). Structural lag: Past and future. In M. W. Riley, R. L. Kahn, & A. Foner (Eds.), *Age and structural lag* (pp. 15-36). New York: Wiley.

Ritvo, R. A., Litwin, A. H., & Butler, L. (Eds.). (1995). *Managing in the age of change: Essential skills to manage today's diverse workforce*. Burr Ridge, IL: NTL Institute/Irwin.

Rolander, R. (1988). Older workers and HRD. *Training and Development Journal, 42*(7), 18-19.

Romzek, B. S. (1989). Personal consequences of employee commitment. *Academy of Management Journal, 32*(3), 649-661.

Rosen, B., & Jerdee, T. H. (1976a). The nature of job-related age stereotypes. *Journal of Applied Psychology, 61*(2), 180-183.

Rosen, B., & Jerdee, T. H. (1976b). The influence of age stereotypes on managerial decisions. *Journal of Applied Psychology, 61*(4), 428-432.

Rosen, B., & Jerdee, T. H. (1985). *Older employees: New roles for valued resources*. Chicago: Dow-Jones/Irwin.

Rosen, B., & Jerdee, T. H. (1988). Managing older workers' careers. *Research in personnel and human resource management, 6*, 37-74.

Rosenbaum, J. E. (1979). Tournament mobility: Career patterns in a corporation. *Administrative Science Quarterly, 24*(2), 220-241.

Rosenthal, C. J. (2000). Aging families: Have current changes and challenges been "oversold"? In E. M. Gee & G. M. Guttman (Eds.), *The overselling of population aging: Apocalyptic demography, intergenerational challenges, and social policy* (pp. 45-63). Toronto, Canada: Oxford University Press.

Rosenthal, C. J., Matthews, S. H., & Marshall, V. W. (1989). Is parent care normative? The experiences of a sample of middle-aged women. *Research on Aging, 11*(2), 244-60.

Rosenthal, R., & Jacobson, L. (1968). *Pygmalion in the classroom: Teacher expectation and pupils' intellectual development*. New York: Holt, Reinhart, & Winston.

Rosow, I. (1976). Status and role change through the life span. In R. E. Binstock & E. Shanas (Eds.), *Handbook of aging and the social sciences* (pp. 457-482). New York: Van Norstrand Reinhold.

Royalty, A. B. (1996). The effects of job turnover on the training of men and women. *Industrial and Labor Relations Review, 49*(3), 506-521.

Ruhm, C. J. (1989). Why older Americans stop working. *Gerontologist, 29*(3), 294-299.

Ruhm, C. J. (1990). Career jobs, bridge employment, and retirement. In P. B. Doeringer (Ed.), *Bridges to retirement: Older workers in a changing labor market* (pp. 92-107). Ithaca, NY: Cornell University, ILR Press.

Rynes, S. L., Bartunek, J. M., & Daft, R. L. (2001). Across the great divide: Knowledge creation and transfer between practitioners and academics. *Academy of Management Journal, 44*(2), 340-355.

Salisbury, D. L. (Ed.). (1998). *The future of medical benefits*. Washington, DC: Employee Benefit Research Institute.

Salisbury, D. L. (1999). *Severing the link between health insurance and employment*. Washington, DC: Employee Benefit Research Institute.

Salisbury, D. L. (2001). No time to snooze: Meeting the needs of an aging work force. *WorldatWork Journal, 10*(4), 12-18. Retrieved March 30, 2003, from http://www.ebri.org/pdfs/ej10n4-2.pdf.

Salopek, J. J. (2000). Retention rodeo. *Training and Development, 54*(4), 20-23.

Salthouse, T. A. (1996). The processing-speed theory of adult age differences in cognition. *Psychological Review, 103*(3), 403-428.

Salthouse, T. A., & Babcock, R. L. (1991). Decomposing adult age differences in working memory. *Developmental Psychology, 27*(5), 763-776.

Savickas, M. L. (1997). Career adaptability: An integrative construct for life-span, life-space theory. *Career Development Quarterly, 45*(3), 247-259.

Schaie, K. W. (1990). Intellectual development in adulthood. In J. E. Birren & K. W. Schaie (Eds.), *Handbook of the psychology of aging* (3rd ed., pp. 183-200). San Diego, CA: Academic Press.

Schaie, K. W., & Schooler, C. (Eds.). (1998). *Impact of work on older adults.* New York: Springer.

Scharlach, A. E. (1994). Caregiving and employment: Competing or complementary roles? *The Gerontologist, 34*(3), 378-385.

Schein, E. H. (1971). The individual, the organization, and the career: A conceptual scheme. *Journal of Applied Behavioral Science, 7*(4), 401-426.

Schein, E. H. (1992). *Organizational culture and leadership* (2nd ed.). San Francisco: Jossey-Bass.

Schein, E. H. (1999). *The corporate culture survival guide: Sense and nonsense about culture change.* San Francisco: Jossey-Bass.

Schnaiberg, A., & Goldenberg, S. (1989). From empty nest to crowded nest: The dynamics of incompletely launched young adults. *Social Problems, 36*(3), 251-69.

Schneider, B. (1987). The people make the place. *Personnel Psychology, 40*(3), 437-453.

Senge, P. M. (1990). *The fifth discipline: The art and practice of the learning organization.* New York: Doubleday.

Senge, P. M. (1998, Summer). The practice of innovation. *Leader to Leader* (No. 9), 16-28.

Shaver, N. (1977). Private industry's investment in older workers continues to pay dividends. *Industrial Gerontology, 4*(2), 133-136.

Shea, G. (1991). *Managing older employees.* San Francisco: Jossey-Bass.

Shearer, R. L, & Steger, J. A. (1975). Manpower obsolescence: A new definition and empirical investigation of personal variables. *Academy of Management Journal, 18*(2), 263-275.

Sheblak, V. (1969). The older worker: Employment and training. *Training and Development Journal, 23*(3), 4-8.

Sheehy, G. (1976). *Passages.* New York: Dutton.

Shields, C. E., Hentges, K., & Yaney, J. P. (1990). The aging employee: Human resource management and health. *Performance and Instruction, 29*(5), 1-6.

Shimamura, A. P., Berry, J. M., Mangels, J. A., Rasting, C. L, & Jurica, P. J. (1995). Memory and cognitive abilities in university professors: Evidence for successful aging. *Psychological Science, 6*(5), 271-277.

Shultz, K. S. (2001). The new contingent workforce: Examining the bridge employment options of mature workers. *International Journal of Organizational Theory and Behavior, 4*(3&4), 247-258.

Shultz, K. S., Sirotnik, B. W., & Bockman, S. E. (2000). An aging workforce in transition: A case study of California. *The Southwest Journal on Aging, 16*(1), 9-17.

Sias, P. M., Kramer, M. W., & Jenkins, E. (1997). A comparison of communication behaviors of temporary employees and new hires. *Communication Research, 24*(6), 731-754.

Simonsen, P. (1997). *Promoting a development culture in your organization: Using career development as a change agent.* Palo Alto, CA: Davies-Black Publishing.

Simpson, P. A., Greller, M. M., & Stroh, L. K. (2002). Variations in human capital investment activity by age. *Journal of Vocational Behavior, 61*(1), 109-138.

Simpson, P. A., & Stroh, L. K. (2001). *Gender and age variation in post-school training.* Paper presented at the 54th annual meeting of the American Gerontological Society, Chicago, IL.

Simpson, P. A. & Stroh, L. K. (2002). Revisiting gender variation in training. *Feminist Economics, 8*(3), 21-53.

Smart, T. (2001, June 4). Not acting their age. *U.S. News & World Report, 130*(22), 57.

Smith, K. G., Smith, K. A., Olian, J. D., Sims, H. P., O'Bannon, D. P., & Scully, J. A. (1994). Top management team demography and processes: The role of social integration and communication. *Administrative Science Quarterly, 39*(3), 412-438.

Smola, K. W., & Sutton, C. D. (2002). Generational differences: Revisiting generational work values for the new millennium. *Journal of Organizational Behavior, 23*, 363-382.

Society for Human Resource Management. (2002). *Workplace forecast: A strategic outlook 2002-2003.* Alexandria, VA: Dave Patel.

Society for Human Resource Management, & AARP. (1998). *SHRM/AARP older workers survey.* Alexandria, VA: SHRM.

Society for Human Resource Management, & Commerce Clearing House (1999, June 16). Wooing good workers in shallow labor pool pushes HR to explore new ways to bait hook. *Human Resources Management Ideas & Trends* (#460-2).

Sommers, D., & Eck, A. (1977). Occupational mobility in the American labor force. *Monthly Labor Review, 10*(1), 3-19.

Sonnenfeld, J., & Kotter, J. P. (1982). The maturation of career theory. *Human Relations, 35*(1), 19-46.

Spence, A. P. (1995). *The biology of human aging* (2nd ed.). Englewood Cliffs, NJ: Prentice Hall.

Spillman, B. C., & Pezzin, L. E. (2000). Potential and active family caregivers: Changing networks and the "sandwich generation." *The Milbank Quarterly, 78*(3), 347-374.

Spirduso, W. W., & MacRae, P. G. (1990). Motor performance and aging. In J. E. Birren & K. W. Schaie (Eds.), *Handbook of the psychology of aging* (3rd ed., pp. 183-200). San Diego, CA: Academic Press.

Spitze, G., & Logan, J. (1990). More evidence on women (and men) in the middle. *Research on Aging, 12*(2), 182-198.

Stabile, S. J. (2002). The behavior of defined contribution plan participants. *New York University Law Review, 77*(1), 71-105.

Stainaker, C. K. (1998). Safety of older workers in the 21st century. *Professional Safety, 43*(6), 28-31.

Steers, R. M. (1977). Antecedents and outcomes of organizational commitment. *Administrative Science Quarterly, 22*(1), 46-56.

Steinhauser, S. (1998, July). Age bias: Is your corporate culture in need of an overhaul? *HR Magazine, 43*(8), 86-91.

Stephens, M. A. P., & Franks, M. (1995). Spillover between daughters' roles as caregiver and wife: Interference or enhancement? *Journal of Gerontology: Psychological Sciences, 50B*(1), P9-P17.

Sterns, H. L. (1986). Training and retraining adults and older adult workers. In J. E. Birren, P. K. Robinson, & J. E. Livingston (Eds.), *Age, health, and employment* (pp. 93-113). Englewood Cliffs, NJ: Prentice Hall.

Sterns, H. L., & Doverspike, D. (1988). Training and developing the older worker: Implications for human resource management. In H. Dennis (Ed.), *Fourteen steps in managing an aging workforce.* Lexington, MA: D. C. Heath.

Sterns, H. L, & Gray, J. H. (1999). Work, leisure, and retirement. In J. Cavanaugh & S. K. Whitbourne (Eds.), *Gerontology: An interdisciplinary perspective* (pp. 355-389). New York: Oxford University Press.

Sterns, H. L., & Huyck, M. H. (2001). The role of work in midlife. In M. E. Lachman (Ed.), *Handbook of midlife development* (pp. 447-486). New York: Wiley.

Sterns, H. L., Junkins, M. P., & Bayer, J. G. (2001). Work and retirement. In B. R. Bonder & M. B. Wagner (Eds.), *Functional performance in older adults* (pp. 179-195). Philadelphia: F. A. Davis.

Sterns, H. L., & McDaniel, M. A. (1994). Job performance and the older worker. In S. E. Rix (Ed.), *Older workers: How do they measure up? An overview of age differences in employee costs and performances* (pp. 27-51). Washington, DC: AARP Public Policy Institute.

Sterns, H. L., & Miklos, S. M. (1995). The aging worker in a changing environment: Organizational and individual issues. *Journal of Vocational Behavior, 47*(3), 248-268.

Sterns, H. L., & Patchett, M. (1984). Technology and the aging adult: Career development and training. In P. K. Robinson, J. E. Livingston, and J. E. Birren (Eds.), *Aging and technological advances* (pp. 261-277). New York: Plenum Press.

Sterns, H. L., & Sterns, A. A. (1995a). Health and the employment capability of older Americans. In S. A. Bass (Ed.), *Older and active: How Americans over 55 are contributing to society* (pp. 10-34). New Haven, CT: Yale University Press.

Sterns, H. L., & Sterns, A. A. (1995b). *Training and careers: Growth and development over fifty years.* Paper presented at the 48th annual meeting of the Gerontological Society of America, Los Angeles.

Sterns, H. L., & Subich, L. M. (2002). Career development in Midcareer. In D. C. Feldman (Ed.), *Work careers: A developmental perspective* (pp. 186-213). San Francisco: Jossey-Bass.

Steuerle, C. E., Spiro, C., & Johnson, R. W. (1999, August 15). *Can Americans work longer?* Straight Talk on Social Security and Retirement Policy, No. 5. Washington, DC: The Urban Institute. Retrieved March 30, 2003, from http://www.urban.org/retirement/st/Straight5.pdf.

Stevens, P. (1998, April). *What works and what doesn't in career development programs.* Paper presented at the annual meeting of the Australian Career Development Association, Sydney Australia.

Stoller, E. P., & Pugliesi, K. L. (1989). Caregivers of the frail elderly. *Journals of Gerontology: Social Sciences, 44*(6), S616-S626.

Straka, J. W. (1992). The demand for older workers: The neglected side of a labor market. *Studies in Income Distribution* (No. 15). Washington, DC: U.S. Department of Health and Human Services.

Strauss, A. L. (1971). *The contexts of social mobility: Ideology and theory.* Chicago: Aldine Publishing.

Stull, D. E., Bowman, K., & Smerglia, V. (1994). Women in the middle: A myth in the making? *Family Relations, 43*(3), 319-324.

Sullivan, S. E., & Duplaga, E. A. (1997). Recruiting and retaining older workers in the new millennium. *Business Horizons, 40*(6), 65-69.

Super, D. E. (1957). *The psychology of careers.* New York: Harper and Row.

Super, D. E. (1984). Career and life development. In D. Brown, L. Brooks, & Associates (Eds.), *Career choice and development* (pp. 192-234). San Francisco: Jossey-Bass.

Tajfel, H. (1978). Social categorization, social identity and social comparison. In H. Tajfel (Ed.), *Differentiation between social groups: Studies in the social psychology of intergroup relations* (pp. 61-76). London: Academic Press.

Taylor, H. (2002, May 15). The new vision of retirement is very different than the traditional image of retirement. *The Harris Poll* (No. 23). Retrieved April 5, 2003, from http://www.harrisinteractive.com/harris_poll/index.asp?PID=301.

Taylor, H. J. F. (2000). Older workers: A valuable resource for the workplace. In W. K. Zinke & S. Tattershall (Eds.), *Working through demographic change* (pp. 5-14). Boulder, CO: Human Resource Services, Inc.

Taylor, M. A., & Doverspike, D. (2002, April). *Recruiting older employees: A multistage model for human resource professionals.* Paper presented at the 17th annual meeting of the Society for Industrial and Organizational Psychology, Toronto, Canada.

Taylor, M. A., & Doverspike, D. (2003). Retirement planning and preparation (Chapter 3). In G. A. Adams & T. A. Beehr (Eds.), *Retirement: Reasons, processes and results.* (pp. 53-82). New York: Springer.

Taylor, M. A., & Shore, L. M. (1995). Predictors of planned retirement age: An application of Beehr's model. *Psychology and Aging, 10*(1), 76-83.

ThirdAge. (1998, June 23). Older workers: Job market of the future. *ThirdAge News & Opinion* (Story 1 of 7). Retrieved March 27, 2003, from http://www.thirdage.com/news/archive/980623-01.html.

Thomas, M. C., & Thomas, T. S. (1990). *Getting commitment at work: A guide for managers and employees.* Chapel Hill, NC: Commitment Press.

Thornburg, L. (1995, February). The age wave hits: What older workers want and need. *HR Magazine, 40*(2), 40-45.

Timmerman, T. A. (2000). Racial diversity, age diversity, interdependence, and team performance. *Small Group Research, 31*(5), 592-606.

Toossi, M. (2002). A century of change: The U.S. labor force, 1950-2050. *Monthly Labor Review, 125*(5), 21-38. Retrieved March 20, 2003, from http://www.bls.gov/opub/mlr/2002/05/art2full.pdf.

Torres-Gil, F. M. (2002). The new aging: Individual and societal responses. *Elder Law Journal, 10*(1), 91-117.

Triandis, H. C. (1995). The importance of contexts in studies of diversity. In S. E. Jackson & M. N. Ruderman (Eds.), *Diversity in work teams: Research paradigms for a changing workplace* (pp. 247-253). Washington, DC: American Psychological Association.

Tsui, A. S., Xin, K. R., & Egan, T. D. (1995). Relational demography: The missing link in vertical dyad linkage. In S. E. Jackson & M. N. Ruderman (Eds.), *Diversity in work teams: Research paradigms for a changing workplace* (pp. 97-129). Washington, DC: American Psychological Association.

Turner, J. C. (1982). Towards a cognitive redefinition of the social group. In H. Tajfel (Ed.), *Social identity and intergroup relations* (pp. 15-40). Cambridge: Cambridge University Press.

Uhlenberg, P. (1996). Mortality decline in the twentieth century and supply of kin over the life course. *The Gerontologist, 36,* 681-685.

United States Board of Trustees of the Federal Old-Age and Survivors Insurance and Disability Insurance Trust Funds (2002). *Annual Report.* Washington, DC: U.S. Government Printing Office. Retrieved March 20, 2003, from http://www.ssa.gov/OACT/TR/TR02/index.html.

United States Bureau of the Census. (1984). *Educational attainment in the United States: March 1981 and 1980* (Current Population Reports, Series P-20, No. 390). Washington, DC: R. R. Bruno.

United States Bureau of the Census. (2000a, January 13). *Census Bureau projects doubling of nation's population* (press release). Washington, DC: U.S. Bureau of the Census. Retrieved May 5, 2003, from http://www.census.gov/Press-Release/www/2000/cb00-05.html.

United States Bureau of the Census. (2000b, March). *Have we reached the top? Educational attainment projections of the U.S. population* (Population Division Working Paper No. 43). Washington, DC: J. C. Day & K. J. Bauman. Retrieved April 16, 2003, from http://www.census.gov/population/www/documentation/twps0043/twps0043.pdf.

United States Bureau of the Census. (2000c, January 13). *Population projections of the United States, 1999 to 2100: Methodology and assumptions* (Population Division Working Paper No. 38). Washington, DC: F. W. Hollmann, T. J. Mulder, & J. E. Kallan. Retrieved April 16, 2003, from http://www.census.gov/population/www/documentation/twps0038.pdf.

United States Bureau of the Census (2001, March). *The hispanic population in the United States: Population characteristics* (Current Population Report P20-535). Washington, DC: M. Therrien & R. R. Ramirez. Retrieved March 20, 2003 from http://www.census.gov/population/socdemo/hispanic/p20-535/p20-535.pdf.

United States Bureau of the Census (2002). *National population projections.* Retrieved March 30, 2003, from http://www.census.gov/population/www/projections/natproj.html.

United States Department of Labor (1999). *Interpretive bulletin relating to participant investment education* (29 C.F.R. section 2509.96-1). Retrieved March 19, 2003, from http://www.dol.gov/dol/allcfr/Title_29/Part_2509/29CFR2509.96-1.htm.

United States House of Representatives, Committee on Ways and Means. (1998). *1998 green book.* Washington, DC: U.S. Government Printing Office.

United States Senate Special Committee on Aging, AARP, the Federal Council on Aging, & the United States Administration on Aging. (1991). *Aging America: Trends and projections.* Washington D.C.: U.S. Department of Health and Human Services.

Useem, M. (1997). Corporate education and training. In C. Kaysen (Ed.), *The American corporation today: Examining the questions of power and efficiency at the century's end* (pp. 292-326). New York: Oxford University Press.

Usui, C. (1998). Gradual retirement: Japanese strategies for older workers. In K. W. Schaie and C. Schooler (Eds.). *Impact of work on older adults* (pp. 45-100). New York: Springer.

Valian, V. (1998). *Why so slow? The advancement of women.* Cambridge, MA: MIT Press.

VanDerhei, J. L., & Holden, S. (2001, November). Plan asset allocation, account balances, and loan activity in 2000. *ICI Perspective, 7*(1). Retrieved March 19, 2003, from http://www.ici.org/pdf/per07-01.pdf.

Van Maanen, J., & Schein, E. H. (1979). Toward a theory of organizational socialization. In L. L. Cummings & B. M. Staw (Ed.), *Research in organizational behavior* (Vol. 1, pp. 209-264). Greenwich, CT: JAI Press.

Veiga, J. F. (1973, January/February). The mobile manager at mid-career. *Harvard Business Review, 51,* 115-119.

Veiga, J. F. (1981). Plateaued versus non-plateaued managers: Career patterns, attitudes, and path potential. *Academy of Management Journal, 24*(3), 566-578.

Veiga, J. F. (1983). Mobility influences during managerial career stages. *Academy of Management Journal, 26*(1), 64-85.

Veneri, C. (1999). Can occupational labor shortages be identified using available data? *Monthly Labor Review, 122*(3), 15-21.

Votruba, J. C. (1990). Strengthening confidence and vitality in midcareer faculty. In S. L. Willis & S. S. Dubin (Eds.), *Maintaining professional competence: Approaches to career enhancement, vitality, and success throughout a work life* (pp. 214-242). San Francisco: Jossey-Bass.

Voydanoff, P. (2002). Linkages between the work-family interface and work, family, and individual outcomes: An integrative model. *Journal of Family Issues, 23*(1), 138-164.

Wagner, W. G., Pfeffer, J., & O'Reilly, C. A. (1984). Organizational demography and turnover in top-management groups. *Administrative Science Quarterly, 29*(1), 74-92.

Waldfogel, J. (1999). Family leave coverage in the 1990s. *Monthly Labor Review, 122*(10), 13-21.

Waldman, D. A., & Avolio, B. J. (1993). Aging and work performance in perspective: Contextual and developmental considerations. *Research in Personnel and Human Resource Management, 11,* 133-162.

Wallace, G. D. (2002, June 17). Just what kind of retiree will you be? *Business Week,* p. 10.

Wallace, P. (1999). *Agequake: Riding the demographic rollercoaster shaking business, finance and our world.* London: Nicholas Brealey Publishing.

Walsh, J. (1995). *Mastering diversity: Managing for success under ADA and other anti-discriminatory laws.* Santa Monica, CA: Merritt.

Walters, J. (2000, March). The employee exodus. *Governing,* pp. 36-38.

Wanberg, C. R, & Kammeyer-Mueller, J. D. (2000). Predictors and outcomes of proactivity in the socialization process. *Journal of Applied Psychology, 85*(3), 373-385.

Ward, R. A., & Spitze, G. D. (1998). Sandwiched marriages: The implications of child and parent relations for marital quality in midlife. *Social Forces, 77*(2), 647-666.

Warner, F. (2002, April). Inside Intel's mentoring movement. *Fast Company, 57,* 116-120.

Wasserman, I. E., Miller, F. A., & Johnson, M. N. (1995). Diversity skills in action: Cross-cultural mentoring. In R. A. Ritvo, A. H. Litwin, & L. Butler (Eds.), *Managing in the age of change: Essential skills to manage today's diverse workforce* (pp. 268-274). Burr Ridge, IL: NTL Institute/Irwin.

Waterman, R. H., Jr. (1994). *What America does right: Learning from companies that put people first.* New York: W. W. Norton.

Waterman, R. H., Waterman, J. A., & Collard, B. A. (1994, July-August). Toward a career-resilient workforce. *Harvard Business Review, 72*(4), 87-95.

Wechsler, D. (1981). *Wechsler Adult Intelligence Scale-Revised.* New York: Psychological Corporation.

Weckerle, J. R., & Shultz, K. S. (1999). Influences on the bridge employment decision among older U.S.A. workers. *Journal of Occupational and Organizational Psychology, 72*(3), 317-330.

Weisbord, M. R. (1987). *Productive workplaces.* San Francisco: Jossey-Bass.

Wellner, A. S. (2002, March). Tapping a silver mine. *HR Magazine, 47*(3), 26-32.

Wharton, A., & Bird, S. (1996). Stand by your man: Homosociality, work groups, and men's perceptions of difference. In C. Cheng (Ed.), *Masculinities in organizations* (pp. 97-114). Thousand Oaks, CA: Sage.

Whiston, S. C., & Brecheisen, B. K. (2002). Practice and research in career counseling and development-2001. *The Career Development Quarterly, 51*(2), 98-154.

Whitbourne, S. (1985). *The aging body: Physiological changes and psychological consequences.* New York: Springer.

Whitely, W., Dougherty, T. W., & Dreher, G. F. (1992). Correlates of career-oriented mentoring for early career managers and professionals. *Journal of Organizational Behavior, 13*(2), 141-154.

Wilensky, H. (1961). Orderly careers and social participation: The impact of work history on social integration in the middle mass. *American Sociological Review, 26,* 521-530.

William M. Mercer (2001). *15th Annual Mercer/Foster Higgins national survey of employer-sponsored health plans 2001.* New York: William M. Mercer. Retrieved March 30, 2003, from http://www.imercer.com/us/imercercommentary/Healthsurvey/BB-final.pdf.

Williams, A., & Nussbaum, J. F. (2001). *Intergenerational communication across the life span.* New Jersey: Lawrence Erlbaum.

Willis, S. L., & Dubin, S. S. (1990). Maintaining professional competence: Directions and possibilities. In S. L. Willis & S. S. Dubin (Eds.), *Maintaining professional competence: Approaches to career enhancement, vitality, and success throughout a work life* (pp. 306-314). San Francisco, CA: Jossey-Bass.

Yeatts, D. E., Folts, W. E., & Knapp, J. (2000). Older workers' adaptation to a changing workplace: Employment issues for the 21st century. *Educational Gerontology, 26*(6), 565-582.

Young-Bruehl, E. (1996). *The anatomy of prejudices.* Cambridge MA: Harvard University Press.

Zacks, R. T., & Hasher, L. (1994). Directed ignoring: Inhibitory regulation of working memory. In D. Dagenbach & T. H. Carr (Eds.), *Inhibitory processes in attention, memory, and language* (pp. 241-264). New York: Academic Press.

Zemke, R., Raines, C., & Filipczak, B. (2000). *Generations at work: Managing the clash of veterans, boomers, Xers and nexters in your workplace.* New York: AMACOM.

Zenger, T. R., & Lawrence, B. S. (1989). Organizational demography: The differential effects of age and tenure distributions on technical communication. *Academy of Management Journal, 32*(2), 353-376.

Zinke, W. K., & Tattershall, S. (Eds.). (2000). *Working through demographic change.* Boulder, CO: Human Resource Services.

Zunker, V. G. (1998). *Career counseling: Applied concepts of life planning* (5th ed.). Pacific Grove, CA: Brooks/Cole.

Author Index

Subject Index